WITHDRAWN
NDSU

FINLAND
AN INTRODUCTION

EDITED BY
SYLVIE NICKELS, HILLAR KALLAS AND
PHILIPPA FRIEDMAN

ILLUSTRATED

PRAEGER PUBLISHERS
NEW YORK · WASHINGTON

BOOKS THAT MATTER

Published in the United States of America in 1973
by Praeger Publishers, Inc., 111 Fourth Avenue,
New York, N.Y. 10003

© George Allen & Unwin Ltd., 1973

This is a substantially revised and expanded edition of a book originally published in 1968 by Frederick A. Praeger and entitled FINLAND: *Creation and Construction*.

All rights reserved

No part of this publication may be reproduced, stored in a retrieval system or transmitted in any form or by any means, electronic, mechanical, photocopying, recording or otherwise, without the prior permission of the Copyright owner.

Library of Congress Catalog Card Number: 72-89453

Printed in Great Britain

ACKNOWLEDGEMENTS

The editors wish to put on record the generous help they have received from many friends in Finland and Britain, especially from the Press Bureau of the Foreign Ministry in Helsinki and the Finnish Embassy in London. The photographs are mostly from the Foreign Ministry collection, with some contributions from Penny Tweedie, J. M. Richards and Sylvie Nickels. The cartoons are by Olavi Hurmerinta, the drawings for the statistical section by Sydney McWilliam and the folder map by T. R. Allen.

For most of the translations we thank D. R. Roper. The extracts from Erik Tawaststjerna's book *Sibelius* on page 235 were translated by Robert Layton whose translation of the whole work will be published by Faber (first volume in 1973). Other translators who have made valuable contributions include John Atkinson, Margaret Sampson, M. A. Branch and Susan Sinisalo. Margaret Parnwell assisted with much impeccable typing.

CONTENTS

ACKNOWLEDGEMENTS 7

A Thousand Years of Finland 17
MIKKO JUVA

Guide Lines 37

Independence and After 40
HEIKKI ESKELINEN

Communism—Finnish Style 63
OLAVI BORG

The Changing Rural Scene 70
W. R. MEAD

Industry and Foreign Trade—Changing Patterns 76
LEIF FAST

The Waterways of Finland 87
W. R. MEAD

The Natural Provinces 92
W. R. MEAD

Urban Portraits 124
W. R. MEAD

The Last Wilderness 129
SYLVIE NICKELS

Wild Life and Nature 137
SEPPO PARTANEN

The Winter Way of Life 142
SEPPO PARTANEN

FINLAND: AN INTRODUCTION

Training the Finnish Soldier 150
KEIJO MIKOLA

The Young and their Education 156
PHILIP BINHAM

On learning Finnish 168
M. A. BRANCH

The Church in Finland 177
JORMA LOUHIVUORI

Two Churches 188
NILS ERIK WICKBERG

Architecture 191
J. M. RICHARDS

Design 202
GEOFFERY BEARD

As Others saw Them 214

Literature and the National Image 219
DAVID BARRETT

New Writers 231
KAI LAITINEN

Sibelius in America and Britain 235
ERIK TAWASTSTJERNA

Before and After Sibelius 242
SEPPO HEIKINHEIMO

Painting and Sculpture 250
JOHN BOULTON SMITH

CONTENTS

The Theatre 257
RITVA HEIKKILÄ
The Year in Finland 263
PHYLLIS CHAPMAN
The Press 271
LANCE KEYWORTH
Finnish Food 278
J. AUDREY ELLISON
Holidays in Finland 284
BENGT PIHLSTRÖM
The Sauna Cult 289
MARJATTA HERVA
Finns Abroad 294
ERKKI SAVOLAINEN
The Finns and the British 299
PHYLLIS CHAPMAN

REFERENCE SECTION
Useful Addresses 306
RIITTA KALLAS
Selected Books 323
YRJÖ AAV
Statistics 343
OLLI SAARIAHO

INDEX 368

PLATES

1. Lakes and forests
2. First flakes in Tapiola
3. Varkaus: raw material for the factories
4. From forest to factory
5. Pyhäkoski power station
6. Winter
7. Sauna: fun for the younger generation
8. The tall forests
9. Lakeside sauna
10. Hydrofoil on the approach to Jyväskylä
11. The *Pommern*
12. Sunworshippers in Helsinki
13. Aerial view of Helsinki
14. Winter fishing through ice
15. Turku cathedral tower and statue of Per Brahe
16. Art and industry in Tampere
17. Tammisaari street scene
18. Sibelius monument
19. The wide horizons of Lapland *between pages 96–7*

20. The church of Sipoo
21. Altar wall of chapel at Otaniemi
22. Nousiainen's thirteenth-century church
23. Interior of Keuruu church
24. Helsinki cathedral
25. National museum, Helsinki
26. Helsinki railway station
27. Parliament House, Helsinki
28. Paimio Sanatorium
29. Chapel near Turku
30. Säynätsalo Civic Centre

FINLAND: AN INTRODUCTION

31. School on Kulosaari Island, Helsinki
32. Tapiola shopping centre
33. Block of flats, Tapiola
34. Atrium houses, Espoo
35. Bank, Eläintarha Park, Helsinki
36. Vuoksenniska church, Imatra
37. Church in Hyvinkää
38. Municipal Theatre, Turku
39. Dipoli, Otaniemi
40. 'Finlandia' concert hall, Helsinki
41. Toronto town hall
42. Cultural Centre, Wolfsburg, Germany   *between pages* 192-3

43. Reindeer round-up
44. Ski-jump
45. Swimming in a clearing in the ice
46. Elementary school
47. Children ski-ing
48. *Vappu* celebrations, May 1st
49. Carpet washing
50. Christmas Eve, Hietaniemi Cemetery, Helsinki
51. Wood-carving from Hollola church
52. Rymättylä church: east wall
53. 'Hihhulit'
54. 'Girls Reading'
55. 'Country Dance'
56. 'Contrapunctus'
57. 'Great Black Woodpecker'
58. 'Death on Skates'
59. 'Head on Black Background'
60. 'Paavo Nurmi'
61. 'Wood'
62. 'Largo' vase

PLATES

63. Ceramic plate
64. Bowl with 'Flora' design
65. Pendant 'Flowering Wall'
66. 'Finnline' stainless steel cutlery
67. 'Paratiisi' printed cotton sateen   *between pages 256–7*

COLOUR PLATES
   United paper mills, Valkeakoski   *facing page* 64
   One of the Lake Saimaa fleet   68
   Finnish icebreaker 'Tarmo'   128
   Winter scene   129
   South harbour waterfront, Helsinki   224
   Morning market, Helsinki   225
   The coming of Autumn in Lapland   288
   On a frozen lake, Lapland   289

A THOUSAND YEARS OF FINLAND

MIKKO JUVA

THE founder of Finland's post-war policy, President Paasikivi, enjoyed the greatest respect and authority as a statesman; he was also well known for his sudden outbursts of anger—sometimes directed against the political immaturity of his countrymen. He is said to have exclaimed once: 'These Finns! What have they achieved? Once they inhabited half Russia. But did they found a state? No! As soon as there was trouble they set sail across the sea to Finland, found a suitable birch grove and built a sauna.'

The idea that the Finns escaped by sea from the migration of peoples and settled by a lakeside sauna is a romantic reconstruction rather than a historical fact. But Paasikivi's assertion still throws a pertinent light on the character and history of the Finns. Due partly to the size of the country and their own small numbers, the Finns have striven throughout their history to live their own lives, avoid assimilation with their neighbours and remain aside from the quarrels of the rest of the world. Right up to the present the forest has been the formative influence in their lives. Their land border in the north and east has always been uninhabited forest and fell, a wilderness such as may still be seen in Lapland and east Finland. This border has been gradually pushed back by settlers from the south-west.

The severity of life in the north and the ever-present forest have moulded the Finnish character. In the backwoods a man must rely on himself, on his own strength and his own inventiveness. The Finns have not known the feeling of solidarity and strength in numbers which are common to village dwellers in the plains.

FINLAND: AN INTRODUCTION

From the time they sailed across the Gulf of Finland from Estonia about 2,000 years ago they have lived in a large country in scattered communities, surrounded by great forests and many waterways. The land was not conquered from other tribes but straight from nature. The few nomadic Lapps that the Finns encountered as they moved in were no problem. There was room for all in the forest, the more so as the Finns brought with them the arts of husbandry, supplementing nature's gifts with dairy produce and crops grown on burnt clearings.

The Finnish settlers avoided the coastal areas where they would have been a prey to the many raiders who sailed the Baltic, preferring the river banks, and then penetrating ever deeper into the interior along the great lakes. In five centuries they spread across south Finland from the west to Lake Ladoga in the east. They still lived in isolation, their only contact with the outside world being the traders who took northern pelts to the markets of Rome, Byzantium and the Frankish kingdom and brought back salt, iron and weapons.

The first thousand years of unwritten history of the Finns in Finland determined their basic character, which has remained constant to the present day. The small-holdings, scattered villages, the vast wilderness, and the natural freedom of the men of the forest, have moulded a self-sufficient, independent and yet a stubborn people. The extremes of the Finnish climate—a dark autumn, bright winter snows, an explosive spring and a short summer of almost continuous daylight—have impressed upon generations of Finns the strength and immutability of the basic forces of life. Hence the respect felt by the Finnish community for their social traditions. But this respect for tradition is linked to a bold readiness to experiment, although the new will not be embraced until it has been tested and found acceptable. It does not mean that the old is rejected, for how can you reject the immutable facts of winter and summer, lake and rock, home fields and virgin forest? The new is accepted because it makes it possible to exploit the old better than before; because it provides the Finns with a new weapon for the old struggle of taming nature and making the north a still better place to live in.

A Free People
Where did the Finns come from? Who are they? These questions have engaged inquiring minds ever since problems of the origin of peoples and their interrelationship began to be discussed. Leaving aside the attempts of Finnish scholars of the early eighteenth century to prove that the Finns were descended from the lost tribes of Israel, we find a most pertinacious theory put forward by J. F. Blumenbach of Göttingen at the end of that century. Blumenbach explained that the Finns were Mongols who had come from Central Asia. This view was based on their non-Indo-European language and on customs which seemed strange in West European eyes.

But the Finns are not Mongols, nor are they Turks as has sometimes been asserted. The most definitive evidence we have on which to decide their origin is their language, which together with Estonian, Hungarian, Lapp and a score of languages spoken by people in north Russia, forms the Finno-Ugric group. We know, however, that a common language does not necessarily imply a common origin: history abounds in examples, and we need mention no more than the Americans and the English, or the French and the Rumanians. Finnish and Lapp are as similar as Swedish and English but anthropologically the Finns bear closer resemblance to the English than to the Lapps. The problem here is to decide whose forefathers acquired a new language. On archaeological evidence we find that the ancestors of the Finns were living in what is now Estonia at least 3,500 years ago. To formulate what we know, rather than speculate on the unknown, we can say that the ancestors of the Finns lived in settlements along the Baltic coast before the Flight from Egypt and before the conquest of Troy. From about the time of Augustus and Nero these same people used to cross the Gulf of Finland each year to the more plentiful fishing and hunting grounds in the north.

Seafaring and sailing were among the more developed skills that the early Finns brought with them when they moved north across the Gulf. Their social organization was that of a typical frontier society in which the family was the unifying element and the spheres of influence were laid down by custom and ancient usage. The lines of communication across the Baltic determined the development of Finnish economic life and social attitudes in a manner common to other Baltic and northern countries. The freemen held assemblies to debate matters of general interest and to resolve their differences. By the end of the tenth century the population had increased so much in the main areas of Finland Proper (the south-western province), Häme (central Finland, in Swedish Tavastland), and Karelia (east Finland) that provincial co-operation in matters of defence and the practice of religion became the rule. This, however, was the extent of Finnish political organization. At this same time Sweden, Denmark and Norway were already federal kingdoms composed of autonomous provinces. No one in Finland had attempted to establish a monarchy. A couple of centuries later political developments in the north had ruled out such a possibility.

Finns and Swedes

A tradition based on pious medieval legend and tales of chivalry relates that the Swedish king St Erik subdued the Finns by force of arms and the English bishop St Henry baptized them. Both Erik and Henry are historical figures and they probably led an expedition to Finland in or about 1155. But the expedition did not introduce Christianity to Finland nor did it lead to the conquest of the country. There had been Christian communities in the country over a hundred years before Henry came. What Henry did was to change a mission field into a bishopric and the opposition to this reorganization led to his martyrdom. Erik's expedition was one of many in the struggles for supremacy in trading operations around the Gulf of Finland waged by East and West, represented here by Novgorod and Sweden, and part of the parallel struggle for ecclesiastical leadership of the new mission fields waged by Byzantium and Rome. The Viking and Varangian expeditions and the opposition they evoked among Finns, Karelians and Balts made the Baltic coasts far from peaceful, especially in the Gulf of Finland. The peoples who lived on the route of plundering adventurers from east and west looked for allies; the Finns allied themselves with the Swedes, the Karelians turned to the Russians.

To the Finns the alliance meant allegiance to Rome and inclusion in the Swedish political system. The province of Finland Proper, nearest to Sweden, was incorporated into the Swedish system early in the thirteenth century, to be followed by Häme (Tavastland) in mid-century, thanks in part to the energy of Bishop Thomas, another churchman of English birth. West Karelia was only brought into the Swedish orbit at the end of the century, after prolonged hostilities with Novgorod. The rest of Karelia, as far east as Lake Onega, fell under the dominion of Novgorod.

That Finland was in alliance with Sweden rather than conquered by her is most clearly demonstrated by the status of the Finnish provinces in the extended Swedish kingdom. The Finns retained control of the land they cultivated, provincial leaders were given a place in the rising nobility, and from the end of the fourteenth century only Finns were appointed to the Finnish see of Turku (Åbo). The towns were international like all medieval towns, but there was a strong Finnish element among the burghers from the start. Only the higher military and political leadership in the main provincial centres was, not unnaturally, in the hands of the Swedish nobility.

Alliance with Sweden was painless because throughout the Middle Ages Sweden still constituted a particularly loose union of provinces, and Finnish society was already similar in structure and permeated by the same northern spirit. Swedes had settled in the Åland Islands before the Finnish alliance, now they came in large numbers to the uninhabited coastal areas of the Gulfs of Finland and Bothnia, to ensure the defence of the new territory. Finn and Swede thus learnt to live together on Finnish soil. Either Finnish or Swedish was spoken according to area in the country districts, but in the towns and among the leading nobility both languages were understood. Swedish was the universal tongue throughout the kingdom and was used by Finns, too, as they gradually learnt to take part in the ordering of public affairs. Finnish was the local tongue spoken by priests, judges and state officials. Legal recognition of Finland's status as the equal of the Swedish provinces was formally granted in 1362, when the Finns obtained the right to participate in the election of the king.

FINLAND: AN INTRODUCTION

Until the seventeenth century membership of the united realm was not particularly irksome to the Finns. Government centralization was minimal and Finnish affairs were largely decided in Finland and in Finnish. Official documents were admittedly in Latin, or in Swedish after the Reformation, but this was all the same to a populace which was illiterate and could rely on clerks and educated people to give them an interpretation in Finnish of the occasional document they might wish to know about. The Reformation did indeed strengthen the position of Finnish in the land. To meet the demand for the Gospel in the vernacular a translation of the New Testament appeared in 1548, and in 1642 the whole Bible was translated into Finnish. A relatively large body of religious literature in Finnish was also produced. Simultaneously, Eastern policy began to be the most important facet of Swedish foreign policy. On several occasions the Finnish authorities had to take an almost independent hand in directing this policy, which increased the importance and self-esteem of the eastern half of the kingdom.

The situation altered with the development of a strong movement towards central government and greater political uniformity during the reign of Gustavus II Adolphus (1611-32). Finland lost her privileged status in many respects and attempts were made to impose conformity with Sweden. The Finnish language was neglected more and more. First it was dropped by the nobility, who withdrew to their estates and spoke Swedish, or left the country and went to Sweden; then the townsfolk followed suit. Even the Academy, founded in Turku (Åbo) in 1640, trained Swedish-speaking officials for public service.

The collapse of Sweden as a great power in the Great Northern War (1700-21) led to a further weakening in the position of Finnish. Just at this time there was a considerable increase in literacy among the people, thanks to an active policy of education instituted by the Church. But there was little for Finns to read except devotional works and almanacs. It seemed to the Finn wrong, not to say insulting, that legal judgments, tax forms and other official documents which concerned him should be written in Swedish, a language he could now decipher but which he did not understand. The acquisition of the Swedish language and attitudes proceeded apace among the upper classes, and the language boundary became an indicator of social standing. It was no longer only the chief representatives of the Swedish state and the artisans and farmers of the coastal areas who spoke Swedish. Tradesmen and minor officials of every sort joined with the owners of small estates in becoming 'Swedish'. Church services were indeed still held in Finnish and the clergy were the only social group that never lost contact with the Finnish-speaking populace, although they too used Swedish as a *lingua franca* among themselves, side by side with Finnish, even in remote parishes where Swedish had scarcely ever been heard before.

Finns and Russians

The first boundary between Swedish domains and the Russian principality of Novgorod was laid down in the Treaty of Pähkinäsaari (known in Russian as Orekhov and later as Schlüsselburg), signed in 1323. Beginning at the river Rajajoki on the Karelian isthmus, north-west of present-day Leningrad, the border passed east of Viipuri (now Vyborg) and continued northeast towards the sea. In the uninhabited wilds the border was indeterminate and was probably never marked on the ground. In later centuries the Finns and their Swedish allies maintained that the border had run up to the Arctic coast, while the Karelians and their Russian allies affirmed it ran westwards to the Gulf of Bothnia. The Russian view appears to have been historically correct, but the actual movement of population proved stronger than an old document. The Finns were not going to let a parchment signed by Sweden and Novgorod deter them from an activity they had pursued for a thousand years—the gathering in of nature's bounty from the rich forests and waterways, and the building of log cabins and saunas further and further to the north-east. The Russians countered this peaceful penetration with destructive raids, beginning a struggle which was to last for centuries. Finnish, Karelian and Russian villages waited their turn to be burnt to the ground.

The eastern border became a scene of bloodshed, and the Russian acquired the reputation of persecutor, an attitude that

FINLAND: AN INTRODUCTION

was to become deeply imprinted in the Finnish consciousness. Defence meant fighting the East and peace meant peace in the East. A first redress of grievances which had become unbearable was obtained in 1595 in the Treaty of Täyssinä (Teushina) by which the border was drawn to run to the Arctic coast and North Finland was recognized to be part of Finland. Soon after this Russia was overtaken by dynastic troubles. Sweden was not slow to take advantage of the situation, sending Jakob de la Gardie ostensibly to support Count Shuisky's claim to the throne. The son of a French officer who had married the natural daughter of John III of Sweden, de la Gardie had been brought up in Finland. With his largely Finnish army he advanced on Moscow, gave battle to the invading Poles under the False Dmitri on the way, and entered Moscow in 1610, an achievement only surpassed by King Sigismund of Poland and Napoleon. It is only fair to say that de la Gardie came as an ally, although he was soon to be involved in hostilities with the Russians in Ingria, near the south-eastern coast of the Gulf of Finland. Peace came in 1617, and by the Treaty of Stolbova the part of Karelia north and west of Lake Ladoga was joined to Finland and Ingria was ceded directly to Sweden. Although the border had now been pushed further east it still cut through areas where Finnish was spoken, and so failed to redeem the hope that all Finnish speakers might be brought under the Swedish crown. The eastern boundary was not to advance for the next three centuries, not until 1920.

The Treaty of Stolbova was also notable for the part in it played by an English mediator at the Russian court. Sent out by James I of England to counter Dutch and Swedish influence and to ensure that the Arctic seaway to Archangel be kept open for British trade, John Merick succeeded in persuading the Russians to oppose Swedo-Finnish attempts to gain a foothold on the Arctic coast.

If language was not a barrier between the King's new subjects and other Finns, religion certainly was. Lutheran Finns moved into the previously Orthodox parishes and their congregations were exhorted to change their religion. Religious persecution increased the people's dissatisfaction with their new masters. When war broke out again in 1656 'Russian' Finns rose up against

'Swedish' Finns and Lutheran and Orthodox villages were burnt to the ground. Once again the Russian advance was repulsed, but as a result of the war the majority of the Orthodox fled to Russia. Five centuries of political and ecclesiastical separation had moulded east and west Finns so differently that they could no longer live together.

Russia's weakness was not to last for ever. At the beginning of the eighteenth century the young Tsar Peter was ready to review his country's borders and extend them to the Baltic again, from which Gustavus II Adolphus had so successfully excluded Russia. The Swedish king, Karl XII, was a headstrong youth who had led his army in many brilliant victories, only to make the mistake of seeking a decisive battle in the heart of Russia. He never got as far as Moscow. His army was defeated at Poltava in 1709. This battle marked the collapse of Sweden's position as a great power, and of Finnish security.

The best Finnish regiments had fallen in Poland, Russia or the Baltic lands, or had been imprisoned in Siberia. In five years the Tsar's armies overran Finland. By the Treaty of Uusikaupunki (Nystad) in 1721 Russia did indeed relinquish most of the country, retaining only Viipuri (Vyborg) and a part of Karelia around Lake Ladoga. But a fundamental change in the Finnish position had taken place. Her own people began to wonder whether an enfeebled Sweden could defend Finland any longer, or whether it would be wiser to accept the inevitable and reconcile themselves to Russian supremacy.

Sweden had indeed succeeded in concluding an alliance with Britain, once the suspicions aroused by Swedish intrigue with the Jacobites had been allayed by the death of Karl XII in 1718. Fear that Russia might now replace Sweden as the master of the Baltic motivated the western members of the anti-Swedish coalition in coming to terms with Sweden. A British fleet in the Baltic under Admiral Norris had even given some assistance against Russian attacks, but preoccupation with trade and the South Sea Bubble inhibited Britain from further support of the Swedish cause.

The Russian occupation of Finland lasted from 1713 to 1721 and is known as the Great Wrath, a term which has come to stand for all that is wretched, cruel and brutal. The Finns were not accustomed to foreign occupation, and the arrival of the feared Russians was a new and terrifying experience. Leading members of the aristocracy and almost all the civil authorities fled the country. The only organization to carry on steadfastly was the Church, which made sure that every parish had at least one clergyman. Terrible stories were heard of the maltreatment, torture and even murder of members of laity and clergy alike. However, most clergymen survived and gained the devotion of their congregations.

The occupation of Finland had been a difficult time but life had continued nonetheless. When the Russians conquered the country a second time two decades later they found a different attitude among the inhabitants. The civil authorities stayed at their posts and the enemy's troops did not have the same opportunity to plunder. By the Treaty of Turku (Åbo), signed in 1743, the Russian border was advanced still further west in south Finland, but once again the occupying forces were withdrawn.

The final conquest was achieved during the Napoleonic Wars, in 1808-9. In alliance with Napoleon, Russia was intent on compelling England's ally, Sweden, to join in the Continental Blockade. As a result of the fighting Finland was occupied by the Russians and this time they did not withdraw. By the Treaty of Hamina (Fredrikshamn) all the Finnish provinces and a part of Västerbotten in Sweden itself were ceded to Russia.

However, the ceded lands were not incorporated into the Russian Empire as Russian provinces. Tsar Alexander I knew that he had not heard the last of Napoleon and it was important that a defeated country as near to his capital as Finland should be pacified. This was best done by offering the Finns better conditions than they had enjoyed under the Swedes. Finnish loyalty was bought at the Diet held in Porvoo (Borgå) in 1809. The country was declared an autonomous Grand Duchy governed by Finns and separate from the Russian government. The Constitution and the entire legislation dating from the Swedish period remained in force. No conscripts were enrolled and taxes were frozen, which over the years meant their virtual reduction.

Thus Finland became a unique state. The laws in force were not the same as in Russia. The country's revenue was employed solely in satisfying its own needs and taxes were no longer collected by authorities in another capital. Russian subjects did not enjoy Finnish nationality but Finns could freely occupy positions in the Russian Empire. In addition the Tsar returned to the Grand Duchy those territories which had been wrested from Finland in the preceding century. When the border was finally marked in Lapland it was drawn several score miles further east in many places. A long period of peace followed and the country's wealth increased. Such was the change in attitude that when the British and French fleets destroyed Russian defences on the Finnish coast during the Crimean War, damaging Finnish property at the same time, there was no mistaking the zeal and conviction with which the Finns took part in repulsing the Western enemy.

Monarch and Subject

The social structure of the nation that had found its living space while allied to Sweden and at war with Russia was based on the independent small farmer. The first settlers who sailed across the Gulf of Finland were free men. So were the generations of Finns who for centuries hacked their way further and further into the virgin forests in the north and east of the country. Free too were the established farmers in the growing villages of the south and south-west. This freedom was based on the farmer's inherited right to own his land, on the principle that taxation was dependent on the taxpayer's agreement, and on the universal right to be allowed one's say in local and provincial courts and, in the last analysis, before the Diet.

When land was cleared for cultivation for the first time it was the property of whoever cleared it, and it passed to his children at death. In this way the land remained in the hands of its cultivators. When freedom from taxation and elevation to the nobility were conferred on certain important landowners from the fourteenth century onwards, in return for cavalry service, this did not give them any rights over their neighbours. Everyone was his own master on his own land.

An organized society must have taxes. We do not know how Finnish tribes paid for the upkeep of their defence castles and religious shrines in the prehistoric era. Church dues are the earliest taxes of which we have records, to be closely followed by Crown imposts in the thirteenth century. Neither authority has relaxed its grip on the Finns since. Until the middle of the sixteenth century, Crown taxes were paid collectively. In the early days of the kingdom it had been agreed that the parish or a section of it should be responsible for a certain annual tax, to be collected by its own nominees and handed over to the Crown bailiff. As the population increased and the parishes became richer the individual's tax burden decreased. From time to time the Crown brought pressure to bear in order to obtain an increase in revenue. An important principle was that the parish collected the taxes itself and its agreement to them was required. In this as in many other fields the Church was cleverer than the Crown. The tithes which it collected in every Christian country had to be paid direct by all householders.

Just as the taxation system encouraged local government, so the administration of justice supported local independence. District justices were eminent local men, and although they were appointed by the Crown from the fourteenth century onwards, only local candidates could be considered for such a responsible office. The judge was assisted by a jury of twelve, who decided on the guilt or innocence of the accused and saw that justice was done in accordance with the people's sense of right and wrong.

State affairs were decided by the king and the much more powerful council, whose members included the bishop of Turku, generally a Finn, and the commanders of the Finnish fortresses, generally Swedes. During the period of internal strife in the fifteenth century, representatives of the common people as well as of the nobility were sometimes invited to join in the council's deliberations. Thus two separate assemblies came into existence, the council and the Diet. In the sixteenth and seventeenth centuries the Diet became representative of the four estates, the farmer taking his regular place beside members of the nobility, the clergy and the burghers.

For two centuries the real reason behind the inclusion of farmers in the Diet was the hope that this would ensure the support of the farming community in times of national emergency and would win their consent to the levying of heavier taxes. The knowledge that they constituted the fourth estate in the realm undoubtedly enhanced their collective self-respect, a feeling hardly shared by the peasants and serfs who were their counterpart in Central Europe.

The Finnish farmer was never a serf. For a short spell during Sweden's ascendancy, when the monarch rewarded noblemen whose help had been decisive in ensuring victory by investing them with fiefs, it had looked as though the nobility might succeed in reducing the farmer to the status of a second-class citizen. But a farmer's hereditary land remained his property despite enfiefment, and although he had to pay Crown taxes and other dues to his lord, the extent of his dues was decided not by the lord but by the Diet. Nor was it permitted to a lord to expel a farmer who met his obligations, no matter how inconvenient the farmer's presence might be. The struggle between poor farmer and rich lord was uneven nevertheless, and there is no telling how it would have ended if the other three estates had not joined forces against the nobility and restored all fiefs to the king, thereby making him an autocrat. Admittedly the estates surrendered all their own rights in favour of an absolute monarch, but they thereby secured for all time the farmer's right to his hereditary plot of land.

The two Karls were the only rulers to enjoy absolute power. Karl XI saved the country and Karl XII destroyed it. After that the people were ready for a change in the system of government. The absolute power of the monarch was exchanged for the absolute power of the estates. The government became entirely dependent on them. When the opposition gained a majority in the Diet it dismissed the council and appointed its own nominees. The Finns were under-represented in all four estates but succeeded in making their presence felt. Political awareness was on the increase and was even noticeable in the Finnish countryside. The Diet was more powerful than any lord and the Finnish farmer could have his say there—provided he spoke in Swedish.

Local self-government suffered a decline in the seventeenth century owing to the increased power of the central government, the altered status of local officials who were now servants of the

Crown, and the change to a system of taxation based on house-ownership. The clergy saved local government by uniting with the farmers. There was no clear boundary between the temporal and the spiritual, and the clergyman, besides being the spiritual father of his parish, was also its guide in worldly matters and the defender of those oppressed by lord or bailiff. The Church was the only institution in which local self-government survived the centralizing policy of the Crown. In the eighteenth century it began to extend its influence again, parish councils taking over responsibility for health measures and the care of the needy, the storing of grain to alleviate famine, and many other matters in addition to purely ecclesiastical affairs. The vicar was *ipso facto* chairman of the parish council although his advice was not always followed by the farmers. As literacy became general just at this time a number of enlightened farmers' leaders made their mark in country parishes, but the scope of their activity was sadly limited by the use of Swedish in public life.

In the towns the system of government by burgomaster and council that had been introduced in the Middle Ages continued almost unchanged for centuries.

A Nation Awakes

With the exception of a small upper class whose speech and mode of thought were Swedish, Finnish society had followed much the same way of life for centuries, jealous of its rights and suspicious of anything new. In the short space of time from about 1840 to 1870 this society underwent a transformation. It is difficult to find simple reasons for this. As so often in history, something which had been developing for several generations was suddenly brought to the surface by favourable stimuli.

There is some uncertainty about who coined the phrase which was to become the motto of the day: 'We are no longer Swedes, we cannot become Russians, let us then be Finns.' There is also some doubt as to what precisely was meant. To each of the three men to whom it has been ascribed it meant something different. To a widely travelled Finnish count Gustaf Mauritz Armfelt the slogan implied a bold political reorientation: pinioned between

Swedish culture and Russian political power, Finland must find its own political identity. To a University lecturer and romanticist of the Turku (Åbo) school, A. I. Arwidsson, it was a call to students to seek out the sources of their nationality in the untapped wealth of the Finnish language and Finnish folklore. To the greatest of the three, the young philosopher and statesman Johan Vilhelm Snellman, it stood for the integration of language and nationhood. The future of Finland therefore depended on Finnish becoming the language of government, public life and education. To achieve this the educated class, estranged from the people by their speech, had to learn Finnish in order that the language of the majority should regain its rightful place.

Snellman was supported by a whole generation of young enthusiasts. Elias Lönnrot made long expeditions to the forest villages of the Finnish and Karelian borderlands, noting down hundreds of folk poems which he then welded into the epic we know as *Kalevala*, first published in 1835. Its publication aroused immediate interest both among educated Finns and in academic circles abroad, besides convincing Finns that their ancestors were not mere forest dwellers, but had been a spiritually gifted race. Matias Alexander Castrén travelled through north Russia and the Siberian tundra and demonstrated how far the Finno-Ugric language group extended. In his poems Johan Ludvig Runeberg sang of Finnish prowess in peace and war. Finally the revolutionary movement in Europe in 1848 stirred Finnish students into demanding national and political liberation in their own country.

The national awakening was in advance of political awareness. Here was further proof that nationhood is not a biological but a historical phenomenon. The overwhelming majority of the educated class and the nobility responded to Snellman's challenge with agreement in principle and with passive expectancy. Their speech did not make them a different nation; constituting 2 per cent of the population the Swedish-speaking gentlefolk felt themselves to be the upper class of the Finnish nation. The humble fishermen and artisans of the coastal regions who spoke Swedish, some 10 per cent of the population, were ignored in this connection. Dissatisfaction among farmers at the continued use of Swedish in courts and government offices made the time ripe for change. In 1863 a law was passed giving Finnish equal status with Swedish in all matters 'concerning the specifically Finnish-speaking population'. A period of twenty years was allowed for the change, and no mention was made of the language to be used in the higher offices of government, but it was a start.

In the same year another great reform was effected. After an interval of over half a century the Tsar summoned the Finnish Diet. The nationalist revival had been accompanied by the growth of strong liberal feeling among the country's leaders. They found it insupportable that political development should be brought to a standstill by the Tsar's neglect of the Diet. Under the constitution the Tsar certainly had the right to summon the Diet or ignore it as he saw fit, but this could no longer satisfy the awakening political consciousness of the Finns, who now wanted a say in their affairs.

Liberal ideas found favour in Russia after the Crimean War, and in the 1860s the new Tsar, Alexander II, agreed to a number of reforms which enjoyed universal approval in Finland. The Diet was to be summoned regularly, elementary schools were established in all parishes, parish and local civil government were separated from each other, the constitutional position of the Church was liberalized. A decisive step was taken towards the granting of liberty to choose one's means of livelihood. The laws were passed by the Finnish Diet and put into effect by the Finnish government in Helsinki. The Finns could now guide their own development in the autonomous Grand Duchy and they often forgot that every law and every reform was in the final analysis dependent on the Russian Tsar's signature.

The idyll was short-lived. Unanimity at home was the first casualty. As long as pro-Finnish sentiments could be expressed in Swedish all was well, but when the law required that documents be produced in Finnish and the Finns demanded that teaching in the schools should be Finnish there were objections. Many members of the upper classes began to notice that they were Swedes after all and urged their fellows to cherish their language and nationality. There was a danger that the nation might split in two, but fortunately it was avoided. Finns and Swedes had become so intermingled over the centuries that the best genealogical authority in the country could not have sorted out the two groups. In the end emotional factors decided who continued to speak Swedish, who learnt Finnish. The liberalization of economic and social life brought a rapid change in the social structure of the country and by the turn of the century the Finnish educated class had grown to such an extent that it outnumbered educated Swedes. Bitter though it sometimes was, the language quarrel did not disrupt the educated class. More and more people became bilingual, marriage frequently brought both sides together, and Russian oppression caused even the extremists to see that they were all in the same boat.

The Road to Independence

Finland's special position had long been a thorn in the flesh of Russian nationalists. It was in any case tiresome that neither Russian money nor stamps were valid on the best bathing beaches near St Petersburg, only twenty miles from the capital and on land that had been conquered by Russian arms. It was irksome too that Russians could not enter the Tsar's service in Finland, and could be sentenced according to the alien Finnish law. The Finns based their political position on absolute loyalty to the Tsar. As long as their relations with the ruler were good they need not bother about his Russian subjects. They seemed even to forget that the Tsar was Russian, thinking of him as 'our Grand Duke' whose all-powerful word kept the malicious Russians in check. The strained political situation in Europe caused by Bismarck led Russia to tighten up her frontier policy. Panslavism was encouraged by imperialistic policies. Under the stress of internal affairs the Tsar quickly sacrificed Finland's special position. In order to ensure the military efficiency of the border defences Finnish autonomy was to be restricted and was to serve the needs of the Empire as a whole.

The February Manifesto of 1899 heralded the policy of Russification. The Finns were astounded. The world had not yet seen Hitler and Nicholas II seemed like the Beast of the Apocalypse. Finnish students skied the length and breadth of the land collecting over half a million signatures for a protest to the Tsar. Some eleven hundred eminent Europeans signed a petition, 'Pro Finlandia', and a deputation headed by a French Senator waited on the Tsar in St Petersburg but was refused an audience. The Finns began a campaign of passive resistance. Officials refused to obey illegal orders and the courts ignored laws and ordinances promulgated on the basis of the February Manifesto and contrary to the constitution. Mahatma Gandhi saw in Finnish disobedience a pattern for his own struggle. But where 300 million Indians succeeded three million Finns failed. Officials were dismissed, political leaders were exiled and an efficient police force kept the country in rein. One man slipped through to revenge some of the exiled leaders. This was Eugen Schauman, and his victim Governor General Bobrikov, one of the most hated men in Finland and author of a new conscription law.

The assassination of Bobrikov in June 1904 and the disasters of the Japanese War (1904–5) were followed by a slight relaxation of Russian pressure. In the ensuing breathing space the Finns reformed their Parliament, with the result that in 1906 they had the most up-to-date parliamentary system in Europe. The franchise was universal on the principle of 'one man one vote', the ballot was secret, representation was proportional, and for the first time in Europe women were given the vote. As a result the working class was brought into the political arena and the Social-democrats gained 40 per cent of the seats in the first Parliament. The reform did not in the least add to the Parliament's real power, although it could with better authority speak in the name of the whole country. The form of government was unaltered and this gave the Tsar almost unlimited power. Once its hold on Russia had been restored the Russian government began to tighten its grip on Finland. Once again Finnish passive resistance was broken. Laws passed by Parliament did not receive the Tsar's assent, and the Finnish Senate was dismissed and replaced by Russians. Finnish autonomy was in practice destroyed, but at the cost of unrelenting hatred of the Russians.

Tradition and Reform

Movements that had a formative influence on European history were also felt in Finland, although generally somewhat later than in Western and Central Europe. The time-lag has also meant a modification and a reduction in the vehemence of these movements, so that Finland has been spared the more disruptive crises of history. Instead of destroying what was old and accepted, Finnish upheavals have built on existing conditions.

There are many examples of the continuity of tradition throughout disturbed times in Finland. The Reformation was considerably milder there than in Central Europe and a shade less radical than in Sweden. In its early stages it was reminiscent of the English Reformation. The historic episcopate and the liturgy based on the Communion were retained, and when the Swedish king, John III, tried to get the Lutheran Church to move a step nearer Catholicism after the Council of Trent, his strongest support came from Finland.

The establishment of a Finnish state by Alexander I in 1809 did not mean a break with tradition. Local and provincial government, schools and the Church, and indeed the entire social system remained unaltered. The only change was that the central offices of government and the Supreme Court, which had been in Sweden, were now replaced by Finnish equivalents, and instead of a king in Stockholm the head of state was a tsar in St Petersburg. It is noteworthy that the Tsar ruled Finland as a constitutional monarch for ninety years; when, after 1899, he began to exercise the prerogatives of an autocratic ruler to which he was accustomed at home, he aroused implacable opposition among the Finns.

Historical continuity is particularly noticeable in the Finnish manifestation of European nationalism. In the middle of the nineteenth century Swedish was the only official language in Finland, although almost 90 per cent of the population spoke Finnish. A language struggle was inevitable and romantic nationalist philosophy supplied the arguments. In theory a struggle between two nationalities, Swedish and Finnish, should have broken out. But this did not happen. The majority of educated Swedish speakers refused to regard themselves as belonging to any other nation than that of their Finnish-speaking countrymen. They were divided on the language question, some learning Finnish but most of them choosing to continue to speak Swedish. However, in course of time many of them became bilingual. Thanks to this the educational tradition which had been Finnish in substance but Swedish in language could be shared equally by both language groups and the Finnish-speaking people did not have to start from scratch and build up a tradition on the basis of a conservative, rural culture.

Let us take a last example from the achievement of Finnish independence. Under Swedish tutelage the Finns learnt to conduct local government. Under the Russians they learnt to govern the whole country. When the ties with Russia were severed Finland had almost all the institutions needed by an independent state, and she had enjoyed a modicum of experience. An army and a foreign policy were all that was lacking. The liberation of the country compelled the Finns to build up the former. The latter was a more exacting requirement and it is only since the Second World War that the Finns have mastered the difficult art of conducting a foreign policy.

But that is another story.

GUIDE LINES

PRESIDENT PAASIKIVI
Independence Day, December 6, 1944

'*Finnish foreign policy is governed by our relations with our great neighbour in the East, the Soviet Union. This is the real problem in our foreign policy and we have to find a solution to it, for the future of our nation depends on it. We have just signed a truce with the Soviet Union. . . . We are all agreed that the provisions of this truce must be conscientiously fulfilled.*'

PRESIDENT PAASIKIVI
on the same day

'*Our social organization and our outlook on life have been determined by nearly 700 years of association with Sweden. This, and the fact that our nation includes a considerable Swedish-speaking population, have led to the establishment of close cultural and economic ties with our western neighbour and with other Scandinavian countries.*'

PRESIDENT PAASIKIVI
to *Dagens Nyheter* reporter, July 31, 1955

'*Good relations with Russia are, and always will be of prime importance to Finland. Geography and history have determined this. In foreign policy we must think geographically, as I have said before, but one cannot repeat it too often. Some people so easily forget to look at the map. And what does history teach us? Although it does not always repeat itself, as was once thought, it is true that all the military engagements that we have been involved in with Russia in the past 250 years have ended in disaster for Finland, whereas we have often achieved worthwhile results when we have met the Russians round a table. In the history of our people the pen has repaired what the sword has broken.'*

>PRESIDENT KEKKONEN
>to the National Press Club, USA, October 17, 1961

'In 1918 we had a civil war. The Finns who fought on the side of the Reds suffered greatly. They too believed they were fighting for Finnish liberty. The memories and bitterness of those days are still with us. Political standpoints acquired as a result of the Civil War have been passed on from father to son. We must also remember that in north and east Finland we have some very poor areas. . . . Life is hard in those parts. There are many people there who support the Finnish People's Democratic Union, and when I have talked to them I have noticed that they do not really know anything about Communism. They vote for the FPDU because they imagine that a change may bring them better living conditions. This attitude is understandable, and one finds it in other places besides north Finland.'

>PRESIDENT KEKKONEN
>to the General Assembly of the United Nations, October 1961

'*We consider that it is our task here to narrow differences, to seek constructive solutions. . . . We believe in the possibility of harmo-*

nizing through conciliation dissimilar interests for the benefit of all. Rather than as judges we see ourselves here as physicians. . . .'

PRESIDENT KEKKONEN
Washington, July 23, 1970

(The USA and the USSR have declared their intention to respect Finland's policy of neutrality.)

'These declarations of policy by the world's two most powerful nations confirm Finland's established position of neutrality. . . . For a country like Finland stability and continuity in external relations are an important advantage. It was therefore in the Finnish interest to extend the Finnish-Soviet Treaty of Friendship, Co-operation and Mutual Assistance without change for a further twenty years. . . . During this period of transition the position of different countries may become subject to uncertainty or speculation. We wish to remove any possible doubt about the consistency of our policy.'

PRESIDENT KEKKONEN
at the White House, USA, July 23, 1970

'It is in our interest to oppose the use or threat of force in international relations wherever it occurs. . . . Finland, as a member of the United Nations, has been and continues to be prepared to do her share in the maintenance of international peace and security. We have contributed men and money to every UN peace-keeping operation.'

'We therefore welcome every constructive effort to replace mutual fear and suspicion by trust and co-operation between all. One means to this end that has been proposed could be the holding of a conference on European security with the participation of all the states involved, including, of course, the United States. We in Finland believe that this is a useful idea, and we have offered to act as hosts for such a conference. . . . We believe Finland would be well qualified for such a role.'

INDEPENDENCE AND AFTER

HEIKKI ESKELINEN

SEVERAL rounds of SALT talks, in which the USA and USSR discussed strategic arms limitations, have taken place in Helsinki since 1969. An interim agreement was signed in the USSR in May, 1972, on anti-ballistic missile systems. The SALT talks held in Helsinki have been among a number of important international conferences for which Finland has provided the setting in recent years.

Not long ago the expression 'Finlandization', meaning the progression of a small state into dependence on a great power neighbour, achieved a certain currency. Lately, however, opinions have been voiced that 'Finlandization' might be best for all Europe. This means the creation of a mutually advantageous co-operation between Western Europe and the USSR (and the group of powers under its leadership) in order to dissipate the atmosphere of mutual fear and to eliminate the threat of war on our continent.

Whatever courses the great power leaders may adopt in furthering their national interests in Europe and in the world, Finland has chosen a policy of her own, which she considers essential to her lasting well-being and to which she is firmly adhering. The lessons of fifty years of independence have been learnt in a hard school. In 1943 Stalin told Roosevelt and Churchill in Teheran, 'The Finns are stubborn. You have to beat sense into their heads with a hammer'. They now seem to have accepted the fact that geography has placed them alongside their great neighbour, sharing with him a frontier 1,000 kilometres (620 miles) long. They want to retain their Western democratic political system, and have gone to war in support of their resolve to maintain their independence—and they have come to realize that a prerequisite for the preservation of their neutrality and detachment from great power disagreements is the confidence of the USSR in their determination and ability to ensure that their territory shall never be used for anti-Soviet ends. They have therefore amalgamated into their traditional outlook on Scandinavian democracy and neutrality the concept of the need to safeguard the security of the Soviet Union's north-western frontier. The world is fortunately starting to understand this outlook. Finland, nevertheless, has had to travel a difficult road before reaching the present situation.

The Background to Independence

Finland is one of the small states whose independence dates from the collapse of three empires in the First World War. It is the only one of those states to have retained the same political structure throughout the storms of the past fifty years. This unique political continuity in an East European country is of course due to more than a happy coincidence of good fortune and good management. Finland's geographical situation next to stable Scandinavian democracies with whom she has shared a common historical tradition since the twelfth century, and her remoteness from the main areas of Russo-German tension, are among the most important causes of her independence. Besides this, Finland was the best prepared of all the states which arose out of the ruins of the Russian, German and Austro-Hungarian Empires. Although national consciousness may have been equally alive in other countries which became independent after the First World War, they lacked the unity of Finland; some were made up of separate areas from different countries, others were the remnants of larger units, while many of them lacked political traditions and institutions of their own. Their social structure was marked by rigid class differences, and they knew little of the tradition of individual freedom common to Northern European countries.

Finland had a comparatively high standard of popular education from the eighteenth century, thanks to the foresight of the Lutheran bishops, and Russian attempts to destroy Finnish autonomy at the end of the nineteenth century evoked opposition from all sectors of the population. From 1906 Finland had the most democratic single-chamber Parliament in Europe. But despite conditions favouring independence, Finland has had a hard struggle to retain her own way of life in our turbulent century, in which so many countries have undergone revolutionary changes. In one respect Finland's success may be compared to England's: they are the only European countries engulfed in the Second World War, whose peoples wholly escaped occupation. Nowadays Finland is the only country with a Western European type of democracy which shares a considerable land frontier with the USSR, a frontier across which there is lively cultural and economic exchange, similar to that uniting Finland with her Scandinavian neighbours and with England and the USA.

In 1914 the outlook was gloomy. Finnish autonomy had been repeatedly violated in the preceding years, after a temporary revival following the Russian rebellion of 1905. News of an Imperial plan for the Russification of Finland, leaked to the public in the autumn of 1914, dashed the last hope that loyalty to Russia during the Great War would lead to the restoration of autonomy. A small circle of Finnish activists had already made plans for armed rebellion and their ranks were now swelled by fresh supporters, especially from among university students.

Immediately after the outbreak of war the activists found support in Germany—they failed to get Swedish support for their plans, due to Sweden's policy of neutrality—and in the next three years some 2,000 young men, mostly students, went to Germany to train for the leadership of an armed rebellion. They formed the 27th Royal Prussian Jäger Battalion and participated to some extent in fighting on the German Eastern Front in Latvia. At home the recruiting officers and the Jägers sent to commit acts of sabotage against the Russians, played cat and mouse with the Russian police. Finns were sent to the Petrograd prisons, but the Russian authorities were humane by comparison with later European occupying forces. However, Finns were no longer trusted, and the occupation was particularly strict at the beginning of the war, when a Swedish or German invasion was expected, aided by the populace.

Not all Finns supported the activists. Many members of the liberal educated class in particular placed their hopes on the Western Powers. It was expected that at the future peace conference they would prevail upon their Russian ally to restore Finnish autonomy, perhaps under new guarantees. Finland should therefore remain firm in her loyalty to Russia despite present sacrifices such as the loss of autonomy and submission to a programme of Russification, all of which the peace conference would reverse. Finland had had no army of her own since the first years of the century, so she was not called upon to shed her blood on the Russian front, but she had to pay for this in millions of marks. There were few volunteers for the Russian army, though a number of Finns traditionally served as officers in it, as well as in the navy, Mannerheim and many others attaining the rank of general or admiral. Russian orders kept Finnish industry busy and defence works occasioned by the fear of a German invasion provided employment for thousands who came in from the country to the cities of west Finland. Even so, there was a general feeling of dismay in the face of Russian oppression. To some this served as an excuse for outrageous swindling, whilst others, counting on a German victory, planned an armed uprising. Elections were duly held in 1916 although Parliament was not summoned. Participation in the elections was small and the result was a surprise: the Socialists gained an absolute majority.

The abolition of the monarchy in the February Revolution of 1917 gave new hope to Russians and Finns alike. The Russian Provisional Government restored Finnish autonomy, and the Finnish socialist and bourgeois parties formed a coalition government. But this was the last time Finns and Russians were to rejoice together. The murder of their officers by Russian troops and the rapid decline in discipline, leading to surprising acts of violence against the civilian population, coupled with mounting political disagreement over the limits of Finland's autonomy, alienated Finnish sympathy. Unrest in Russia was reflected in events in Finland. The men employed on defence works were left without a job by the cessation of the work, Finnish industry suffered a decline due to absence of orders from an increasingly chaotic Russian army, and food imports from Russia ceased, leading to shortages and rising prices. Workers in the cities were haunted by the spectre of famine.

There were also social grievances, even though autonomy had allowed Finland to develop faster than Russia. The Tsar had refused to ratify several reforms during the period of Russification and during the war the work of Parliament had come to a standstill. Supported by headstrong Russian troops and in contact with the Petrograd Bolsheviks, the more extreme Finnish Socialists demanded far-reaching changes. An eight-hour day for industry and a wholly democratic organization of local government were agreed by Parliament, but in the summer of 1917 strikes broke out among agricultural workers and violent clashes ensued.

An immediate source of disagreement between Finnish and Russian officials, once the initial revolutionary ardour had subsided, was the wielding of supreme power in Finnish affairs, previously the prerogative of the Tsar. The Finns wanted complete control of everything except foreign affairs and the armed forces, and complete independence was openly advocated in speeches and newspapers from the spring of 1917 onwards. The Russian Provisional Government considered that it retained control until the Constituent Assembly should be given the right to decide on any change in the relationship with Finland. The attitude of the Provisional Government was strengthened by the 100,000-strong army of occupation and the bulk of the Baltic Fleet, which was in Helsinki. However, the Finnish Socialists entered into negotiations with the Petrograd Bolsheviks, who had declared themselves in favour of self-determination for non-Russian nationalities, and in conjunction with right-wing protagonists of Finnish independence they got a bill through Parliament in July 1917 giving Finland complete control of her affairs.

Meanwhile, a Bolshevik coup in Petrograd misfired and Lenin took refuge in Finland (once again). In Petrograd the Provisional Government declared the Finnish Parliament dissolved. Fearing that parliamentary rule would mean socialist rule and seeing the inevitability of submission to Russian force of arms, the representatives of bourgeois parties in the Finnish Senate, or Government, accepted the dissolution. Thereupon the Socialists left the Government and formed an implacable opposition.

The elections of autumn 1917 were a shock to the Socialists, who expected continuing advance for their party. Participation was much greater than before and the majority of the new voters proved to be anti-socialist. The Socialists lost their majority, which led to increased revolutionary activity in their ranks. Leading positions in the party passed to more extreme members and at the Finnish Socialist Party congress a Russian emissary, Joseph Stalin, called for a social revolution.

The violent acts committed by undisciplined Russian troops and the disturbances of the summer of 1917 led to the formation of volunteer corps of National Guards to replace the Tsarist police. The activists intended to drive the Russians out of the country with the help of these guards and the Germans. But Germany was waiting to see what happened; she had withdrawn the Finnish Jäger battalion from the front after the Russian Revolution and kept it standing idle in Latvia. In the autumn the revolutionary Socialists began to form their own volunteer corps of Red Guards, obtaining arms from the Russian troops. In November the extreme Socialists declared a general strike, during which violent disturbances and confrontations of National and Red Guards occurred.

In October the Bolshevik coup in Petrograd succeeded. Once again the Finnish Parliament declared it was the sole repository of supreme power in Finnish affairs. Led by Svinhufvud, hero of the days of passive resistance, the bourgeois Senate submitted to Parliament the formal declaration of independence and it was approved on December 6th. Now under Lenin's leadership, Russia recognized Finnish independence on January 4, 1918, as did France—with whom Finland had close cultural ties—and Germany and Sweden.

Independence Achieved

Despite the desire of all parties for independence the country was internally divided against itself. In one respect it was near to the English parliamentary system of two large parties—on the one hand a bourgeois block, on the other the Socialist Party. But although socialist parties in the different European countries at war had shared in the national coalition governments, they had not yet become accustomed to the idea of constantly operating as reform parties in bourgeois society, entering the government and observing parliamentary procedure. The situation in Finland was in advance of the times; with almost half the seats in Parliament many of the Socialists were impatient to govern. The social order was of greater importance to them than the popular mandate. Once the more extreme elements had obtained leading positions in the party, the Socialists planned their coup. At the same time the bourgeois Government prepared to expel the Russian troops which Lenin still had not withdrawn. This was originally planned to be done without German help, under the leadership of General Mannerheim, now back from Russia. On the very night, in January 1918, that Mannerheim's National Guards began to disarm Russian garrisons in north Finland, the Red signal of revolt flared up from the roof of the workers' headquarters in Helsinki. Some members of the legal Government fled to Vaasa which became the centre of 'White' Finland, while the Socialist People's Commission took command of Helsinki.

A front line between the two sides was soon established, leaving the larger cities and the best farmland in the hands of the 'Reds'. But they were handicapped by a strike of civil servants and by the lack of experienced leaders. They received only limited assistance from the Russian troops, except for a quantity of arms, and after the Peace of Brest-Litovsk between Russia and Germany, all Russian troops were withdrawn. The Whites had the services of Finnish officers from the Tsarist army and the Jäger battalion which Germany had now repatriated. Mannerheim had the help of Swedish staff officers at his headquarters and some hundreds of Swedish volunteers joined the ranks. Mannerheim intended to put down the rebellion without further foreign aid. Svinhufvud—who had remained in hiding in Helsinki, where he feared the establishment of a terrorist regime—made a dramatic escape to German-held Tallinn on an icebreaker seized from the Russians, and proceeded to Berlin to plead for German aid. Aid came in April, in the form of one division under General von der Goltz, but by this time a decisive battle had been fought at Tampere and the Reds had been defeated. Mannerheim led the victory parade in Helsinki in May.

The Whites considered they were fighting a war of liberation against the Russians and their lackeys, whilst the Reds maintained they were just as much in favour of independence as the Whites and that the war was a civil war. Both views are now felt to be historically justified, the terms used depending on the angle from which one regards the events.

The outcome of the war and the presence of German troops in the country strengthened the position of the Right. Plans were laid to invite a German prince to ascend the Finnish throne, but the defeat of Germany altered this and the constitution which was ratified by Mannerheim as acting head of state in the summer of 1919 confirmed the republicanism of the 1917 declaration of independence. The first President was the liberal Ståhlberg, a professor of law who had been a loyalist and had opposed the Jäger movement. He made it his task to reinforce the constitution and reconcile opposing sides in the Civil War.

At the end of the war the Red leaders fled to Russia, where they founded the Finnish Communist Party in the summer of 1918. A revolutionary programme was announced and underground preparations for an armed revolt were put in hand. The Social-democrat wing, which had largely remained aside from the revolt, re-established the Social-democrat Party in the same summer. In local elections in December they gained majorities in some localities. In the national elections in the spring of 1919 they obtained 40 per cent of the seats. A Social-democrat became speaker in 1921. In 1920, Communist thought was also permitted public expression in the Press and in a party organization under a cover name.

The new republic had some unresolved points of dispute with its neighbours. Sweden's neutral stand in the war of liberation and her attempt to gain control of the Åland Islands had given rise to bitter feelings towards the former mother country. Like other Swedish areas along the coast, the islands had been part of

FINLAND: AN INTRODUCTION

Finland even under the Swedish Crown, before 1809. Memories of the nationality struggle in Finland itself added fuel to the fire. The oldest Finnish institutions of higher education were barely fifty years old, and the acceptance of Finnish as equivalent to Swedish in public offices had been even more recent. Swedish speakers still held a conspicuously high proportion of positions of importance, in both cultural and economic life. A consequence of this was the rise of the 'True Finnish' movement among young educated Finns and farmers. By the middle of the thirties the language quarrel had died down, partly because Finns had gained positions of importance corresponding approximately to their numbers, partly because a new political menace from outside demanded a closing of the ranks. Although Parliament had a majority of Finnish speakers from the start, the language laws were particularly liberal and have served as a model for other countries. The Swedish language, whose speakers then numbered 10 per cent of the population (less now), was given the status of the second national language. Wide autonomy was granted to the Åland Islands and the League of Nations declared in favour of Finnish ownership.

The area inhabited by Finns and closely related peoples stretches far over the eastern border into East Karelia. In the Tsarist period the frontier was open and contact was maintained by trade and intermarriage. The Karelian backwoods were the last stronghold of ancient Finnish folk poetry. In the mid-nineteenth century Finnish collectors of folk poetry stirred the national consciousness, which in turn aroused sterner measures of Russification. In the post-revolutionary chaos the tiny East Karelian nation also made a bid for self-determination. The leaders of the movement had been trained in Finland and were at first aided by Finnish soldiers. In 1918, while war was still being fought in Finland, Mannerheim sent a small force over the border. From then on until the recovery of Russia in 1922, when Soviet forces expelled the last 'White' Karelians and Finns, intermittent battles were fought with varying success. Power politics played their part, Germany and Britain each seeing its interests threatened by the other. A British expedition landed at Murmansk and at one time held the area with White Russians. The East Karelian

INDEPENDENCE AND AFTER

question, ranging from the settlement of refugees on Finnish territory to the setting up of an autonomous Finnish Communist administration in East Karelia, bedevilled Russo-Finnish relations until the end of the Second World War.

The British were seen in force in the Gulf of Finland in the summer of 1919, when the fate of Petrograd was in the balance. Admiral Cowan's fleet visited Helsinki and more easterly ports, whence British torpedo boats made a daring attack on the naval base of Kronstadt. When, twenty years after Cowan's departure, the outlines of another vast conflict began to appear, Soviet military men could hardly ignore this episode. The consequences were to prove disastrous for Finland. Yet Finland had not taken part in the intervention in 1919.

Finland's southern neighbour and related nation, Estonia, had also declared its independence, and Finnish volunteers had joined in the fight against the Bolsheviks in 1918-19. In 1920 separate peace treaties were signed between the USSR on the one hand and Finland, Estonia, Latvia and Lithuania on the other, Poland following a year later. All these countries had been part of the Tsarist Empire, but with differing status, Finland freest of them all. They all feared the threat from the East again once Russia recovered her strength. Finland attempted to maintain a correct attitude towards Russia although the East Karelian question and Russian direction of the Finnish Communist Party's underground activity inflamed public opinion. In foreign policy Finland turned from the pro-German attitude of 1918 and the dependence on British protection of 1919 to the exploration of Baltic co-operation. However, disillusionment was soon felt at a prospect which might involve Finland in Central European disturbances, and in 1922 Parliament rejected the pact that the foreign minister had signed in Warsaw. After this, links with nations to the south were largely of a cultural nature, particularly close in the case of Estonia. Like the rest of Europe, Finland looked to the League to defend the rights of small nations. She was a member of the Council from 1927 to 1930 and made a notable proposal for an international fund to assist victims of aggression. Opposition by Britain, who would have had to foot the largest bill, led to abandonment of the plan.

FINLAND: AN INTRODUCTION

The first years of independence saw several reforms in social conditions. Farmers who rented their land were given the right to buy it, with financial help from the state. Laws relating to compulsory schooling and religious freedom were passed and the social services were enlarged. Economic development proceeded rapidly as Britain came to occupy first place in Finnish trade. With the exception of small groups of extremists the nation began to be welded into one unit.

There was a rapid change towards the end of the twenties. Domestic conditions led to an economic decline in 1928, a year before the world slump, which only made things worse. Bankruptcy, compulsory auctions, unemployment, declining wages, all became stark reality, Simultaneously the Communists stepped up their agitation in accordance with the tactics of the Comintern and a general strike was attempted in 1929. In the unions the Communists first acquired positions of leadership, then exerted pressure on 'white' workers. A series of short-lived governments and unstable coalitions in the twenties were grist to the mill of all opponents of parliamentary government.

The first open conflict occurred in November 1929 in Lapua, a village in southern Ostrobothnia. Right-wing extremists tore the red shirts off participants in a Young Communist provincial congress. 'Lapua' groups were formed in popular meetings all over the country. The movement had a nationalist and religious basis. Communists were regarded as hirelings of a foreign power, on the basis of the events of 1918, and their attitude to religion was particularly deplored. Widespread demands for the banning of the Communist Party were met by its proscription in 1930, although it had received 13·5 per cent of the votes in the 1929 elections under a different guise. The Lapua extremists remained unsatisfied; they proceeded to kidnap and beat-up Communists, and even forced ex-President Ståhlberg into a car and drove him to the neighbourhood of the Russo-Finnish frontier. These actions soon brought disrepute on the perpetrators, and the united opposition of Social-democrats, Liberals and the Swedish Party, together with increasing support from Conservatives and Agrarians, led to the decline of the movement. It came to an end with a rebellious meeting at Mäntsälä, near Helsinki, in 1932, when the handful of rebels was forced to surrender without bloodshed. The IKL (Patriotic People's Movement) which took its place proved equally unsuccessful, its strength in Parliament declining from fourteen members in 1934 to eight (out of 200) in 1939.

From 1933 onwards Finland's economy recovered more rapidly than that of many countries. Exports increased and were of a higher category, with paper and cellulose replacing raw timber as the main item. This recovery was achieved by pre-Keynesian methods, and the orthodox attitude was evident in Finland's repayment (unique among debtor states) of the American debt incurred during the First World War. In a country short of capital greater material advantage might have been obtained by investing the money in productive machinery, but the goodwill engendered by this repayment was of incalculable value to Finland in subsequent trials. Increased production brought a rising standard of living to all sections of the population and political passions became less violent, so that the twentieth anniversary of independence could be celebrated in 1937 in an atmosphere of mutual understanding by Swedish and Finnish speakers, socialists and bourgeois alike.

In the early thirties (1932 for Finland), the USSR signed non-aggression pacts with her western and southern neighbours. In 1934 she entered the League of Nations where Litvinov put forward his thesis of collective security. Nothing came of it and the fate of Ethiopia, whom the League was powerless to help, showed small nations the dangers of the international situation. Finland had tried to build her security on an illusion. The Anglo-German naval agreement of 1935 evoked counter measures from Russia. The Soviet envoy in Helsinki informed Finland that if war broke out between the USSR and other great powers, Finland would be occupied, for which the Red Army would require six days. The 'Eastern threat' that extreme Finnish nationalists had spoken of since 1918 was now brought to the fore by power politics.

Finland attempted to convince Russia of her earnest desire to remain neutral. Seeing the failure of the League she chose the path of alignment with traditionally neutral Scandinavia. On December 5, 1935 Parliament unanimously approved a statement that

FINLAND: AN INTRODUCTION

Finnish foreign policy was to be on Scandinavian lines. On the radio the three Scandinavian prime ministers welcomed Finland into their company. With the rise of Hitler the Social-democrats acquired a more positive attitude to the country's defence and last-minute attempts to strengthen it were put in hand. It has been said that the USSR might never have attacked Finland if she had been convinced of Finland's ability to defend herself against a possible German landing—a conviction she certainly could not have in view of the weakness of Finnish armament. Finland proposed co-operation with Sweden for the defence of the Åland Islands, which were demilitarized by international agreement, but the criticism voiced by both Stalin and Hitler caused Sweden to reject the plan, leaving Finland isolated.

From the autumn of 1938, international politics moved precipitately towards war. The Munich Agreement gave Hitler the Sudetenland and six months later he marched on Prague. England's guarantee to Poland followed, and the Western Powers sent their negotiators to Moscow. At the end of August 1939 the Russo-German Non-aggression Pact relieved Hitler of the fear of war on two fronts while Stalin obtained two years' grace. In a secret protocol the dictators divided Europe between themselves. After the two armies had met on the demarcation line in Poland in the middle of September, Stalin began to put into effect his part of the deal in Northern Europe. Estonia, Latvia and Lithuania were compelled to sign agreements permitting the Red Army to establish bases on their territory. At the beginning of October Finland was asked to send negotiators to Moscow. The demands for territorial concessions in the Karelian isthmus, known of old, were now more extensive than previously. The frontier suggested would have pierced the modest Finnish defence system, while a new demand was for a naval base on the northern coast at the entrance to the Gulf of Finland. The Red Army was concentrated on the frontier and Molotov rejected Swedish and American offers of mediation. Mobilization was ordered in Finland as early as October. The pact between Stalin and Hitler had united extremists of both sides with the rest of the nation, which now formed a single unit, conscious of its destiny and awaiting the judgment of history.

INDEPENDENCE AND AFTER

The Winter War
There were indeed many Finns who had an almost biblical view of history: it was their conviction that God or some cosmic forum saw to it that wrong did not win. Such idealism helped a weak party in an uneven struggle. There were other illusions to nourish people's confidence. It was especially difficult for Social-democrats to believe that a socialist state would unleash an unprovoked attack. Some held that this was merely a war of nerves; there would be no attack provided Finland remained firm. The last illusion was that the Western Powers would not stand back while Finland fought for her existence.

The small concessions made by the Finns in the Moscow negotiations were not enough. The Government felt unable to go further in spite of Mannerheim's advice. At the end of November Molotov accused Finland of staging a border incident. He refused to allow either joint investigation or arbitration and denounced the Non-aggression Pact. An ultimatum might have persuaded the Government to reconsider its position but none was received. On November 20th, the Red Army invaded Finland and Finnish towns were bombed, without a declaration of war. On the following day a 'government' of emigré Finnish Communists led by Otto Kuusinen was set up in Terijoki, a village on the border, and a treaty of union with the USSR was signed, whereby *inter alia* the greater part of East Karelia was united with Finland. Thereafter the Soviet Union did not consider itself at war with Finland—it was giving aid to the Terijoki Government at its request. The last act of the League of Nations was to expel the USSR for its attack on Finland.

Instead of the walkover the Red Army expected on invading Finland they experienced 105 days of hard fighting, during which the Finns were helped by the difficult terrain, to which they were accustomed, and the exceptionally hard winter. Foreign aid was almost negligible, except for arms and volunteers from Sweden. At first the invader was repulsed on all fronts and lost heavily in the pincer movements in the forests north of Lake Ladoga. February saw the beginning of a six weeks' battle on the Karelian isthmus in which the Finns fought without reserves of men or ammunition and were driven back from their defence lines to the outskirts of Viipuri. With the unexpected prolongation of the struggle Britain and France planned to send aid but the project came to nothing because the Scandinavian countries refused to permit transit of troops.

Although disenchantment was felt in Finland at the time, later events showed that this was a wise decision. The Finnish Government was under no illusions concerning Western promises and in March 1940 it signed the onerous Peace of Moscow. Some 11 per cent of Finnish territory was surrendered, moving the frontier in the south-east to where it had been at the time of Peter the Great. The surrender of property amounted to 12 per cent of the national wealth. In the south-west, the port of Hanko and the surrounding area were leased to Russia as a naval base. The entire population of the ceded areas, 422,000 in all, left their homes and moved into a shrunken Finland. Their resettlement was made a matter of national responsibility, farmers receiving land requisitioned from large landowners, while other property owners were compensated on a sliding scale according to their losses. The whole operation was financed by an extraordinary property tax levied in 1940, and again in 1945.

The end of the Winter War found Finland in a difficult position. Normal international trade was disrupted by the European war. Before the war Finland had been largely self-supporting in food and had even exported dairy produce, but this was due to extensive use of imported fertilizer. In the later war years grain had to be imported, and this was obtained from Germany. The only home-produced fuel was wood, while lubricants, medical supplies and industrial equipment all had to be imported. The British Navicert system permitted a trickle of supplies to be brought in via Petsamo on the Arctic coast. After the occupation of Norway, which brought the Germans dangerously close to this route, and especially after Russia broke off trade relations in January 1941, Finland was dependent on Sweden and Germany.

An Uneasy Peace and the Second Finnish War

Finnish security continued to pose a problem. Discussions with Norway and Sweden on the formation of a Northern defence union were frustrated by Molotov's veto and Norway remained alone to face the German invasion. In the summer of 1940 the possibility of a Swedo-Finnish political union was explored but in December Molotov announced that this would be an infringement of the Treaty of Moscow.

Throughout 1940 and 1941 Soviet-Finnish relations were extremely tense, with the Soviet Union making fresh demands, such as the use of the waters of the Vuoksi river or the return of property removed from the surrendered territories. The Petsamo nickel mines proved a particularly troublesome problem. The Anglo-Canadian Mond Corporation had installed new plant shortly before the war. Apart from what she obtained from the Soviet Union this was the only source of supply easily available to Germany. The Soviet Union was not satisfied with equal rights of purchase with Germany but wanted to acquire the lease of the mines. Negotiations in Moscow were in the hands of the Finnish envoy Paasikivi, who had also conducted the 1939 negotiations. They dragged on until the spring of 1941 with no result, punctuated by various crises. In August 1940 it had been rumoured in diplomatic circles that a new attack on Finland was planned and Hitler ordered his army in Norway to be ready to seize the nickel mines. The Soviet Union's dissatisfaction was finally made plain in January 1941 by curtailment of trade relations, jeopardizing Finnish supplies of wheat.

In July 1940, the Red Army completed the occupation of the Baltic States and their new governments requested union with the USSR, a request that was readily granted, while a Soviet ultimatum to Rumania forced the surrender of Bessarabia and Northern Bukovina. There was great activity among extreme left-wing circles in Finland at this time due perhaps to a suspicion that union with the Eastern neighbour was imminent. At this juncture the Soviet Union chose to demand transit rights over the Finnish railway system to the naval base at Hanko, just when Sweden had granted Germany limited transit facilities to Norway. Agreement between Finland and the USSR was reached in September 1940, at the moment when Germany was turning her attention to the East.

Following his defeat in the Battle of Britain, Hitler ordered an investigation of the possibilities of attack in the East. Up to this time Germany had shown no interest in Finland, in accordance with the 1939 pact. In Finland even the Coalition Government of the Winter War period had not included a representative of the extreme Right, and the leaders of the Government were Liberals and Social-democrats of Western orientation. Now that she was planning an Eastern campaign Germany turned her attention to Finland and Rumania, both of whom had suffered losses to the Russians. Indication of the change came in the releasing of Finnish armament purchases in countries occupied by Germany, in a German promise to sell arms to Finland, and in a request that German soldiers on leave might be allowed transit through Finland to north Norway. The request was clearly political, for the small numbers involved could easily have travelled through Scandinavia. Finland acceded to the request, hoping that Germany's evident interest in Finland would deter the Russians from making any further demands. So it happened that from September 1940 there were both Russian and German troops in transit through Finland. As the signs of war became clearer the situation became more irksome.

In April 1941 the Soviet Union speeded up deliveries to Germany and instituted a phase of more cordial relations with Finland, restoring grain deliveries. But Finland had experienced too much, and been drawn too far in the wake of Germany for a sudden change in the Russian attitude to dispel the doubts of her leaders concerning the USSR. Germany claimed to be representing Finland in far-reaching discussions with the USSR, who wanted, according to Germany, a free hand to deal with Finland in the same way as with the Baltic States. Early in June Germany informed Finland that war with the USSR was most probable and military talks were initiated, Finland insisting that she would fight only if attacked. But whatever the form of works in the negotiations, Finland was in fact in a cleft stick. Not to have negotiated with Germany would have deprived her of any influence on the course of events, left her open to occupation and might have turned the country into the battlefield of two foreign armies. If that had not happened a difficult supply position would have created conditions under which Germany could have compelled Finland to enter the war on less favourable terms.

INDEPENDENCE AND AFTER

The Soviet Union fulfilled the terms for Finnish entry on June 25, 1941, when several Finnish towns were bombed. A unilateral statement in Hitler's speech on the declaration of war on Russia, claiming that Finland was joining the campaign, may have misled the Russians, although Britain stated several times during the early days that Finland was neutral. The Russians may also have drawn conclusions from the arrival of German divisions in Finnish Lapland. It has also been claimed that the Luftwaffe provoked the Russian attacks by flying over Leningrad and the Hanko base in such a way as to appear to have come from Finnish airfields. And Britain, although she went a long way in her understanding of Finland's desire to remain neutral, had thrown Finland completely into the arms of Germany only a week earlier by ceasing shipments to Petsamo.

With Russian troops heavily engaged further south, Finland rapidly regained control of the territories ceded in 1940. Nazi plans to destroy Leningrad were not shared by Mannerheim, who preferred to advance into East Karelia and settle down to a holding operation. Mannerheim politely refused Churchill's request that Finland cease her advance, although he avoided cutting the Murmansk railway. Britain was compelled to declare war on Finland in December 1941 in order to satisfy her Russian ally. However, Finland was never at war with the United States and Free France.

After Stalingrad it was clear that a German defeat was only a matter of time, but it was not easy for Finland to extricate herself from the war. Food stocks were strictly regulated by the Germans so that no reserves could be built up. Finnish sympathy for victims of the Nazis in Norway and Estonia was one cause of strained relations between the two co-belligerents. Nor was the plight of European Jews ignored in Finland, where Jewish men served in the army like any other Finn. German attempts to get back several hundred Jewish refugees who had escaped from central Europe were thwarted at the last moment by the granting of Finnish nationality. In north Finland the Germans were virtually in charge although they did not interfere with the Finnish civil administration.

Peace feelers put out in 1943 showed the Russian demands to

be so extreme that they could not be considered. Hoping that East Karelia would be a good bargaining counter in future negotiations, Finland waited for a weakening of Germany's hold on her. However, a surprise attack by the Red Army along the Karelian isthmus on June 9, 1944 compelled a rapid evacuation of troops from East Karelia. After twelve days of fierce fighting against an enemy vastly superior in numbers the Finns were driven back north of Viipuri, where a new defence line was established. In return for supplying arms Germany insisted on a political agreement with Finland. This difficulty was solved by President Ryti signing a letter on his own behalf in an effort to buy time for a negotiated peace with Russia. He thereby violated the Constitution. By July the battles around Lake Ladoga were dying down—the Russians had to move troops and arms for their drive on Berlin—and in August the Finns repulsed the last Russian attempt to surround the Finnish army north-east of Lake Ladoga. This created the necessary conditions for negotiations and Finland was informed via Sweden that the Soviet Union had reconsidered its earlier demand for unconditional surrender and now offered a truce, admittedly on stern conditions.

President Ryti resigned at the beginning of August and was replaced by Mannerheim, who informed the Germans that the agreement with Ryti was no longer valid. A cease-fire came into operation on September 4, 1944 and the truce was signed in Moscow a fortnight later, to be ratified by the Treaty of Paris in 1947. Finland ceded to Russia the same territory as in the Peace of Moscow of 1940, plus the nickel mines of Petsamo, thus losing her outlet to the Arctic Ocean. A base at Porkkala, nearer to Helsinki, was leased instead of Hanko, and reparations to the value of 300 million dollars at 1938 values were to be paid in industrial products. German property was to be made over to Russia, and German troops were to be interned or driven out if they did not leave voluntarily within two weeks. This they did not do, and fighting between Finns and their former brothers-in-arms continued through the autumn in Lapland from where the civilian population had been evacuated to the south or to Sweden. By December most of the area had been cleared of Germans, except for some bases in north-west Lapland which they held until April 1945. In their retreat they wrought destruction on all that lay in their path and planted millions of mines.

Post-war Recovery

Finland's losses in the entire war period amounted to 86,000 dead (of whom 84,000 were soldiers and only 2,000 civilians), 60,000 disabled, a refugee population of 400,000, and a devastated northern half of the country. Food supplies were negligible, industrial plant run down, and the country had to pay relatively the severest reparations in history, the total involved amounting to at least 1,000 million post-war dollars. But what was most important of all had been saved—political independence and the nation's liberty.

Participation in elections since the war has been 10 to 20 per cent greater than pre-war, partly due to the enfranchisement of the extreme left in the now legal Communist Party. In the immediate post-war years the Communists expressed their resentment at the treatment meted out to them in pre-war years by staging strikes and demonstrations, but they have since accommodated themselves better to a developing Finnish democracy, playing their part as a radical opposition. From 1944 to 1948 and again from 1966 to 1970 they have been represented in a coalition government of left and centre parties.

In foreign policy a complete reorientation was necessary after the war. This was achieved gradually, under the leadership of Paasikivi, who was Prime Minister immediately after the war and President from 1946 to 1956. Even in the early days of this century Paasikivi had been among those who strove to reconcile Finnish autonomy with the demands of Russian security. But the view generally held before the war was that Finland was a Western outpost against the East. The experience of the two wars demonstrated the error of this view.

Paasikivi's new aim was to ensure Finnish security and at the same time convince the Soviet Union that Finnish territory would not be used as a base for an attack on Leningrad. He held that the USSR's interest in Finland was purely military. The war had dispelled any illusions that Moscow may have had in the thirties about the desire of the Finnish working class and Finnish farmers to be governed by that well-known Finnish member of the Comintern, Otto Kuusinen. It was therefore of prime importance to reconcile the Soviet Union's concern for the defence of its north-west frontier with the preservation of a Western type of democracy in Finland. During the past twenty-five years, under the leadership first of President Paasikivi, then of President Kekkonen, this new line in Finnish foreign policy has led to the creation of a spirit of trust and co-operation with Russia.

Sweden and America gave incalculable assistance in the development of Finnish industry to meet the reparations requirements, and a lively trade with Russia and Britain was soon established. Immediately after the war, Britain regained her traditional position as Finland's main trading partner. Realizing that Russia did not regard Marshall Aid with favour, Finland made no attempt to obtain it.

After the Prague revolution of 1948 the USSR invited Finland to discuss the signing of a treaty of friendship and aid, similar to the treaties entered into with Hungary and Rumania. Despite doubts expressed by some outsiders, the ensuing treaty takes full account of the special relationship between Finland and the USSR, and differs from the treaties with other East European countries. Finland is made responsible for the defence of her own territory only, and if Soviet assistance is required this is to be given in a manner to be agreed upon by both parties. Finland's desire to keep out of the disagreements of the Great Powers is expressly recognized and in a later statement the Soviet Union has explained that the treaty is in effect a guarantee of neutrality.

The Berlin crisis of 1948-9 did not directly affect Finland, but the second crisis of 1961 led to a proposal from the USSR for consultations in the spirit of the Treaty of Friendship, Co-operation and Mutual Assistance. After personal negotiation by President Kekkonen the demand for consultations was withdrawn.

In the fifties, most Western powers publicly expressed their understanding of Finnish neutrality. In 1952 the last reparations delivery sailed from Finnish waters and in 1956 the USSR returned the base at Porkkala to Finland, in advance of time. In the same year Finland joined the Nordic Council, whose aims are the co-ordination of legal, social and cultural matters in the Northern countries. She was also allowed to join the United Nations (great power disagreement over the policy of admissions had blocked the way to all new members, including Finland, for almost ten years). Since then Finnish UN military contingents have been stationed along the Suez Canal and in Sinai and are at present performing peace-keeping duties in Cyprus. Oustanding contributions to the United Nations have been made by the late Mr Sakari Tuomioja, a diplomat, and General A. E. Martola. The country's policy of scrupulous neutrality in UN questions earned her a seat on the Security Council and led her UN Ambassador, Mr Max Jakobson, into the forefront of today's UN scene.

In 1961 Finland joined EFTA as an associate member on special terms which safeguarded the interests of her vital trade with the East. In 1972, arrangements were negotiated with the Common Market, which has assured Finland of its understanding for her special position. She is also a member of OECD and conversations are likewise in progress for closer co-operation with COMECON, although the economic systems of its consituent states diverge from hers.

Finland's traditional partners are the United Kingdom and West Germany, both essential customers for her forest products. Additionally, exports of her highly developed industries and in particular her fashion goods have gratifyingly increased. At the same time trade eastwards has been lively and co-operation close. Examples of this have been a number of important Finnish building projects on Soviet soil, the construction of the country's first atomic power stations with the aid of Soviet techniques and the current plan to procure Soviet natural gas for use in Finnish industry.

On the Russian side a unique arrangement has been the grant of transit rights through the Saimaa Canal, joining the Gulf of Finland to the lake system—a route severed by the establishment of new frontiers in 1940 and 1944. So far the traffic has not reached its target—land transport has developed substantially during the past 25 years—but the Canal and its bridges leading eastwards symbolize the development of Finland's position. The

FINLAND: AN INTRODUCTION

Finns, in fact, no longer see their country as an outpost of the West but as a bridge uniting two cultures, promoting co-operation advantageous to all. Yet they will remain—like other nations—firm in their attachment to their own special national character and their traditional Western democratic system.

COMMUNISM—FINNISH STYLE

OLAVI BORG

Finland is the third European non-Communist country, after France and Italy, in which the Communists have become a major political party, playing an important national role. Support for Socialism in Finland goes back to the beginning of the century; Communism proper has had its adherents since the early twenties. However, unlike France and Italy, the constitution and political structure of the country have remained unchanged over more than five decades of independence. Party dividing lines and indeed party support in Finland are still largely based on traditional class differences and economic contrasts.

Nevertheless these lines are starting to blur, as emerged unmistakably in the parliamentary elections of 1966 and 1970, which produced big increases in the numbers of floating uncommitted voters.

All the usual groupings of the multi-party state are represented: Conservatives, Liberals and Agrarians; and moderate and radical Socialists, i.e. Social-democrats and Communists. Since the end of the Second World War, Finnish Communism has had approximately the same degree of support as the Social-democrat Party. Midway between these two is the small Social-democratic League, which entered the political arena in the fifties.

At about this time there also appeared a new Agrarian group, the Finnish Small-holders Party, which later changed its name to the Finnish Rural Party. Populist and poujadist in outlook, the party made headway in the 1968 communal elections and in the 1970 General Election secured over 10 per cent of all votes cast.

Finland can be divided into two fundamentally different parts:

the well-developed, urbanized and industrialized 'welfare-Finland' of the south and west, and the under-developed, agrarian 'development-area-Finland' of the north and east. As support for Communism is strong in both these areas, students of politics have had to admit the inadequacy of the usual theories that Communist support springs only from bad social conditions. A special feature of Finnish Communism is that Communists have been members of the government, first in the exceptional political circumstances immediately after the war, and during the fifties and sixties under normal conditions.

Finnish Communism has its roots in the Marxist ideology which spread to Finland at the end of the last century from Central Europe, particularly Germany and Austria. With its image of the ideal community and its plausible explanation of deep social inequality, Marxism was enthusiastically adopted by the industrial working class and the many artisans, tenant farmers and labourers who together made up more than 70 per cent of the population in 1890. The Socialist ideology not only explained to them the causes of social injustice; it also seemed to offer a simple way out.

The Socialist break-through came in 1907, when 70 per cent of the population voted in the first elections to a single-chamber Parliament under conditions of universal suffrage. The Finnish Social-democrat Party won 80 of the 200 seats. This was evidence of the change in the political climate due both to social development and to the worsening of relations between the autonomous Grand Duchy of Finland and Tsarist Russia. However, the Social-democrat Party programme did not embrace the Communist dogma of the dictatorship of the proletariat any more than it accepted the necessity of a revolution to promote Socialism, doctrines which Lenin in particular developed from the writings of Marx and Engels and published in 1903.

As an organization the Finnish Communist movement did not come into being until fifteen years later, as a result of what Finns call 'the events of 1918'. Having declared itself independent of Russia on December 6, 1917, Finland became involved in a short but bitter civil war between 'Reds' and 'Whites' in the early months of 1918. When this ended in victory for the Whites,

United paper mills, Valkeakoski

One of the Lake Saimaa fleet, near Savonlinna

many of the Red leaders fled to the new-born USSR. These men, many of whom had been active in the unified working-class party that existed before the war, founded the Finnish Communist Party in exile at the end of August 1918. They based their programme on uncompromisingly revolutionary Marxist-Leninist doctrine. The close relationship between Lenin and Otto Ville Kuusinen, for many decades the real leader of the party, and Kuusinen's high position in the Comintern and afterwards in the Russian Communist Party itself, had an important bearing on the status of the Finnish Communist Party.

But a party in exile soon loses contact with the political realities of the home country. For a while after its foundation the Finnish Communist Party tried to initiate a new revolutionary movement in Finland, but its banning from all parliamentary, co-operative and trade-union activities had the effect of reducing its popularity. In 1920 an undercover Communist Party was formed which tried to combine illegal underground activity with parliamentary action in conformity with the policy then laid down by the Comintern. This Socialist Working People's Party achieved marked success in the elections in 1922, when it gained 14·8 per cent of the votes on its first appearance at the hustings, but it was banned from parliamentary activity in 1923 and all its deputies were imprisoned despite parliamentary immunity. The group appeared under different names in elections up to the end of the twenties, winning between 10 and 15 per cent of the votes. Parliamentary support for Finnish Communism thus had its origins in the 1920s.

As right-wing radicalism gained ground in Europe a similar process was at work in Finland. At the beginning of the thirties all Communist activity was made illegal by the 'Communist laws'. The Party went underground, where it was to remain for a long time. In subsequent elections up to the outbreak of the Second World War the Communists transferred their support more and more to the Social-democrats.

At the outbreak of the Winter War a Finnish government, composed of exiled Finnish Communist leaders, was formed at Terijoki, a village on the Karelian isthmus occupied by Russian troops. The Terijoki government had no political standing in

Finland and the decision demonstrated a misjudgment of the Finnish internal situation. The political and historical background to this episode is still in dispute among researchers.

When Finland signed the armistice with Russia in September 1944 the Finnish Communist Party was legalized and it resumed activity at once, using another name for tactical reasons. In order to gain a wider base it joined with dissident left-wing Socialist groups to form the Finnish People's Democratic Union. This union was the first well-organized attempt to put into effect in post-war Europe the new Communist Party lines and Yrjö Leino, one of the most prominent leaders of the Union, was the first Communist minister in a non-Communist country in Europe. Under close Communist control, though without the outward appearance of Communism, the Union has represented left-wing radicals in the Finnish Parliament since the war.

The basic objective of the Finnish People's Democratic Union was to unite all left-wing groups and even 'progressives' on the left-wing of non-Socialist parties, in support of a policy of radical national reform. But when the Communists took over the leadership from the start, other groups which might have co-operated soon seceded from it. The outcome was that the Finnish People's Democratic Union became a party organization in its own right, partly parallel to, partly within the real Communist Party, yet clearly broader than it. The Finnish Communist Party is in fact a corporate member of the FPDU with a membership of its own of about 55,000 in 1966. The Finnish Women's Democratic League and the small Academic Socialist Society belong to the FPDU. Total membership of the Union including Communists, is about 150,000. In accordance with the rules about 90 per cent of the members of Parliament representing the FPDU are members of the Communist Party. During the two decades following 1945, support for the FPDU was steady, ranging from a peak level of 23·5 per cent in that year to a lowest level of 20 per cent in 1948. Examination of voting trends and results since then have shown an initial slight decline which was followed, in the General Election of 1966, by a marked diminution in support for the group (in 1970 they received only 16·6 per cent of the votes).

The Finnish People's Democratic Union was represented in all three governments in the years immediately after the war. In the last of these governments, which lasted from 1946 to 1948, the Union had six ministers, including the Prime Minister, Mauno Pekkala. For the next eighteen years the Union was in opposition, then in 1966 it joined the Social-democrats and the Centre Party (previously the Agrarians) to form a 'National Front' government of centre and left-wing elements, in which it had three ministers. Although this administration came to an end following the presidential election of 1968, its successor resembled it in composition and pursued a similar political line. In all, the two 'National Front' governments lasted some four years.

The new administration which took office after the General Election of 1970 once more included Communists, their sixth cabinet participation. Its salient feature was that it was the broadest-based government in the country's history, covering the political spectrum from bourgeois liberals and conservatives of the centre to 'revisionist' and 'dogmatist' Communists. However, the very width of its political compass attenuated its effectiveness and led to its downfall. The immediate cause of its collapse came from the Communists themselves, whose inter-party disagreements finally made them go into opposition.

We have alluded to the strength of Communism both in the prosperous south and west of Finland and in the poorer north and east. The sociologist Erik Allardt has spoken of the dual nature of left-wing radicalism in Finland and coined the terms *industrial Communism* and *backwoods Communism*. These two varieties of radicalism, though acknowledging the same political ideology, arise out of two very different social sources. The mark of industrial Communism is that its strength is founded on the historical tradition surrounding events such as the Civil War of 1918, on the forces that supported the unified Socialist Party before independence, and on class conflicts. It cannot be said to have any direct connection with the economic insecurity brought about by unemployment and poverty.

Backwoods Communism, on the other hand, appears to thrive in conditions of economic insecurity, particularly when there is unemployment. The effects of the world slump of the thirties and of endemic unemployment in north and east Finland after the Second World War support this thesis. Backwoods Communism is a much younger phenomenon than industrial Communism, the result mainly of the spread of radicalism among small farmers and forest workers after the Second World War, when they were drawn into social and political life. Of the other political parties in north and east Finland, the former Agrarian (present Centre) Party in particular took a radical line, recalling in some respects the social agrarianism found for instance in certain Canadian provinces. Finnish Communism is primarily a movement of social protest. The rank and file are not well versed in the party ideology but vote for the party to show their opposition to existing conditions. They tend to be conservative and nationalistic in their attitudes. The revivalist movement known as 'Laestadianism' thrives in just the same areas as does backwoods Communism. Sectarianism and Communism offer these people much the same kind of opportunity to protest. So, too, does a new populist party, the Rural Party, which is already eroding the backwoods Communist vote.

Industrial Communism is a radical, left-wing movement deeply rooted in Finnish life. It is not an exceptional political attitude to be explained away on grounds of either personal or social disturbance, which is the traditional explanation of support for Communism. The protagonists of Communism in the developed areas of the country are by no means the rootless social outcasts they are sometimes said to be. Communism is an established way of life which is gradually gaining acceptance by society. Even so, left-wing radicalism and its organizations form a kind of political and social minority culture, still divorced from the national culture as a whole. The integration of this minority culture with the rest of Finnish society, even provided that it acknowledges the democratic constitution of the country and its tradition of liberty, is something about which Finns are still divided. It is however obvious that progress is in the direction of mutual reconciliation, leading to national integration.

This division extends also to the Communists themselves who, as we have seen, on one occasion considered the unity of the party more important than participation in the government and, by implication, than reconciliation with other sectors.

How the Communists will come to terms with this dilemma will emerge only in the future. Meanwhile, national harmony is the acknowledged political goal, and it seems clear that mutual reconciliation and integration must eventually be achieved.

THE CHANGING RURAL SCENE

W. R. MEAD

It is estimated that Finland has about 800,000 hectares of cultivated land in excess of its needs. In addition, since output is likely to increase more than consumption, another 100,000 hectares may well become redundant between 1970 and 1980. Given the present level of demand for farm products the biggest Finnish farming problem of the decade is to identify the least efficient farmed land and allocate it to other uses.

How has this unusual situation developed? The pattern of Finnish farming, static for many generations, has gone through many changes in the last fifty years. The farmer has always been crucial for Finland because he has provided the country's food. His lot has always been hazardous because Finland lies on the physical limits of field husbandry. When Finland escaped from the stage of subsistence farming into an exchange economy, Finnish farmers found themselves on the economic margin as well as the physical margin of production. An added difficulty was the structure of Finnish farming. Finland is proverbially a country of small-holdings operated by owner occupiers. A key figure in Finnish society is the talonpoika (bonde, in Swedish)—once mistranslated as peasant, better interpreted as yeoman. His isolated home, with the large farm buildings that represent such a high capital outlay, is usually in the midst of a holding consolidated during earlier land reforms. Its forest area generally far exceeds the cropped land.

In proportion to the total population of Finland, the farm community is relatively high, though declining. Farmers constitute a sufficiently important element in society to maintain their own powerful political party. Despite the increased drift from the land during the last generation, strong family links with farming remain among townsfolk. For most Finns, farming is more than a way of making a living. The philosophy of the early twentieth-century social scientist Hannes Gebhardt still colours contemporary Finnish attitudes—'Woe to the people and the country that loses its feeling for the soil.'

Finland has experienced a major agrarian revolution since the First World War. The deficiencies that once stamped it a famine land have been converted into surpluses in a number of fields of production—this at the same time as rapid population increase. The reasons for these surpluses are chiefly physical and technical, but they are inseparable from education and organization. The physical circumstances of Finnish farming have been greatly improved through increased fertilization (with artificial fertilizers principally of domestic origin), more effective drainage (especially of sub-soil drainage in the place of the widespread open ditch), breeding of more resistant swifter-ripening and heavier-yielding grains, the promotion of grassland husbandry, more effective systems of rotation, the development of better strains of animals, the rise of poultry farming, mink farming and horticulture.

Side by side with these improvements, Finnish farming has been speedily mechanized: the tractor has largely replaced the horse; bulldozers have transformed land clearance, road building and drainage. Mechanization has been speeded by reducing the size (and consequently cost) of farm equipment such as milking machines and combine harvesters and by the establishment of domestic plants for their manufacture. Rationalization of farm buildings may have reduced the picturesqueness of many holdings, but has increased their efficiency. Educational institutions and advisory services have speeded the diffusion of ideas and techniques. Not surprisingly a country which, despite physical handicaps, has achieved both diversification of production and flexibility in management has attracted the attention of world organizations.

Agricultural transformation has been the more impressive because it has taken place in spite of the fundamental disturbance to the farming structure caused by territorial losses in 1944 and the resettlement of a tenth of the population. Most displaced people were farmers. Some were accommodated on holdings carved out of existing farms, and efficiency was seriously impaired as a result. Others, amounting to some 10,000 farming families, were settled on new holdings which were cleared from woodlands in Europe's greatest colonization programme of the century. The resettlement operation was a major national effort in which society had to be put before economy, and massive diversion of capital resources from more profitable to less profitable uses was unavoidable.

As in most European countries, farming in Finland is inseparable from systems of farm support. Indeed, it has been facetiously remarked that much of Finnish farm enterprise is by courtesy of the government. Certainly, direct and indirect subsidies have played a large part in expanding and sustaining production. As Finns plan the future development of their country with increasing care, the agricultural sector has come under growing scrutiny. Finland's predominantly industrial and urban community argues for diversion of investment from farm investment into more efficient areas of production and for the release of farmed land for more profitable employment. Both energy and persuasive power are needed to change an established system. The situation is the more difficult to redress because support for farming has been strongest in the least favoured parts of the country, where a radical political outlook goes hand in hand with relative poverty. As in Sweden, the low income farms of the north, with their large families and poor tax potentials, are vulnerable to economic arguments.

One function of agricultural economists is to plan the most rational use of farm resources. Ideally, at both the domestic and world levels, each area should produce the goods for which it has the greatest natural advantages. For Finland, it is clearly advantageous to concentrate on livestock, hardier grains, hay and potatoes. Moreover, within Finland, production is more favoured in the south than in the north. Not only do the northlands yield less for a greater effort, but the risk of summer frosts, early snowfalls, and spring floods is higher and the need for compensation heavier than in the south. For various reasons, much energy and capital have been employed to promote farming, especially dairying, in northern Finland, but it is difficult for Finland to compete in the international dairy market. The most logical location for milk production is in the south-western third near to the largest centres of domestic consumption.

Withdrawal, in one sense or another, is a recurrent Finnish phenomenon. But it is withdrawal as a prelude to a new advance that lies behind the philosophy of the legislation that provides for the reduction of the cultivated area. In the Agricultural Law of April, 1969, priority was given to the withdrawal from production of holdings with 2–15 hectares of cultivated land and to those belonging to farmers over 55 years of age. Owners who withdraw land from cultivation receive appropriate annual compensation provided that they prevent weed growth on it and do not allow their farm buildings to be leased for agricultural purposes. Nor may they lease, exchange or sell their farm property without permission. By the end of 1970, more than 100,000 hectares of land had been taken out of cultivation. On some of this timber will be planted, but most for the time being will remain uncropped, on the same principle as the American soil bank scheme.

Ironically, the agency through which this exercise is being undertaken is the same Ministry of Colonization that carried through the great programme of resettlement and land reclamation after the Second World War. Moreover, it was through this programme that a considerable number of the farms in the critical size category were created.

Current rationalization in Finnish farming has other objectives. One is to reduce the number of milk cows by 40,000 annually in the period 1969–74 in order to bring the supply of dairy products more closely into line with demand. A second is to purchase any farm or farmland which comes on to the market and which can be either beneficially withdrawn from production or, through consolidation, used to increase the size of farm units. A third is to intensify forest farming and help to remedy a situation where timber growth lags behind timber needs. Sixty-five per cent of Finland's forests are privately owned—many by people who have left the countryside for the towns. Finland's softwood timber potential is high, but the quality of many privately-owned stands falls short of that of company- or state-owned woodlands. The forest component on the Finnish farm has an improved status. In 1970 the Ministry of Agriculture itself became the Ministry of Agriculture and Forestry.

These changing features of and shifting attitudes to Finnish farming, inseparable from the relatively declining role of agriculture in the national economy and from the growing crisis in softwood production, are also related to Finnish economic integration with the other Scandinavian countries. Production costs of the principal commodities deriving from Finland's farms are all much higher than those of Denmark and most of them are higher than those of Sweden. It becomes increasingly desirable to exploit the advantages of softwood production and to review the comparative disadvantages of farm production.

The successes of Finnish farming in the twentieth century are explained at two levels. First—and at the practical level—the *farmer himself shares with Finland's indigenous flora and fauna a stubborn vitality.* This natural inheritance, deriving from generations of living close to the land, is coupled with a resilience nurtured by the need for regular adjustment to the vagaries of international circumstance. Secondly—and at the theoretical level—so many of Finland's agricultural planners have their personal roots in the land and have maintained the confidence of the mass of Finnish farmers when presenting their recommendations. Finland must be unique in the number of adjustments that its farming community has had to make in the space of the last generation. The resulting experience and expertise are not narrowly restricted to Finland, but are capable of transference to other situations and other places.

INDUSTRY AND FOREIGN TRADE—CHANGING PATTERNS

LEIF FAST

THE expression that you cannot see the wood for the trees must surely have originated in Finland—someone once worked out the annual growth of spruce and pine alone is enough to encircle the world with a wall three feet high and three feet wide. But after all, in this vast country of forests and lakes there are barely five million Finns, so it is still something of a surprise and an achievement that Finnish exports of paper and board are the second largest in the world, that Finland competes with Japan as the world's largest exporter of plywood and that she is the third largest exporter of woodpulp. Many famous newspapers use Finnish newsprint, such as *The Times*, the *New York Times*, and the West German magazine, *Stern*.

Exports are the lifeline on which depends Finland's high standard of living—among the first fifteen in the world. Finnish businessmen and manufacturers are well aware of this and there is a go-and-get-it dynamism about their approach to their problems. Finnish-built paper machines account for fifteen per cent of the new machines built for the world paper industry. More than half the icebreakers built in the world since the Second World War come from one Finnish firm—Wärtsilä.

There are also the entirely new industries which have put Finland on the map in recent years—Finnish fashion, ready-to-wear clothes, textiles, furniture, shoes, jewellery, glass, and, of course, saunas—and the attempt, not always successful, to export with them the Finnish way of life. The common factor in all these new ventures is Finnish Design.

Finally, the Finns have exported themselves and their expertise. To-day Finnish wood-processing plants are in operation in Britain and the United States, in nearly all the Common Market countries, as well as in the Middle East, Africa and Latin America. For instance, there is the plant set up in British Columbia, Canada, right in the heart of Finland's biggest competitor in this field. Four leading Finnish companies, Enso-Gutzeit, Kymi Oy, Tampella, and Myllykosken Paperitehdas, combined to start Eurocan Pulp and Paper Ltd, and founded what has become the largest Scandinavian enterprise in the North American continent. Production started in 1971 and a special Finnish sales organization now markets Eurocan's board, kraft paper, pulp and sawn timber all over North America.

There is a Finnish tractor plant in Brazil, a cable factory in Turkey, a lift-making plant in Spain, a factory in Holland turning out aluminium products—these are typical examples of Finnish activities abroad in the 1970s. Broadening their base of operations, specializing, and going out into the world are the watchwords of Finnish exporters today.

But let us start from the beginning, and the beginning is the forest industry which even today is the starting point for any description of industrial Finland.

The Forest Industry

The Finnish forest industry has one of the highest productivity rates in the world, higher than that of the corresponding industries in the other Scandinavian countries or in the USA, and it is still rising. In the past ten years the Finnish pulp and paper industries have increased their production by as much as they did during the whole of the preceding hundred years. The forest industry as a whole still retains its unchallenged position as the country's leading export industry, providing 55 per cent of Finnish exports.

It has, not unnaturally, set its stamp on the communities in which it is based. Its dependence on the lakes and rivers of Finland for floating its logs and for water power is reflected in place names—this is the reason why today so many of the townships where works are situated have names which end in -koski (-rapids). Many of the townships are still dominated by one big company. This is the case, for instance, with such places as Tervakoski, Valkeakoski, Myllykoski and Kuusankoski, to name only a few.

Kuusankoski, in south-eastern Finland, is perhaps one of the most typical of Finnish paper manufacturing communities. The first paper mill was established there in 1873 and to this day practically all the 20,000 inhabitants of Kuusankoski are dependent on one big employer, the Kymi Company. They earn their living in Kymi and they live, in all probability, in houses of their own built on ground leased by Kymi. The smell of the sulphite factory permeates virtually every corner, both literally and metaphorically.

Different surroundings have made it possible for other districts gradually to develop more diversified kinds of production, but the basic characteristics remain the same.

One of the main discussion points in Finland during the past ten years has been the yield of the forests. Can it be increased? For some years the rate of cutting was greater than the growth rate, but after a few years of an intensive reafforestation—the so-called 'Mera' programme—the situation is already much better than the pessimists thought possible five years ago. If everything continues to go according to plan, the yield of the forests will be considerably increased, i.e. by about 10 per cent during the next five years, and will be more than doubled during the next couple of generations. In the meantime, while the Finnish forests are drained, treated with artificial manure and the exploitation of the timber is intensified, shortages have to be made good by imports—mainly from the Soviet Union but also to some extent from Sweden.

The Finnish forest industry has a highly developed research organization and this is undoubtedly one of the reasons why it has been able to reach the position it holds today; though this position is also due to a sound policy with regard to its raw materials, the size of the various units involved, and a highly developed integration of production and 'know-how' which has grown out of generations of experience. For more than half a century the Finnish Pulp and Paper Research Institute near Helsinki has been commissioned by individual companies to carry out short-term research and quality checks as well as medium- to long-term research. The Institute also undertakes basic research.

The main aim of the Finnish forest industry is gradually to improve its manufacturing standards so as to be able to cope increasingly with more highly developed products. At present, newsprint still accounts for more than 50 per cent of the total production and export of paper, but during the next few years it is expected that more emphasis will be laid on better quality, surface-treated paper. Production is still dominated by bulk goods, but speciality products such as wrappings and wood chips are playing an ever more important part.

Some interesting new products have already been developed. By treating wood with plastic it has, for instance, been possible to produce parquet flooring of a remarkably lasting type and at the same time to preserve the natural beauty of the wood. Have a look at the parquet floor at Helsinki Air Terminal the next time you come to Finland. A couple of million people walk on it each year, but the manufacturers claim that it will look exactly the same in the year 2000.

The Finnish forest industry began to establish itself abroad at an early stage. The new plant in Canada already mentioned is said to be the largest Scandinavian establishment ever set up in North America. The reason for this development is twofold, partly the enormous resources of the Canadian forests and partly to safeguard Finland's position in the traditional markets of North America. This is surely sufficient proof, if proof is needed, that the Finnish forest industry is an expanding industry, not only in Finland, but internationally.

Other Resources

Finnish iron ore deposits are sufficient to meet about 50 per cent of the country's needs although it must be admitted that they are not always competitive in price.

The copper deposits are well known and are the largest in

Western Europe. In addition, geological research in recent years has revealed surprisingly good deposits of other kinds. There are considerable quantities of zinc and nickel, even by comparison with other countries, and important alloys, such as chromium, cobalt, titanium and vanadium. On the other hand the country has no deposits of coal, oil, or natural gas and its resources of water-power have to all intents and purposes reached the limit of exploitation. Future needs will have to be met by atomic power. The first atomic power station in Finland is being built by the Russians and will be ready in 1975, but some fifty per cent of the total value of the equipment is being provided by Finnish industry. In addition, following the example of Western Germany and Austria, it is planned to import natural gas by pipeline from the Soviet Union.

Finland is sparsely populated and its total labour force is not very large but, unlike Sweden, it still has some reserves of labour in the north and east, which may well prove extremely valuable as industry continues to expand. The standard of education is also relatively high.

The Metal Industry

The records both in value and in employment figures are held by the metal and engineering industries, though it must be recognized that they owe a great deal of their success to the forest industry. Right from the start they specialized in machinery and equipment for use in that industry. Achievements in other branches of the metal industry are also largely due to the special conditions of Finnish climate and geography.

The greatest increases in recent years have been in the basic metal industries. The production of steel-plate was begun by Rautaruukki in north-west Finland in 1967 and sheet-steel is the next item on their programme. Outokumpu, the well-known copper firm, has also become an important producer of nickel and, in addition, during the last few years this firm has made a start on the refinement of several new metals such as chromium, cobalt and zinc.

An important addition to the engineering industry was

achieved when a new car factory was founded in Uusikaupunki (Nystad) in western Finland in 1969 by a combine of the Swedish Saab company and the Finnish Valmet. It was also towards the end of the 1960s that the manufacturing and marketing of the total output of lifts in the Scandinavian countries was concentrated on the Finnish firm of Kone. This step is expected to treble the production of lifts in Finland during the next few years.

These two examples illustrate one method used by the Finnish engineering industry in its attempts to strengthen its competitive position—co-operation with the other Scandinavian countries, especially Sweden. Another method can be seen in the energetic efforts being made to expand even further the sub-contracting system within the metal industry throughout the Nordic countries. Finland's delivery of parts for atomic power stations being erected in Sweden is also an interesting co-operative project.

It is essential for Finnish trade that the shipping routes are open throughout the year and this requires a powerful fleet of icebreakers. The Finnish ship-building industry is now the unchallenged leader in this sphere.

Dominated by the three companies of Wärtsilä, Rauma-Repola and Valmet, the Finnish ship-building industry has in general gone a long way on the road to specialization. It builds container ships and refrigerator ships as well as passenger ferries and luxury liners for cruises. The last are specially designed for cruising in the Caribbean.

Increasing activity in the engineering and ship-building industries has also had the effect of raising production in the electronics industry. Practically everything which is needed for the production, transmission and exploitation of electric power is manufactured in Finland. Atomic energy also plays its part today. Domestic appliances such as Rosenlew's and Upo's refrigerators, Strömberg's and Upo's electric cookers and radio and television receivers produced by a variety of manufacturers now control 70–80 per cent of the home market and hold a strong position in the Scandinavian market as a whole. Colour television sets manufactured by Salora have even gained a footing in Britain.

Developments in the metal and engineering industries can be seen as typical of a transformation which is taking place in the whole of Finnish industry. In brief, the three main factors involved are a broadening of the base of any given industry, specialization and internationalization.

The Chemical Industry

Production in the chemical industry has since the mid 1950s increased by 10 per cent each year. Those who work in it speak of it as the key industry of Finland's future. They may be right.

The state sector, which in general controls only 15 per cent of Finnish industrial production, holds a strong position in the chemical industry. Neste, the biggest oil refinery in Scandinavia, and Rikkihappo, producer of sulphuric acid, superphosphates and nitrogen fertilizers are both state-owned companies. The cellulose and paper industries, which are predominantly in private hands, are also of great importance for the chemical industry, and the forest industries provide chemical products such as ethyl alcohol, pine oil, turpentine, lignite, etc. All are important exports, even if the man in the street does not know much about them.

Finland provides many examples of the way in which publicly- and privately-owned sectors can work together. There is, for instance, the newly founded petrochemical company, Pekema, which manufactures the raw materials for plastics. The ownership in this company is shared on a 50/50 basis between state-owned and privately-owned companies.

The main field of expansion in the chemical industry in the next few years is obviously going to be in the production of basic chemicals and in the paint, medicine and technochemical industries. The considerable effort which has gone into the development and expansion of the nitrogen-based industry will continue.

The Design and Know-How Industries

During the last twenty years a completely new group of industries has put Finland's name on the world map. Finnish design has become a strong selling point in an ever toughening international market, and in Finland itself the expression 'new exports' has become the new ideal.

INDUSTRY AND FOREIGN TRADE—CHANGING PATTERNS

The common denominator for all these activities in Finland as in so many other countries, is a fortunate combination of tradition and a go-ahead spirit. Finnish design was fortunate in that it entered the field early and succeeded in choosing the right path, that of simplicity and exclusiveness. It is no accident that Finland's design industry has adopted an individual role. For a small country with small production units compared with other countries and with relatively high production costs it is the only way.

Finnish industry, once known mainly for its timber products, has developed yet another branch in the 'know-how' industry. Jaakko Pöyry, for instance, is one of those who is now selling know-how about the forestry industry to South America and the Far East as well as to Sweden. Petri Bryk has developed a completely new method, known as the flash melting method, for the production of copper of a very high degree of purity. Licence agreements for this method have been reached with copper manufacturers throughout the world.

Small firms with the right kind of initiative and inspiration have also made some interesting inroads on the international market. A cheap and simple meteorological radio balloon for wind direction plotting, made by Professor Vilho Väisälä, is today manufactured by Vaisala Oy, who have their own works in South Africa and South America, among other places, and completely control the world market in this speciality product. The Rapala trolling spoon developed by Lauri Rapala and his sons has had remarkable success in luring American fish. The American angling trade caught on and, in spite of many extensions, this family firm is now barely able to keep up with the apparently insatiable demand from America alone.

Finland's many lakes and enormous archipelago have helped to preserve the art of boat building to a greater extent than in most other countries, and the firm of Nautor on Finland's west coast is one of many small-boat builders who export 90 per cent to 100 per cent of their output.

When it comes to the manufacture of sauna ovens and complete saunas the manufacturers are too numerous to mention, and every true Finn still finds it mortifying that the Swedes got in first with the registration of the name Sauna Ltd in the USA.

FINLAND: AN INTRODUCTION

Foreign Trade
Finland's economy, like that of so many other small countries, is in the main dependent on its export trade. On average Finland exports a fifth of its national product and a quarter of its industrial output. Industry accounts for 95 per cent of total exports.

Of this total the forest industry accounts for 55 per cent, the metal industry for 25 per cent and other industries for 15 per cent. The remaining 5 per cent is accounted for by agriculture and forestry. It is interesting to note that in spite of an absolute increase in the exports of the forest industries their proportion of total exports has decreased while that of the metal industries and other industries has increased.

Finland's most important imports are machinery and equipment, chemicals, fuel, steel and iron and certain other raw materials. Investment goods and a group of other necessities for their own production account for three-quarters of Finnish imports, while consumption goods, including cars, account for one quarter.

For a country like Finland widely diversified foreign trade is vital. Nevertheless, association with EFTA has brought about a degree of reorientation. In general trade with the EFTA countries has been strengthened at the expense of other markets.

During the period from 1960 to 1970 exports to the EFTA countries increased from 34 to 44 per cent of total exports, while those to EEC countries and to Eastern Europe fell to a quarter and sixth respectively. As a result of Finland's association with EFTA, exports to the EFTA countries have been considerably diversified and EFTA has become, apart from Eastern Europe, the most important export market for the metal industry. There has been no comparable development in Finnish exports to Common Market countries, which are still predominantly products of the forestry industry.

Correspondingly, Finland's imports from the EFTA countries have increased from 30 to 39 per cent of total imports, while imports from the EEC countries and Eastern Europe have again decreased to just over a quarter and a sixth respectively. Machinery and investment goods are strongly represented in imports from the Common Market countries while imports from the Soviet

Union are still, in spite of intensive attempts to diversify, dominated by fuel and raw materials.

The increase in Finnish trade with the other Scandinavian countries has been particularly notable in recent years, and Sweden has become Finland's leading trading partner. Next in importance come Britain, Western Germany and the USSR.

Co-operation between Finnish industry and industry in other Scandinavian countries arises out of their geographical and historical relationship. From time to time there has been lively discussion on the need to institutionalize Nordic co-operation. This was the case, for instance, towards the end of the 1960s. In spite of this, industrial co-operation between the Nordic countries has developed without any very pronounced formal framework.

Finland's association with EFTA in 1959 took the form of a customs agreement designed to safeguard her industries in her most important export markets. The increased competition in the home market which resulted from the EFTA agreement also provided a much-needed spur to Finnish industry.

Plans for the creation of a Nordic Economic Union foundered because Finland felt that her neutrality was threatened, while certain other countries looked upon Nordek as a gateway to the Common Market. Finland's main object, therefore, during this period of continuing integration in Europe, and as the expansion of the EEC takes place, is to safe-guard the advantages of EFTA membership in so far as this can be combined with the maintenance of neutrality. Finland's negotiations towards a solution to the EEC problem are likely to enter a more active phase as the problems connected with the applicant countries are solved. It is in the interest of Finnish industry that trade with Eastern Europe should also expand.

Looking to the Future

Success depends largely on the extent to which it is possible to eliminate bottle-necks which, in spite of everything, do occur and tend to slow up production on the national level. For a small country the financing of investments and the putting into practice of the results of work done on technical research and development is a heavy burden, as are some of the internal problems which will have to be solved if Finland is to continue to be competitive in international terms.

One of the organizations which attempts to solve some of these problems is the Finnish National Fund for Research and Development, better known under its Finnish initials SITRA. The Fund was started by the Finnish Parliament at the time of the 50th anniversary of Finland's independence. SITRA has carried out research on the present condition and future prospects of various branches of industry and has financed economic research projects involving a too high degree of risk for private industry to undertake. Typical examples of the wide-spread interests covered by SITRA are the financial contributions which the fund has made, for instance, among many others, to the development of a new steering system for ships in difficult ice conditions, to research into air pollution and to the formulation of new guide lines for town planning in Finland.

According to research carried out by, amongst others, the Federation of Finnish Industries, the chemical industry is expected to have the fastest growth rate of all the Finnish industries, and it is estimated that from 1965 to 1980 production will have increased fivefold. The metal industry is also expected to have a growth rate faster than that of industry in general. Expansion is increasing in the forestry industry as well but—for natural reasons—at a somewhat slower rate; though, as a result of modernization and new investment, the paper and board industry, for example, is expected to increase its output by 45 per cent by 1974.

It is forecasts such as these and the developments of recent years which form the basis of great expectations for the future.

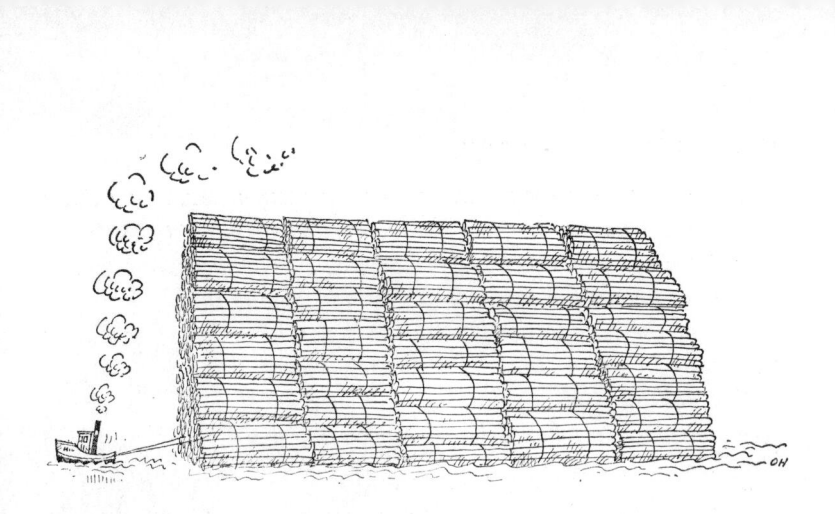

THE WATERWAYS OF FINLAND

W. R. MEAD

In few areas of the world are land and water intermingled so freely as in Finland. This means that water has played and continues to play an important part in communications, both locally and nationally. Eight per cent of Finland's surface area is covered by water and this figure excludes the labyrinthine archipelago channels inside Baltic territorial waters. Mikkeli, with 24 per cent aqueous area, is the most watery province. The largest of the inland water masses is Lake Saimaa which is 4,400 square kilometres in area and drains 16 per cent of the country. In Finland, water has been the historic medium of summer transport, and it continues to play an important role for transport purposes. Water, in general, becomes ice in winter—a morphological change which introduces a whole range of communicational adjustments. The adjustments were more positive for Finland in the days before the combustion engine than they are today.

FINLAND: AN INTRODUCTION

The coasts have their fairways—some plotted since the Middle Ages, others passed on from one generation of pilots to the next. The fairways are deceptively dangerous. 'He would be a rare pilot who knows the entrance to any port among them', wrote the author of the text to accompany the Atlas Maritimus et Commercialis *in 1723. Finland's skerries, indeed, have been a protective vallum against coastal assault in time of war. The skerry reconnaissance, conducted largely under the direction of N. G. af Schultén at the end of the eighteenth century is a chapter in its own right in the charting of Finland's waterways. Given the present-day size of shipping, the need for continuous overseas winter communication and the new technical means of keeping open winter channels, the dredging and improvement of protected skerry fairways has assumed a new importance—more important in many ways than the opening of new interior lines of communication.*

Finland's rivers, like those of Norway and Sweden, but unlike those of most Western Europe, are youthful and immature in both transverse section and profile. They are intercepted by waterfalls, rapids, boulder-strewn stretches and shallows. This is partly related to the fact that as the land has risen from the sea, they have cut down differentially into the hard granite bedrock. In their natural condition they are mostly non-navigable—or when they have been navigated, they have presented hazards and obstacles which have opposed large-scale use. Most of Finland's rivers are quite short. Exceptional in size is the Kemi, though the Vuoksi has the largest drainage basin.

Until the coming of rail and motorized road transport, the rivers provided the principal routes of movement of forest products—from logs to refined pitch and tar. The Oulu river was a great route for the picturesque but expensive transport of tar and the navigators of the tar boats were local heroes. These swift watercourses exhilarated some. Jacob Stenius wrote of 'swinging round a hundred bends—with unbelievable speed, more like the flight of birds'. Contrastingly, travellers to north Finland, such as Edward Clarke, swiftly became aware of the exertions of punting and portaging up the Tornio river. Until very recent years rivers such as Tenojoki on the Norwegian boundary, still provided the only summer routes for movement of mail and domestic necessities.

Finland's principal navigable waterways are its lake systems. The varied local forms of rowing boats reached their most elaborate expression in the church boats. These, the author of John Murray's Handbook for Travellers advised in 1849, were 'pulled by about twenty women, while an equal number of men smoked their pipes in the stern'. The older parishes of lakeland Finland developed shapes sympathetically responsive to local lake basins—waterways uniting, woods dividing people. Paradoxically, the waterways united people even more effectively when they were frozen in winter, for then, direct sleigh routes across them could be employed. Winter roads continue to be used over the frozen waterways. In the lake districts over a hundred ferry routes come to a standstill and buses drive over ice which may be several feet thick. In parts of the archipelago, special winter roads are cleared by snow ploughs to provide motorways to offshore islands.

The coming of steam, from the 1840s onwards, called for an increasingly thorough survey of channels, and the construction of beacons, seamarks and buoys, together with the preparation of navigational charts. It was already clear that modification of Finland's waterways was needed in the interests of efficiency. Finnish leaders followed with keen interest the way in which Western Europe played with artificial waterways. Canal mania struck Finland, although because of the lack of capital the impact was milder than in Britain, France and Germany.

In the lake districts, a number of lesser canals were successfully completed—Vesijärvi and Kalkkinen canals on Lake Päijänne, Konnus and Taipale canals on Saimaa. They remain vital channels in Finland's interior waterways. So, too, does the network of man-made timber flumes through which the life blood of the Finnish economy flows.

By the end of the nineteenth century, lake routes reached a peak of importance in Finland's network of interior communications.

FINLAND: AN INTRODUCTION

Old timetables testify to the summertime effectiveness and efficiency of the tall-funnelled steamships which collected farm products and were veritable royal mail lines. The lake boats, originally burning wood fuel, but now powered by oil, still serve as pleasure craft for tourists as well as playing a minor commercial role. Despite the glamour of the hydrofoil, they still retain their tourist appeal.

In 1856, Finland's largest lake was linked to the inner reaches of Viipuri Bay by a 56-kilometre canal. Two-and-a-half centuries earlier, Pontus de la Gardie had initiated excavations, but the 'old ditch of Pontus' came to nothing. Following financial appropriations equal to the Finnish budget for an entire fiscal year the route from saltwater to Saimaa was dug by several thousand labourers over ten successive summers. Models of Neptune and Väinämöinen presided jointly when Alexander II opened the waterways; and as traffic began to flow through it, even customs houses blossomed in Finland's lakeland ports, as they sensed the remote pulse of the outer world's trade. The Saimaa Canal was bisected by the new Soviet boundary resulting from the Peace Settlement of 1944, but negotiations with Russia resulted in the reopening of the waterway in 1968.

Reconstruction of the canal has been Finland's largest single investment since the Second World War. The balance sheet of the enterprise is not easy to estimate. In theory, the canal gives seagoing shipping of up to 3,500 tons access to navigable waterways totalling some 3,700 kilometres and extending north to Pielisjärvi by way of the canalized Pielis river. In so doing it offers an alternative water route to the Baltic for timber exports which are currently transported by lorry from the harbours of the Saimaa system to the ports of Hamina and Kotka. It also provides a tourist route from Viipuri to Lauritsala—a minor St Lawrence waterway in appearance, with miraculously managed locks and sky-high bridges.

Beyond this, its practical value must yet be fully demonstrated. Most of the timber moving along it (and it has yet to surpass in volume the pre-war figure) could move at least as cheaply by road. The operating costs of the canal are equal to those of the rest of

Finland's artificial waterways collectively—and the volume of shipping and commodities that it handles is less. Naturally, Saimaa canal is closed by ice from November to April, and its Baltic outlet cannot be kept open as are the east Finnish ports of Kotka and Hamina. In many ways, the canal appears to be a folie de grandeur. Yet, there have been and remain invisible items on the balance sheet. During its construction, the canal absorbed much otherwise unemployed labour. More importantly, the challenge that its reconstruction offered to Finnish technicians and the demands that it made of the Finnish metallurgical and engineering industries have fostered expertise which can be employed elsewhere and equipment which can be applied in other situations. It intrigues foreign visitors and has become something of a tourist attraction. Finally, Saimaa Canal has an international importance as a link between Finland and the USSR. In its own right it is a symbol of co-operation between the two countries.

Finland's waterways occupy a different status in the economy today from that of half a century ago. They provide transport routes which are subject to increasing competition from road haulage. Their inconsistency is one problem. Waterways are seasonally idle, subject to spring flooding and intermittent deficiency of flow. The hydrographer is sensitive to their behaviour: so is the economist. Yet they must remain partly complementary to other forms of transport. And if the day comes when logs no longer cavort in their rapids or move imperceptibly in bundles over their broad lake surfaces, there will still remain a lively demand for the waterways. For pleasure-boating has seized the Finns, so that motor boats and high-speed launches—let alone yachts—have already given a new value to the inland waters.

THE NATURAL PROVINCES

W. R. MEAD

'**P**LAIN John Bull dismisses the Finnish landscape as monotonous', wrote Selina Bunbury of her *Summer in Northern Europe* in 1856. If the marked regional contrasts which characterize Britain, France, Germany and Belgium are the criteria adopted for landscape appreciation, 'plain John Bull' is right; for Finland lacks the diversity of rock and relief which accord variety to their countrysides. Different criteria must be employed to appreciate the contrasts distinguishable within Finland. For Selina Bunbury the Finnish landscape was not monotonous—'There is always some new shape, some curious appearance, some changing effect to appeal to the eye.' She touched upon the essential fact that the Finnish scene is a study in *nuances* and that appreciation of local variety is the key to its understanding.

Local variety results from a limited number of features which repeat themselves in an infinity of size and shape over short distances. The themes upon which the variations are played are granite, sand and clay; water, peat and fen. And to each of these natural habitats belongs a different plant association. Among vegetation, woodland dominates: among natural features, water. Water yields everywhere to woodland. If it be true, as Sir John Lubbock wrote that, 'without water no landscape is complete', the Finnish landscape might lay claim to be one of the most complete in the world.

Yet, for all its completeness, the attractions of the scene are elusive, unless viewed in the right circumstances. Its vital detail

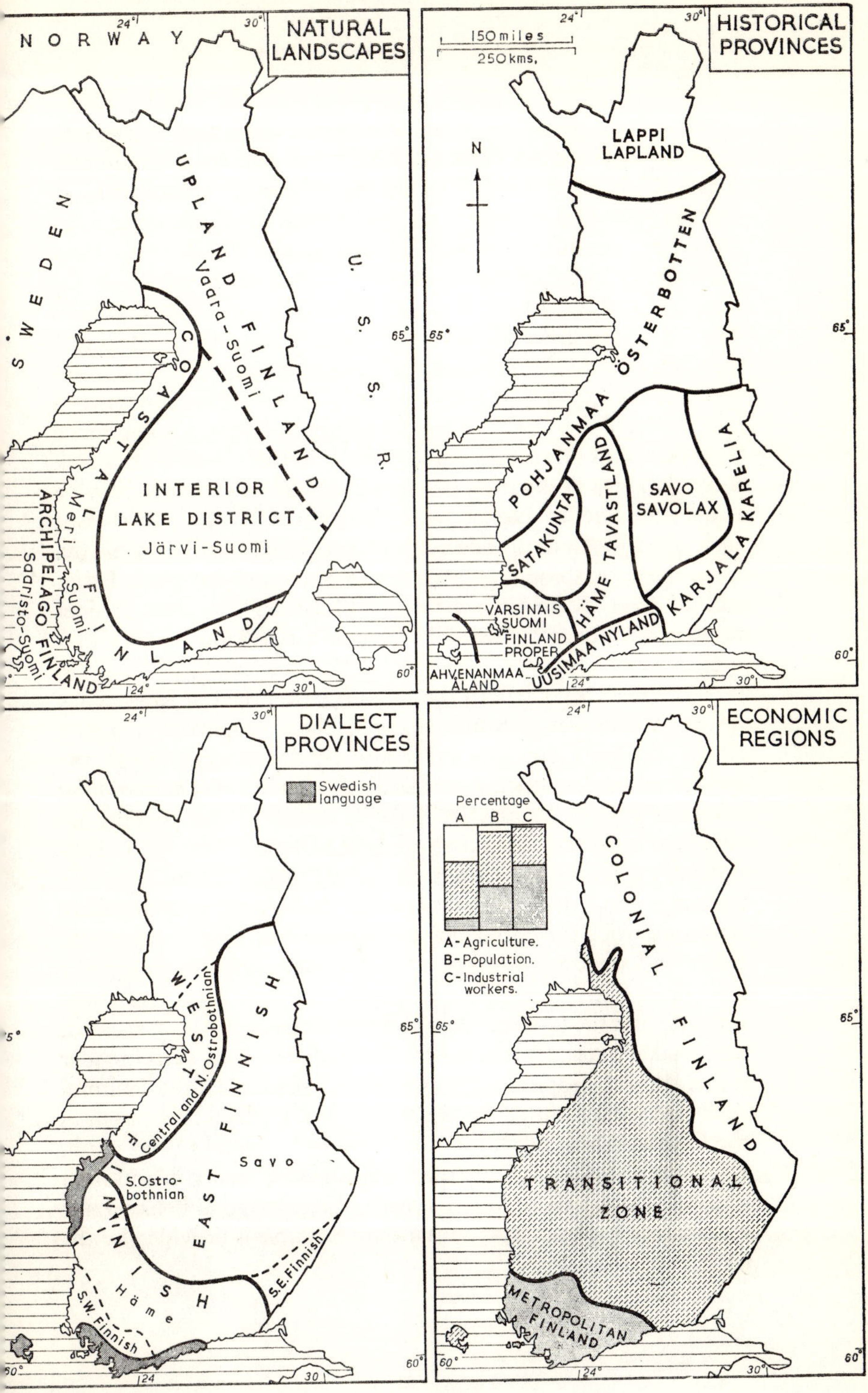

NATURAL LANDSCAPES
NORWAY
SWEDEN
U.S.S.R.
UPLAND FINLAND
Vaara-Suomi
COASTAL FINLAND
Meri-Suomi
INTERIOR LAKE DISTRICT
Järvi-Suomi
ARCHIPELAGO FINLAND
Saaristo-Suomi
24°
30°
65°
60°
HISTORICAL PROVINCES
150 miles
250 kms.
N
LAPPI
LAPLAND
ÖSTERBOTTEN
POHJANMAA
SATAKUNTA
HÄME TAVASTLAND
SAVO
SAVOLAX
KARJALA KARELIA
VARSINAIS SUOMI
FINLAND PROPER
UUSIMAA NYLAND
AHVENANMAA
ÅLAND
DIALECT PROVINCES
Swedish language
WEST FINNISH
Central and N. Ostrobothnian
S.Ostro-bothnian
EAST FINNISH
Savo
Häme
S.W. Finnish
S.E. Finnish
ECONOMIC REGIONS
Percentage
A B C
A - Agriculture.
B - Population.
C - Industrial workers.
COLONIAL FINLAND
TRANSITIONAL ZONE
METROPOLITAN FINLAND

is lost as it flashes by the window of a car. Its features merge into a mosaic of a wholly different kind when seen from an aircraft. They can be appreciated best by more leisurely means of locomotion—from a rowing-boat, a summer stroll along country tracks, an autumn day's berry picking in the woods or a winter traverse by ski. Eighteenth-century travellers in search of the mood of a landscape never sought more diligently for heightened effect than the more sensitive Finns who still go barefoot so that they may enjoy the summer contrasts of feeling between warm sand, smooth rock, soft moss or prickly pine needle. Few visitors have extracted more enjoyment from the Finnish countryside than Mrs Alec Tweedie, who wrote a minor classic of her trek through it by horse and cart in 1898. Horse and sleigh provide equal moments of exhilaration. Unfortunately, the pleasures of such rustic methods of transport are increasingly hard to come by. Yet Finland is a country in which to stand and stare—or, better still, to sit and stare from the deck of a leisurely steamer. It hides itself from those who would cover its length and breadth in a week.

To appreciate variety in the Finnish scene, then, it is necessary to adopt different perspectives from those employed in many lands. Yet there are regional landscape differences, though the natural provinces which they create have less distinct personalities than the *pays* of France. In Finland, the same components are common to all the natural regions, but they are blended in substantially different proportions in each of them. This accounts for the contrasting physical qualities of the Baltic archipelagos (where water and rock are dominant) and the interior landscapes (where water and trees are dominant), the south-eastern plains (on the broad claylands of which arable land takes the lead over other features) and the northern fells (where the arctic scrub of the cold desert takes over). Each area has islands of the others in its broader scene. In sub-tropical July, there are patches of agricultural opulence strung out along the course of a Lapland river, such as the Ounas, which recall the rural riches of Finland's deep south. By contrast, wherever a stretch of bogland occurs in southern Finland, there is to be found a piece of country that behaves like a miniature Lapland. The outstanding example is provided by the barren stretches of Suomenselkä in southern Ostrobothnia, which are commonly called Satakunta Lapland.

Variety in the Finnish scene is largely an expression of three influences which meet and mingle above the fractured granites, the 'Penelope's web' of glacial land forms, the younger sediments laid down by sea and lake, and the humus of the peatland. The influences may be identified according to the compass as westerly, easterly and northerly: they may be called maritime, continental and arctic respectively. Each makes its contribution to Finland's climate, the seasonal variations of which are so great that they completely transform its landscapes.

The climate is dominated by high latitude, for much of Finland lies in the sub-arctic, where winter takes precedence over summer. Finland also experiences a pronounced annual rhythm of daylight and darkness. Short, dark winter days are balanced against nightless summer days. But the length of the period when water is sheathed by ice and when snow squeaks beneath the runner varies considerably in a country which extends through ten degrees of latitude.

The northerly component in Finland's climate is modified by the influence of the ocean to the west and the Eurasian continent to the east. As with the rest of Scandinavia, Finland is sensitive to the weather patterns which move eastwards across the Atlantic. Its southern third, in particular, is familiar with the succession of dull and cloudy, bright and sunny weather common to much of north-west Europe. The westerly influence modifies the severity of winter, but it may also reduce the sunshine totals in summer. By contrast, the barometric high pressures of the continent counteract maritime influences, so that Finland may suffer winters of Siberian intensity (as in 1966) and summers of considerable heat (as in 1959). The power of the eastern high pressure systems is usually sufficiently strong to eliminate the modifying effect of the Baltic Sea.

Plant and animal life is a reflection of these controls. Species common to western Europe, eastern Europe and the sub-arctic mingle in Finland. Nevertheless, by comparison with Norway, Sweden and Denmark, variety in Finland's flora and fauna is more limited. A short growing season, the low temperatures of the harder winters, the risk of spring and summer frosts—all reduce the range of plant life.

Fauna are restricted in variety. Most herbivores, for example, are at a distinct disadvantage where grazing or browsing activity is restricted for the greater part of the year. Squirrel, hare and elk range over considerable areas in search of food. The reindeer is the best adapted inhabitant of the north country, which has abundant wild deer as well as domesticated herds. In winter, reindeer move from the fells to the woodlands, where the snow lies less deep and the mosses upon which they feed can be more easily obtained. Northern and eastern Finland are subject to invasion by bear and wolf, which prey upon domestic as well as wild animals. Some creatures, such as the bear, retire to lairs in a condition of winter torpor; others, such as the hedgehog, practise true hibernation. Bird life is more easily adaptable and is largely migratory.

Climatic influences, with their associated flora and fauna, play upon a land area which has three different environments. They are the environments of the coastal plain, with its associated archipelagos, of the lake plateau and of the north country. The features of the human landscape tend to exaggerate the inherent differences of the natural setting. At the same time, human attitudes deriving from the different landscapes cannot be written off as old-fashioned environmentalist dogma. There is no denying that the sea has affected the attitudes of the coastal Finns as the lakes have those of central Finland. In addition, the natural provinces have fostered and sustained quite well-defined local patriotisms.

The contrast between the long-occupied and well-developed landscapes of the south-western half of Finland and the thinly-peopled and under-developed territories of its north-eastern half encouraged J. G. Granö to make a distinction between *Luonnon-Suomi* and *Kulttuuri-Suomi*. They may be paraphrased respectively as the area where the features of the natural landscape prevail over those of the humanized landscape and the area where a man-modified landscape predominates. Although there has been a widespread assault on the north-eastern wastelands in the post-war years, Finland remains one of the few countries in Europe

1. Lakes and forests

2. First flakes in Tapiola

Varkaus: raw
material for the
factories

From forest to
factory

5. Pyhäkoski power station, part of the Oulu river development (architect, Aarne Ervi)

Winter

Sauna: fun for the younger generation

8. The tall forests

9. Lake-side sauna

10. Hydrofoil on the approach to Jyväskylä

11. One of the last of the windjammers, the *Pommern*, now a museum ship at Mariehamn, Åland islands

12. Sunworshippers in Helsinki

13. Aerial view of Helsinki: South Harbour in centre

14. Winter fishing through the ice

15. Turku cathedral tower and statue of Per Brahe

16. Art and industry in Tampere (sculpture by Wäinö Aaltonen)

17. Tammisaari street scene

18. Sibelius Monument by Eila Hiltunen, in Helsinki

19. The wide horizons of Lapland

which has extensive virgin lands. It balances sophistication in its coastal zone and primeval wilderness in the depths of its interior.

COASTAL FINLAND

The Archipelagos

Finland is a country which has been born of water. Since it began to emerge from the edge of the Quaternary ice sheet 10,000 years ago, it has been continuously rich in islands. The outlines of Finland have changed profoundly in the interval; they continue to change actively. Land uplift, probably its most intriguing natural phenomenon, continues apace. The process is most clearly visible in the archipelago zone. The degree of uplift varies from 25 centimetres a century in the south-west to a maximum of 80 centimetres in the Vaasa archipelago. Here, in the lifetime of a man, new islands emerge from the virtually tideless sea; isthmuses change the outlines of the mainland; inlets and shallows become salt-marsh and are reclaimed as arable. Here, too, freeze and thaw processes can prise open fissures in rocks. It is not unusual for a man to remember a four-foot-wide crack opening in a granite rock in forty or fifty years.

The entire Finnish coast is paralleled by an island zone. The zone reaches its greatest breadth and complexity in the south-west. The world has no richer *skärgård* (*saaristo*, as it is called in Finnish) than that which proliferates in Åland and Turunmaa. They are granite islands—but granites which weather locally by exfoliation (peeling off like flaky pastry), by chemical weathering (so that their surfaces may look as if peppered by shot), by water action (so that they assume shapes as if rounded by a sculptor). The south-western island groups enjoy the most favoured climate in Finland and are washed by coastal waters where the salinity is greatest.

Finland's offshore islands are numbered by tens of thousands— the Åland archipelago alone has nearly seven thousand. G. H. Millar, the eighteenth-century encyclopaedist, called them 'The Cyclades of the North'. Nowhere in Finland is there such a rich flora as in the wooded meadowlands of the Åland and Turku archipelagos. Here, oak woods and hazel groves have an under-flora which breaks into an early summer exuberance of anemone, primrose, viola, bluebell and lily-of-the-valley, yielding on the bouldered seashore to the crouching, wind-trimmed wild rose, wild red currant and raspberry; giving way on the rock outcrops of the mainland to the fleshy sedums and the incrusted lichens; merging into the pine woods by way of grassy clearings full of lime-loving scabious and knapweed and pricked with spry junipers. 'Had but genius and poetry comprised to render every cliff and promontory immortal' they would be world-renowned commented G. H. Millar. Titania and Oberon could have had no more fitting setting for their encounters.

The skerries have a rich bird life. Seabirds move to the ice edge in winter. Waterfowl, rearing their families in the boulder-strewn shallows, move out in the autumn. The islands are sportsman's country, with widespread duck and more restricted wild goose (in the island of Hailuoto, for example) as the bag.

The islands are also a natural home for fishermen, with the Baltic herring as the principal catch. Smoking, pickling and canning are other skerry pursuits. The archipelagos of Åland and Turku harbour the greater part of Finland's fishing fleet. The trim decked-vessels, which are mostly co-operatively owned, indicate the increasingly professional character of fishing. They are replacing the smaller open boats which have operated since time immemorial. The bigger ships are more economic to operate, undertake longer journeys and are more seaworthy. Island graveyards, the yellowing pages of church registers, and the lonely monuments scattered among the winking lighthouses and seamarks of the outermost skerries—all tell of the toll of the sea. Formerly, the seal was also widely hunted for fur, meat and train-oil. Seals remain abundant in the Bothnian Gulf, though they are rare in the south-west.

The setting of the south-western archipelagos in relation to the outlines of the Baltic Sea, the harvest of the surrounding waters and the relative reliability of yields from the limited but fertile farmland, encouraged early occupation. Åland and Turku archipelagos provided a natural causeway for colonial settlers who moved from Sweden to Finland and, as a result of land upheaval, the succession of their prehistoric settlements (with Bronze Age remains at the highest altitudes) can be traced down-slope. Åland province alone claims more than 10,000 burial mounds, ranging from simple long and round barrows to elaborate boat burial sites comparable with those in Gotland. Treasure trove reflects early trading contacts with many lands.

The archipelagos at Finland's south-western approaches received the first foreign impulses to affect Finland, and they were among the earliest Christianized parts of the country. They harbour the ruins of early monastic cells, such as the Franciscan remains by Kökar graveyard; while timber fragments and post holes beneath the floor of Saltvik's medieval church tell of an even earlier stave building. In shape, the sturdy speckled stone churches suggest architectural affinities with those of Gotland and central Sweden.

The influence of Sweden is dominant in the western isles. Not surprisingly, the Swedish language is strongly entrenched in them. Finnish is a language as foreign to the Ålanders as Swedish is to the countryside of Karelia. The independent qualities which characterize island people are powerfully expressed in the Ålanders, whose province is autonomous within the Finnish state. The landscape is imprinted with a distinctive folk culture, which is identified in building styles (from house types to windmills), in farm equipment and working practices, and most expressively in the midsummer poles. Other Finnish island clusters also have their own expressions of identity.

In the days when subsistence farming dominated the Finnish economy and when self-sufficiency was the order of the day, the archipelagos enjoyed a security that interior Finland frequently lacked. They might have 'to search between the rock and water for farmland', as a nineteenth-century author put it, but the soil yielded generously. As trading emerged, they added to their wealth by promoting share-owned trading vessels, while many farmers' sons joined the ships' crews of other nations. Finnish sailors were accounted the finest in the Tsar's domains and nineteenth-century reports from the British Board of Trade spoke of them no less highly. The islands continue to provide the bulk of the recruits for Finland's mercantile marine. The substantial supplements which they have brought to the islands' income help

FINLAND: AN INTRODUCTION

to explain the juxtaposition of the handsome farmhouses and outbuildings with the small landed holdings.

The continuingly strong association of Finland with the sea aids the islanders. They manifest it practically as well as romantically. Practically, it is summarized in the columns of the newspaper *Ålands Tidning*, which lists the location of a registered tonnage that amounts to nearly a third of Finland's total of more than a million tons. Romantically, it is evident in many ways. The tall ships with their memorable names—*Moshulu, L'Avenir*—have acquired a legendary quality. There are plenty of retired seamen whose blood still pulses with the sea fever of their days before the mast and whose white-wood cottages enshrine souvenirs from exotic lands. There are books to recall the heyday of the Åland clippers (Elis Karlsson's *Mother Sea* has passages as powerful as anything written by Henry Dana; Pamela Ericsson's *Herzogin Cecilie* touches colourfully upon life ashore as well as afloat). There is a captive four-master in Mariehamn harbour which is a part of the town's maritime museum. There is a collection of figureheads and log books from Åland ships that have sailed the seven seas.

The modern demand for social and other services among the scattered island communities has led to widespread desertion of the less accessible islands. These islands can only be supplied with electricity, telephones, schools, mail and medical care if there is heavy subsidy. In the contemporary Finnish welfare state, they constitute problem areas no less than Finland's remote mainland frontier territories. Their scattered resources do not provide a satisfactory basis for the large-scale activities that characterize the contemporary Finnish economic structure. In addition, their situation when the ice cover neither bears nor breaks interrupts the continuity of operations that is so vital to business efficiency.

Adjustment to the changed status and situation has taken two forms. First, there has been a substantial migration within the archipelagos—a retreat from the less accessible to the more accessible locations. Secondly, there has been emigration. The islands have an established tradition of emigration. From Åland it flows principally to the Swedish mainland—some of it is permanent, some short-term. From Turku archipelago movement

THE NATURAL PROVINCES

is mostly to the Finnish mainland; from Vaasa archipelago, to the coastal cities of Vestrobothnia.

These features have been intermittently complemented by short-period migrations to the islands which have their origins in contrasted motives. One motive is military; the other, recreational.

Finland's offshore islands have had their fair share of military garrisons, and they contain some of her most impressive military ruins. The most extensive of them are found on the islands clustered at the approaches to Helsinki. Suomenlinna—Sveaborg to its founding genius Augustin Ehrensvärd—was in succession a Swedish, Russian and Finnish fortress. Here, Gustavus III's monumental gateway leads to a tourist restaurant in the fortified granite ramparts, but Elias Martin's eighteenth-century paintings of the navy yards can still be recognized in the outlines of the shipyard, and stiff-jointed cannons cast in Tsarist foundries point their rusted nozzles seaward. A scatter of lesser forts is found in the archipelagos. But, as was commonly remarked in former times, their fortification was scarcely necessary because of the natural hazards of their treacherous channels.

Åland has long been a cynosure of strategists, who have added to the scenic qualities of the islands with their fortresses. One of Finland's most formidable medieval forts, Kastelholm, is central to the main island. The complex of fortifications built by the Russians at Bomarsund in the 1830s and destroyed by the British and the French fleets in 1854, remains an impressively picturesque ruin. Prästö's cemeteries for Orthodox, Catholic, Jew and Mohammedan bear testimony to the cosmopolitan armies which military service brought on duty to the islands. Åland has been demilitarized and neutralized since their day.

Save for those travellers who suffered nightmares during their winter passages, the archipelagos have always impressed visitors by their scenic qualities. For K. A. Tavaststjerna, summer days in the skerries were 'echoes from the land of dreams'. Finnish coastal waters have long been a haunt of yachtsmen—international as well as national. But the coming of the motor boat has transformed summer appreciation of them, giving rise to a vast seasonal invasion. In the inner skerries, summer cottages proliferate so that there may be daily as well as weekend commuting between large coastal cities and their tributary islands. In the outer skerries, deserted farmsteads are being restored to their former estate by holiday-makers. A network of ferries also brings a summer surge of visitors. Åland receives hundreds of thousands. Visitors to the islands are principally from mainland Finland. They come to see them because they recognize in them a different landscape and circumstance from their own home areas. By the act of their coming, they help still more to distinguish the island way of life from that of the mainland.

Metropolitan Finland

Finland, the independent state, was born in the coastal plains of its Baltic littoral. Most of its town-dwellers have always lived in the Baltic ports and they have especially concentrated in those of the south and south-west. Finland's first point of administrative control and cultural development was Turku (Åbo), which became the capital when the country was a Duchy of Sweden. It is located at the mouth of the Aurajoki, one of the many modest rivers which flow across Finland's coastal lowlands. A splendidly restored medieval castle dominates Turku's seaward approaches: on the landward side are the relics of a prehistoric strongpoint, Vanhalinna. Turku became Finland's first place of religious pilgrimage. It has a sturdy cathedral reminiscent of those in the Hanseatic cities of north Germany and is the seat of the archbishop. Finland's first university was founded here in 1640.

Today, the prospect of the city is no less appealing; the setting no less significant. Disastrous fires have destroyed its old buildings, but the restored and protected neo-classical façades of the early nineteenth-century city give a distinct atmosphere to the leafy 'Latin quarter' on the Aura river's left bank. The Luostarinmäki handicraft museum and the spacious cobblestoned market place recall that workshop industry and trading are deeply rooted here. Travellers long used Turku as a resting point on the trunk road—Finland's 'royal road'—which linked Stockholm and St Petersburg, and it remains Finland's chief passenger terminal. Old-established shipyards ring with a clangour and riveting for the export market, and *Suomen Joutsen*, the four-masted naval training ship, lies white and splendid at anchor. Turku is also central to the granary of Finland. Black windmill sails still sketch a silhouette on Myllymäki, but the harvest of the hinterland is now stored in the silos and ground in the imposing co-operative mills at Raisio.

The entire area tributary to Turku has an air of maturity and well-being. The strongly humanized landscape is inseparable from the antiquity of its settlement. Much of the countryside has been cleared and cultivated for more than a thousand years. Medieval churches are clustered thickly in it, their network of parish boundaries tracing a finer mesh than anywhere else in Finland. To the Swedish-speaking Finns, this part of peninsular Finland is known as 'the corner of the estates'. It contains scores of old-established manor houses, many still owned by the descendants of the original nobles to whom lands were given in the sixteenth and seventeenth centuries. Although most of the estates have been shorn of their large acreages, their richly varied and commodious living quarters, their lofty barns and immense stone stables remain. The avenues of linden, maple, mountain ash—even oak—which mark their approaches recall those of Swedish Uppland. Some estates are surrounded by parklands in varying degrees of maintenance or neglect: all have features which reflect West European ideas and fashions from a century and a half ago.

It is natural that the south-west corner should absorb and diffuse the ideas and techniques of other lands. It reacted at an early stage to agricultural improvements—in stock, crop and equipment. Pehr Kalm established Finland's first botanical garden on the banks of the Aura: contemporary Finland's principal horticultural research institute is at Piikkiö, 30 kilometres to its east. The British Board of Agriculture was emulated by the foundation in Turku of the Finnish Economic Society in 1797. The first improved European cattle were imported to Turku six generations ago. From the estate owners the new methods and techniques filtered through to the yeomen farmers. The principal orchards of Finland are also found in the south-west. Today, the south-west's intensive agriculture is based upon a scale of mechanization, of investment in deep drainage, of co-operative marketing schemes, of factory processing of farm produce which is unsurpassed in Finland.

The transformation of farming and industry went hand in hand. As a result, the south-west landscape displays the country's greatest variety of industrial establishments. The birth of industry is inseparable from mining. In the south-west, Finland had its own modest region of mining and metallurgy, repeating on a smaller scale that of adjacent Sweden. In the little fault-guided valleys (*sprickdalar*, as they are picturesquely called in Swedish) ores were worked and metal goods were produced with the aid of charcoal and carefully controlled water power. The legacy of this activity remains in such patriarchal establishments as Fiskars, Billnäs and Dalsbruk. Under the paternalism of the von Julin family, Fiskars was one of the most vigorous centres of diffusion of technical ideas in the early nineteenth century. There is also limestone at Parainen (Pargas), the basis for the country's cement industry.

The mature development of the countryside extends northwards from Turku through so-called *Vakka Suomi* and on to the Kokemäki river, which drains the lakes of Häme, to the port of Pori. The area embraces the quiet little seaport of Uusikaupunki (Nystad), which gave its name to the uneasy peace of 1721. Nearby, in the old town of Rauma (Raumo) wooden houses line the twisting medieval lanes and a tradition of domestic lace-making survives; but the sounds and smells of copper working and of wood processing are its twentieth-century characteristics.

Eastwards the development of the coastal plains extends to the Russian border. Successive little rivers open up fertile valleys behind old-established settlements such as Tammisaari (Ekenäs) on Pojoviken, Porvoo (Borgå) with its steep-roofed cathedral and Loviisa (Lovisa) with its old frontier ramparts. The largest of the rivers entering the Gulf of Finland is the Kymi (Kymmene), outlet for Lake Päijänne. Its succession of rapids support softwood processing industries and lead to Finland's largest export harbour, Kotka. Kotka is a new town which has spread around the fretted estuary of Kymijoki, welcoming a great variety of foreign shipping in its shallow roadsteads, thrusting its mill chimneys ever higher into the air. The past is invisible. Yet in adjacent Ruotsinsalmi (Svensksund) scores of Russian and Swedish naval vessels lie on the seabed. These remains of a historic battle in 1789 have only recently been probed by amateur divers.

It is difficult to escape from the military relics around Finland's coastal plains. The star-shaped plan of Hamina (Fredrikshamn) recalls its former military function. Hanko (Hangö), where peninsular Finland juts farther west, also had its military moment and Mr Punch recorded it in 1854. But it is more renowned as an old bathing resort, with sandy beaches and verandahed villas. Hanko is also Finland's most favoured winter port. Its lighthouse, Finland's Pharos, is the subject of one of the earliest poems learnt in the schoolroom.

Finland continues to be administered from the coast. Old Helsingfors was established more than 400 years ago, but was called upon to fulfil a completely different function after 1812. For political reasons, the administration was transferred from Turku, so that Helsinki became the new capital of the Russian Grand Duchy and was given a monumental neo-classical centre. The sea winds blow through the city and international shipping penetrates to its heart. Helsinki is Finland's largest port and its most cosmopolitan city. It gathers together the talents of the country, even if Finns are least Finnish when they assemble in it. It deals with the world, and its hinterland is all Finland. Most of Finland's coastal cities are living expressions of the piece of country which they serve; but Helsinki dominates the local scene. It is Finland's principal centre of wealth and its chief centre of manufacturing.

It is not inappropriate to speak of Finland's coastal zone as its 'golden horseshoe'. The fact emerges most clearly in the metropolitan south and south-west. When the grain is hoisted upon the forest of harvest pikes (or is bagged in the field by the combine harvester), the stubble is golden, the rowan tree drips red, the maples are yellow and orange; when cattle are sleek in the clover pastures and the caged mink dart in their gleaming thousands; when the early September gardens are in their final flush of sunflowers and dahlias around copper or saffron-painted farmsteads, it is easy to write Georgics about the coastal plains. From the discerning churchmen who established one of Finland's earliest religious houses at Naantali (Nådendal) to the president who enjoys a summer villa across the sound at Kultaranta (literally 'the gold coast'), those who have lived here must have occasionally sensed the illusion of a golden age.

Ostrobothnia

Ostrobothnia, Pohjanmaa to the Finns, also has its coastal zone. It is a land of little relief, but it is a land of many rivers. Its southern coastal plains, the broadest in Finland, are traversed by a distinct series of parallel-flowing rivers which originate in Suomenselkä, the height of land. Between the Oulu valley and the Swedish border, the character of the rivers changes. Oulujoki, its formerly impressive falls now harnessed for power, is Finland's most majestic river. Crowded beyond its broad and rapid-strewn estuary and along a low-lying coast are those of the Iijoki, Simojoki, Kemijoki and Tornionjoki.

Ostrobothnia's shoreline is one of the most actively changing in Finland. The waves of a tideless sea break upon its emergent coast. They strike erratic blocks as big as haystacks, boulders of widely varied origin, and broad sandy beaches littered with driftwood fantasies. And the winds play with wandering dunes, the ancestors of which have been long since fixed deeply in the hinterland. In winter, the frozen sea may form a bridge to Sweden across the Quarken. It is May before the ice honeycombs, rots and sinks beneath the waves.

The shallow river valleys of Ostrobothnia look wealthiest in the south, where old-established farming settlements in parishes such as Isokyrö, Lapua and Kauhava form close-knit communities. Northwards they are succeeded by a pattern of narrow, fertile valley and broad barren interfluve. The original parishes, elongated along the axes of the watercourses, supported church villages such as Kalajoki on the seaboard, and a thin scatter of farmsteads stretching upstream to the watershed. At the approaches to the Oulu valley, peatlands become more extensive. In Liminka parish they are seamed with dark drainage ditches, stretch billiard-table flat as far as the eye can see and are scattered with so many hay storage sheds that local people speak of 'the sea of haybarns'.

THE NATURAL PROVINCES

Ostrobothnia has always looked to the sea. Its ports, principally seventeenth-century foundations, found in naval stores the basis of their early prosperity. For several centuries, the woodlands of Ostrobothnia were denuded to meet the demands of the tar pit, the products of which were barrelled and principally despatched to Great Britain, France and the Netherlands. Ships were also built for export. 'Good, long yellow deals' (as the London traders Rew, Prescott and Co. described them) were sawn by the rough blades of watermills on the sites of rapids. At the mouths of the Ii, Kemi and Oulu rivers, salmon and whitefish were smoked and dried for exchange. Salted butter, hides and skins were also traded. Distinctive merchant houses grew up to lend their particular flavour to ports such as Pietarsaari (Jakobstad) with the Malm trading house, Raahe (Brahestad) with Sovelius's merchant house, or Kaskinen (Kaskö) the foundation of Pehr Bladh. The sons of merchant traders came to ports, such as Liverpool, Hamburg and Bordeaux, to learn how the wider world conducted its business and to establish their connections.

The ports of Ostrobothnia continue to display the exotic in their manufactures (from cigarettes to guitars) and to pay homage to a past epoch in their trade by incorporating the word 'tar' in street name and hotel name. Their local wealth is reflected in the well-furnished seaboard churches, the handsome clapboard houses of retired sea captains and the commercial archives tucked away in town libraries.

Vaasa (Vasa) has always been the focus of Ostrobothnia's coast, though Oulu (Uleåborg) has the largest export harbour. Prehistoric finds point to an early recognition of the virtues of Vaasa and a medieval castle at Korsholma (Korsholm) confirmed them. Vaasa became the provincial capital and objective of successive Russian invasions, while its hinterland emerged as a legendary tract in Finnish history. It is in keeping with the spirit of Ostrobothnia that Vaasa has a sturdy monument to the White Guard, who used it as the spearhead of their campaign of 1918. Oulu is a natural complement to Vaasa. The smell of industrial wealth hangs over and around it. In this respect it resembles Kotka. On the seaward side, lighters which look like Noah's arks, carry exports to flotillas of foreign vessels moored in the roadsteads.

FINLAND: AN INTRODUCTION

The tall chimneys of the softwood processing factories are matched by those of fertilizer plants. To the south-west burn the furnaces of northern Finland's steel plant of Rautaruukki. As in nearby Kemi, the hum of generators comes from rapids imprisoned close to the town centre. Oulu also has the most northern university in the world.

Swedish- and Finnish-speaking peoples mingle in coastal Ostrobothnia, the immensely diversified local place names of which tell of their successive advances and retreats. Partly because of a shortage of farmland, partly because of the nature of inheritance laws and partly because of the outward-looking character of the seacoast peoples, Ostrobothnia has considerable population mobility. Emigration, directed principally to North America, reached a peak at the turn of the century. Swedish Bothnia also claims permanent as well as seasonal migrants, while thousands of Ostrobothnians (and their horses) have traditionally migrated as lumberjacks to north Finland during the winter. Pressure on the land, with consequent sub-division of holdings, has also encouraged such intensive enterprises as fur farming and greenhouse cultivation.

LAKELAND FINLAND

The Central Lakes

Since the outer world first began to pay attention to Finland, its lakes have made the primary impact. No one really knows how many there are. It depends how they are defined and counted. There is, however, an identifiable Lake Plateau, low in elevation, which covers the greater part of southern Finland and where water as an element in the landscape reaches its climax. The names of its great lakes have been known to European mapmakers for several centuries. They are Finnish names, such as Saimaa, Päijänne, Näsijärvi. The short, turbulent watercourses which drain the lakes to the sea have Swedish as well as Finnish names. The lakes are shallow, diminish in area with the passage of the centuries and have their own archipelagos. They are surrounded by suites of terraces which trace former water levels. In the lake district, the more remarkable legacies of the Ice Age also stand manifest. They are dominated by the long, sinuous esker ridges, rising scores of feet above the lake surface, generally clad with lofty pines and flanked by sandy beaches. Such ridges as Punkaharju, Pyynikki and Pulkkila are nationally-renowned.

In the lake districts the forest plays a more prominent role than round the coasts. To the east and north-east, it is absolutely dominant. There is a bold contrast between the extensive farmlands of western Häme and the oases of cultivation in south Karelia, where the most striking human features are the hill-top farmsteads. The harvest of the woodland has always taken precedence over that of the field. Historically, the pelts of woodland animals were synonymous with money and the coat of arms of Savo (a fully-drawn bow) symbolized the hunter.

Today, the great rafts of bundled timber, drawn at a snail's pace across the broad lakes by patient tugs, are the principal wealth. This is also pastoral country. It is no longer pastoral as in Albert Edelfelt's canvases, with cattle roaming open range and dairy maids milking in a wildwood clearing over which smoke drifts combat insect clouds. It is a highly-organized animal husbandry, more appealing to the economist than to the artist, with co-operative creameries and slaughter-houses processing animal products with proverbial Scandinavian efficiency.

Lakeland Finland has its urban as well as rural pursuits. They usually focus upon strategic routeways in the lake systems, and in historical or market centres. Among them, Tampere (Tammerfors) in the south-west has surpassed Turku as Finland's second city. It is a personable and progressive city, with a bishopric and a university. As an industrial town, it is not much more than six generations old. A statue erected by the firm *Suomen Trikoo* symbolizes the principal source of its wealth. Other lands may speak of the golden fleece or the golden hoof, but the riches of Tampere, which is Scandinavia's principal textile city, are summed up by a maiden twisting a golden thread. Tampere has engineering workshops too, yet it contrives to present the face of a garden city. Indeed, all the lakeland towns are garden cities.

Each town has distinctive as well as common features. Mikkeli (St Michel) has Marshal Mannerheim's underground headquarters, now converted into a splendid store for provincial archives. Jyväskylä has Aalto's university buildings. Kuopio has Puijo hill and tower, and its cosy old yards behind wooden houses off cobbled streets. Hämeenlinna (Tavastehus) contrasts the solid mass of its castle and the intimacy of Sibelius's birthplace. Lahti has one of Finland's dizziest ski jumps from which to survey its swiftly expanding urban panorama. There are also 'company' towns, such as Jämsänkoski and Valkeakoski, focusing upon factories. Mills, of world stature, are nowhere more heavily concentrated than along the south shore of Saimaa. And there are the occasional towers of mine shafts, as at Outokumpu which possesses a source of copper of European magnitude.

The personality of the lake districts resides in their people as well as in their pursuits, which changes from west to east. The eastern shores and tributary lakes are inhabited primarily by Karelians, whose historic province has changed in outline with the changing fortunes of Finland. The peoples of Häme (*Hämäläiset*) and of Savo (*Savolaiset*) are in many ways the most Finnish of the Finns. As with all Finnish regional groups, they have retained a strong folk culture. It is seen in architecture, lake boats, farm implements, domestic utensils and textiles. There has been a tradition of birch-bark work and wood carving, of spinning (both flax and wool) and of weaving, especially of the *ryijy* hand-made wall hangings. Savo has distinctive foods, too. There is *kalakukko*, or fish pie—rye-crusted and layered with lake fish, and fat bacon. Together with adjacent Karelia, Savo rejoices in a tract of country where the arctic strawberry grows.

In Savo, the Lutheran Church assumes a stricter, even pietist bent. At the same time, a broad country humour, beloved of theatre comedians, comes readily to Savo people and to their relatives in northerly Kainuu. They are ponderous people, often the butt of the sophisticated wit that characterizes metropolitan Finland. To the Ostrobothnians, who consider themselves the 'toilers' of the Finnish world, the men of Savo are mere 'anglers'. Their collective wisdom has been assembled in books, the proverbs of which spring out of the earth: 'Who will hold up the cat's tail, if not the cat himself?'

The scattered farmstead prevails. Häme and north Savo farms

have gently sloping, open-ditched clay fields. In Mikkeli province, boulder-ridden lands are frequent. Boulder walls and heaps testify to an added burden imposed upon generations of land reclaimers. The frame farmhouses are hedged about by lilac and shaded by bird trees ('the tree where the cuckoo sings' in the vernacular), their large living rooms have immense brick or plaster ovens. The lakeshore or streamside *sauna* emits its sweet incense of pine smoke, though the Savolainen prides himself on his *savusauna* or smoke *sauna*, inside which the precious aroma is preserved. Nowhere is the evocation of archaic Finland stronger than in this national institution.

Dwellings multiply at the approaches to the leafy church villages. These villages are the local service centres with cooperative mills, creameries, stores and perhaps slaughter-houses. They occupy the middle of parishes whose boundaries are drawn round the diffuse watersheds of lake systems rather than through their water basins. Once a year they may provide the setting for one of the country fairs that are common to all of Finland with their prize stock and garden produce, preserves and domestic handicrafts, brass bands and banners, coffee-drinking and picnics, exhortations and orations, accordions and naphtha flares, swings and merry-go-rounds.

The fairs are shop windows in which the latest farm equipment is displayed and where advisers of the regional agricultural societies discuss the most recent scientific ideas. The noise of motorized equipment—saw, tractor, outboard motor, skidoo—prevails over the neigh of the horse. The outboard motor is needed to tie together the daily business of the great lake archipelagos as well as for mere pleasure. The wicker-work and chicken-wire of the white-painted, tall-chimneyed lake steamers is now left for the tourist to relish; the slender church-boats, with a dozen pairs of oars, are retired in museums. Tractor and lorry now gather together farm produce for the markets of the world; mobile shops bring the produce of the world to the farmhouse doorstep. The devices and desires of the twentieth century are everywhere; yet, at the same time, it is almost as easy as in Runeberg's day to slip into the deep tranquillity of Saarijärvi's unspoilt woods.

FINLAND: AN INTRODUCTION

Karelia

All Finland's provinces have their particular crests and colours. Karelia's coat of arms shows two mailed fists raised in the act of combat. The colours of the Karelian flag are red and black. They are fitting colours for this the most eastern part of Finland. For Karelia is a province which has been born and reborn of fire. Fire has played a threefold role in the forging of its personality.

First, Karelia is a land of fire in a purely physical sense. As with its neighbouring province of Savo, it is one of Finland's great softwood reservoirs. In the frequently hot and dry summers of eastern Finland, pine and spruce woods become tinder dry. Forest fires, mostly started by lightning in the great thunderstorms which build up after midsummer, were a constant threat to the goods and chattels of early settlers. The tell-tale plumes of smoke, spotted at an early stage from fire towers or helicopters, no longer develop into the menacing clouds which formerly blotted out the sun over countryside miles from the scene of the holocaust.

From the earlier stages of Karelian settlement, until the late nineteenth century, fire was an aid to farming. Much Karelian farmland was born of fire, for slashing-and-burning was the principal method of augmenting cropland. The rotational firing of woodland, at roughly 25-year intervals, provided the principal seedbed for barley, rye and turnips. It was already evident to some mid-nineteenth-century visionaries that, by firing the forest, farmers were burning wealth and sowing poverty. Ecological consequences of the practice are still widespread in Karelia. Spruce and pine, secondary in the ecological succession, only slowly replace the primary colonists—birch, aspen and alder.

In the second place, Karelia is a land of fire in a military sense. As borderland people, most generations of Karelians have suffered a baptism of fire. The earliest public documents referring to the province speak of invasion, destruction and pillage. Symbolic of Karelia's attempts to resist assault from the East are the remains of frontier outposts such as Viipuri (Vyborg) castle, bastion of a city no longer a part of Finland, and Olavinlinna (Olofsborg) at Savonlinna (Nyslott), the largest medieval fortress in Scandinavia. Most church archives record sagas of destruction, while many beacon hills (*palomäki*, in Finnish) recall systems of signalling by smoke and fire in former times of invasion. As in Roman days, frontier farmsteads were often allocated to local soldiery, in order to strengthen their resolve on the frontiers of the empire. Nor was the resumption of an official peace a guarantee of security for villagers, as is illustrated by the eighteenth-century harrying of Kuusamo settlers from the East.

The Karelians have been accustomed both to the swing of frontiers across their territory and to migration. Shifts in frontiers have not infrequently been a response to international pressures, for Karelia is on the Eastern marchland of Europe as well as on the eastern borders of Finland. Consequent changes of allegiance have resulted in ethnographic modifications. Not only has there been appreciable local admixture of Russian people along the border, there has also been absorption of their customs and practices. Externally, this is most evident in church life, for Karelia has proportionately the largest number of Orthodox adherents of any Finnish province. Historic religious houses, such as Valamo or Konevitsa, are now on the Russian side of the border. Only vestiges of their former glory and colour have been carried to present-day retreats in Heinävesi and Ilomantsi and the Orthodox Church museum in Kuopio. Double crosses and censers, ikons and elaborate vestments contrast with the simplicity of the Lutheran Church. Local farm architecture, language forms, superstitions and customs also reflect former Russian influences.

As a territory of invasion and counter-invasion, Karelia is a province in whose history the Book of Exodus is writ large. Lamentation was never more profound than during 1940 and 1944. By the Armistice of 1944 and the ensuing Peace Settlement of 1947, the historic province of Karelia was bisected. Ladogan Karelia and the isthmian lands with Viipuri, all of which had been reunited with the Grand Duchy in 1812, were detached from Finland. All but a handful of the 430,000 inhabitants left the ceded territories for resettlement in other parts of Finland. The migration, of livestock as well as of people, had to be undertaken in a matter of days. The resettlement took seven years.

The diaspora of a tenth of Finland's population resulted in the creation of more than 30,000 new farms—a full third of which had to be pioneered from the forest. Only a small proportion of the Karelian evacuees moved into the rump. Most were widely dispersed between town and country districts. Ethnographic differences between people in the evacuation and reception areas gave rise to problems of adjustment. Simultaneously, the lost lands of Karelia assumed a legendary quality in the eyes of those who had left them. In the Lost Eden, the river fish were bigger and tastier, the fruit harvest was more abundant, the harvest of field crops was more secure. For the older generation, only the land that had been given up could ever be called home.

There is a third sense in which fire colours the image of Karelia. Tongues of fire also run through it in a literal sense. Karelia, being possessed of a powerful tradition of oral poetry, has propagated and harboured a greater wealth of folklore and folk tale than any other part of Finland. From the eighteenth century onwards, scholars who made journeys into its interior called the attention of the outer world to its rich stores of native poetry. Henrik Gabriel Porthan the celebrated rector of Turku university, produced the first extended study of the subject nearly 200 years ago. But the first collector to fire popular interest was Elias Lönnrot who from his home in Kajaani in the 1830s, made a series of travels into Finnish Karelia and the adjacent Russian province. The poems which he collected from the inner recesses of the province were arranged in a composite form to be known throughout the world as *Kalevala*. In it, pastoral and domestic episodes prevail over battles and epic heroes. Karelian studies were points of departure for a number of Finland's best-known scholars. Men such as Castrén, Sjögren and Europaeus sought a fuller understanding of the Finns by linguistic, toponymic and ethnographic investigations among their kith and kin in Russia. The subsequent romanticization of *Kalevala* exaggerated the mental image of Karelia held by most Finns. Artists, such as Gallen-Kallela; poets, such as Eino Leino; musicians, such as Sibelius and Järnefelt, helped to invest Finland's easternmost province with a romantic glamour.

Karelia has been ridden hard by the horsemen of the apocalypse, but its resulting experiences have neither taken possession of its popular lore nor stultified plans for its development. Communications, critical for its material advance, have been a concern common to militarist, merchant, farmer and manufacturer. Outstanding in the history of Karelian communications has been the saga of Saimaa canal. Saimaa, Finland's largest lake, has its outlet through the Vuoksi river. The river traverses isthmian Karelia in a series of rapids among which the tumultuous Imatrankoski is distinguished by stars in international guidebooks. From the seventeenth century onwards, visionaries had schemes for striking a canal from Saimaa shore to Viipuri Bay. Excavations, said to have been begun by Pontus de la Gardie, can still be seen. In 1856, Saimaa canal was completed: it gave to eastern Finland a direct link with the outer sea. The canal played a considerable role in broadening the horizons of nineteenth-century Karelia; but it fell into disuse when bisected by the 1944 boundary. In 1968, it was reopened as the most extravagant and impressive single structure in Finland.

The bisection of Karelia, the loss of its historic towns to the Soviet Union, the dispersal of the majority of its people and improved communications have all reduced the distinctiveness of the province. Yet, certain qualities are inherent in the rump that remains. They derive from two facts. First, Karelia is sufficiently extensive to have known extreme isolation within itself as well as within Finland. Secondly, Karelia differs from the rest of Finland in its cosmopolitan qualities. The peoples of isthmian Karelia absorbed Dutch and German merchants, Swedish administrators, Scottish mercenaries, West European entrepreneurs, Russian summer migrants, Armenian and Georgian pedlars and a fair share of gypsies.

Not surprisingly, the more tranquil western Finns ascribe to them a pronounced vivacity. To Topelius, the Karelians were a compound of 'fundamental restlessness and Biarmian tractability'. The precariousness of life in a frontier zone may help to account for the stronger emotional expression. 'They weep by day, but laugh by night', an observer said of the Karelians during their exodus in 1944. An element of fatalism may also have the same roots. 'When black bread gives out, eat white', is a Karelian saying not unrelated to their history. By repute Karelia is a more colourful province than other provinces and its people are more

FINLAND: AN INTRODUCTION

mercurial than most Finns. Karelia provides a foil to Finland. Its peoples—who are of the stuff that makes martyrs, mystics, musicians and mountebanks—have provided and continue to provide a leaven.

THE NORTH COUNTRY

Nearly half Finland's land area can be described as north country, for the northerly characteristics are not confined to the area beyond the Arctic Circle. The north country includes the most elevated parts of Finland. Administratively, it has been a territory of Lappmarks, tied to administrative centres on the coast and resembling its Swedish counterpart. It is a country recent in permanent occupation. In 1542, Gustavus Vasa declared that all land not privately owned belonged to the Crown. As a result, most of the northern third of Finland belongs to the state.

The north country is also international border country. Until the beginning of the nineteenth century, Lapland was a great no-man's-land through which there were no precisely defined boundaries. The northern marches of the Fennoscandian peninsula, occupied principally by migrant Lapps, upon whose reindeer pastures pioneers intruded from the eighteenth century onwards, were not given formal boundaries until after Finland became a Russian duchy in 1809. The Lapp inhabitants of north Finland had been subject to the competitive forays of Swedish, Danish and Russian tax collectors and to the rival persuasions of Orthodox and Lutheran missionaries. Christianity made slow headway in the thinly-peopled wilderness. The present-day western boundary of north Finland was demarcated between 1824 and 1825: the eastern boundary in 1827. The northern boundary has been less stable. From the mid-nineteenth century onwards a Finnish corridor to the Arctic Ocean was debated. This became a reality from 1920 to 1940, after which the Petsamo Corridor reverted to Russia. So, too, did the eastern halves of Salla and Kuusamo parishes.

Topelius ascribed many of Finland's problems to what he called 'the old giant of the north'—cold. From the north the Ice Age advanced and to it the ice sheet retreated. Winter still advances southwards from the fells and lingers longest in them. The six or more weeks of midwinter twilight are relieved by the shifting curtains of the *aurora borealis*, and by moonlight made more intense by reflection from the snow. Most of north Finland sees the midnight sun; but frost lurks even in summer.

As a result of a cold climate, the north country spans a significant frontier. The timber line passes through it and the limits of tolerance of many boreal forest plants occur within it. The pine, advancing farther north along the valleys and farther up the hillside than the spruce, is the last of the tall timber trees to succumb. The fells are clothed with birch, willow and alder scrub which diminishes to a dwarf carpet before yielding to the mosses and lichens of the rock-shattered heights. Below and above the tree line, north Finland has extensive swamps, and about a third of its area is covered with bogland. The vast expanses of swamp are the least attractive elements in the northern landscape.

The pace of vegetative life is more sluggish than elsewhere in Finland. Trees grow more slowly and reproduce less quickly. Contrastingly, in the realm of insect life, the processes of the life cycle are accelerated so that they may be completed in the brief summer season. In such an environment, flora and fauna are especially sensitive to any longer period changes in climate.

North Finland is a country of great rivers. Finland's longest and most impressive rivers belong to it. The most elaborate network is that of the Kemi. To its west, is Tornionjoki which, with its tributary Könkämäjoki, is the boundary river shared with Sweden. All of these rivers empty into the virtually freshwater Bothnian gulf. But the character of north Finland derives in part from the fact that its rivers also find their way to other seas. North of the height of land, Finland has a broad flank which drains to the Arctic Ocean. Paatsjoki (Pasvik, to the Norwegians) is one outlet; though Finland also shares with Norway the handsome trough of the Tenojoki (Tanaelv, in Norwegian). To the northeast, a series of rivers has been superimposed upon the rugged fells of Salla and Kuusamo parishes to carve dramatic gorges through to Russian Karelia. Kitkajoki and Oulankajoki are not only geomorphological curiosities, but among the most unspoiled torrents in the country.

FINLAND: AN INTRODUCTION

The rivers were the pioneer routes of entry and north Finland is one of Europe's few remaining pioneer areas. By the mid-eighteenth century colonists had penetrated the upper reaches of the Oulu, Kemi and Tornio valleys. Subsistence farming prevailed—rye, barley, oats, turnips yielded meagrely, and the potato arrived only 200 years ago. The bark of trees was pulverized to help out the grain supply in years of shortage. 'The primeval home of bark bread' was K. A. Tavaststjerna's epithet for Kuusamo. Game animals, fish and birds were abundant in the northern wilderness. Dried, salted or frozen, they provided basic constituents in the diet. The summer yielded a generous harvest of berries; the autumn woodlands, an equally rich crop of mushrooms. Animal fodder, to meet the needs of the long winter indoors was gleaned everywhere. Pelteries were important for trading as well as for clothing.

Two centuries of occupation have given a mature appearance to the river valleys. Torni valley, for example, displays, well-tended land and property, linked by the ubiquitous telephone and electricity, and a lively traffic upon the highway belies its remote setting. In addition, the presence of an international boundary pricks the national pride of both Finn and Swede so that both put on a correspondingly brighter face.

A different type of organization and a new sense of immediacy characterize contemporary pioneering. They are expressed in planned community enterprise instead of the piecemeal and haphazard activities of individuals; in the direct assault on virgin territory by giant land clearance machines and powerful ditch diggers; in the immediate erection of prefabricated dwelling units. Surveyors and engineers form the advance guards of enterprises planned by the state. For political reasons, it is also good to people the empty lands of the north.

The rate of population growth is such that settlement not only continues to expand in the north, but a substantial population outflow to the kindlier south can also be supported. But to stabilize the settlement of the north country, an increasing variety of artificial supports must be given. Industry and agriculture benefit from transport subsidies. Civil servants and teachers living in isolated areas are compensated according to the distance that they must travel to towns and cities. They also have allowances for the extra clothing and heating needed to offset the winter.

Twentieth-century pioneer communities look more to other resources than to farmlands—to forests, mines and water power. The revaluation of Lapland's forests has spurred more careful management of labour as well as of trees. Programmes of woodland improvement belong to the summer, when poor quality stands are replaced by new seeds and seedlings, when seed is collected from the best tree stands, when ditches are dug and roads made. Management of labour is of primary concern in winter. Lappi and Oulu counties receive Finland's greatest immigration of lumberjacks. Despite mechanization, winter felling needs more men than north Finland can supply locally: nor can tractors entirely supplant the hardy, blond-maned horses.

The surveyor and engineer are concerned principally with communications. Finland's rivers are not navigable, railways barely penetrate into the 'colonial' territories of the north, so that 'roads to resources' are a critical preliminary to pioneering. In no part of Finland has such an extensive network of new roads been constructed as in the north land. In view of their purpose, it is more important to sketch in a large number of dirt and gravel roads than to provide a smaller length of first-class highways. This holds in spite of the havoc played with unsurfaced highways during the six weeks or more of the thaw.

Among the resources to which roads lead are the hydro-electric power sites. The north country has Finland's greatest power potential—partly because of its higher relief. Its development was delayed not only because of limited capital, but also because of former problems of long-distance transmission of power. The Kemi river system is Finland's richest in power potential. Plans for its development call for fully twenty power plants, with associated dams and storage lakes. The water power sites along Oulujoki have all been harnessed; but those along the border rivers await international decisions. The experiences of hydro-electric engineers in north Finland have extended beyond the national borders; they have constructed plants on the Paatsjoki and Tulomajoki for the Soviet Union. Maintenance engineers constitute a new type of recruit to the northland. Indeed, the

FINLAND: AN INTRODUCTION

transformation of Finland's northernmost provinces can only be accomplished by the provision of a technical elite.

As in the past, the advance occasions conflict with the prior inhabitants. The Lapps have retreated in response. Although economist and ethnographer alike may recognize an official Lapp area, it is an area continually eroded to meet the convenience of the burgeoning commercial economy. The Lapps, who number 2,500, constitute an extremely small minority and they occupy a very extensive area. Numbers engaged in traditional reindeer herding are minimal. The tourist, looking for reindeer Lapps in Finland, might more easily find the proverbial needle in the haystack. In the image of Finland (or Norway, or Sweden) they have made and continue to make an impact out of all proportion to their numbers and significance. Their traditional economy is still found; but it is intruded upon by the machines and services of the twentieth century. Snow-scooter and factory-made clothing rival the historic sled and picturesque garments. Reindeer skins flap from the awnings of tourist booths: reindeer meat is processed in co-operative slaughter-houses. Perhaps the ultimate degradation of the noble beast is the smoked sausage. The true reindeer husbandman, 'Bedouin-proud' as H. G. Porthan portrayed this denizen of the cold desert, is a disappearing phenomenon. All around the edges of the reindeer pastures, the Lapp has adopted a sedentary life, with Finnish colonists, dependent upon the ubiquitous state subsidies.

'To him that hath shall be given and from him that hath not shall be taken away even that which he hath.' It is in keeping with this scriptural truth that the inhabitants of the north country were among the hardest hit of all Finns in the Second World War. During the last bitter days, they shared the experiences of the Norwegians and suffered a scorched-earth policy at the hands of the retreating German Army. Consequently, in Finland at large, reconstruction was most costly where it was most urgent. One result of this experience was that much of north Finland was given a new look. There is a Canadian brightness (sometimes verging on North American brashness) about most towns and villages. Rovaniemi, astride a Kemi river which has suggestions of a minor Mackenzie, epitomizes this mood.

THE NATURAL PROVINCES

The north country is not without its human problems. In the same way as soil and climate conspire to twist and contort its antique woodlands into fantasies which might be attributed to trolldom, so the isolation and hardships of many generations have left their mark upon its people. Thus, the north country has a proportionately higher incidence of diseases associated with malnutrition than most of Finland; while its inhabitants are more inclined to extreme expressions in politics and religion than Finns at large. Nor has the wizardry of the Lapp been entirely explained away by twentieth-century science.

The north country is a country of exploration, of conservation, of experimentation and of inspiration. It is likely to remain a land of primary industry; yet, in the provision of raw materials, exploitation yields to conservation. Fortunately, its softwood resources were delayed in their utilization until such time as the significance of a planned husbandry had been established. The exploitation of hydro-electric energy was conveniently postponed until unitary plans for entire valleys could be implemented. Its extensive wastes have yet to be intensively surveyed for likely minerals. The thin scatter of mining communities is scarcely expressive of its hidden wealth. Experiment in their planning and development is also a challenge. Mineral deposits are exhaustible. The deserted settlement and the ghost town may yet enter the northern scene.

Finland's north country also inspires. It has an army of enthusiasts who accept its challenges and who challenge its causes in the national forum. It has eloquent artistic and literary apologists who are inspired by its moods and scenes—from Outakka, who has portrayed a gallery of Lappish faces, to Gallen-Kallela, whose woodpeckers and hoary pines reflect a craggy antiquity, from the realism of Eino Leino who has wrestled poetically with winter darkness to the neo-romanticism of Yrjö Kokko's *Way of Four Winds*. For the rest of Finland, Lapland has always been a legend spelling enchantment and mystery rather than hardship and penury. The north is a source of inspiration to the Finn as the west is to Americans. And, however hard the physical frontier may be, life is renewed upon it.

Finally, the north exhilarates because it is a national playground.

FINLAND: AN INTRODUCTION

In a countryside which retains elements of neolithic culture, all may play at living in archaic times. They may savour the silver beaches of Kuusamo's lakelets, tumbling torrents such as Pihtsosköngäs, the aromatic heights of the hump-backed fells, the dusty highway that leads along the spacious Tornio valley to the grandeurs of the Norwegian border country, the cloven rifts of Kevojoki canyon or the chapelet of lakes along Lemmenjoki (where alluvial gold is still panned). And under the March sun the snow-clad fells reach another climax of attraction.

Thus, while the resources of the northland are undergoing fundamental revaluation in the light of technical change, they are also experiencing a reinterpretation in the spiritual life of the nation. The rigours of the north persist, but a little of the rhetoric of the south has done much to change the attitude to them.

A Country on the Defensive

As a nation, Finland's attitudes are coloured by interests and outlooks which are a combined expression of archipelago (in Finnish, Saaristo-Suomi), peninsula (Suomenniemi), lakeland (Järvi-Suomi) and interior upland (Selkä-Suomi). Each component of the national scene complements the other. Finland displays inward-looking characteristics and outward-looking characteristics and national policies reflect the tug-of-war between them. The nation's authority has been born by the sea—in peninsular Finland, with its capital cities and ports. It is maintained through the sea, because the country can only live by overseas exchange. But Finland's strength is rooted in the interior forests and lakes. The old Adam of Finland is a man of the lakes. And he is a woodlander, too—a hunter as well as a fisher.

Yet if regional differences prompt differences of opinion, the unity of the nation demands that they should be subordinated to broader considerations. These derive from the land at large rather than the constituent landscapes. First, all parts of Finland have a northern setting. Accordingly, as Zachris Topelius wrote a century ago, 'Our country is set by nature on the defensive'. All parts of Finland are aware of climatic restraints and only the degree of restraint distinguishes them.

THE NATURAL PROVINCES

The second broader consideration for the land and landscapes of Finland is that they can only be fully explained in a European context. The nature and intensity of the influences exerted upon Finland from European sources also vary regionally. While Finland occupies one of Europe's oldest and most stable geological areas, it is one of the most recent areas of the continent to be permanently occupied. If political instability and independence are to be explained largely by a frontier situation on the marchlands of Western Europe, the retarded economic evolution of Finland is inseparable from a location removed from the cultural and economic hearths of the continent. Cultural and innovation waves from the outer world have long broken upon Finland's south and west fringes. It is only in recent decades that their effects have been fully transmitted to the interior.

This delayed development had two advantages which largely compensate for the earlier disadvantages of Finland's setting in Europe. First, it enabled the accumulation of Finland's past cultures to remain largely undisturbed until their value could be appreciated in the context of independent nationhood. Secondly, urbanization and industrialization were retarded in Finland until other countries had wrestled and solved some of the basic problems associated with them. Accordingly, Finland avoided many of the social and economic difficulties suffered in Western Europe through the rise of factories and the precipitate movement of people to the towns.

In brief, then, the land and landscapes of Finland which were subject to relatively little change from their early occupation until about a century ago, have experienced transformation at a North American or Australian speed. By Old World standards they have passed through a very great deal of change in a very short time. And the fact is clearly inscribed upon them.

URBAN PORTRAITS

W. R. MEAD

Although some Finnish towns have roots that go back centuries, few reflect this in visible remains. There are several explanations. First, Finland has always had a scanty population and town settlements were insignificant until the late eighteenth century. Secondly, Finland formerly had little of the labour needed to erect large stone or brick buildings and little money to spend on them, so that few lasting structures were built save churches and castles. Thirdly, while coastal towns began to multiply in the seventeenth century, they were mostly constructed of wood. The scourge of fire played regular havoc with them, independently of the natural process of timber decay. Brick and stucco awaited the nineteenth century, and even then their use was relatively isolated. Finally, urbanization was late to develop in Finland. This fact is inseparable from the delayed impact upon Finland of the technical changes that have become collectively known as the Industrial Revolution.

The principal result of all these facts is that, save where they are centred about a medieval church or a rare castle (as for example at Savonlinna, Hämeenlinna or Kajaani) Finnish towns are distinguished by an air of modernity. They are old towns by New World standards; new towns by Old World standards. But as places in which to live, they combine the best of both worlds. Where there are older features that merit preservation, they are the objects of studied care. Examples are provided by the 'empire line' of many buildings in Turku's older sector, the classical façades of Kristiinankaupunki, Porvoo cathedral precinct, Hamina's octagonally devised town centre, Uusikaarlepyy's picturesque main street, the environs of Tammisaari church and Rauma old town. Where new features in the townscape emerge, there is frequently a conscious attempt to harmonize these with the natural setting. A Scandinavian appreciation of the need for planning leads to a balance of economy and amenity. For Finnish towns are Scandinavian towns. Yet, although they have Scandinavian characteristics, variations on them and innovations springing from them give rise to Finnish distinctiveness.

The most common feature of the established Finnish town is the grid-iron street plan. Its geometry does not resemble in detail that of the American or Canadian town, but it gives rise to similar rectangular blocks of property. This feature is rooted in the fire hazard to wooden properties. Turku suffered the most disastrous destruction of any Finnish city in 1827. Pori and Vaasa were similarly devastated in 1852. Some towns, such as Oulu, went so far as to employ a watchman, who blew his horn at intervals throughout the night from the church tower to reassure the citizens that all was well. Late eighteenth-century and early nineteenth-century legislation paid careful attention to the spacing of buildings and the layout of urban lots. Their original form may still be seen in the older sections of some of the provincial capitals. In Kuopio and Mikkeli, administrative offices, churches and other public buildings, parks and market places are fitted neatly into the gridiron plan. The town gård, the usual type of dwelling unit, occupied a well-defined share of a rectangular lot, the yards and gardens of which were enclosed by a clapboard fence. It remains a dominant feature of many smaller towns and is only just disappearing from Turku and Tampere.

Indeed, in Finland's urban scene, the age of timber still seems near at hand. Light grey zinc replaces the black-tarred roof of older dwellings, yet it does not detract from their general impression of warmth. Timber has an abiding cosiness which brick may acquire in time but which concrete never wholly achieves. No matter how shabby or down-at-heel wooden properties may be they rarely lack interest. It is because they are the products of personal craftsmanship.

Personalities may sometimes stamp their impression upon the features of a city. The classical core of Helsinki is the product of the joint endeavour of Engel (the architect) and Ehrenström (the planner). In its initial stages of growth the new capital was the most spacious and airy of all Finnish towns. Visitors drew it in their sketchbooks and recorded their impressions of it in their diaries. For Xavier Marmier in 1843, its 'aspect [suggested] at every step the imprint of a vast empire'. In Helsinki, the Finns first waged urban war on rock. The echoing explosions of blasted granite are continuingly familiar sounds for Finnish town-dwellers. Helsinki's original plan took two generations to complete. Then industry overtook trading and administration. This called for the establishment of industrial precincts in the 1880s. Planned industrial sectors remain a feature of the expanding capital which expects to have a population of 600,000 by 1980.

Formal planning has acquired a variety of meanings in twentieth-century Finland. It may mean the planning of completely new settlements. Pre-eminent among them is the satellite city of Tapiola, west of Helsinki, though other satellites are planned to accommodate the south-westward drift of population. It may mean the introduction of planned sections to older cities, and the corresponding *imprint of a vigorous planning personality as with Alvar Aalto's design for Oulu's island settlement. It may mean planning for complete reconstruction, as with Rovaniemi following its wartime destruction. Or, it may spring from the need to integrate housing and new industrial plants, as at Sunila, near Kotka, or in the new Porkkala industrial area. And, always, planning makes provision for the incorporation of 'set pieces' in the heroic style, such as Säynätsalo civic centre near Jyväskylä.*

Space relations and amenity values have changed with urban growth in Finland. Land has become more valuable and the urban panorama has acquired a correspondingly more lively vertical expression. Finnish towns have avoided suburbia, but the residential precincts which are its counterpart and in which living space is coldly calculated in square metres, have a habit of repeating themselves throughout the country. They are identical from Åland to the Arctic. Yet they are saved from monotony by the broad spaces that surround them. From the beginning of town planning, the disproportionately broad streets were planted with rows or avenues of trees. Present-day town-dwellers enjoy them in their maturity. The tradition is established. Today, in areas scheduled for urban expansion, timber stands are carefully incorporated into the building plans and (despite land prices) landscaping assumes extravagant proportions.

Identity in the features of many Finnish urban profiles results from the fact that much development has taken place in a short time. The Finns have only become a nation of town-dwellers in the last generation. But if the contemporary in architectural style prevails, they have been able to profit from the mistakes of those who have preceded them in their urban migration. In addition to the changing profiles of town, the old-established hierarchy of town size has been altered. Some cities have grown more vigorously than others. Tampere has overtaken Turku in size: Lahti has emerged as Finland's most swiftly expanding city.

Old maps of Finland yield a harvest of towns that never existed (like old mariners' charts with their mythical isles). Some show a town called Arctopolis. Finland has no Arctopolis today, but it has continuing need to create new towns in its northland. One day, a new urban morphology will emerge in high latitudes—one which differs from that in lower latitudes. Finnish Lapland might conceive a new bastion built against winter to accommodate a few thousand families of administrators, foresters, miners. It would be a miracle of compression, eschewing the extravagant use of cold wasteland that wind-chills the pedestrian in Rovaniemi or Kemijärvi. It would be a 'bastide' town—taking as its model the medieval walled towns of south-west France. Where lofty flats did not flank its periphery, it would be glass-walled and it would have heated warrens of narrow streets. Vehicles would move beneath them. A ski jump would project from its wall of glass. And, in summer, as is the practice of all Finnish town-dwellers, its residents would desert their winter palace for cabins in the wilderness. A 'summer' Helsinki (especially in the neighbouring archipelagos) balances the permanent residence in the city. The pattern would have to be repeated in the new Arctopolis.

Icebreaker *Tarmo* at work

Winter scene

THE LAST WILDERNESS

SYLVIE NICKELS

Rovaniemi might well spell disillusion to many first-time visitors to Lapland. It is hard to combat those confused preconceived ideas—and some of Finland's publicity abroad does not always help—of frozen wastes and empty horizons where a perpetual sun shines down on bounding herds of reindeer and rather small people in colourful costumes. So the tourists arrive, trigger-fingers poised over their cameras, eager for their first sight of brightly-dressed Lapps in a sort of Arctic version of a mid-west shanty town.

Instead, what they see are the white blocks and glassy façades of a modern city; what they find are shops stocked with the kind of goods to be found in any prosperous community anywhere in the world, hotels of which any major tourist centre would be proud, restaurants, coffee bars, cinemas, museums, schools, one of the best-designed libraries (by Alvar Aalto) in Europe, and an ultra-modern concert and congress centre under construction. Should they stay only a day or two, as many do, they may see neither Lapp nor reindeer, unless they drive to the Arctic Circle hut, five miles north of the city, where one or two are, as it were, permanently available.

Rovaniemi, of course, is no more Lapland than London is England or New York is America. The Lapps, the reindeer, the desolate face of the wilderness, the great untamed beauty of forest and fell, they are all there in the nearly 40,000 square miles of the province of Lappi (Finnish Lapland). So is the sheer, hard unromantic grind of learning to live with some of the hardest conditions Nature can impose—and of making a living to provide the necessary comforts for those long, cold, dark months of the sub-Arctic winter.

But if the shiny face of Rovaniemi is deceptive, if it conceals a complexity of problems, it is also here in the province's administrative capital that much is reflected of the region's chequered story. Lapland's boom came in the early post-war years, ironically founded on the devastation thrust upon it by a war whose power games were far removed from this remote corner of the map. When the treaty terms enforced by Russia in 1944 turned German co-belligerents into enemies, retreating troops left a trail of destruction, tens of thousands of forest acres were burned, farms and villages razed. Among them was Rovaniemi.

In 1940, Rovaniemi was little more than a village itself, with a population of under 7,000. The ruins had hardly stopped smouldering before the inhabitants returned here, as elsewhere, to remould the face of Lapland. An army of architects, builders, engineers and road workers descended on the province. Work was plentiful—and purposeful. By 1950, Rovaniemi had doubled its population; by 1970 it was quadrupled to nearly 28,000. Alas, by then, too, the frenzy of rebuilding was over. Other factors were contributing to a change in the whole economic pattern. An ugly rise in unemployment figures reached a peak in 1968, with an average for the province of nearly 6,000 a month. People began to leave in search of work, some moving to south Finland, many to Sweden.

There were—and still are—pessimists who say Lapland will be empty in two decades; but an empty Lapland seems hardly likely to be in anyone's interests. Optimists—realistic ones who are in a position to know—say there is no reason why Lapland should not comfortably support its present population of around 200,000. At the moment, there seems to be more than a small hope for their optimism. The average monthly unemployment figures dropped in 1970 to 3,400; the exodus to the south and to Sweden continues, but on a smaller scale.

A major reason for hope lies in recent government policies towards assisting the so-called 'developing' areas, of which Finnish Lapland forms a substantial part. The most recent of these policies, formulated in 1969, offers concrete assistance in terms of tax concessions, low-interest loans, and a special fund for encouraging industrial development in these areas. As important a factor as any from Lapland's point of view is the provision of improved facilities for higher education—in particular vocational training—which should considerably stem the flow of young people heading south for this purpose: a flow which earlier accounted for 50 per cent of the movement of youth away from Lapland. With a lack of bureaucratic red tape that would be remarkable in any country, a large new trade school had already come into operation in Rovaniemi in the latter part of 1971.

These schools will provide training that had earlier not existed for specialized occupations. But it is, as usual, a question of whether the egg or the chicken comes first. Industrial development may have been hampered by lack of trained personnel, but a new skilled labour pool also needs steady outlets into which it can flow. Even in the jet age Lapland remains a long way from anywhere—to a southern Finn as remote as is Shetland to a Londoner; there is hardly likely to be an industrial revolution. Nevertheless, a sturdy industrial tradition exists, and potential developments, especially with regard to mineral resources, are as yet in their infancy.

The main need is for a complete rethink concerning the direction in which Lapland's economy can progress to best advantage. Available figures for employment over recent years show a reversal in the whole pattern of labour distribution, notably in the ratio of industry to forestry and agriculture. The number employed in the latter branches, for example, dropped from 36,000 in 1961 to 21,600 in 1969, while figures for industry in the corresponding period rose from 11,000 to 13,000. This change is due in part to the increased mechanization of methods of forestry and in part to the realization that fruitless subsidies of agriculture—especially when in the whole country there is agricultural overproduction—are not the answer to Lapland's problems. All the same, in some respects, Lapland's special conditions do show some advantages: for example, in the quality and yield per acre of potatoes which substantially exceed those of the south.

New or expanding industries, properly rationalized, however, can offer a far more predictable solution, unaffected by climatic vicissitudes and governed only by availability of skilled labour, raw materials and the ability to compete on the open market

FINLAND: AN INTRODUCTION

Over recent years, there have been steady if slow signs of this expansion: in pulp and timber, as for example in the great mills of Veitsiluoto Oy, and Kemi Oy; in the expanding textile mills, factories and brewery of Tornio; in the recent introduction of cement production north of Kolari; and in continued hydro-electric developments which have added a network of power stations as well as great new lakes—such as in the Vuotso area—to the Lapland map.

One of the brightest hopes for Lapland's future lies in tapping its undoubted and considerable mineral potential. Most of the nation's mineral research effort is now focused on Lapland, both by the state's Geological Research Institute and by such companies as Outokumpu and Rautaruukki, which figure among Europe's larger mining interests. The subject is by no means a new one. The whole geological construction of this northern roof of Europe, the vast wealth already exploited in Sweden, Norway and Finland herself holds great promise. The iron mines of Kolari and between Rovaniemi and Kemijärvi are old established; some are almost worked out, but others are ready to replace them. A new vanadium mine opens at Posio, about eighty miles north-east of Rovaniemi in 1972. A chrome mine—the mineral discovered near Kemi not by one of the research giants but by an amateur geologist—came into operation in the late 1960s and has resulted in a refinery in Tornio; a factory for high quality alloy steel is a further repercussion. The search for minerals is encouraged at all levels, with special rewards offered by communes for discoveries made on their territory.

But there is an equal need to encourage small enterprises that will offer greater diversity of employment. One success story in this respect is that of the Marttiini family whose ramifications have initiated a variety of businesses with sound Lapland roots. Puukkotehdas Oy is one which specializes in all types of knives and exports over a thousand a day to the United States alone; the same family is concerned with developing a marble quarry south of Rovaniemi, and with the manufacture of machinery for the forest industries. The souvenir business is well established and expanding in both Tornio and Rovaniemi, especially in traditional Lapp products which find a ready market in the big stores of Helsinki and elsewhere. Luxury fur farms—fox, chinchilla and notably mink—are making a small but important contribution to general expansion. A factory concerned with pipe insulation was successfully established in Rovaniemi in the late 1960s.

Not all experiments, of course, have been successful. A highly ambitious project was devised to create a vast recreation centre on the outskirts of Rovaniemi; based on Lapland's traditional associations with Santa Claus, this was to be known as Joulumaa or Christmasland, even supplying its own passports as well as a whole population of new Disney-like characters in the form of toys and fairy tales. The project failed because of lack of funds through the sheer vastness of the undertaking, though it has been revived on a more modest scale, under the sponsorship of a member of parliament.

What though of reindeer breeding, the traditional occupation associated by every foreigner with Lapland? The reindeer are still there in as great a number as ever—about one for each of Finnish Lapland's 200,000 inhabitants. Their economic importance with the rise in the value of reindeer meat, has even increased, though the way of life associated with them has undergone radical changes. Nowadays reindeer-breeding is a highly organized business, with the province divided into fifty-eight grazing districts and each of the 17,000 reindeer owners belonging to a central reindeer owners' association, or Paliskunta. This provides their liaison with the state (for it is the Ministry of Agriculture in Helsinki which decides on the number of reindeer that can graze each year in any district, albeit based on information supplied by the Paliskunta); it deals, too, with the budget and practical organization required for research, building new fencing, maintaining corrals for the annual round-ups, paying the herdsmen, etc.

Finland has more reindeer than either Sweden or Norway, but unlike in Sweden, reindeer ownership is not limited to the Lapps, who number a small minority of only 2,500 in Finland compared with far greater totals in Sweden and especially Norway. About a third of Finland's reindeer are owned by Lapps, and in all 2,500–3,000 families are estimated to make their living from reindeer. But the seasonal rhythm is slowly undergoing changes in the interests of simple economics: the quality—and the price—of reindeer meat is higher in autumn and drops in winter. The colourful winter round-ups when the herds are gathered in corrals in a spray of snow and pounding hoofs against the pastel tones of the Arctic mid-winter day are being replaced by autumn round-ups which make more economic sense. Even in the remoter fastnesses of northern Lapland, the traditional and colourful reindeer-drawn *pulkka* (boat-shaped sledge on one runner) has all but been replaced by the unbeautiful, noisy but practical motorized sledge. And inevitably as Lapp youth attending state schools learn new ways, their identity with their own culture is sadly superseded by a taste for pop music and the international fashions of their contemporaries the world over.

Despite this, much of the old cultural pattern still exists, as anyone who has attended a Lapp wedding ceremony or church festival or even simply taken to his own feet and wandered away from the limited tourist trails will know. The traditions, hospitality and sterling qualities of the Lapps and northern Finns *are* unique. And it is of concern not only to the Finns, but also to neighbouring Norwegians and Swedes that some kind of economic and cultural unity should be preserved.

Nordkalotten (Pohjoiskalotti in Finnish) is the umbrella name for the vast provinces which form the geographical northern limits of Europe and, in principle, extend across the corresponding adjoining regions of Russia. Some serious organized attempts have been made over recent years to co-ordinate the interests of these areas in both the cultural and commercial fields. Conferences ranging over a wide variety of subjects from reindeer breeding and tourism to education and economic co-operation have produced at least some practical results, especially in the field of tourism. They have also taken other forms: a retraining centre, for example, at Övertorneå just across the river border with Sweden. With an intake of 210 students, the costs of this higher education centre are shared by Norway, Sweden and Finland. Other forms of co-operation include a water-purifying plant (between the communes of Haparanda and Tornio) and many small local enterprises shared by communes across their respective borders. There is, in any case, a free flow of labour between the northern countries, and expanding communications will encourage the tendency. Today, a growing network of roads links areas that earlier could only be reached on foot, by ski or by boat according to season.

These improved contacts are increasingly reflected in all directions. In addition to Finnish-built power stations across the eastern border, there is now also a steady flow of tourists (as yet, albeit, limited to Finns) who can buy a package deal to Murmansk.

The general boom in tourism has been one of the greatest developments in Lapland during the last decade. The number of visitors more than doubled between 1960 and 1970 when it reached an estimated total of 500,000 for the province, 25-30 per cent of which were foreigners, including an impressive array of heads of state. A dozen years ago, the number of tourist hotels could have been counted on the fingers of one hand. Today at least a score of hotels offer the kind of facilities of which any major European resort could be proud. In addition, as many holiday villages in attractive log cabin style set on lake or river shore against a wilderness backdrop of forest or fell, mark the presence of the world's biggest industry in this far-flung corner of the map. Ski- and chair-lifts stride up fell slopes that were once largely the preserve of reindeer and ptarmigan. New roads bore across virgin forests where centuries ago the Lapps worshipped ancient gods in seclusion, and better communications have meant a flow of visitors on a variety of circular north-Scandinavian trips that did not exist ten years ago.

Nor is this limited to main roads. The gold-washing area in the upper reaches of Lemmenjoki (literally, River of Love), southwest of Inari, is now on a regular schedule by tourist boat from Inari's tourist hotel. Sevettijärvi, a remote Skolt Lapp settlement north-east of Kaamanen towards the Russian border, was until recently accessible only by boat in summer, by ski or snow-bus in winter. Now it is served by regular buses and offers its visitors accommodation in a log cabin holiday village.

Many will think it is sad, but Lapland, too, has learned the commercial value of its tourist potential. You can now pan for

FINLAND: AN INTRODUCTION

gold for a nominal fee, only a short distance off the Arctic Highway, near Vuotso. You can learn to drive reindeer at Pohtimolampi, fifteen miles north of Rovaniemi. You can attend motor sledge races. You can have every comfort of the 1970s against a setting that is only one step removed from the last Ice Age. You can, in short, experience what might be called 'instant Lapland'—and probably have very little idea of what it is really all about.

Yet its true seekers have only to expend a little energy, leave the road, shoulder their rucksacks, be prepared to sit and listen rather than to question and demand in order to come in contact with a way of life that has no parallel anywhere, certainly not in Europe. It is this which has drawn a small but caring minority of settlers from other parts of Finland, even from other lands, who find values that do not exist elsewhere and who are prepared to accept the harsher challenges that Lapland offers. For them, as for many of Lapland's inhabitants, the changes are sad. But most will accept that they are essential if Europe's last wilderness is to survive as a living place.

WILD LIFE AND NATURE

SEPPO PARTANEN

Flying across Finland from south to north, the traveller's first surprise is probably the size of the country. It is 724 miles from one end to the other, the sixth largest nation in Europe and nearly one and a half times the size of the United Kingdom. The term 'Little Finland' is therefore very much a misnomer.

The summer trip will also give him a good idea of Finland's scenery and countryside. From the air it all looks rather like a half-finished jigsaw puzzle. The completed bits are mostly green—the deep emerald of the pine and spruce forests, the lush pale meadow green of the fields—and these areas are in the minority. Most of what the passenger sees is sky-blue, the watery sapphire

FINLAND: AN INTRODUCTION

hue of thousands of lakes, rivers, ponds and sea. The lakes tend to be narrow and labyrinthine, studded with a profusion of small islands, many uninhabited and most quite unspoilt—the bits of the puzzle that are usually left to the last because they are difficult to fit in. The towns and the villages tend to concentrate either where water systems meet or on rocky promontories, lake shores or islands.

What will the visitor find when he reaches his destination? Leaving aside the fact that the airport staff at Ivalo, nearly 200 miles inside the Arctic Circle, may have to chase reindeer off the runway before his plane can land, there should be plenty to please and even astonish the traveller, whether he be naturalist, nature lover, or just plain tourist.

Take for instance the four species of beasts of prey. The largest is the bear, and in the barren wastelands and tundra of Lapland and eastern Finland there are between two and four hundred of them. Apart from other restrictions, they may be hunted only from mid-May to mid-October and this protects them during their winter hibernation. In 1968, seventy-four were killed and two were trapped alive. All this is far different from the ravages of the early nineteenth century, when one famous hunter alone accounted for over two hundred. Today the state has to pay compensation every year to owners of reindeer herds for their losses from bears, and the damage they inflict may well be even greater for the herds roam wild and some of the massacred animals are never found.

As an interesting side issue, the bear became at one time, shortly after Finland's independence, a focus of lively political argument. Always popularly considered the king of Finnish beasts, there were those who wanted it put on the national coat of arms. In the event the bear lost out, and today the country's armorial bearings still carry a stranger from far off and warmer lands: the lion.

However, it is not the bear that is the greatest enemy of the reindeer, but the wolverine, weighing only some 45 pounds, which can nevertheless kill several head in one attack. This predator, of which some forty to sixty are believed to be left, jumps

138

on its prey from an overhanging branch and severs its jugular vein with its teeth.

To Finns the wolf presents a very different picture from something in a Disney cartoon. True, in the lifetime of the present generation at least, no Little Red Riding Hood has been gobbled up, nor for that matter has her Grandmother either. However, wolves do occasionally attack children in the countryside and they also kill livestock. Most of them come over the eastern frontier from the Soviet Union. They are great wanderers and have been seen near the centres of habitation in southern Finland. Commonly, when their tracks appear in the snow, the entire male population of the district turns out to hunt them and a number is shot every year in this way.

The fourth beast of prey, the lynx, is becoming a rarity and is now protected throughout the country. There are at present about one hundred of these ferocious animals and, in exceptional cases only where they attack reindeer, permission is given to hunt them.

The two most important of the non-predators are the elk and the reindeer. The latter is a domestic herd animal, found mostly in the vast Lapland tundra where, until recently, its meat, hide and bones were essential to the survival of its Lapp and Finnish owners. The elk, on the other hand, wanders wild far to the south, right to the shores of the Gulf of Finland; it even occasionally appears in city streets, from where it is the job of the police or firemen to cajole it back to the woods. A few decades ago, the animal was being hunted almost to extinction, but as a result of vigorous protection measures it has now re-established itself, and elk warning signs are quite common on Finnish roads. The incautious motorist who disregards them soon learns, after the bonnet of his car has been dented by a collision with several hundredweight of antlered quadruped, to pay attention to their admonitions.

Many other wild animals are found in the Finnish forests and not only there. In 1970, the municipality of Helsinki carried out a

FINLAND: AN INTRODUCTION

survey of wild life in its area. In spite of the fact that vacant building land has almost vanished, they found families of elk, foxes, badgers and hare still living within the precincts of the city.

In the peace and stillness of the forest, the hiker may see a weasel or marten raiding a nest, an otter building its dam or a vixen teaching its cubs to stalk a bird. Earlier, in the Lake Saimaa region of eastern Finland, he might have found the majestic eagle, the wild reindeer (forebear of the present domesticated species) and, on the lake shore, the seal. Regrettably, during the last few decades these three have been dying out. Finally, there are the famous lemmings, of whose strange suicidal mass migrations everyone must have now heard.

For centuries the Finn has taken the unspoilt beauty and apparently limitless natural amenities of his countryside for granted. It was, he felt, part of his heritage and not subject to the laws of change. Not, that is, until recently. For the sad fact is that even this impressive treasure-house of wild life—more varied than any to be found elsewhere in Western Europe—is today facing the same threats of pollution that have long been worrying the governments of less-favoured countries. Some of the reasons have already been implied; to these one must add the use of harmful chemical fertilizers, disastrous oil tanker strandings, wasteful use of forest resources, and many others. The cumulative effect is now beginning to show.

It is therefore encouraging to record that the trend is not all adverse. Public awareness is being aroused; housewives are seriously thinking about changing their brand of detergent to avoid polluting waterways; young radicals put up conservation posters in Helsinki streets; for the first time a car has been smashed up in a city square in protest. The plain fact is that Finland, too, has felt the influence of International Conservation Year. What is the country's official conservation policy, and what has it achieved so far?

The division of Finland between industrial and rural areas is plain enough. The latter are to be found in the huge agricultural and forest regions of the east and north—the regions which people are abandoning in search of work. Conservation policy has two aims, to keep industrial growth out and preserve unspoilt what is left of the superb rural sectors. Thus, no less than 750,000 acres (or 1.1 per cent of the area of the whole country) enjoy protection of some kind. The most important are the National Reserves, covering about 220,000 acres, set aside for public recreation. In addition there are fifteen National Parks, comprising 100,000 acres, intended primarily for scientific research, though anybody may hike there and the trails are all signposted. However, both reserves and parks are in wild country and cars may drive up only to their perimeters. The Forestry Commission in charge of state forest land has banned felling in 308 virgin forest sectors, totalling 120,000 acres, and partial felling in a further 175,000 acres. There are also forty-five private conservation areas of various types.

Finally, at the close of the International Conservation year, the authorities set up a permanent advisory committee, composed of all interested bodies, to deal with every aspect of national conservation problems. Legal steps have since been taken to limit hunting and protect wild life, especially rare wild life. There is also a proposal to establish a joint Finnish-Norwegian national park.

This, then, is the Finnish wild life scene: a richness and variety such as few, if any, European countries can match, with unencumbered access for the visitor or tourist; some admitted pollution problems beginning to cause concern; and an increasingly well-informed public opinion supporting government conservation measures.

THE WINTER WAY OF LIFE

SEPPO PARTANEN

Snow, ice, cold—brisk and sharp—these are winter's everyday realities to the Finns; the hard frost is a call to work, pleasure and exercise, an invitation to slip out from the warm fireside.

The earliest snowfall comes to Lapland in September or October; by Christmas the whole land is under snow. The whiteness of Christmas symbolizes the beauty and innocence of the Christmas message while the spring ceremonies of the first of May mark the final victory over winter. In April, in most places, the snow is melting away; but in the very north of Lapland you can still find snow in the forests and the shady gullies of the fells as late as June. March is the month of deepest snow, averaging eighteen inches to three feet. In the south there are three to six months of snow; north of the Arctic Circle it can last six to eight months.

Meteorologically, winter starts when the average temperature for the day sinks below zero centigrade: usually October in Lapland, November elsewhere. In April the average temperature for the day climbs back above zero. The coldest month is February, when the day's average is around $-10°C$. Over several decades the average minimum temperature recorded for the month has been $-25°C$ to $-39°C$.

Finns work through the winter and take their annual holiday in the three summer months. The pattern has, it is true, been changing: employers have been encouraging winter holidays by making them 50 per cent longer than summer ones. The schools are closed for the three summer months, but they have a week's ski-ing holiday in February or March as well, to refresh the boys and girls for the heavy spring term. Many children go up to the northern holiday centres for this week of ski-ing.

Country youngsters often ski to school. City children hump

their skis and skates to school for their athletics periods. They ski themselves to the limit in the school championships and, in the evening, desert their homework for the tobogganing slopes, skating rinks and ski-tracks. Out of these early pastimes the adult world has created a great structure of winter happenings.

Shrove Tuesday is the climax of winter activities in Finland. December and January are the year's midnight; in Lapland the sun does not appear above the horizon, and even in the south the days are a dull grey. Lapp folklore records a peculiar illness endemic to this time of year—'arctic hysteria', caused by the 24-hour gloom: depression, the horrors and the shakes. You cured it by creeping up behind the patient and putting your fingers over his eyes.

Shrovetide is, of course, the feast starting off the Catholic Lent, and Finland enriched it with some of its old pagan beliefs, customs and omens. Spinning was forbidden, otherwise the sheep would sicken in the summer; you should not speak in the sauna if you did not want to be attacked by swarms of mosquitoes in the summer; you ate lots of fat so that you would not have a lean year; and on the annual toboggan day, when the whole village turned out together, they shouted, as they hurtled down the slopes, 'Long linen and fine hemp', to ensure an abundant crop the following summer. Shrove Tuesday lost its ecclesiastical character and has turned into a cheerful winter carnival for the young. In the country, young people take their toboggans to the hillsides and dance in the evening. In the towns they go to the children's parks and swoop down the slopes on toboggans and on hardboard and plastic sheets. Then they set off for the bars, discothéques and restaurants to eat the traditional Shrove dishes: pea soup, hot milk and buns stuffed with marzipan. The evening ends, as carnivals do everywhere in the world, with dancing.

The Finns are said to have been born with skis on. Ski-ing is still the main winter sport, as the example of President Kekkonen —now in his seventies—shows. Not only does he do his daily stint on skis, but every winter he takes off on a 60–120 mile ski-trip over the Lapp fells. Finnish skiers have always won great victories in ski-competitions, hunting, trekking, and especially at war in long-distance ski patrols behind the lines.

FINLAND: AN INTRODUCTION

Ski-ing is an important keep-fit exercise for the ordinary person. Even in the centre of Helsinki, with its half-million inhabitants, you can put on your skis, glide through the parks into the suburbs and off into the open country. On the city's outskirts are illuminated ski-tracks where people can lick themselves into shape after the day's work. Communities all over the country challenge each other to so-called 'people's' races, where to qualify you have to ski at least three miles. Finland and Sweden have had international meetings on the same lines. In these kinds of competition, ten to twenty million results are judged good enough for registration each year.

Besides these, ski-treks 30–125 miles long, are arranged at the week-ends. Thousands take part. Trips into the Lapland wilderness, like President Kekkonen's, are very popular. Travel organizations arrange guided trips, 50–100 miles long, lasting a week, through spectacular landscapes of snowy wastes and steep fells. These tours are possible because, even in the most desolate places, the state has built log cabins for everybody's use, with heating equipment, a cooking stove, utensils and bunks. March and April are the best months, when the afternoon sun softens the snowcrust and the night frost freezes it over with a thin layer of ice which carries the skier and speeds him on his way.

Finland's great winter sports meetings are the equivalent of major horse-racing events in England. The world's best winter sportsmen come to show what they can do, and along troop the country's leading politicians, the foreign diplomats, publicity-seekers and thousands of ordinary people. The parade of winter fashion is just as important as the sport, with society-editors and fashion-columnists looking just as keenly as the sports writers to observe what people are wearing and who is with whom.

Skiers are amongst the most prized of Finland's athletes. In 1970, the sports editors chose Kalevi Oikarainen as athlete of the year, for his world championship victory in the fifty-kilometre ski-ing event, even though equally important victories were won in both motor-racing and other sports.

Slalom and downhill runs have developed alongside cross-country ski-ing, largely at the instigation of the younger generation. Though slalom has been practised in Finland since the 1930s, it only reached the general public in the 1960s, when slalom slopes began to be cleared and ski-lifts constructed all over the country. They have already reached the hundred-mark. The longest and most gruelling slopes are on the Lapp fells, with runs of up to two miles. Lapland also has the country's only slopes fulfilling international competition standards. Nowadays Finland's holiday centres entice tourists, alpine-fashion, with modern lifts, express slalom courses and romantic après-ski programmes.

Winter encouraged other peculiar means of transport too: reindeer, for instance, though nowadays Finnish children only know reindeer as Father Christmas's steeds. A trained reindeer gelding was harnessed to a sleigh or a flat-bottomed wooden sledge. During the period of hard-frozen snow, both reindeer and sledge could get up a fine speed over an unbroken surface. The driver sat in the first sledge, to which were attached ten to twelve more reindeer-drawn freight-sleighs. In this way a nomadic Lapp could drive all his property around the fells alongside his herds of reindeer. Nowadays reindeer-owners herd their beasts with skidoos or motor-sleds. These are popular with tourists too; you can get to the farthest fishing rivers in them across the Lapland wilderness. Reindeer-driving has also revived for the tourists, who now have the chance of qualifying for reindeer driving-licences in some tourist centres. In late winter, reindeer safaris are organized lasting two to seven days; each member has a reindeer and sledge, and the safari is led by a Lapp versed in reindeer and the terrain. Nights are spent in cabins on the fells.

Before the tyranny of the motor car, the kick-sleigh was used for short distances in towns and villages—and is by no means yet obsolete. This is a chair-like vehicle on two long iron runners, curving up at the front like skis. You lean on handrests above the chairback, place one leg on one runner and scoot with the other along the icy street. You can get up an impresseive speed going downhill on a slippery road. Children, shopping and even girl friends can be placed on the chair itself. I went to school by kick-sleigh myself, and it used to animate the whole village, especially the pupils of the girls' school. This, in fact, was secretly in my mind. You see, a kick-sleigh can have fatal consequences as it can be propelled by two people side by side.

FINLAND: AN INTRODUCTION

The most philosophical of winter pursuits is fishing through a hole in the ice. Since the Finnish disposition is in general contemplative, hole-fishing is well patronized. You bore a hole in a frozen river, lake or sea, sit down by the hole, drop some bait into the water on the end of a line and start to unravel the problems of space, time and the human condition. If a fish bites, your rod registers a slight tremor and then it is time to abandon philosophy and start pulling. And you may be lucky enough to catch a perch, pike, burbot, trout, grayling or salmon.

Anyone can do this if they have a state fishing licence in their pocket and a permit from the owner of the waters. The only equipment necessary is a hook and line, warm clothes and a camp stool. Angling clubs arrange week-end competitions, which are often so well patronized that prize winners can get a car, a television set, an automatic washing machine or a motor-sled out of the funds collected from the cheap entry tickets.

Twenty-five per cent of motorists put their cars away during the winter months. The first snows invariably fall one day before drivers have managed to put their winter tyres on. Traffic is a skidding chaos that day, but Finnish drivers quickly learn to manoeuvre on iced and snowy roads. Thus, road accidents are less frequent during the winter. Road deaths in 1968 worked out as follows: January, 53; February, 59; March, 51; and April, 57. The sombre time is summer, when all the cars are out and speeds are greatest, and, moreover, pedestrians and motorists are often holidaymakers unfamiliar with local roads. In 1968, summer deaths were as follows: June, 82; July, 99; and August, 94.

The Finnish Government's civil engineering department spends £3,000,000 on road maintenance in the winter: that is 15 per cent of the government's total maintenance expenditure. It costs this to plough the snow away from almost six million miles of highways and by-ways. Road scrapers shear the ice off over two million miles throughout the winter, and fences protect over one thousand five hundred miles of road from drifting snow.

Some £800,000 are spent each winter on treating slippery roads. Motoring organizations and the government officials responsible for road maintenance have been quarrelling for years about whether salt should be used for melting snow off the roads.

THE WINTER WAY OF LIFE

The motoring organizations are usually opposed to salt because of its corroding effect. In the winter of 1970, the civil servants gave in for the first time by leaving certain sections of road unsalted, but during the Christmas traffic many drivers were observed to be avoiding the unsalted but slippery and icy roads. Thus danger was considered more of a threat than car depreciation due to salt.

Snow is also ploughed away to clear roads over the ice to various islands in the sea and the lakes, and thus allow the islanders to maintain road-contact with the mainland for several months. Many winters, at the narrowest point of the Gulf of Bothnia, a road has been cleared over the ice all the way from Finland to Sweden.

Finnish motor-racing has a secret weapon: the ice-track. Local authorities and motoring organizations arrange for a track to be ploughed on the ice, $\frac{3}{4}$ mile to $1\frac{1}{4}$ miles long and from ten to thirty yards wide, with several bends and curves. Drivers gather there in the evenings and on Sundays to practise their skill on slippery surfaces. As the ice-track is bordered by a snow embankment several yards high, the course is quite safe: even if you slip off the track at high speed you only cause a 'snowstorm'. In this way, a driver learns to recognize his car's first symptoms of skid and to control them, a useful attribute even for ordinary driving. Since 1966 'Talja', the Finnish organization responsible for safety on the roads, has trained approximately 1,400 driving instructors on winter-driving courses, including both theory and practical experience on the ice-track.

Ice-track driving has become a popular national sport and about two hundred events are arranged up and down the country each winter. Standard cars are fitted with spiked or studded tyres and the competitors circle the ice-track five to ten times. Participants sometimes crash into each other, the snow thrashes up on the bends, cars often flip over and skid along on their roofs, and the crowd enjoys itself. Motor-racing aces and ordinary drivers compete in separate classes. There are also 'microcar' ice-races. A 'microcar' is a reduced chassis driven by a motorbike or moped engine, with tiny wheels, a very low-set seat and a windshield. Microcar-driving is open to young people too, as a driving licence is not required on the ice-track. Often they construct their own microcars in their school or community recreation-club workshops.

Car-rallies are another entertainment and delight of the Finns. Finnish drivers' victories in international rallies have infected the whole country with rally-fever. The special feature of the Finnish winter and spring rallies has been said to be the amount of time cars spend in the air as they negotiate the fast courses. This 'jumping' has aroused a lot of comment abroad, brought in thousands of spectators and earned Finnish rally-drivers the common nickname of 'the Flying Finn'. Several rally races are held in Finland each winter, attracting nearly all the best Scandinavian drivers, though up to now these events have not become international news.

Finnish rally-drivers have been disciplined in their art by hard winters. This is shown by their high score of victories in the snowy parts of the Monte Carlo rally in recent years. Major car manufacturers have also seen the advantages of the Finnish winter and are testing out their new prototypes on the Lapland highways.

Ace Finnish rally-drivers were placed in the first five in the 1970 London-Mexico rally: the winner was Hannu Mikkola, the third was Rauno Aaltonen and the fifth Timo Mäkinen. Of the same group are Simo Lampinen and Leo Kinnunen, a star performer in international track-racing. Many younger drivers are already competing with these on equal terms in the home rallies. And a new generation of Finnish rally-drivers is growing up in the park sand pits where miniature Mikkolas, Mäkinens, Kinnunens, Lampinens and Aaltonens whizz contending round the tracks. The great point at dispute in these clashes is who shall have the right to use which famous name.

Winter holds many humorous episodes for the car-owner too. One morning I left my car by the kerb in front of my flat in Helsinki. There had been heavy snow a few days earlier and now the temperature had risen above zero, making the roads treacherously slippery. At the office, I got an urgent call from the person I used to kick-sleigh with: I had forgotten to leave her the car-keys, she said, in some alarm, and a great mass of snow was glaciering slowly down the roof of the house and was just about to submerge my car. I tore round in a taxi, just in time to leap into my car and drive it out of the way. A great bulk of hundredweights of wet snow came flopping down into the street, sorely disappointing the crowd that had eagerly gathered.

TRAINING THE FINNISH SOLDIER

KEIJO MIKOLA

A weasel in a ruin, so runs a Finnish proverb, is worth five elsewhere. In English, the comparison would perhaps be with the gadfly who, like the guerrilla fighter, buzzes in and out so fast that he seems to be everywhere at once.

This was how Finnish troops in the winter of 1939–40 harried the sensitive flanks of the advancing Soviet columns in the forests of Karelia. Accustomed to mobility almost from birth, they were trained to cover ground quickly and hold extensive areas in small strength. In a country a third as big again as Britain but with only one tenth of its manpower, rapid movement is the sine qua non of the military art.

The country's economic resources do not allow her to solve her mobility problems by motorizing the entire army. In any case, the motor vehicle is not suited for use on the sparse road network. Large territories between these roads are best controlled by ski troops in winter and infantry in summer, with scouts on bicycles making use of forest tracks. Most of the terrain is tree-covered and strewn with ice-age boulders, and there is a profusion of marshes and swamps which can be traversed only in single file. As terra firma often narrows into strips between the waterways, it is easy to predict the direction and route of massive forces on the move.

Finnish effectives are trained to fight in lightly-armed units over this type of country, harrying enemy patrols and lines of supply advancing on the roads, while more heavily armed contingents, with superior technical equipment, are used to block the advance itself. In winter this means, in practical terms, training to cover daily stretches of twenty to thirty miles on skis, and in summer to cycle from sixty to ninety miles. Such groups must learn to be self-supporting under all possible conditions. For backwoods travel of this kind they must carry all they need in the way of equipment and supplies either on their backs or their bicycles or, in winter, on sledges drawn by the men themselves. In addition to training in these skills, the warm light summer nights and the ice-cold winter snows involve very special problems of movement and weapon usage.

Conditions also vary widely in different parts of the country. What has been said above is relevant mainly to Lapland and other parts of northern Finland, where uninhabited forests and treacherous swamps are more widespread, and also to central Finland, fragmented by large patches of water. But in southern Finland the population is denser, the roads more numerous and the cultivated area bigger; and these surroundings favour large armoured formations. On the other hand the south—and particularly the southwest—coast is guarded by one of the most labyrinthine archipelagos in the whole of Europe. This, in effect, ties a hostile offensive to lines of attack where progress is difficult. Even sterner is the task of breaking through the island network since the Finns have mastered the art of using it for defensive purposes. Part of the troops are trained as coastal infantrymen to cover the maze of channels and narrows in fast boats based on rocky island strong-points. To a defender the archipelago offers many advan-

FINLAND: AN INTRODUCTION

tages, including naturally protected outposts and countless coastal inlets, from whence a comparatively weak force can seriously impede an unsuspecting and powerful intruder. The naval forces draw their reinforcements largely from fisher-folk and other seafarers.

Every Finnish male is called up at the age of twenty to serve a compulsory term of from eight to eleven months training in the armed forces. His liability to military service starts in fact when he is seventeen, and he remains in the reserve until he is fifty, or in the case of officers to the age of sixty. During this period he is required to serve a total of from forty to one hundred days on refresher courses or learning to use and service new weapons.

Finnish military instruction is limited by international agreement to activity within the state frontiers. Training covers every branch of weaponry used by a modern army. The most important force is the infantry, comprising six brigades and ten battalions, including armoured and parachute formations, as well as specialist contingents for arctic and coastal warfare. The field artillery contains ten motorized batteries. This arm of the service has a great tradition of high-accuracy gunnery, which is still the aim of the training. The Finns are also excellent marksmen with light weapons. The seven batteries of coastal artillery, some of them mobile, based on heavily fortified island strongpoints, are responsible for the defence of the principal outposts in the archipelago.

The brigades have their own signal and sapper units, but in addition specialists in these techniques are trained for command duties in signals regiments and engineer battalions. Anti-aircraft units defending industrial and populated areas also operate either in brigades or as individual batteries.

The airforce, consisting mainly of fighters, is divided into three squadrons to ensure readiness to cover the whole country. The core of the navy consists of two modern gunboats, supported by a number of light fast craft. This force is greatly helped by the availability of reefs and shallow water for mine-laying. The main bases are in Turku and Porkkala.

Geographically, the country is divided into seven military districts, embracing all the foregoing, though the naval and air forces have independent commands. The district commanders are in charge of peacetime effectives, reserves and local defence staffs, ensuring combat readiness both nationally and locally in the event of a threat of war. In particular, the defence forces in various areas are geared to repel a surprise attack independently and without delay. The frontier guard, an elite body, specially trained for guerrilla action, which in peace-time is under the jurisdiction of the Ministry of the Interior, would in that event be seconded to the regular army.

Conscripts receive their training in the formations described above. Each group has a school for non-commissioned officers where the latter—about 20 per cent of each annual intake—receive instruction in the duties of subordinate command and other special tasks. Men drafted to reserve officer training also go through the n.c.o. school. There are even instructional units for such specialized skills as radar and meteorology, while for regular-army personnel elementary, intermediate and advanced tuition is furnished by appropriate establishments covering general duties and various types of weapons.

In the event of hostilities, the reserve officer role is decisive. During the last war Finnish reserve officers proved excellent company commanders, and some even made outstanding battalion commanders. This suits the national character; the Finn is a practical individual and his best military qualities emerge when operating in a small independent group. About 10 per cent of the annual call-up go to the Military Reserve Officer School or to the reserve officer classes of the naval and airforce academies.

By modern standards the services are comparatively lightly armed, a consequence both of the country's economic and industrial resources and of local conditions. Thus, the nation has evolved an arms industry adapted to the requirements of her soil and climate—a widely-known automatic pistol, new assault weapons, efficient machine and anti-tank guns—as well as such ancillary equipment as winter camping gear. Domestic industry can provide all these. The heavier armament output is smaller, but it too is enough (with some reinforcements from foreign sources) to equip a striking force capable of giving sufficient support to lightly-armed but well trained groups to make life intolerable to an invader.

Under the Peace Treaty (Paris 1947) Finland's peacetime armed services are fixed at a ceiling of 41,900 men—34,000 military, 4,500 naval and 3,000 airforce. There are also limits on certain types of arms, in particular for the naval and air branches, and non-service military instruction is barred. Since the weapons denied to Finland are in any case mainly those possessed by the great powers, these limitations have not substantially affected service development. For mobilization the most important consideration is that, while observing the global ceiling, all age groups should receive full and continuous reserve training. However, the organization of large-scale manoeuvres, affording practice in operations at wartime strengths, is difficult for economic and other reasons. Finns in general consider it a matter of honour to observe written undertakings; but they are also prepared to fulfil their obligations by the voluntary maintenance of their military skills. They therefore find irksome the restraints on defence preparedness caused by the prohibition of training outside the service establishments. Reservists, both commissioned and non-commissioned, conscious of their wartime leadership responsibilities, would like to undergo refresher courses in voluntary organizations of their own.

The Finn sets store by his national independence, aspires to defend it and hankers after means to sustain the appropriate skills. He appreciates that experience in fighting on his own soil gives him an advantage denied to an invader. It has been said of him that, as a soldier, he is phlegmatic and not easily amenable to discipline, but that in battle he is fast, tough and intelligent, in fact an opponent to be reckoned with. He is independent by nature and somewhat of a loner, and therefore finds it difficult to submit to the restrictions of peacetime soldiering. In actual combat, however, he feels free to use his own initiative and employ to the *full his physical and mental aptitudes in contributing to the defence of his homeland.*

He has a large area to protect, but his knowledge of it is profound. Its range of specialized conditions covers the whole spectrum from the near-empty European Arctic to the heavily populated farmlands and myriad islands of the Baltic shores.

THE YOUNG AND THEIR EDUCATION

PHILIP BINHAM

To be able to understand the young Finn, we must have some idea of the world he lives in. And since his world is largely school, the Finnish educational world seems the best place to start. The keyword in Finnish education in the seventies is reform, and the biggest reform in progress is the changing of the basic education process through which all Finns must pass.

The present school system has not had a real shake-up for a long time. And education is something that the Finns—like the Scots—take very seriously indeed. Not that they always take to it with ease. The classic attitude of the Finnish schoolboy can be found in the classic Finnish novel *Seven Brothers* by Aleksis Kivi. In this story of the early-nineteenth-century backwoods, the brothers—aged between eighteen and twenty-five—are ordered to attend school by the local vicar in order to learn their alphabet. Their attitude is summed up in Juhani's terse statement, 'Impossible to learn to read.'

It was prescribed in the Church law of Sweden-Finland in 1686 that everyone should learn to read and learn by heart a considerable number of religious texts. The penalties for non-compliance were formidable. An illiterate person was not allowed to enjoy civic rights or to marry. More recently Finland has been proud to point to one of the lowest illiteracy rates in the world. Finns will tell you that the reason for this is that Finnish orthography is phonetic. Any foreigner who has tried to learn Finnish will be inclined to consider it a miracle that anyone learns to read at all.

The spreading of school education, and thus of teaching in the Finnish language, was slow, however. Towards the end of the nineteenth century, the idea of extending folk education beyond religious teaching was first publicly expressed. Progress was hampered by the fact that the Russian tsars did not favour a high standard of folk education. In 1863 the first seminar for folk-school teachers was started at Jyväskylä—still an important education centre—and in 1866 the Senate finally passed a law for the setting up of folk schools. It was not until Independence was declared that a universal School Attendance Act was passed. The present *kansakoulu*—folk or elementary school—starts at the age of seven. Fifteen is the lowest school-leaving age; there is an examination at the age of eleven in which the successful candidates go on to secondary school. For those who stay on at elementary school there are practical subjects (including forestry).

Everything at the elementary school is free—free books, free meals, free medical and dental treatment, and for children living more than three miles from school (the rule rather than the exception in the more remote districts) free transport. Clothes and shoes are also provided for needy pupils. The size of schools varies considerably, from several hundred pupils in the cities to twenty on islands in the archipelago. Most schools in Finland, incidentally, are housed in rather modern buildings—many of them built since the war. Their elegance and disregard for cost by British standards reflect the authority of the Finnish architect.

The examination at the age of eleven is chiefly in writing and arithmetic. Those who do well enough in this—a little over a half of all children—go on to *oppikoulu* ('learning school'). This secondary school is divided into two: the first five years of *keskikoulu*—'middle school', and the remaining three of *lukio*, a sort of senior high school.

Under the new system, much of this will be changed. Instead of the elementary and middle schools, there will be the new *peruskoulu*. This means literally 'basic school', but the term is being generally translated into English as 'comprehensive school'. It is not, however, quite the same as the British-style comprehensive school. The new Finnish version will be attended by all Finnish children for nine years, from the time when they begin school, and, as in the present elementary schools, all will be free for all. Local authorities will be responsible for them.

FINLAND: AN INTRODUCTION

A few of these comprehensive schools have already got under way; the original plan was to have the whole system changed by 1980, but now efforts are being made to speed up the process by at least five years. The situation has become more urgent because of the very rapid increase in entries to the fee-paying secondary schools; under the present system, something like 80 per cent of all children are expected to attend them by 1975.

The new comprehensive school differs from the traditional junior secondary or middle school in that emphasis is shifted from intellectual attainment to the development of the whole personality. At lower levels—the first six classes—all pupils study the same subjects, but in the last three classes there are optional subjects and courses of varying intensity to choose from. Also, pupils are allowed considerable mobility—they may even switch courses in mid-term.

In a country like Finland, a knowledge of foreign languages is vital. Indeed, one of the most striking aspects of the Finnish secondary school has been the amount of time it devotes to languages. Now, Finland will join Iceland as the only countries in Scandinavia—perhaps in the world—where two foreign languages are taught to the whole nation.

The idea of a foreign language for all is a very radical one. Learning languages has had certain class associations in Finland—one is reminded of those French-speaking Russians in Tolstoy and Turgenev. One of the characters in a play by the modern dramatist, school-teacher and psychologist Walentin Chorell says: 'Proletariat—don't you know what proletariat means? It means people who always use butter for cooking and can't speak English'.

Comprehensive school pupils will start one main language in the third class, and a second subsidiary language in the seventh. Most schools will offer Swedish and English; in a few, German, Russian or French will be taught. For those who have temporary difficulties, supplementary instruction in the mother tongue, mathematics and foreign languages will be given. So far, there have been complaints of lack of material for this remedial work.

The comprehensive school idea has come under very heavy fire. The bright pupils will suffer, say the critics. It is impossible to educate the whole population. And so on. The defence claims that all the children of the future must have a higher standard of knowledge for the country to achieve greater productivity. They must be taught how to spend their growing leisure time. They need to understand the workings of their increasingly complex society to preserve its democratic nature. And then, democracy itself—it is only fair that everyone should be given equal opportunities.

For the time being, *lukio*—the senior secondary school—will remain unchanged. About one-third of the secondary schools are state owned. The rest, known as private schools, are partly owned by local communities, partly privately owned. All of them receive a high proportion of their expenses from the state. The original private schools were often founded in the nineteenth century because state schools were Swedish-speaking. In fact, it was not until 1858 that the first Finnish-language secondary school was established—at Jyväskylä again. The proportion of Swedish-language secondary schools is still high compared with that of Swedish-speaking citizens.

Lukio, which is attended by about a quarter of each age group, culminates in the *ylioppilastutkinto*, a matriculation examination which is taken at around the age of nineteen, partly ensures university entrance, and entitles those who pass it to wear the student cap so favoured in Scandinavia.

The pressure of this examination is such that no time can be spared for individual study, and the *ylioppilastutkinto* is followed each year with the breathless interest of a national sporting event. Many of those who have once taken it go through every word of the exams, which the newspapers print in full. Immediately after the exam, the pupil's own teacher goes through the paper, and gives his mark, which he tells to the pupil.

The papers are then sent to a board, who have the final say, while the candidates wait, hoping the teacher was too pessimistic (or not too optimistic). Finnish pupils are very marks-conscious, remembering clearly many years later what they got in their matric. It is characteristic of the Finnish love of statistics and precise figures that end-of-term averages (all marks out of ten) are worked out by the teacher to two places of decimals.

Another result of the matriculation exam is that little time is given to oral practice in foreign languages or to discussion in general; nor does the authoritarian attitude of many teachers improve matters. The results can be seen in the awkward reserve of university students, their difficulties in discussion and in offering personal judgments, though how far this is due to other social factors it is hard to say. But the remark of a Finnish student to an American teacher who expressed his exasperation with his uncommunicative class is perhaps worth considering: 'If no one speaks it is also possible that someone is thinking.'

According to Paavo Koli, a former Rector of Tampere University, young Finns are further handicapped by poor ability to work together. There is too much stress on individual sports in their education, and the present system of selection is too competitive. Paradoxically, they have difficulties in individual thinking and performance. He deplores the lack of public discussion and informed opinion. 'The Finnish way of bringing up children has been so far, both at home and at school, a unique combination of authoritarianism and encouragement of initiative and independence.'

It is hoped that the new comprehensive schools will help to change all this. Also, there is talk of radically changing the matriculation exam or even of doing away with it completely. No clear plan has yet emerged.

The alternative to going to secondary school is to attend a vocational school. Vocational education was sharply expanded in 1947 because of the need to fulfil war reparations to the Soviet Union, and the consequent demand for increased skilled labour. General vocational schools have mainly been the responsibility of local authorities. They have specialized in metal work, machine repair, electricity, woodwork, building and construction, clothing and foods. By the end of 1969 there were over 40,000 students in such schools. Other types of vocational schools and colleges have taught public health and nursing, technology and commerce. A topical problem is the lack of suitable vocational training in the remoter, more sparsely populated districts.

It seems that the boom in vocational schooling will continue: forecasts estimate that by 1985 half the working population will have received such schooling—the corresponding figure in 1960 was less than one-sixth.

The urge for reform is carried over from the schools into the universities. Finland has been fortunate in having had very little student violence, but students and educational authorities have been pressing for change for some time.

What happens to the young Finn who has got his student cap and wants to continue his studies? If he has good enough marks in his matric and (for many university departments) in an entrance exam, he may enter a university. These are mostly state institutions, and studies are free, or very reasonable by British or American standards.

The earliest university in Finland was a Swedish-speaking Academy at Turku, founded in 1640 and transferred to Helsinki in 1828. Today, the largest by far is the bilingual Helsinki University, with well over 20,000 students. There are Finnish-language universities at Turku, Oulu, Tampere and Jyväskylä. There is a new one for eastern Finland shared between the towns of Joensuu, Kuopio and Lappeenranta. A new Swedish-language university was founded in Turku in 1919. All are expanding vigorously. They are mainly concerned with teaching, a fact bitterly resented by many Finnish academics, who believe that far more money and interest should be given to research. The standard at Finnish universities is high—in most fields it takes at least four years to get a degree; in many, much longer.

One reason why university studies tend to take a long time is that very many students work, not only during the long summer vacation (there are only two terms in the Finnish education system) but also during term time. The campus system is rare and on the whole unpopular with students. A notable exception is the Finnish Institute of Technology, breeding ground for Finnish architects and engineers.

The jump from school to university is a big one. From the carefully-guided mass drive for the student cap, the schoolboys and girls are expected to leap straight into the adult responsibility of 'academic freedom', with few obligatory lectures, and exams that can be taken 'when the student feels he is ready for them'. One result of this sudden permission to go to the devil their own way is that some, unable to acquire the necessary self-discipline, fall into outer darkness; you may find them one day teaching at some *kansakoulu* in Lapland.

A lot of people get a university-level education in Finland. The 'student class' includes four per cent of the population, and the annual intake is nearing 13,000. The increase in total numbers has been very steep (15,000 in 1950, 55,000 in 1970), and consequently the student/teacher ratio is often unsatisfactory. Plans call for 75,000 new student places by 1981, with the emphasis on medicine, science and technology. An American-style credit system is being introduced, with a wide choice of subjects offered, each worth so many units of academic credit or 'points'. Students must amass a certain number of points to get their degree. This system will offer a wider choice of studies, but will reduce academic freedom, as the points normally bear a relation to the number of hours of instruction attended.

Although students have not resorted to violence, they have stated their desires vociferously enough. In particular, they want to have a hand in the making of decisions that concern themselves. The content of these demands has changed interestingly in recent years. In 1968, students asked for a system where voting for decision-making posts and bodies would be proportional: one-third each for professors, students, and junior teachers and others. At the time the professors, most of whom have been accustomed to a Germanic, authoritarian academic world which still often insists on students standing up when the professor enters the room, rigidly opposed the proposal. Within a year or two, the professors were supporting such a quota scheme but the students, goaded to militancy, wanted nothing less than 'one man, one vote'. This is the obverse side of the famous Finnish *sisu*—a sort of passionate pigheadedness that sometimes makes one wonder how the Finnish world can possibly work. It is perhaps worth noting that *kompromissi* is a dirty word for most Finns.

Students have made demands in other fields, too. They want a student salary, places to live, and the right to start a family while they are studying. At present, they are chiefly financed by their parents or by their own earnings. There are an increasing number of special state-guaranteed loans at three per cent interest, but very few scholarships.

Health and medicine have been well looked after by the students themselves. Finnish students have wealthy, efficiently centralized unions, and these have established the Student Health Service Foundation. The unions also provide meals and dwellings for students, while the universities themselves have done very little in this sphere. But living quarters are in short supply. Renting a room is difficult and often costly. There are some student hostels, but not enough by far. Salaries are still a thing of the future.

A notable feature of Finnish student life is that a good half of all students are women. Of these a third drop out before taking their degree—mainly because they marry. The number of married students of both sexes is high. All the same, quite a lot of Finnish women who get married either before or after taking their degrees go on to a career in fields where English women would be rarities. Most dentists in Finland are women, there are many women architects and quite a few engineers. Nowadays many women go on working even when they have young children, partly no doubt for the extra income, but even more because 'a woman should do something more than wash dishes'. There still remain fields where women have yet to penetrate successfully; there are, for example, few Finnish female business executives. And although there are many women teachers, few academic doctors are women, and there are even fewer professors.

On the whole, the Finnish student is a serious person, who respects his studies and is in turn respected as an integral part of Finnish society. As early as 1898, Angel Ganivet remarked in his *Cartas Finlandesas* that 'a Finnish student is socially and economically someone'. As a nation, Finns show considerable respect for learning and for academically distinguished persons, witness their frequent use of academic titles such as *maisteri* (M.A.) and *insinööri* (M.Sc. Eng.) instead of Mr or Miss. It is not easy to find Finnish equivalents for 'egghead' or 'philistine'. Such conceptions are foreign to Finnish thinking.

The respect for learning is reflected also in the many forms of adult education, both vocational and non-vocational. The largest organizations today are the *kansalaisopistot* (civic institutes) and *työväenopistot* (workers' institutes), which together catered for a quarter of a million students in 1969-70. Then there are the *opintokerhot*—study circles consisting of five to twenty-five adults, often run by volunteer ideological organizations—said to include nearly a hundred thousand participants.

Many Finns continue to study something all their lives. One interesting form of study is provided by the Finnish-British Societies, of which there are over sixty dotted around the country. Each year many of these societies, with the help of the British Council, get a young Englishman or woman to come out as teacher-secretary of the society.

But to return to youth, for whom this formidable education programme has mainly been designed. We have glimpsed the young Finns, silent and (more or less) attentive before their all-powerful teachers, triumphant in their white caps, working and sometimes playing their way through the academic maze. What are they really like? How do they react to the education they are offered, what are they like out of school, what else are they offered by way of youth services, clubs and the like?

We might begin with little Maija and Kalle, bright two-year-old dumplings bundled up in countless layers of winter clothing, rolling in helpless glee in the snow along with twenty other little balls, all presided over by a 'park aunt' whose task it is to keep them herded and happy for a couple of hours while mother works or shops. Already they are shy, their shrieks and tears suddenly stilled by a stranger's footfall.

When Kalle and Maija are seven they are dumped without preparation into 'real' school, with proper lessons, discipline, even homework. They probably go off to school at 8 a.m.—starting early is very common in the Finnish educational system in general. The Finns, adults and children, are much less bothered about early mornings and late nights than English people, possibly because of seasonal variations in daylight hours.

As they grow up, little occurs to lessen their reserve towards strangers, adults, teachers, even each other. Although they get plenty of homework at school, Maija and Kalle have a leisure problem like anyone else. What steps have been taken to channel their energies?

At some of the secondary schools there are fairly active clubs of various kinds, including the *teini* clubs. Oddly enough, *teini* does not come from 'teenager'; it is an old expression, taken from the Swedish *djäkne*, for the poor scholars of Turku who used to troop around the countryside singing in order to collect money for their studies. These clubs have their own central newspaper, *Teinilehti*, whose voice is surprisingly adult, although more than half the paper is written by schoolboys and girls. It is criticized by adults and headmasters for its radical politics, its attacks on the established Church, and for outspoken proposals such as that unmarried pregnant girls should be allowed to continue their school studies. One of *Teinilehti's* constant cries is for more 'democracy' in schools.

Outside school and the universities, the most popular young people's clubs—especially for boys—are the innumerable sports clubs. Next come the political youth organizations and the *Kristillinen Nuorisoliitto* (Christian Youth Association). Both of these claim around a quarter of a million members. Then there are the *nuorisoseurat*—youth clubs, which are part of the idealistic *Suomen Nuorisoliitto*. These clubs have a long tradition. They flourish in the countryside, and are highly organized. Temperance is considered of great importance—all leaders and officials must be entirely teetotal. The *nuorisoseurat* may be considered a bit naive by Helsinki *teinit*, but they still draw in a hundred thousand members.

At the universities, club activity until recently was mainly in the hands of the student 'corporations', membership of which was based on the part of the country from which students came. But lately they have lost their importance, and political parties and activities have taken their place. In general, students have moved left. They have also become more international. Compared with their parents, who find it difficult to forget their fears of Russia, they feel secure. *Isänmaallisuus*—love of the fatherland—has been partly replaced by international idealism. President Kekkonen, with his line of peaceful coexistence with both East and West, has both supported and won the support of the students.

FINLAND: AN INTRODUCTION

Finnish youth has shown its international aspirations in its support for non-independent peoples, and its demands for more overseas development aid in the national budget. Pacifism has also been a central theme of the more radical student voices.

But, in spite of pacifist talk, there has not been much protest against the military service which all young Finnish men must perform, for a period varying between eight months and a year. Nor do parents deplore this duty, which is considered important in 'making a man' of their son. He probably benefits from getting away from his mother, who tends to spoil her boy, fussing over his feeding and seldom requesting, expecting or getting help from him in the house. Perhaps military service makes Finnish men easier husbands.

Those who have passed their matric usually become officers. In some cases, completion of military service counts as a credit towards being accepted to a university or college. There is no corresponding credit for women.

The young Finn often starts doing a job during the three months summer holidays while still at school. At the university, as we have seen, he quite often continues to work during term-time. He does not wash dishes or wait at table in the college restaurant or work at a down-town supermarket, like an American student: usually he takes some sort of an office job, though during the summer you may see, for instance, women students tending parks.

Women often go abroad during the summer to do housework, help at Butlin's camps and so on, mainly to improve their foreign languages. It is unfortunate that, whereas it is easy for both men and women to get good temporary employment in Germany, it is much less easy for young Finns to get a reasonable vacation job in England.

All through their lives, Finns spend part of their summer in their own countryside. Very few become so urbanized that they do not love their lakes and feel at home in their forests. If the young Finn is not taught to co-operate, he does know how to be self-sufficient, and is seldom lonely in the sense of just needing other people around him. This strength he partly draws from his relation with his sparsely-populated country.

THE YOUNG AND THEIR EDUCATION

The picture I have sketched reveals a nucleus of young people who are serious, often politically and socially active, even with violent opinions. They are accustomed to working at a job from an early age. They are reserved, awkward in debate, aware of the need for cooperation but not quite ready to put it into practice. Sometimes they drink hard to get over their 'complexes'. Not a very different picture from that of earlier generations. The respect for learning and the desire to learn, which penetrate deep down into Finnish society, appearing in the old, vanishing culture of the Swedish families and in the strivings of the sons and daughters of small farmers and factory workers, still strongly persist. These young Finns will want more learning and social education for their children, and it looks as though they will get what they want.

ON LEARNING FINNISH

M. A. BRANCH

Since the turn of the century writers have been telling us of the immense problems of learning the Finnish language. Travel books have done much to propagate this idea and some reference to the 'difficulty' of Finnish seems to be a necessary feature of such works. It has been variously compared to Chinese, Russian, Basque, and Gaelic. It has been said to be short in adjectives and adverbs because the Finns are 'a nation little given to gush'. It has been attributed with a case system ranging from fourteen to eighteen cases—hardly the kind of statement to encourage someone smarting from memories of Latin or Greek. One writer, having pontificated on the 'difficulties' of Finnish, tried to illustrate his point by quoting a specimen of the language: the passage quoted turns out to be five lines of Swedish warning the occupant of a hotel room not to smoke in bed.

Certainly Finnish is not an easy language, but I would hesitate to claim that its inherent difficulties are such as to set it apart from other European languages. After all, the Finnish child takes no longer over learning to speak than the child of any other nation. In its linguistic perspective Finnish is one of the six Baltic-Finnic languages, which themselves belong to a larger grouping known as Finno-Ugrian. The languages of this group are spoken by more than 21 million people of which the largest unit comprises the Hungarians (approximately 13 million including those outside Hungary). Finnish is spoken by about 5 millions if we include the Finnish-speaking population of North America. The other Finno-Ugrian languages, apart from most of the Lapp languages, are spoken in the USSR. There are twelve main linguistic groups scattered over northern Russia and their numbers range from about 100 Votes in Ingria to more than a million and a quarter Mordvins in central European Russia and almost a million Estonians.

In terms of linguistic development Finnish and Hungarian, which represent opposite extremes of the Finno-Ugrian group, are separated by some five thousand years. They share very little common vocabulary and are in no way mutually comprehensible. Nevertheless, they have retained some cohesion of structure, though it requires a linguistic training of several years before this will be apparent.

Let me agree that it is very difficult, if not impossible, to acquire a 'skimming knowledge' of Finnish sufficient to gather the gist of a passage or to make oneself understood, a method of language learning that many people claim to have followed with French or German. The genetic relationship that English shares with other Indo-European languages, such as French or German, certainly makes a superficial familiarity of this kind possible. This is not so with Finnish with its entirely different structural and lexical origin. Even words borrowed by Finnish from Indo-European sources often change beyond recognition, e.g. raamattu *'Bible' which shares a common origin with English* grammar*; or* olut

FINLAND: AN INTRODUCTION

'beer' which derives from the same word as English ale. Recent borrowings are more easily recognized, e.g. pankki 'bank', baari 'bar', or pamfletti on pop 'the pamphlet is all the rage' (a headline noted from a publisher's catalogue), though the 'skimmer' would find even this superficial similarity little help in a declined form, e.g. pamfleteissa on paljon popia!

Unfortunately, many people assume that if a 'skimming knowledge' is hard to acquire, the later stage must be all the harder. This is to misunderstand the process of language learning. The 'skimmer's' approach is founded on what is superficially similar between languages and overlooks two important facts: words of common origin preserving some surface similarity have often undergone far-reaching semantic change and the extent of even surface similarity is in any case very limited. Any language is difficult if one wants to learn to speak and write according to the standards of educated speakers of that language. The only positive value of surface similarity is the psychological reassurance it gives.

Although the practical difficulties of learning Finnish—lack of textbooks and qualified teachers—have diminished, the reputation lives on. On becoming interested in Finland most people read one or two popular books about the country. If they go on to study Finnish, they are already psychologically prepared for trouble. When they find the language difficult—as they do—they see this as confirming the reputation and often give up there and then. This process involves a degree of double-think, since Finnish can only be especially 'difficult' if compared with a norm that is 'easy'. And what is that norm? Generally, French, German or any other language studied at school. Yet, after only a few lessons of Finnish many people are ready to dismiss it as extraordinarily 'difficult' forgetting that it took five to six years of compulsory school lessons several hours a week to reach (or not to reach) some standard of proficiency in the 'easy' norm!

On starting Finnish, on the other hand, the learner is surprised to find that the pronunciation has none of the pitfalls of English or French; nor does it demand the phonetic gymnastics of Russian.

The orthography is by and large phonetic and, as the main stress of a Finnish word is always on its first syllable, one is spared the tortuous vacillations of English stress as in refúse (*noun*) and refúse (*verb*). Contrary to English, however, one must follow the written form of a word very closely; to pronounce a short sound long or a long sound short (a short sound is one letter, a long sound the letter written twice) will alter the meaning of a word, often with unfortunate results as in tapamme 'we kill' and tapaamme 'we meet'. The ratio of consonants to vowels in Finnish is very balanced so that awkward consonant clusters such as occur in German and the Slavonic languages are avoided. Finnish is the only European language with a higher proportion of vowels to consonants, a characteristic to which many people ascribe the musical quality of the language.

It usually comes as something of a surprise to find that Finnish has no articles, no grammatical gender and not even a future tense to contend with. Moreover, the reassuring factor of predictability applies equally to the rules of grammer which, by and large, do not need exceptions to prove them.

The most striking feature about Finnish is the extensive use made of suffixes. Even the so called 'case system' (*fifteen* 'cases' currently in active use) I prefer to see as a collection of suffixes rather than as 'cases', which tend to evoke misleading association with the numerous declensions of Latin and Greek. The Finnish 'case'-suffixes express a range of ideas: the function of nominative, accusative and genitive, and the adverbial concepts of 'in', 'on', 'into', 'on to', 'out of', 'off of', 'without', 'together with', 'by means of', 'amount of', and 'change of form'. There is only one declension and the only structural difference between singular and plural in the 'case system' is the insertion of the plural suffix (*with appropriate sound changes*); unlike Latin, the 'case'-suffix itself does not change. Other adverbial concepts such as 'behind', 'beside' are expressed by postpositions (i.e. prepositions that follow the word qualified) and even occasionally by prepositions.

A generalized way of looking at Finnish is as a collection of abstracted 'concept roots' and suffixes. By adding certain suffixes these roots acquire nominal or verbal qualities to which further suffixes are added to express a whole range of ideas and to link the word thus formed to other words in the sentence.

The following examples will illustrate how, at its simplest level, this process works. Taking the 'concept root' laul-, an abstracted form expressing 'singing', we can make it into a noun by adding -u: laulu 'song'. To say 'in my song', we add the appropriate suffixes -ssa 'in' and -ni 'my': laulussani. The whole concept can be made plural by adding the plural suffix -i-: lauluissani. To make the same 'concept root' into a verb there are several approaches. One is to add -aa: laulaa 'to sing' and another -eskella: lauleskella 'to sing often'. The present tense and person are again formed by adding appropriate suffixes: -a- and -t: laulat 'you sing', or -e- and -t: lauleskelet 'you often sing'. And so on.

Far more space than is available here would be needed to describe Finnish adequately and I must emphasize that I have limited myself to stating the most general principles. There is a great deal to learn before one can effectively work these principles and in attacking the idea that Finnish is extraordinarily difficult, I do not want to give the impression that it is easy; the correct use of the partitive 'case' alone is a mystery even to many Finns (it is comforting, therefore, to know that the definitive work on the subject was written by an Englishman). The student will find Finnish as difficult as any other language.

Finnish presents the beginner with a vast number of rules for sound change and grammar which must be mastered. But it rewards the learner by having very few exceptions to these rules. I share Professor Björn Collinder's view that the more grammar a language has, the more it can be systematized; and the more it can be systematized, the easier it is to learn well. As Professor Collinder points out: 'In this sense Finnish must be much easier to a Chinese or Indonesian than is English or French.' Support for this argument comes from an American scholar who many years ago drew attention to the fact that English is one of the languages that least lends itself to systematization and that consequently: 'Foreigners learning English have to absorb it unconsciously—a process requiring years—by dint of constant exposure to bombardment by spoken English in large chunks.' Yet foreigners do learn English. Hence if these theories are correct, it follows that given adequate facilities the English can learn Finnish.

My teaching experience of the last few years has proved the case to my own satisfaction. I only hope that as more people acquire a command of the language, the traditional, forbidding reputation of Finnish will be forgotten. After all, how better can a Finnophile demonstrate his enthusiasm and affection for Finland and the Finns than by making the effort to learn their language. The linguistic burden of Anglo-Finnish communication has been left to the Finns for long enough.

WHERE TO STUDY FINNISH

UNITED KINGDOM

Degree courses

1. Starting in October 1973, the University of London School of Slavonic and East European Studies plans to introduce courses leading to B.A. degrees in Finnish Language and Literature and in Finnish studies. (Further information from: *M.A. Branch, School of Slavonic and East European Studies, University of London, London WC1E 7HU.*)
2. Finnic linguistics can be studied as part of the B.A. in Hungarian Language and Literature at the University of London School of Slavonic and East European Studies. (Further information from: *The Secretary Registrar, School of Slavonic and East European Studies, University of London, London WC1E 7HU.*)
3. Finnish language and literature can be studied as part of the B.A.

in Scandinavian Studies at University College, London. (Further information from: *Director of Studies, Department of Scandinavian Studies, University College London, Gower Street, London WC1.*)
4. Language courses and a seminar in Finnish literature in translation can be taken as credits towards B.A. degrees in Aspects of European Studies at the University of East Anglia. (Further information from: *Admissions Clerk, School of European Studies, University of East Anglia, University Plain, Norwich NOR 88C.*)
5. Research into subjects related to Finland can be offered for the degrees of M.A., M.Phil. and Ph.D. at a number of universities. (For further information write in the first instance to: *School of Slavonic and East European Studies, University of London, London WC1E 7HU.*)

Evening classes

School of Slavonic and East European Studies, University of London, London, WC1E 7HU. Intermediate course and Finnish Literature Seminar. (Further information from: *The Secretary/Registrar.*)

Central London Polytechnic, Red Lion Square, London, WC1R 4SR. Beginners course, Elementary course. (Further information from: *The Registrar.*)

Goldsmiths' College, Lewisham Way, London S.E.14. Beginners course with occasional background lectures. (Further information from: *Director, Department of Adult Studies.*)

Chelsea-Westminster Institute, St Matthew's School, Old Pye Street, London S.W.1. Beginners course in Finnish conversation. (Further information from: *Principal, Chelsea-Westminster Institute, Marlborough Street, Sloane Avenue, London S.W.3.*)

Clarendon College of Further Education, Pelham Avenue, Nottingham. Beginners course. (Further information from: *Principal.*)

University of Reading Scandinavian Circle, University of Reading, Whiteknights, Reading RG6 2AA. Beginners course. (Further information from: *Secretary, University of Reading Scandinavian Circle.*)

Facilities for learning Finnish change from year to year and an up-to-date information bulletin is available free on request from *Dr M. A. Branch, School of Slavonic and East European Studies, University of London, London WC1E 7HU.*

ON LEARNING FINNISH

UNITED STATES

New York

Columbia University, New York, N.Y. 10027. Graduate courses (M.A. and Ph.D. candidates) and Undergraduate courses (credited towards B.A. degrees). Also Elementary, Intermediate and Advanced language courses. (Further information from: *Professor Robert Austerlitz, 404 Philosophy Hall, Columbia University.*)

Indiana

Indiana University, Bloomington, Indiana 47401. Introductory and Advanced language courses, Ref. U331, U431. (Further information from: *Department of Uralic and Altaic Studies, Goodbody Hall.*)

Michigan

Finnish Center Association of Detroit, Michigan. Beginners and Intermediate evening classes. (Further information from: *Mrs Viola Pudas, M.A., 18611 Rutherford Avenue, Detroit, Michigan 48235.*)

Suomi College, Hancock, Michigan 49940. Beginners evening course. (Further information from: *M. Järvenranta, M.P.Sc., Suomi College.*)

Portage Lake Community School, Houghton, Michigan 49931. Two Beginners and two Intermediate evening courses. (Further information from: *M.Järvenranta, M.P.Sc., Suomi College, Hancock, Michigan 49940.*)

Northern Michigan University, Marquette, Michigan. Two Elementary and two Intermediate language courses, Ref. FN100, FN101, FN200, FN201. (Further information from: *J. Watanen, Northern Michigan University.*)

Texas

University of Texas at Austin, College of Arts and Sciences, Austin, Texas 78712. Structure of Finnish: phonology and syntax for students of general linguistics. (Further information from: *Department of Linguistics.*)

FINLAND

The Finnish Ministry of Education publishes an annual bulletin *Finland, Language and Culture* which includes details of Finnish summer courses for foreigners. Copies of the bulletin can be obtained from: *Opetusministeriö, Rauhankatu 4, Helsinki 17.*

FINLAND: AN INTRODUCTION

From time to time Finnish courses for foreigners are held at the universities of Helsinki, Turku, Jyäskylä and Oulu. Further information can be had by writing to the Finnish departments of these universities (the name of the department, university and appropriate town are sufficient address).

THE CHURCH IN FINLAND

JORMA LOUHIVUORI

A NEWSPAPER cartoonist a few years back depicted an essential feature of the church's image in public discussion today. Gazing at his ancient country church, a clergyman remarks, 'Well, at least its a convenient scapegoat for everybody else's sins of omission.' The drawing appeared at a time when the clergy were a focus for widespread and trenchant criticism. As in other western states, the body of divines had become part of the national establishment—an institution holding a key position in both the material and spiritual life of the community. Public stricture is proof, in the best sense, that this situation persists and is considered crucial.

Since 95 per cent of the population are Christians, the reasons are clear. Ecclesiastically the nation is very homogeneous, 92.7 per cent being members of the principal National Church, the Evangelical-Lutheran Church of Finland. Despite all the reproaches levelled at her, there are few apostates. Foreign observers are surprised to learn that at the General Election the great majority of the 420,000 Communist voters were church members, many of them professing Christians. They pay Church taxes, get married in church, have their children baptized and send them to Sunday school. The proportion of civil marriage ceremonies has, in fact, declined and in 1968 was only 8 per cent. Those over 20 years old who have abandoned religion are a bare 180,000.

Although the established church bears the name of the great German reformer, Martin Luther, Christianity in Finland has venerable roots springing from a wider European heritage. For instance, despite the country's relative remoteness, three English churchmen played an important role in the foundation of the

Christian church in the twelfth and thirteenth centuries. The best known is Bishop Henry, who has been described as the Apostle of Finland and who subsequently became the patron saint of the Finnish Church. He arrived in Finland in about 1155 with a crusading party led by the Swedish King Erik, and stayed behind with his followers to tend the new Church when the other crusaders returned to Sweden. The story of Bishop Henry's tragic death on the ice of Lake Köyliö, which ended his short life's work in Finland, has become a classic topic for after-dinner speeches on Anglo-Finnish occasions.

The Finns had come under the influence of Christianity, both from East and West, before the crusade, and it must therefore be regarded as a move in the game of power politics being played by the Eastern and Western Churches. One of the most eminent leaders in this religious cold war was another Englishman, the cardinal legate Nicholas, formerly Nicholas Breakspear, who in 1154 became Pope Adrian IV, the only Englishman ever to hold this high office. Cardinal Nicholas was sent to Scandinavia by the Pope to counter the growing influence of the Eastern Church, which had brought Christianity to Russia and was showing interest in Northern Europe. After setting up an archbishopric in Norway in 1152—an honour Norway shared with Ireland—Cardinal Nicholas proceeded to Sweden to negotiate the establishment of a Church province for the Swedes. One may assume that the Swedes were pressed into missionary work in Finland, still ecclesiastically unorganized and engaged in considerable trading with north Russian towns. Tradition has it that Bishop Henry was one of the Cardinal's retinue on this occasion, a couple of years before his own journey to Finland. Thus the Finns were put on the map by the West and shown a glimpse of their future role in a land bordering on East and West.

Early in the thirteenth century a third Englishman, Thomas, was appointed the first Bishop of Finland, in about 1220. His continental outlook and upbringing were of great advantage to him in carrying out missionary work in his new home country, but Swedish efforts to extend the Western Church's domain eastwards evoked the opposition of Russian princes and the Eastern Church. The Swedish forces were defeated on the ice of the River Neva by Alexander Nevsky. Five years later Bishop Thomas retired to a monastery in Sweden, where he died in 1248. He had given the Church new life in its battle against heathenism and had raised it from a position of insecurity to one of power and respect.

When Finland's eastern frontier was first officially drawn, about a hundred years later, it marked the division between the spheres of influence of the Churches of Rome and Byzantium. Subsequent shifts in the frontier have disturbed the ecclesiastical unity of east Finland. Consequently there are now two National Churches: the Evangelical-Lutheran Church of Finland, to which the main part of the population belongs, and the Orthodox Church of Finland, accounting for 1.5 per cent.

Martin Luther's ideas reached the kingdom of Sweden-Finland at the same time as they spread to England. His rugged individualism seemed most suited to the way of life developing in the midst of the Finnish forests. The reformer of the Finnish Church was Mikael Agricola, who went to Wittenberg to study under Luther three years after Thomas Cranmer had left Germany to become Archbishop of Canterbury.

A basic tenet of the Reformation was the translation of the Bible into the vernacular. Ten years after Tyndale completed his English translation, Agricola began translating the New Testament into Finnish. All the most important books required by the Church, beginning with an alphabet book, came from the pen of Agricola. In addition to the New Testament he translated almost a quarter of the Old Testament. Nearly 100 years passed, however, before the whole Bible appeared in Finnish, in 1642.

Although Finns gained a reputation as fighters in Gustav Adolphus's day, the Reformation proceeded without violence. Reform was slow, and it took over a century for the nation to adopt the principles of the Reformation in its religious life. Evidence of this peaceful transition is seen in the pre-Reformation traditions still alive in Finland. Various 'names-day' customs are found in different parts of the country. The present Finnish calendar is based on the saints' calendar of the Middle Ages, each day being allotted to a different name. Another custom which has survived from before the Reformation is seen when a housewife draws the sign of the cross in the dough she has prepared for baking. The St Thomas's cross, which is now a popular Christmas decoration, is still seen drawn on doorposts on St Thomas's day.

Ancient objects and decorations have been preserved in many medieval churches, chasubles are still worn by the clergy at services, and the bishop's staff, cross, cope and mitre have been retained. However, the inner life of the Church, which reflects the spiritual life of the people, shows that the Lutheran Reformation has taken deep root in the soul of the nation.

In England one is often asked, 'What Church do you belong to?' In Finland, where only very few people belong to some other denomination, the question is irrelevant and rarely heard. There is a Roman Catholic Church with about 2,000 members and a seat in Helsinki, created in 1957. The Anglican Church in Helsinki has a long history in developing contacts between England and Finland.

Finland has been called the world's most Lutheran country. This may be nominally true, but membership of the Church is often conventional. Registration of births was in the past always done by the Church, after the christening ceremony, and this has remained customary even after legislation to ensure complete religious freedom. Inhabitants of remote rural areas often have difficulty in bringing their children to a church or parsonage for christening in winter. They wait for the spring, or for a clergyman to visit the district. Baptism and registration of birth may therefore have to wait several months. Keeping the register gives the clergy work to do which is not essential to the running of the Church, but it has the advantage of bringing them into daily contact with a great many people. There is a civil register for those who do not wish to be on the Church register and it now records about 5·5 per cent of the population.

From time immemorial a freeman in Finland had the right to take part in formulating decisions on communal matters. All parishioners who are over twenty-one and have been confirmed may join in the election of the clergy, the precentor and the organist in their own parish. Before the election the chapter selects the three most suitable candidates for the job from among the applicants. The local press publishes opinions for and against, and lively discussion ensues after the candidates have conducted their obligatory services. The parishioners may avail themselves of their right to nominate a fourth candidate if he has the support of 20 per cent of their number. A candidate nominated in this way must obtain more than half the votes polled in order to be elected. Otherwise the candidate polling most votes is elected. There are no sinecures in the Church, and the parish always chooses its own servants.

Many other offices are filled by direct suffrage. Since 1970, there have been elections for parish councillors and vestrymen just as for State and Local Government. Selection committees composed of parishioners enter their own lists of candidates. Political and other emblems may not, however, be used at these elections. The replacement of the former general parish council by this new system aroused great public interest. Various social groups, in particular the political parties, started to display a heightened interest in ecclesiastical affairs and in securing representation on the parish administrative bodies.

The country is divided into eight dioceses, seven Finnish and one Swedish. The parishes where the majority language is Swedish, all in west or south Finland, belong to the Swedish diocese. The diocese is administered by a bishop and chapter. In spite of the Reformation, Finnish bishops enjoy *Successio apostolica* although this does not carry theological significance in our Church. Bishops still make official visitations to their parishes, where they inspect local institutions. To treat someone 'like the bishop at the vicarage' is still a common saying when great hospitality is shown to visitors. A feature the Anglican and Finnish Churches have in common is the nomination of bishops by the Head of State. In England, however, the Prime Minister does not disclose whom he will propose to the Monarch for appointment, whereas in Finland the clergy of a bishopric join lay representatives chosen by the parishes to elect three candidates, and from these the President usually appoints the one who obtained most votes.

The highest administrative organ in the Church is the Church Assembly. Three-fifths of the members of this 'single-chamber parliament' are laymen and two-fifths clergymen. Although the

FINLAND: AN INTRODUCTION

assembly is the final authority on all matters solely affecting the Church, changes in Church law have to be submitted to Parliament for approval. Parliament cannot itself initiate changes and can only approve or reject proposals. There is remarkable agreement between Church and state on the administration of Church law, although during recent years the ties between them have been much criticized. Attempts have been made to prove that the state restrains the Church and prevents it from being true to its real nature. It is interesting to note that Parliament has shown greater conservatism in the handling of ecclesiastical matters than the clergy, generally blamed for their conservatism. So long as the greater part of the population belongs to the Church, the state for its part acknowledges and values the Church's function in the community. Religious instruction is given in all schools, military chaplains serve in the army under the leadership of a field bishop, the state supports hospital and prison chaplains, is responsible for diocesan expenditure and maintains theological faculties in the universities. Parliament opens and closes its sessions with a service, and the government, regardless of political colour, allots four days a year for thanksgiving, penitence and prayer.

During recent years these lay and clerical sectors have been the object of much sharp criticism by young radical groups who, in the name of democracy and free-thinking, have aimed at dislodging religious activity from schools, armed forces, hospitals and prisons alike. Typical of the trend in public opinion towards secularization has been the suppression of religious instruction in the current comprehensive reorganization of education.

Early Finnish churches were modest and sturdy, generally built of granite with low walls and steeply raked roofs. Many of them have naive murals, among the best of which are those at Hattula and Lohja. The simple lines of Turku Cathedral, built in the thirteenth century, set it apart from the great Gothic cathedrals of Western Europe. Wooden churches became common in Finland in later centuries, but few have survived the ravages of fire and war. Modern church architecture has produced buildings which provide a focus for the life of the parish on weekdays as well as Sundays. New churches have clubrooms, classrooms, rooms for hobbies and gymnasia.

In a land of thousands of lakes, waterways were the natural transport links before roads existed and churches were built to be accessible by water from various parts of the parish. In the lake districts people went to church in long boats, some of which had up to sixty oars and held over a hundred people. Upkeep of the boats was usually financed by a farmers' syndicate. On trips lasting several hours there was a good deal of singing, and a rich hoard of religious and secular songs was handed down from one generation to the next. Since the advent of the motor, church boats have been relegated to museums, but sometimes during summer festivals they are again brought into use.

Although Finns are still 'church people' according to some statistics, only 4 per cent of them attend church on Sundays. Why is this? Distance is a decisive factor. A man from north Lapland once told me that the journey from his village to the nearest church was 120 miles. When I expressed dismay at this he consoled me saying: 'There is at least this to be said for it—with a journey like that before you, you don't go and get married without thinking about it very carefully.' Finland's largest parish is Inari in Lapland. It covers about 10,000 square miles and has about 7,000 inhabitants. Velkua in the Turku archipelago has 263 inhabitants in a parish containing 265 islands. Journeys to church in the country are often difficult and in some places become impossible in winter.

These conditions have meant that parish work is not concentrated in a comparatively small area around the church as in more populous countries, but extends far across lakes and into forests, to wherever people live. Services may be held in homes, schools or other suitable places. Christenings and marriages may be celebrated in the main room of a farm. The parish meeting may even be held on the rocky bank of an island or in the natural temple of a birch grove. Parishioners can also hold prayer meetings in their homes without a priest. In these 'house meetings' Bible readings and hymns are interspersed with short spontaneous talks given by any who wish. Although such meetings do not

FINLAND: AN INTRODUCTION

figure in statistics of church attendance, they are an essential part of the spiritual life of the nation.

Neither the Dissenters' Law of 1889 nor the law of 1923 ensuring complete religious freedom caused any real break-away from the Church. One reason was that the powerful revivalist movements of the eighteenth and nineteenth centuries remained within the Church. The first leaders of these movements were chiefly laymen and the clergy often opposed them. The state, too, tried to suppress them and public meetings were forbidden, but despite sentences passed on them, members of the movements declared: 'As long as the Creed and the Lord's Prayer are said in the church, we recognize it as our own.' In their independent struggles the revivalist leaders rediscovered for the Church some of Luther's basic principles. The most important of the revivalists are the Pietists, the Evangelicals and the Laestadians, all represented throughout the country, although their hold is stronger in the countryside than in towns and industrial areas.

These spiritual movements have reinforced a sense of social responsibility already present in the Finnish *'talkoo'* spirit. This is seen in the custom of helping any family or individual in difficulties by the concerted efforts of the whole village or parish. If a farmer has fallen ill, others in the village will help his family reap the harvest; if a widow or invalid has lost a home through some catastrophe, the men of the village will build the victim a new house. Many a chapel and village hall has been built in this way. Outside the main door of some old churches one may see the figure of a beggar carved in wood, standing anything from five to eight feet high, with outstretched hand or hat in which there is a slit for money. Before the days of the welfare state this was one means of collecting for the poor. The state now makes provision for invalids, old people, widows and others in need, but the Church still supplements this work. Every parish and village has its Deacon's committee, ready to render assistance to the needy. There are about 7,000 such committees in the country.

'The priest's sack is bottomless' runs an old adage, referring probably to the extent of the dues which all householders once had to pay to the Church. Nowadays the Church is entitled to collect taxes from all tax-paying members of the parish and from business undertakings. The Church tax is about 1 per cent of taxable income and goes to either the Lutheran or Orthodox Church, according to the taxpayer's religion. A positive aspect of ecclesiastical taxation is the assurance of a regular income, relieving the clergy of any need to curry favour among their parishioners. Church ordinances lay down the uses to which the taxes shall be put and guard against abuse. Parishes nowadays own very little land or other fixed assets. A negative aspect of taxation is that it does not encourage charity. However, much of the Church's social and missionary work at home and abroad is supported almost entirely by voluntary gifts.

With few exceptions, cemeteries are owned and cared for by the parishes. Respect for the dead is one of the oldest of Finnish traditions and is manifest in the reverence with which graves and cemeteries are tended. A central position in the churchyard is usually reserved for those fallen in battle. In the country parishes it is customary to set aside a special day in spring for dressing the graves and in summer many parishes have a churchyard festival. On Hallowe'en the graves are again decorated with flowers and candles. Christmas Eve especially is an unforgettable sight. Candles flicker on the snow-covered graves, lighting up the Christmas flowers and lending sparkle to the snow. Dark spruce and slender birch complete the picture. Into this enchanted landscape come relatives and friends of the dead, paying their Christmas visit to the graveside.

The Finnish words for *Bible*, *cross* and *priest* are Slavonic in origin and were probably introduced by the Orthodox Church. Orthodoxy was dominant in East Karelia from an early date, while the rest of Finland was subject to civilizing influences from the West. The Finnish Orthodox Church now has 70,000 members, with an archiepiscopal see and a seminary in Kuopio. Monasteries have always played an important part in Orthodoxy. One of the most famous of them, Valamo, was in the territory ceded to Russia after the last war. The monks were resettled in Heinävesi, where they now have their Uusi (New) Valamo, not far from Konevitsa monastery and Lintula convent, both similarly evacuated from Karelia.

There have been times when the Finns have wanted to repudiate their divided national life, wishing to see themselves solely as heirs of the West. This attitude is now changing. Both national Churches, the Lutheran and the Orthodox, are active participants in world-wide ecumenical work. Thanks to this, Orthodox Karelians have found acceptance in Lutheran areas, and their spontaneity and gaiety have brought a leaven to the proverbial solemnity of the Finns.

Industrialization and urbanization have altered people's attitude to the Church. In an attempt to meet the criticisms levelled at it by young people of today, the Church has developed many new forms of activity. Youth work has been extended and the Church's own training centres prepare youth leaders for the parishes. The office of Church lector has been created, a post open to women theologians qualified for pastoral and social work with women and young people. In the larger cities family guidance centres have been set up, where specially trained clergymen and doctors advise on marital and educational problems. In the industrial field seminars are arranged under the leadership of industrial pastors to discuss industrial problems. A Church Information Centre works closely with the press and is largely responsible for religious programmes on radio and television. An impartial investigation has shown that ever-larger numbers listen to these programmes. Several parishes now run courses and arrange holidays for people of all ages and professions. The recently founded Church Research Institute is studying the fields in which the work of the Church could be improved and expanded.

Finland's long connection with Sweden led to the forging of permanent links with the Lutheran Church in Scandinavia. The Finnish Lutheran Church maintains close contact with the Lutheran Church in Germany and America, and is actively engaged in the work of the World Council of Churches and the Lutheran World Federation, of which Professor Mikko Juva, Rector of Helsinki University, is a president. England has proved a fertile source of ideas for many forms of evangelical and social work. The Finnish Bible Society was founded by John Paterson in 1812, and writers such as Bunyan, Baxter and Wilcox have been widely read in Finland. Since 1936 members of the Anglican or the Finnish Church may be admitted to communion in each other's churches. A similar agreement was reached with the Church of Scotland in 1955. Anglican bishops have taken part in the consecration of bishops in Finnish churches and Finnish bishops have been invited to the Lambeth Conference. All this has greatly strengthened the bonds between our Churches.

TWO CHURCHES

NILS ERIK WICKBERG

If you look for the characteristics of old Finnish architecture you are struck, above all, by its great simplicity. Situated far away from the main stream of European culture, Finland was incorporated completely into Western Christendom only in the year 1300. With her sparse population, and few towns, most of which would have been regarded in wealthier countries as not much more than insignificant villages, she would seem to have offered poor soil for art to grow in. Against this background the seventy or so medieval churches are an astonishing achievement. In a country with no previous buildings in stone they must have been regarded as miracles.

However, the simplicity made necessary by poverty was not an entirely negative factor. The builders of the medieval stone churches and of the seventeenth and eighteenth century timbered churches knew well how to make a virtue of necessity. In the flat Finnish countryside where the view is restricted by backdrops of forest, the simple rectangle and the great steep saddle roof of the medieval church were completely dominant.

Near Helsinki is the old church at Sipoo (Plate 20). Like the more famous one at Hattula, near Hämeenlinna, and the fine timbered eighteenth-century churches at Keuruu and Petäjävesi in central Finland, it is now used only occasionally in the summer. It is not one of the largest among medieval Finnish churches, but its calm, fine proportions, its detached bell-tower which is also the entrance to the churchyard, and its surrounding leafy trees form a grouping of unusual harmony. Above the stout protective walls built of irregular blocks of granite, can be seen the fine brick ornamentation of the western gable. The interior is a unique combination of two and three-aisled design: shafts of light fall through narrow openings set in the two west pillars and through these the three-aisled choir is vaguely visible, its centre aisle richly decorated in a star design. The painted décor is not quite as magnificent as in the Hattula church where all surfaces except the floor are covered with large-scale figures. At Sipoo the arches have been decorated with simple, slightly clumsy arabesques contrasting strangely with the firm heavy walls. The absence of an organ-loft and of pews, and the primitive cobbled stone floor emphasize the atmosphere of abandonment.

There is a marked contrast between such Finnish granite churches from the fourteenth century, with unbroken wall surfaces and a few rather small windows, and contemporary West European churches where the walls have been dissolved into vast areas of glass. The withdrawal from the world around is an ancient reaction which, however, accords with the often bleak Finnish climate. Illuminated by candles, such a church interior must have appeared like a Garden of Eden against the backcloth of the snow and wintry darkness.

The Finnish character's closeness to nature is a fact often and generally recognized. But to Finns their relationship with nature has not only been a matter of mystic feeling, a magic communion;

nature has also been a troublesome adversary who must needs be conquered in a stubborn struggle, and made to serve. In our modern welfare state this need is not as great as it was even fifty years ago. But the feeling of oneness with nature remains.

A beautiful example of an effort to make a church form part of the forested countryside is the Institute of Technology Chapel at Otaniemi to the west of Helsinki (Plate 21). It was built in 1956 and 1957 and is based on designs by two architects, Kaija and Heikki Siren. In spite of the entirely modern shapes and forms, there is something of ancient Finnish church building tradition in the simple cube of the chapel and its unity with the countryside around. In the forest, brick walls and pole fencing surround the forecourt where the self-contained bell scaffolding stands. Entrance into the tall, spacious church is by a low hall. The side walls and floor are red brick, the roof-truss construction is of an open design.

One feature which is not present in any of the old churches but which is characteristic of the feeling for nature in our day is the altar wall; it consists of a single large window, behind which the forest and an open air cross together form a picture varying with the season and the light. Such a theme would not be possible in a town, but here where the ground falls steeply away from the window wall and human beings seldom pass by, it is acceptable and right. In this case, it was no longer a problem of finding protection against an inhospitable climate and hostile demoniac forces in nature but, on the contrary, of bringing the countryside into the church to use it as a peace-giving element helping the visitor's mind to meditation. The theme may have reached Europe from classical Japanese architecture, but perhaps it is not pure coincidence that it was in Finland it was used in a Christian church.

ARCHITECTURE

J. M. RICHARDS

THOSE who are interested in architecture make pilgrimages, if they can, to Finland, just as people who are interested in wild animals make for the game-parks of East Africa and those interested in wine make for Burgundy or Bordeaux. Finland has been famous for its architecture for so many years that it no longer causes surprise that a relatively poor and thinly populated country on the northern fringe of the habitable world should excel in an art usually associated with great centres of urban culture and with countries rich in historical precedent.

Finland is so remarkable an exception that it is interesting to try to analyse the circumstances that have made it so. Initially, the high reputation of modern Finnish architecture was established in Europe through the work of Alvar Aalto, whose strikingly original and technically inventive buildings became known abroad around 1930; and it was established in America largely through Eliel Saarinen, who migrated there from Helsinki in 1923, after winning the second prize in the competition for the Chicago Tribune Tower the previous year. Saarinen's buildings afterwards became somewhat pallid and academic, but as a teacher at Cranbrook Academy, Michigan, he was a powerful liberalizing influence in a country still at that time—in spite of the presence of one of the world's most far-seeing architectural prophets, Frank Lloyd Wright—closely tied to eclecticism and historicism.

So Eliel Saarinen (born 1873) and Alvar Aalto (born 1898) are the two world-famous names in Finnish architecture, the former self-exiled until his death in 1950; the latter, in spite of having designed buildings in many parts of the world, always deeply involved in the life and landscape of his own country. Indeed, except for a period in America after the war when he taught at, and designed one building for, Massachusetts Institute of Technology, he has never left it for any length of time.

So great, however, has Aalto's celebrity become that it is necessary to emphasize that his achievements have not been the only ones to impress the world in the past half-century. Architectural pilgrims to Finland seek out Aalto's buildings and find much to admire in them, but what they find even more remarkable is the high quality of so much of the rest of Finnish architecture: its technical proficiency, inventive use of materials and sensitive relationship to landscape, and the regard in which the art of architecture is held. All are attributes that countries with longer traditions and greater resources find it difficult to rival.

To this, Aalto has made his own essential contribution, and it is probable that without his leadership and example so high a standard would not yet have been achieved. But modern Finnish architecture is more than one man thick; indeed it is remarkable, considering Aalto's genius and reputation, how few architects of a later generation have based their work on his.

What the best of them do have in common with him is a close relationship with—a subconscious awareness of—the historical factors that have shaped Finland herself and the temperament of her people. Modern Finnish architecture cannot be understood except in relation to the climate, the sparsity of resources and the continuous struggle, political and economic, of which the history of Finland has consisted. To these must be added, as contributory factors, the status and organization of the architectural profession and one psychological asset: the fact that success breeds success. It creates a kind of confidence in the air, so that when a profession knows what is expected from it, that very expectation keeps aspirations, and the resultant standards, high.

In analysing in more detail the special quality of their architecture, one must therefore start with the Finnish people themselves, whose temperament, and the historical strains they have been subjected to, have moulded their achievements throughout the eight centuries or more since architecture began in hard-won clearings in the harsh northern wilderness. For the celebrated modern Finnish architecture was not created out of nothing. It

20. The fifteenth-century church of Sipoo (p. 189)
21. The altar wall of the chapel at Otaniemi (architects, Kaija and Heikki Siren) (p. 190)

22. Nousiainen's thirteenth-century church, near Turku
23. The interior of Keuruu church, 1758

24. Helsinki cathedral

25. National Museum, Helsinki (architects, Gesellius, Lindgren, Saarinen, 1901: 1905–12)

26. Helsinki railway station (architect, Eliel Saarinen, 1904: 1906–14)
27. Parliament House, Helsinki (architect, J. S. Sirén, 1924–30)

28. Paimio Sanatorium by Alvar Aalto, 1929–1933 (p. 194)

29. Chapel near Turku, by Erik Bryggman, 1939-41 (p. 196)

30. The Säynätsalo Civic Centre, by Alvar Aalto, 1951 (p. 194)

31. School on Kulosaari Island, Helsinki, by Jorma Järvi, 1955

32. Tapiola Shopping Centre, by Aarne Ervi, *1961* (p. *195*)
33. A block of flats, Tapiola, by Viljo Revell, *1955* (p. *198*)

34. Atrium houses, Espoo, by Jaakko Laapotti and Toivo Korhonen, 1959
35. Bank, Eläintarha Park, Helsinki, by Kaija and Heikki Siren (1968) (p. 199). The building also houses, offices shops and a medical centre.

36. Vuoksenniska church, Imatra, by Alvar Aalto, 1959 (p. 195)
37. Church in Hyvinkää, by Aarno Ruusuvuori, 1961 (p. 200)

38. Municipal Theatre, Turku, by Risto-Veikko Luukkonen and Helmer Stenros, 1962 (p. 200)

39. Dipoli, Otaniemi, by Reima Pietilä and Raili Paatelainen, 1966 (p. 194)

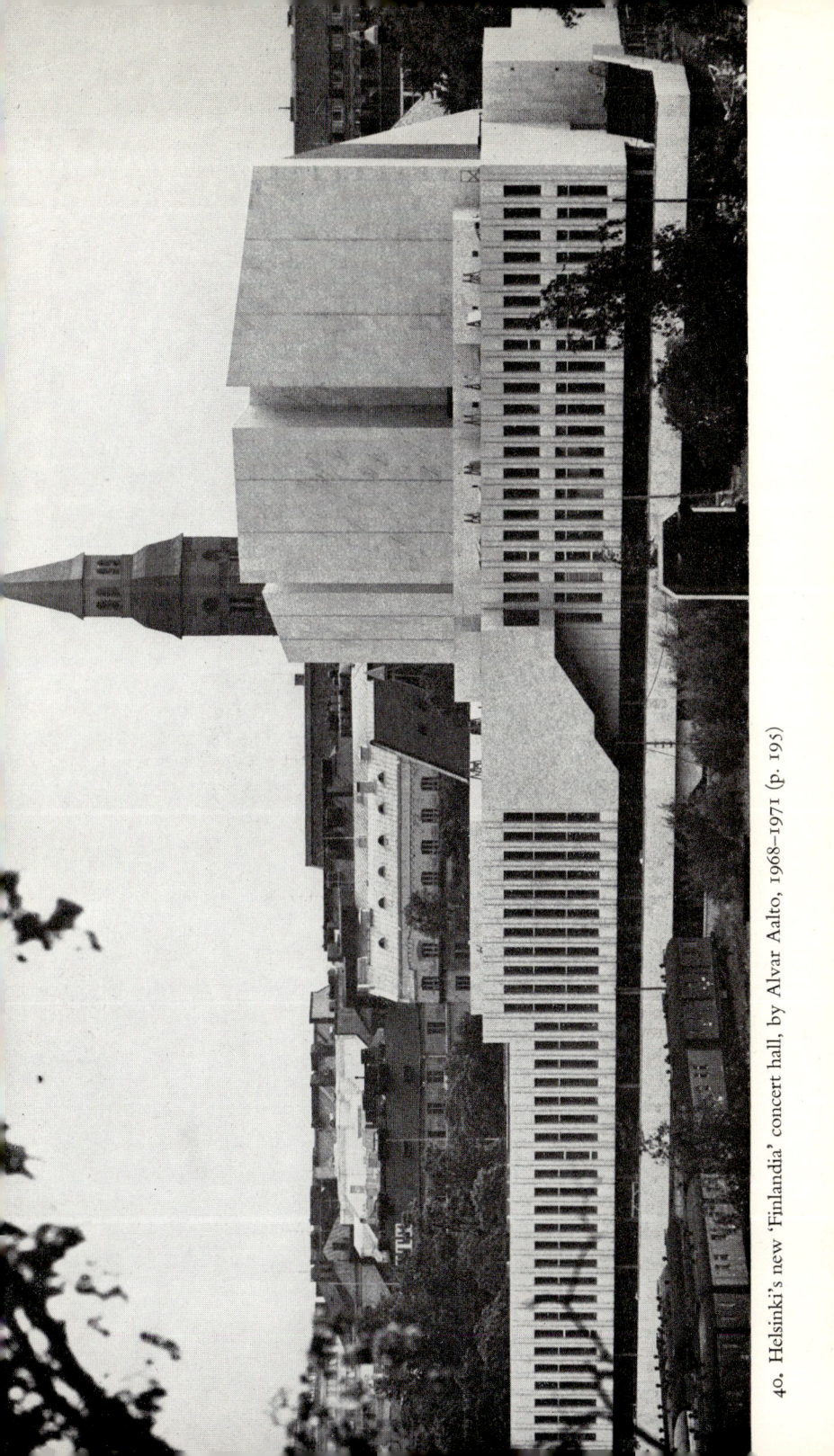

40. Helsinki's new 'Finlandia' concert hall, by Alvar Aalto, 1968–1971 (p. 195)

41. Toronto Town Hall, by Viljo Revell and John B. Parkin Associates, built 1964 (p. 199)

42. Cultural Centre, Wolfsburg Germany, by Alvar Aalto, 1958–62 (p. 199)

is the climax of a long local tradition, which has naturally been modified by new technologies, but which continues to reflect the special characteristics of the Finnish situation.

The earlier Finnish architecture is not widely known. It includes no world-famous monuments and, because of the vulnerability to fire and decay of the timber out of which much of it was constructed, it has survived only sporadically. But if we seek the examples that do survive, we find in them qualities that the modern architecture unconsciously echoes. The gabled medieval churches that add distinction and a point of focus to many Finnish villages may be taken as an instance of a style of architecture determined by the special conditions in which the Finnish people are compelled to build. These churches are simple and unpretentious—the needs of a hard-working community of foresters and fishermen would not require otherwise—and are typically constructed of unsquared field-stones and heavy timbers, with high steep roofs designed to throw off the snow. They make a plain geometrical statement that gains in vigour and effectiveness by having few embellishments. They are visibly a part of the landscape of pine and birch trees, outcrops of grey or pinkish rock, tufted grass and rough stone walls in which they stand.

These features: bold geometry, a limited range of materials and colours and (when building in a rural setting) a close relationship to an only partially tamed landscape, characterize many of the modern buildings also. They are qualities that emerge from the centuries-long struggle—which modern science may have ameliorated but certainly has not brought to an end—to contend with a severe climate, which at all times of the year remains close to the architect's consciousness, and with limited economic and material resources. The challenge these offer to the designer have made him aware of Nature as something he has to withstand rather than luxuriate in; it has demanded that he puts functional needs first and has imposed on him a clear, direct relationship between means and ends.

Even when, in the present century, more scientific building techniques supplanted the adze and saw and the mason's chisel, the principle remained. When Aalto built, in 1929, his masterpiece of reinforced concrete construction, the tuberculosis sanatorium at Paimio, deep in the pine forests east of Turku, he instinctively made of it a spare, bony structure, expressive of the nature of the material but reflecting also the Finnish tradition whereby stress is laid on the essentials rather than the elaborations of architecture. The plan of Paimio, moreover, in the way it spreads its wings to welcome the life-enhancing sun, not only provides for the needs of the patients but symbolizes the significance for the Finns of the elemental gifts, grudgingly bestowed on them, of sun and light and warmth.

This intense consciousness of life as a contest against nature, besides endowing much of Finnish architecture with its organic quality—in the sense that the American architect, Frank Lloyd Wright, used the word, to mean sympathetic to natural processes instead of aloof from them—often gives it a romanticism, a sense of losing itself in the potentialities of a particular situation. We see it in Aalto's civic group at Säynätsalo or in the way he has brought the surrounding pine-forest right into the staircase-hall of his university building at Jyväskylä by the use of a sheer glass wall. But romanticism is acceptable in architecture only when it is a by-product of a genuine discipline. If, instead, it is allowed to become an objective in itself, romanticism soon degenerates into artfulness.

We can see this process at work in the designs of some of Aalto's followers. Dipoli, the student union building at the technical university at Otaniemi, added only four or five years ago by Reima Pietilä, is a striking design with its vigorous concrete slab roof and its use of rounded natural boulders that appear to be incorporated in the building itself; yet the very skill with which this has been contrived gives it a self-consciously theatrical air. The same can be said, in spite of the fascination of the conception, of the touristically popular Temppeliaukio church in Helsinki (by the brothers Suomalainen), excavated out of the solid rock. A tendency for the organic idiom that Aalto handled with such restraint and discipline to become sentimentalized is perhaps one of the factors that drove the more perceptive of the generation that followed Aalto—led by Viljo Revell and taught by Aulis Blomstedt—towards a more severe and classical modern idiom.

In any case the Aalto buildings just referred to occupy a rural setting. In spite of his international reputation it was not until many years after Aalto had built the Paimio sanatorium, Säynätsalo and the country houses that brought him fame that he was given a commission in the city of Helsinki. This may have been symbolically just, since town architecture was alien to the long Finnish tradition—Finland had no towns of any size until a century ago—but it makes it difficult to compare Aalto's achievements with those of other great architects for whom an evident relationship with nature was not the essence of most of their designs.

When Aalto did first build in the city—the Rautatalo building in Helsinki, 1955—he showed in a different way his inventive awareness of the challenge offered by the Finnish climate. The building encloses a high top-lighted hall—a kind of roofed-in courtyard—surrounded by shops and cafés and, above these, by galleries giving access to the upper floors. It is an imaginative device for allowing normal urban activities to be pursued while protected from the severest weather; a device which, surprisingly, has not been developed on a wider scale. However, some of the vast shopping complexes designed by Revell—and after his death by his partner Heikki Castrén, in Helsinki, Turku and Vaasa—are planned with the same need in mind, as is Aarne Ervi's latest building at Tapiola with its galleried central concourses.

Aalto's Rautatalo street façade is sensitively handled but strictly rectilinear, and with none of that feeling for free-flowing geometrical forms characteristic of his other work. His subsequent buildings, however, whether urban or rural, are highly idiosyncratic and exploit this feeling to the full. The most successful, perhaps, are his brick-walled House of Culture in Helsinki (1958), his main building for the Institute of Technology at Otaniemi (1964), his church at Vuoksenniska (1959) and his civic centre at Seinäjoki (1964). Some of his other recent work, including the prominently-sited Enso-Gutzeit office-building facing Helsinki's South Harbour, have disappointed many of his admirers, but in his very latest building, his 'Finlandia' concert hall in Hesperia Park, Helsinki, his handling of space and restrained use of luxurious materials are again worthy of his international reputation. The Seinäjoki civic centre, with its exterior covering of ceramic tiles, illustrates his inventiveness in the use of new materials, which has been one of his claims to continuing fame since he changed the whole world's conception of modern furniture around 1930 by developing new techniques of laminating and bending plywood. Aalto's work as a furniture designer has always been integral with his work as an architect; his influential and much-imitated sprung plywood chairs and stools, for example, made their first appearance in his Paimio sanatorium, referred to above, and his library at Viipuri of 1930, now in Soviet territory.

Timber is of course the material with which Finnish architecture is most closely associated—the basis of the country's economy as well as the dominating constituent of its scenery. The range and virtuosity with which it is handled is evident everywhere: in open carpentered roofs, like that in the Sirens' student restaurant at Otaniemi, in ribbed wall surfaces like those which Lindegren and Jäntti added in 1952 to Helsinki's Olympic stadium, and, of course, in innumerable examples of interiors and their furnishings which show a craftsmanlike familiarity with the essential nature of the material.

Another factor that gives its special character to Finnish architecture is the sense of independence that the Finns have shown throughout their history; an emotion which, paradoxically, has led them both to assert their national individuality and—since the first World War—to adhere unequivocably to the international modern architectural movement. This latter perhaps signified for them their hard-won freedom to choose the most forward-looking path for themselves instead of accepting the position, culturally, of an appendage to a larger power.

At that time Finland's positive contribution to modern architecture consisted of the early works of Aalto and the sincere but somewhat more orthodox works of a handful of other progressive architects such as Erik Bryggman and Erkki Huttunen—who, incidentally, was one of the first to experiment with prefabricated houses in timber, designed for factory production. It was after the Second World War that Finnish architecture began to produce the varied body of work that has given the country its present reputation—but not immediately after. To begin with, so acute was the need for housing, aggravated by the problems of refugee settlement and of re-establishing industrial production, that professional skills were mostly concentrated on planning and reconstruction generally. From Turku and Helsinki in the south to Oulu and Rovaniemi in the distant north, plans for expansion and redevelopment were drawn up and have for the most part been gradually implemented. This phase coincided with the increasing urbanization of Finnish life; but the provision of housing in the needful quantities did not result—because of lack of time, vision, experience—in great architectural achievements.

But soon a new generation of architects showed that the pre-war distinction and integrity of design had not been lost. Their subsequent achievements, based on the same qualities that I have already described—a direct response to the challenge of climate and resources and an inherited tradition of simple geometrical expression—have been encouraged by two professional factors that have given the more forward-looking Finnish architects the wide support they have needed. These two factors are first the high regard in which the architect is held in Finland, which safeguards him to some extent against the interference of ignorant clients and officials and gives him more control than in many countries over the interiors and furnishings of his buildings, and secondly the widespread use of the competition system.

Nearly every important new building in Finland is the subject of an architectural competition, which gives the young architect an early opportunity of making his mark, prevents too many of the commissions from being concentrated in the hands of a few successful architects and—perhaps most useful of all—keeps the general public informed and interested in architectural developments through competitions and their results being regularly reported in the press. The system has also, of course, its drawbacks, one being the undue preference it induces for the striking image or idea, as against the more thoroughly but impersonally worked-out solution to a given problem whose merits may not be so immediately apparent. Nevertheless, the prevalence of competitions is a beneficial element of the Finnish architectural scene and the envy of other nations.

Thus was launched, soon after the war, the architectural

FINLAND: AN INTRODUCTION

enterprise that has received more attention from visitors to Finland than any other: the dormitory town of Tapiola. A competition for the layout of this new town, situated west of Helsinki, was held in 1950 and won by Aarne Ervi, who also designed its main administrative and shopping centre. The town houses nearly 17,000 people, occupying three neighbourhoods each with a mixture of small houses and high blocks of flats, set among trees with a sensitive relationship of planting and the landscape characteristically Finnish. It is regarded as a model of its kind, the only general criticism being that the central green space, separating the neighbourhoods from the town centre, is so large as to create a sense of diffusion at the very point where urban concentration would have been desirable.

In 1952 another event took place that provided a stimulus for modern Finnish architecture: the Olympic Games at Helsinki. Viljo Revell built for the administration of the Games a handsome building on the waterfront (destined later to be part offices and part the Palace Hotel). It was again the outcome of a competition, and its severe lines and plainness of finish, though to some extent due to post-war austerities, established Revell as a new leader capable of maintaining Finland's place in the main stream of European architecture with a rationalist approach to design which has been dominant ever since.

Like every country in the world Finland has its proportion of poorly designed buildings, and in the sphere of town planning there are policies and tendencies that give rise to misgivings. But the country's general architectural standards are as high as anywhere in the world, and undoubtedly higher than those of any country with Finland's limited resources. Housing, educational, religious, industrial and institutional buildings can all show outstanding examples. Finland was one of the first countries to give factories—in her case paper and wood-pulp mills—serious architectural attention. On the other hand, it is remarkable that the city office-tower which, with its emphasis on verticality and and its fully glazed walls, is popularly associated with the idea of modern architecture, plays no such prominent role in Finland. There are massive commercial buildings in the larger cities, like those by Revell and Castrén already referred to and the circular banking headquarters, surrounded by shops and offices, at Eläintarha Park, Helsinki, by Kaija and Heikki Siren; but Finnish cities do not yet suffer under the indignity of tall business buildings dominating the skyline which cannot claim either civic or social justification for doing so.

The changes that can be observed in modern Finnish architecture since its earlier days are nevertheless partly due to building activity being more concentrated in the towns, though Aalto has successfully used in town architecture the favourite idiom of his middle period, based on the use of red brick with copper trim. Those younger architects, too, who have adhered more closely to the international idiom still seem able—even in an urban setting—to exploit their inherent sense of geometry and restraint in the treatment of materials.

Perhaps the fact that the subtleties of the relationship between materials and setting mean so much to the Finns can be used to explain why even the most distinguished Finnish architects, when invited to design abroad, have not been at their best. Aalto's dormitory for the Massachusetts Institute of Technology, his housing and civic buildings at Berlin and Wolfsburg, his office tower at Bremen and Revell's Toronto city hall (the result of victory in an international competition) all have their qualities; but they are not handled with the assurance and sensitivity typical of their architects when working in the conditions peculiar to their country and stimulated by the challenges they find there.

Memorable exceptions are the two temporary exhibition pavilions that Aalto designed for the great Paris Exhibition of 1937 and the New York World Fair of 1939. Their imaginative and technically inventive use of timber was a revelation to the world, and it was these buildings more than any other that first drew international attention to Finnish virtuosity in using timber and Finnish design in timber products such as furniture.

The modern visitor to Finland, if he wants to study the country's architecture at its best, must travel from the Baltic Sea to within the Arctic Circle. It is one of the characteristics of the present Finnish scene that the best architecture is now so widely distributed that nearly every town possesses modern buildings of interest, and many towns—new as well as old—can boast buildings of real distinction. For example, the quickly expanding industrial town of Kouvola, in south-eastern Finland, has just completed a highly sophisticated, beautifully modulated, town hall and civic offices by Saarnio and Leiviskä, and the somewhat older industrial town of Lahti has a bank by Revell notable for its original and spacious interior. These are only two examples among many.

The quality of some industrial buildings, even those of thirty years ago, has already been referred to; the tradition continues, as in the exemplary design of the milk-depots and processing plants of the Valio company—a type of building not notable elsewhere for such thoughtful design. Examples, by the architects Mäkinen and Sääksvuori, can be seen outside Turku, Lahti and Vaasa.

The greatest concentration of interesting modern architecture is naturally to be found, however, in Helsinki. Here the architectural pilgrim can also familiarize himself with other significant contributions Finland has made to European architectural history: the neo-classical buildings of the Empire period—dominated by the giant figure of Carl Ludwig Engel (1778-1840)—and the National-Romantic period, with a flavour of Art Nouveau, which reflects the passionate drive towards self-expression and cultural liberation that emerged among the Finnish people at the end of the last century. Second only to Helsinki in the quality and variety of their modern buildings are Turku—the ancient capital—Tampere and the educational centre of Jyväskylä.

In all these places the architects whose work should be sought out, besides those already named, include Aarno Ruusuvuori, whose churches at Hyvinkää in central southern Finland and at Huutoniemi near the west coast, are worth a special journey to see; Timo Penttilä, architect of the new city theatre at Helsinki, spread along a hillside in Eläintarha Park; and Pekka Pitkänen whose grey concrete crematorium in the suburbs of Turku, set in a smoothly modelled landscape, creates an atmosphere of calm and dignity.

Also at Turku are the recently completed Sibelius museum by Baeckman, a number of sober, well-related university buildings by Ervi, Pitkänen, Baeckman and others, and the civic theatre by

Luukkonen and Stenros, who also designed the theatre at Kuopio. Near the Turku theatre is a somewhat sombre group of municipal offices making, like the theatre, lavish use of copper, and a museum devoted to the work of the sculptor Aaltonen. At Tampere outstanding buildings are the university institute, the first major building by Toivo Korhonen—another of the second-generation architects who are maintaining Finland's reputation internationally—and the ambitious, lofty Kaleva church by Reima Pietilä.

This essay could easily become a catalogue of names and places, but modern Finnish buildings, rather than being listed and described, should be visited. Thus, they can be seen in relation to the life they serve and to the pride and practicality of the Finns, from which the architecture derives its quality but which can only be fully appreciated when travelling among them.

DESIGN

GEOFFREY BEARD

It is not easy to define 'good design', and most people accept that Scandinavian products are blessed with it but what it consists of does not matter to them. The requirements of design have been analysed as needing to take note of principles of arrangement, geometrical relationships, strengths, access, cost and appearance. In Scandinavia the processes leading to this acceptance have emerged in the past fifty years. They are, naturally enough, those which have gradually accepted form and function as vital elements necessary to the creation of any workable industrial design. In Finland the process would have been much more complicated but for the existence of 'Ornamo'—the Society of Decorative Artists, founded in September, 1911.

For a long period prior to this there had been groups of people in Finland interested in arts and crafts. They had contributed to the foundation of the important Finnish Society of Crafts and Design, and its design school. Many of Ornamo's members attended this school—later the Institute of Crafts and Design—and their professional skills were put to the realization of Ornamo's aims of developing domestic crafts and design, promoting co-operation between artists and improving the ability of its members to deal with such matters. That it did so can be instanced by the career of its member Arttu Brummer (1891–1951), who joined Ornamo in 1912. Reference is soon made to him when talking to any of the Finnish designers he trained in Helsinki, and his glass bowl named 'Finlandia', made by Riihimäen Lasi Oy in 1945, was selected in 1960 as the 'object of the decade'. In his forty years of association with the improvement of design-standards Brummer, together with his pupil Gunnel Nyman (1909–48), remained true to Ornamo's ideals and put them actively into practice. There were also encouraging signs that the strongly progressive movement taking place in Scandinavian art handicrafts was not limited only to the revival of the techniques and forms of national handicrafts, but also showed strong signs of a new and independent flowering starting from the complete mastery of the forms.

From the conversations and ideas of intellectuals gathering among objects created for national fairs and competitions it became possible gradually to raise the artistic standards of industrial products. That this took place for the most part against the restrictions imposed on national life by an unwilling adherence to Russia says much for the Finnish character. The emergence of the country as an independent republic after World War I culminated in a number of similar important steps forward. It became possible for artists and designers to form plans for the great exhibitions in Paris (1925) and Barcelona (1929) with a devotion and detachment born of the new status. Some of the search for new design talent was also encouraged by one of the first of the big utility glass competitions: that organized in 1928 by Riihimäen Lasi Oy, one of Finland's three major glassworks.

The aim of the competition was to find new designs for suites of household glass made in cheap soda form and without any additional cutting or engraving. This left the shape to be exploited and the competition was won by Henry Ericsson (1898–1933) a painter and graphic artist as well as a glass designer. He joined Riihimäen Lasi Oy as head designer and in this capacity produced many special pieces, of which the tall engraved goblet presented to the City of Barcelona at the time of the important exhibition there in 1929, is the best known. But when Ericsson was killed in an accident his place was not easy to fill—Finnish glass by Iittala at the Barcelona exhibition for example was, for the most part, copied from traditional styles, with an excess of decoration.

The emergence of Finland's importance as a nation with a conscience for design started to come about in the early 1930s. Some of the early impetus was undoubtedly owed to the foundation of the Milan Triennales. Finnish handwoven textiles, glass, ceramics and furniture aroused great interest at the 1933 Triennale. The Finnish architect Alvar Aalto's plywood chairs on show there were a novelty (despite the existence of plywood mills in Finland since 1912), but within a year or two, by 1935, his cantilevered chairs (made by Artek of Helsinki) were successfully exploiting all the characteristics of bent plywood and laminated birch. By forming the laminated layers with the wood grain of each running in the same direction great strength, as well as a spring-like quality, was achieved, matching the best efforts in metal and wood of the German 'giants' Mies van der Rohe and Marcel Breuer.

It was significant for Finland's future in the manufacture of furniture that the international acclaim of Aalto's work was well supported in Finland by Ornamo. In its own annual exhibition of 1934 it concentrated an important section on 'Furniture On Sale in Shops'—the way was open for design in the industrial context to develop from a modest home industry, and to take advantage of increasing international affluence. It did not do so without some suspicion on the part of Finnish employers themselves. The Finnish textile industry for example, which now forms the fourth largest production group after wood, metal and foodstuffs, had a long tradition spanning some 200 years. The producers brought their pattern collections from New York, Paris, Vienna and occasionally from Sweden and England. These were then adapted to suit the national taste and designers were still an unnecessary luxury.

Finland had admittedly gone through more difficult times than its Western neighbours but a greater awareness of artistic abilities seemed to be present in the ceramics it made. The Arabia porcelain manufactory had originally been a subsidiary of the old Swedish factory of Rörstrand, founded in the eighteenth century. By 1874 the inaptly named 'Arabia' had been set up in Helsinki, but until 1916 it was still controlled from Sweden. Only the fortunate transfer from Rörstrand in 1895 of the young artist Thure Öberg (1871–1935) allowed any artistic progress to be made. He became the representative of the new art-nouveau and arts and crafts styles, and introduced many new decorative processes and materials. His contemporary A. W. Finch (1854–1930, who worked for several years in the furniture and ceramics factory in Porvoo founded by Louis Sparre, and operated completely in the crafts spirit of William Morris) was, as a ceramic artist, also much in advance of his time. Finch's work as a teacher at the Institute of Industrial Arts in Helsinki allows us to consider him, with ample justification, as the founder of modern Finnish ceramics.

The later artistic achievements at Arabia owe much to Öberg's and Finch's example, and the technical and artistic importance of the firm gained in strength through the thirties. Some of this was undoubtedly due to the formal setting-up of an art department in 1932, and to its employment from 1924 of artists such as Friedl Kjellberg, (she retired in 1970 after forty-six years at Arabia); Toini Muona (retired 1969), Aune Siimes (1909–64), Michael Schilkin (1900–62) and Birger Kaipiainen. At the 1937 Paris Exhibition, Schilkin won a gold medal, and Siimes and Kjellberg a silver one. Their associations at this time with the Swedish artist Tyra Lundgren, who had worked in France and Italy, also provided Arabia with an extremely valuable international stimulus in what, for designers in Finland, were the 'break-through' years of acceptance.

It is easy to be complacent about the introduction of freedom to design and the gradual impact designers have had on the special provinces of the factory engineers and the marketing teams. It was not accomplished without friction and antagonism, and managements had to make determined efforts to see the problems objectively, and then lead the way with understanding. Closer co-operation between industry and art college became necessary, in order that a sound technical knowledge in practical and theoretical terms could become part of the designers' preparations for their careers.

Finland provides a hundred superb examples at every turn of designers who did this. It might be invidious to single out names, but those of Marjatta Metsovaara-Van Havere (who heads her own firm of weavers of textiles for interior decoration), Tapio Wirkkala, (who works free-lance for Iittala Glass, among many others), Timo Sarpaneva, Eero Aarnio, Kaj Franck, Bertel Gardberg... the list soon spans the alphabet with ease. The products themselves have obtained a world-wide market. Metsovaara teamed up with the artist designer Maj Kuhlefelt to introduce the colour-harmony fashion line, 'Finn-Flare'. Wirkkala produced many splendid designs for Iittala as well as for the

FINLAND: AN INTRODUCTION

German porcelain firm of Rosenthal. Sarpaneva has ranged over an enormous free-lance range of door handles, glass, packing-papers, textiles, and Gardberg's cutlery is almost too elegant for us to believe it is also functionally balanced, and sharp. Two events highlighted the success of these new designs: the Milan Triennale of 1951 planned by Wirkkala, and Kaj Franck's plea for the object, not the designer's name, to be considered as paramount. The two are at opposite ends of the straight line which has led to the meteoric rise and acclaim of Finnish design and its exponents.

Part of the story is based on the assumption that an object which is correct in function should be as correct in aesthetic terms also. It was not easy for manufacturers to accept this, and in some parts of the world it is still unacceptable. But purposeful designers in close collaboration with industry can even make an outboard motor, a hunting rifle or a bidet look good! The manufacturer for his part is pleased to advertise—as Ammus-Sytytin Oy of Rauma did in 1964 for Eero Rislakki's 'Belinda' Coffee Pot and 'Tytti' Percolator—'these examples of our production have gained favour with the purchasing public in many countries thanks to their pleasing appearance'. It can all be seen to splendid advantage in the decor and fittings of the flagships of the Finnish shipping lines. They take abroad the message of the 'Finnish Design' line in a colourful and functional way with attractive decor, and pleasing crockery, linen and cutlery.

At the Ninth and Tenth Milan Triennales in 1951 and 1954 the overall responsibility for the Finnish sections was entrusted to Tapio Wirkkala (b. 1915). The enthusiastic reception of the displays enhanced not only his own, already considerable, reputation but also signified an international acclaim of Finnish design and crafts. Of fifty-seven Grand Prix awarded at Milan in 1951 Finland gained six, of which three went to Wirkkala and one to his wife the Arabia ceramist, Rut Bryk. A *ryijy* rug (representative of a centuries-old tradition that can be quickly assessed in Osakeyhtiö Neovius's *ryijy* showroom in Helsinki) by Eeva Brummer, and one of Dora Jung's great tapestries made up the medal-bedecked group. At the 1954 Triennale, six out of a total of twenty-eight Grand Prix went to Finland; in 1957, six out of a total of twentyfive; in 1960, nine Gold Medals of the fifty awarded. However, although the pattern has been repeated faithfully, the dangers of this adulation of the designer have been recognized by some critics.

The most percipient of these is Kaj Franck (b. 1911) whose skill as a glass designer for Wärtsila's subsidiary, Nuutajärvi, has won him world-wide acclaim. In glass and ceramics he has pioneered the application of good design to the utilitarian object, to the point where, in respect of mass-produced goods he advocates that 'instead of resting on the designer's name the product must stand on its own merits of which the design is an essential part'. Anonymity for mass production, and a restoration of a perspective in relating design to the whole story may be only first imaginative steps in a new direction. Franck's own splendid work will always command respect long before and after the natural human instinct of enquiry has started up or exhausted itself. With his younger colleague, Oiva Toikka (b. 1931), the Lunning prize-winner for 1970, Franck has however been able, under his own name, to work also on solitary creations, 'the result of the creating artist's vision of beauty', by forming many unique, 'one-only' pieces of glass. It seems completely acceptable and desirable that these pieces should bear the names of the artists involved.

On September 14, 1961 the fiftieth Anniversary of Ornamo was celebrated in an exhibition of which Wirkkala had been unanimously elected architect. For the first time it became possible to present ten silver spheres, (designed by Wirkkala's younger colleague, Timo Sarpaneva, b. 1926) to firms and associations 'in recognition of their valuable contribution to Finnish crafts and design'. The remainder of this chapter is given over to an analysis of the contributions the main sectors of industry have been able to make in bringing the good name of Finland's well designed products into the competitive years of the seventies.

It should be said at once that at a time—the early fifties—when government support for the arts had to be earned and encouraged the great industrial firms such as Arabia and Iittala gave considerable assistance. They aided the process whereby the foundations of many trades—glassmaking had been carried on since the late

FINLAND: AN INTRODUCTION

seventeenth century and the making of rugs since the fifteenth—could be used as a springboard to launch more daring and innovative ideas for present-day markets. With their rich hauls of Triennale prizes the designers and their professional societies pulled sharply away from the rich over-decorated pastures of the past. The Society of Crafts and Design appointed a forceful and knowledgeable personality, Olof Gummerus to lead it. In the way that Finch, Ericsson, Gallen-Kallela, Brummer, Nyman and others had all played their vital parts in the past, Finland of the present owes much to Gummerus and his far-reaching policies. Not least of the successes was a manifold increase in the state subsidy to his society, and the establishment of good working relationships with the vital Ministries of Foreign Affairs and Education. There is now even the Finnish President's Export Prize, awarded annually.

The various market surveys which the government and private associations carry out on Finnish products constantly stress some such phrase as this: 'experience shows that the most successful export products are those for which the first stage of consumer selection depends on appearance and external quality'. Price is also naturally important but not the only consideration in determining choice. The plastics industry expects to grow now at the rate of 20 per cent per annum: textiles, clothing, footwear, glass and furniture expect by the 1980s to be maintaining a 4–7 per cent annual growth rate. They merit a, regrettably brief, look.

It is a long haul from the pioneer Finnish plastics factory of 1921 making buttons to the present eminence of the industry: the use of plastics has quadrupled in the years 1965–70. In the realm of plastic fabrics ties do, of course, exist with the successful fashion industry. The four outstanding manufacturers of plastic fabrics, Oy Finlayson-Forssa at Forssa; Förenade Plastfabriker at Vaasa; Oy Hemming's at Kuopio and Friman at Äetsä, between them make up articles such as fabric raincoats, tablecloths, upholstery materials, as well as providing the raw materials for further processing such as bags, tarpaulins, bookbinding requisites and so on. The versatile free-lance designer, Timo Sarpaneva, whose work we have already briefly mentioned, has provided designs for Finlayson's Kerni range—'Kerni is more than a plastic tablecloth'—and with its attractive floral design it is easy to believe that it is. In the polythene sheet industry most of us have seen or used one of Finnair's plastic carrier bags, which in a design by Ilkka Jortikka, won the 'Eurostar' prize of the European Packaging Federation for Kalvopakkaus Oy in 1968. Since 1958, when Eurostar prizes were inaugurated, Finnish packs have won a total of fifteen awards.

Some part of this is due to the considerable efforts made by Finnish manufacturers and their designers to provide suitable packs—often gift packs—for the objects they design and make. Plastics naturally play their considerable part in this. The great Rosenlew Group, together with Amerplast of Tampere monopolize the plastic bag trade—with perhaps 300 million bags a year. Rosenlew use Sarpaneva's design services to dictate colour and pattern; to their wrapping paper ranges he has introduced a wonderfully colourful set, ranging across the spectrum. A pack, whether it is of plastic film, paper or card must protect the product against dirt and breakage, facilitate storage and speed up service at the retail level. It must also be distinguishable from other competing products so that the object will sell. The Finnish Packaging Association organizes an annual competition to stimulate the supply of effective designs for packages and packaging series. Arabia, among others, has opened a new department with the responsibility of 'fitting' their gifts to the right pack.

In the development of domestic designs in plastic Finland has few, if any, equals. Olof Bäckström's 'Fiskamin' plastic tableware for the Fiskars Group, in heat-hardened melamac, withstands rough handling, looks good, and is functional. This is equally true of Yki Nummi's acrylic ranges, including light fittings, for Sanka Oy, which require considerable skills to manufacture. Plastic also reaches over into the large-scale trade in children's toys and furniture—many of them in wood—and many of them with an educational purpose. Jukka toys by Juho Jussila Oy are already well known: designers Anna Tauriala, Jorma Vennola and Pekka Korpijaakko have also drawn out 'Poppa' play furniture and other educational toys for Aarikka, Korhonen Oy and several other firms.

Finnish-made clothing has long been able to build up on the

FINLAND: AN INTRODUCTION

splendid achievements of the firms of Marimekko, internationally known since 1961, and of Vuokko. In its own right its exports have 'mounted' over 600 per cent in the years 1962–70: all based, according to the Central Federation of Finnish Clothing Industries on 'fashion, quality and price in that order'. The leather fashions of Kaarina Hellemaa (Modeurope chose four of her Matisse colours for their international colour chart of six colours in all), ranging from thick suedes to dyed soft chamois, put themselves at the head of a long line of distinguished names. And what fashion demands in fabric the textile industry does its best to supply.

It will be obvious that with at least 260 Finnish textile manufacturing units, from specialized plants on the smallest scale to integrated companies, including some of the largest in Scandinavia, a few words here are hardly adequate. Tampella's range alone demands a book to itself. Serious enquirers in any case will be orientated enough to approach either The Finnish Foreign Trade Association in Helsinki, one of the over thirty commercial sections of the relevant Finnish Embassies, or check directly with the trade association—in this instance the Association of Finnish Textile Industries.

I own to a sneaking fascination with the way Finland's many talented jewellers and silversmiths, led by Björn Weckström (b. 1935) and Bertel Gardberg (b. 1916), have created, or adapted many of their pieces with fashions in mind. While Weckström may now be setting his space jewellery in transparent blocks of acrylic plastic there are others like Seppo Tamminen who, with his bronze and silver work, carries into his pieces a touch of the Orient. He makes jewellery for young people of all ages who want something exotic but inexpensive to wear. Rita Salo is fascinated by form and movement, and is now collaborating with a dress factory for her mass-produced jewellery to be an integral part of the finished outfit. Paula Häiväoja, by contrast to silversmith-trained Salo, trained firstly as a dress-designer, and still owning her own boutique, now works in silver. Craftsmen-made shoulder ornaments, buckles, bracelets and rings are made to suit a modern style of dress—jewellery in a striking, emancipated mood—and among the most important of all contributions to the arts, in precious and semi-precious metals.

DESIGN

A chapter on Finnish design that bypasses its glass and ceramic products in detail may be almost unforgiveable. I have however devoted much attention to the subject elsewhere, Kerttu Niilonen's excellent book on Finnish Glass (Tammi: 1967) is readily available, and Arabia, with its frequent house-journal *Ceramics and Glass* is its own best advocate. What would be inexcusable would be avoidance of mention of the furniture industry. The trade literature will tell us that Finland's 200 furniture factories include two of Scandinavia's largest, where mass production on an international scale is possible. These highly mechanized and rationalized production methods are a powerful asset in executing orders for contract furnishing. Add to that 'purity of line' and 'freshness of colour' and the brochures are almost lyrical. If one merely lists the six firms who took part in the Fourteenth Triennale at Milan there is still injustice! However, Asko, Haimi, Korhonen, Lepokalusto, Studio Nurmesniemi and Skanno were there and thereby demand attention.

Mention has been made of Alvar Aalto's important step in founding (with three others, including his wife), the house-furnishing and industrial art firm of Artek in 1935. Still in active existence it provides a link with his world-famous laminated wood furniture of the '30s and the important industry of today. Some of the early emphasis on mass-production to a good design came from Werner West (1890–1959) who designed for the Helsinki department store of Stockmann. The talented glass-designer Gunnel Nyman was also originally a furniture designer. They provide the link to the dominant names of the present, who as well as using timber have branched out into plastic and glass-fibre applications. The firm of Asko Osakeyhtiö in its fifty-odd years of existence, has moved from its joiners' workshop start to a 20-acre production plant at Lahti, and some forty-seven Asko-stores throughout Finland. Eero Aarnio, one of several free-lance designers working for Asko, designed the famous 'Globe' chair for them—a glass-fibre shell, aluminium base, and padding of polyfoam and Dacron. Antti Nurmesniemi, who won acclaim for his Finnish setting at the 1960 Milan Triennale, has produced much in moulded plywood for Vilka Oy, and for his own studio range.

FINLAND: AN INTRODUCTION

The idea of 'easy-assemble' furniture offers many possibilities for homes in town or country, and for hotels, motels, reception areas; thus P. J. Wainio designed the 'Finno' range for Vilka Oy, which also uses a wide variety of furnishing materials varying from cotton to leather. This combination of wood and textiles is widely applied—the pine furniture by Pirkko Stenros, allied to textiles by Marjatta Metsovaara-Van Havere is particularly successful. Made by Muurame it may be seen and enjoyed to advantage at the Ruuponsaari Holiday Village, near Jyväskylä. This is extended into the extensive lines of 'please-yourself—keep the home young' furniture designed by Totti Laakso for Skanno. Wooden frames are bright vinyl-covered, with loose cotton covers allowing flexibility to change the mind—'some dark morning we may wish to make our home different. So away with the old sun-yellow sofa covers... and we surprise the family with a new grass-green sofa'. These element-built pieces, assembled at home as the owner wishes, and available in endless permutations to fit the most difficult corners is one of Finland's imaginative answers. Its furniture industry, in my opinion, does a great deal to uphold the high standards of Finnish design.

Among the plethora of objects provided for a world which has come to accept these high standards from Finland, almost without question, there may be some which do not stand the pace. The Informative Labelling Association tries to safeguard the accuracy of information given to the public. The object of this state-supported, official and impartial body is to guide and promote informative labelling in Finland along with uniform standards for the benefit and guidance of consumers. The label provides information on the essential utility features of the product. When different manufacturers use the same formula for similar groups of products, the consumer receives information about the various competing products which helps him make comparisons and decide which of them is the most suitable and the best buy.

The use of automatic dishwashers on a large scale has also caused research to be undertaken by the Finnish Research Institute of Engineering in Agriculture and Forestry on the various makes. The glass, ceramic, metal, plastic and wood manufacturing industries are all concerned in the results obtained. Arabia for example intends to stamp its future ceramic products, as appropriate, with the legend 'Dishwasher-proof'—in Finnish, Swedish and English. A collector's mark all its own!

A last few words, however, still need to be said, and were more adequately phrased in 1961 by Benedict Zilliacus, an editor of *Hufvudstadsbladet* in Helsinki.

'We proudly assume that the rest of Scandinavia can learn something from our fresh and untrammelled creativeness in alliance with Nature, but at the same time we must admit that there is a new test before us. We need to think how to guide our art-craftsmanship away from the ill-considered, the over-aesthetic, the dehumanized, towards something less productive of limelight and gold medals but much more representative of our actual capacity'.

The signs are that this cautionary tale is almost learned. The growing significance of EFTA and EEC markets as outlets for everything made has raised home standards. The future may be viewed with guarded optimism and, helped by the daily therapy of the slogan, and the act—'happiness is a real Finnish Sauna'—even in terms of euphoria.

AS OTHERS SAW THEM

GEORGE NORTH
The description of Swedland, Gotland, and Finland, 1561

'*Finlande is called a fayre countrye, because it is more pleasanter than Swecia.* ... *Much wine is transported thither, out of Spayne, by the sea Balthic, which the people of the Countrye much desireth, onely to exhillerat their myndes.* ... *This countrye doth excell Swecia, in corn and grain, both for plenty and goodness, because it is for the most part playne, and not so fenny nor hylly as Swecia* is. . . . The Finnons have continual warres wyth the Muscovites in the arm or bosome of the sea Finnonicus: using in Summer the ayde of Shyppes, and in Wynter they combat upon the Ice . . .'

>JAMES THOMSON
>The Seasons, 1730
'Not such the sons of Lapland: wisely
they despise th'insensate barbarous trade of war,
They ask no more than Nature gives,
they love their mountains and enjoy their storms.'

>JOHN STORY
>Travels through Sweden, 1632
'Next in order follows Finland, which some think to be so called in comparison of Sweden, as tho' it did in fruitfulness far exceed it, (who are foully deceived; for it is more probable, that it was first called Fiendland by reasons of the great hostility those Finlanders exercised against this nation, so long as they were commanded by a king of their own). This country abounds in corn, pasture, fish and fowl; and, finally, in such things as are most necessary for the life of man. The people are very laborious, and able to endure hardship. Of old they were esteemed the mildest among all the Scanzian people; howbeit, at this day, they are somewhat harsher; and their valour in war was well witnessed in the memorable battle fought near Leipsick in Misnia. They have a peculiar language of their own . . .'

>MADAME DE STAËL
>Dix années d'exil (written 1812)
'They try to cultivate the mind a little there, but bears and wolves come so close in winter that all thought is of necessity concentrated on how to attain a tolerable physical existence.'

>MRS ALEC TWEEDIE
>Through Finland in Carts, 1897
'Finland is not the home of barbarians, as some folk imagine,

neither do Polar bears walk continually about the streets, nor reindeer pull sledges in summer,—items that have several times been suggested to the writer!'

VOLTAIRE
Histoire de Charles XII, 1731

'The Kingdom which is made up of Sweden and Finland is, according to our measurement, about 200 leagues broad and 300 long, and stretches from south to north as far as the 55th degree or thereabouts. The climate is severe; there is scarcely any spring or autumn, but there are nine months of winter in the year.... The people ... live to a good old age when they do not undermine their constitutions by the abuse of strong drink, which northern nations seem to crave the more because they have been denied them by Nature.'

ANGEL GANIVET
Cartas finlandesas, 1896–97

'The Finn is the most watery person in Europe.'

OLAUS MAGNUS
Historia de gentibus septentrionalibus, 1555

'The Finnish people are so experienced in the shipwright's craft that they can build vessels which are as strong and durable, yes, perhaps even better than those which I have seen built by the Venetians with their brilliant gifts in this field.'

A. M. C. CLIVE-BAYLEY
Vignettes from Finland, or Twelve Months in Strawberry Land, 1895

'It would be difficult to find a town (Helsinki) of 80,000 inhabitants in England so clean, so bright, with such museums, libraries, and public buildings. Even Bedford is not as educational as Helsing-

fors, nor is Brighton so well served with social amusements, concerts and theatres.'

KONSTANTIN BATYUSHKOV
Extracts from a Russian Officer's letters on Finland, 1809

'*Boredom crawls over the snow wastes and one can truly say that life in this wild, barren solitude, without books, without company and often without aquavit is so miserable that we cannot tell whether it is Wednesday or Sunday.*'

ALEXANDER SERGEYEVICH PUSHKIN
in a poem, 1833

(*referring to Finland*): '*Nature's unhappy stepson . . .* '

EDWARD CLARKE
Travels in various countries of Europe, Asia and Africa, Part III: Scandinavia, 1819

'*The atmosphere (in Åland) was so clear and dry, that, being well clothed, the effect of it was charming. An intensity of general cheerfulness seemed to keep pace with the intensity of the season. Brilliant skies; horses neighing and dancing; peasants laughing and singing—"Fine snow! brave winter!" Merry making in all the villages. Festival days, with unclouded suns; nights of inconceivable splendour and ineffable brightness; the glorious firmament displaying one uninterrupted flood of light, heightened by an aurora borealis, while boundless fields of snow reflected every ray.*'

WILLIAM SANSOM
The Icicle and the Sun, 1957

'*Sometimes it seems, looking round in a restaurant, that every second person is an intellectual acutely meditating. There is about this mood an air different from the tense and formal silence of a Swede, or from the actively planning silence of the North German.'*

GEORGES DUHAMEL
Chant du Nord, 1929

'*Countries are like people: by their very existence they exalt or deflate the opinions one would like to have of oneself. When I return from Finland, I feel younger and livelier; I make great plans, I like many things in the world and, what is more, I like myself a little better.*'

WINSTON CHURCHILL
Broadcast speech, January 20, 1940

'*Finland alone—in danger of death, superb, sublime Finland!— shows what free men can do.*'

LITERATURE AND THE NATIONAL IMAGE

DAVID BARRETT

IT is in its literature that a nation finds its own image. In the case of the Finns, whose literature can hardly be said to have begun till the nineteenth century, this image-creating function quickly assumed an altogether unusual importance and became a vital factor in the political as well as the intellectual life of the people. The moulding of such an image was a necessary part of the movement towards independent nationhood, and as this movement gathered speed Finnish writers came more and more under the spell of the national image that had been built up, so that even after independence had been achieved they found it difficult to escape from it. The result, noticeable by any foreign visitor to Finland in the 1930s and 1940s, was an extraordinary consistency in the view of the 'national character' taken by Finns of all types and classes. It was with this image of themselves that the Finns entered the Winter War of 1939–40 and tackled the tasks of reparation in the later 1940s; and it is only in very recent years that Finnish writers have attempted to modify the picture so compellingly painted by their predecessors. Even so, much of the nineteenth-century image persists.

During the six centuries of Swedish rule, which ended in 1809, Finnish literature can hardly be said to have existed at all. In the early days of the Reformation a few learned Finns, educated abroad, had seen the necessity of translating the scriptures into the language of the common people, as was being done elsewhere. A Finnish New Testament, translated by Bishop Mikael Agricola, a disciple of Luther, had appeared in 1548; and during the next hundred years this had been followed by a number of other religious works and collections of hymns, mostly translated, but including some attempts at original versification in Finnish. The programme had culminated in the publication of a complete Finnish Bible in 1642. But apart from isolated efforts at prose and verse composition by a few learned individuals such as Daniel Juslenius (1676–1752), this had been virtually all. There were no Finnish schools at all. Academic education was conducted in Latin; Swedish was the language of administration and of all cultured society, and a knowledge of that tongue was essential to acquire a salaried post or any education worth the name. Only the priests and the law-court interpreters were required to know Finnish.

It was something, however, that most of the Finnish-speaking peasants and backwoodsmen who comprised the bulk of the population outside the towns were able to hear the scriptures read in their own language, and no doubt the abler priests were quick to develop an effective style of pulpit oratory. Moreover, from the late seventeenth century onwards parish authorities were required by the Church to ensure that all candidates for confirmation could read and write. As a result the parish reading class became an important, if not always a popular, feature of rural life, and although the instruction given was very elementary (little more than the ability to read the catechism was required) this institution undoubtedly created a tradition of literacy among the peasantry, even in the poorest and most remote areas.

The change from Swedish to Russian rule in 1809 was regarded by many as a change for the better. Instead of being a rather neglected part of the kingdom of Sweden, Finland became an autonomous territory, admittedly ruled by a Grand Duke who happened also to be Tsar of Russia, but retaining its own Swedish laws, its own Church and—in theory at least—its own parliamentary institutions. The Finns, whether they spoke Finnish or Swedish, were suddenly forced to realize that they were on their own: Finland was a separate entity and had a frontier round it. In cultural and political circles (which were still, of course, almost exclusively Swedish-speaking) the search for a national identity became a psychological necessity.

The age of romanticism had by now begun in Europe, and

signs of its influence had begun to appear in Sweden and Finland before the end of the eighteenth century. Writers and scholars in many countries had begun to take an interest in ancient ballads and folk poetry, and this had led a number of people in Finland to begin examining the folk poems and legends that existed in great abundance in the Finnish language. Particular interest had been aroused by the researches of Henrik Gabriel Porthan, whose thesis *On Finnish Poetry* (1766) had dealt in some detail with the form and content of the folk poetry known to him. Porthan was also a linguist and historian, and as a result of his influence quite a few enthusiasts began to study the Finnish language and to tour the countryside in search of traditional songs and tales. They were not slow to note the obvious antiquity of much of the poetry they discovered, with its curious mixture of pagan and Christian elements; but even more remarkable was the high poetic value of the material, revealing (as it seemed to them) a streak almost of genius in the unschooled peasantry that had created it. The word 'Finn', on educated lips, began to take on a less derogatory meaning—instead of meaning 'boorish backwoodsman' it awakened thoughts of an ancient culture, a tradition of peasant wisdom and spontaneous artistic creation.

There was one sphere, at least, in which the virtues of the Finns had made themselves evident in a more tangible way. For centuries they had had to take their part in fighting the Swedish king's enemies, and of the quality of the Finns as soldiers nobody had any doubt. The study of folklore was all very well for people who had lived in the countryside and knew the nuances of the language, but for many Finlanders who taught, spoke and felt in Swedish it could never be an absorbing passion. But tales, more or less true, could be told of the courage and heroism of Finnish individuals both in peace and in war, and when at length the new nationalistic feeling began to find expression in literature, round about the 1840s, this was one of its dominant themes.

Meanwhile, during the early years of the new regime, very little change had taken place in the official attitude to the Finnish language. The country was run, under its Russian Governor, by Swedish-speaking civil servants; in 1840 there was still hardly a single Finnish school in the whole country, the university was still exclusively Swedish-speaking, and few of the judges and law-court officials knew any Finnish at all. There was still practically no literature in the language, though a number of attempts had been made to start newspapers in Finnish; some of these had been remarkably successful for a time, but sooner or later they had almost invariably come up against the censorship or other forms of opposition and been forced to cease publication. Yet in spite of conservatism in high places, and cautiousness or even hostility on the part of the Church, the movement for the recognition of Finnish and for its development as a national language had been steadily gaining support.

The strength of the opposition is understandable enough. Quite apart from the entrenched position of the Swedish-speaking officials and intelligentsia—nobody but a crazy enthusiast would wish to change his native language—there was little concrete evidence that the Finnish language *could* be developed into a vehicle suited to all the needs of a civilized modern state. Despite all the efforts of von Becker and other journalistic pioneers, such Finnish prose as had been attempted was for the most part stiff and ponderous, its syntax intractable and even its vocabulary undecided—for there was still much dispute as to which dialect should be adopted. As for poetry, the problem of fitting Finnish stresses and quantities to borrowed metrical forms and rhyme schemes had not yet been satisfactorily solved, and attempts to write sophisticated poetry in the unrhymed trochaic metre of the folk poems had not been particularly successful either.

So it is not really surprising that when the nationalist movement began to gain impetus, towards the middle of the century, it should have found expression very largely in Swedish. (For a parallel we need only recall that Yeats, Synge, and many other representatives of the Irish revival, wrote exclusively in English.) Of the three great men whose names are associated with the birth of Finnish national literature, two—Runeberg and Topelius—wrote in Swedish.

Johan Ludvig Runeberg, a sea-captain's son from a west coast town, would have been a poet of considerable stature even if he had remained all his life in a purely urban and Swedish-speaking environment. But while he was still an undergraduate his holiday work as a private tutor took him to the rural parish of Saarijärvi, where he came into touch with a way of life and a type of character that impressed him deeply. He wrote a long article on the subject, and his picture of the Finnish character soon began to find expression in poems such as *Paavo of Saarijärvi*, *Elk Hunt on Skis* and *Christmas Evening*. His greatest and most popular work was *Tales of Ensign Stål*, a collection of lyrical ballads describing the deeds and adventures of Finnish soldiers in wartime. Runeberg's poems achieve an apparently effortless simplicity and clarity which make them both readable and memorable: he combines the idealism of the romantic with a classical discipline and sense of form. The poems were widely read, and Runeberg's somewhat idealized picture of the Finnish character—simple, blunt, inarticulate, indrawn, yet stubbornly loyal, honest and courageous—imposed itself irresistibly.

The 'Ensign Stål' poems began to appear in 1848. Three years later Zachris Topelius began the publication of a series of historical tales in prose, entitled *Tales of a Field Surgeon*. Topelius, a prolific writer both in prose and in verse, was a full-blooded romantic. His novels and stories gave the Finns a sense of their history, while his poems gave expression to much that was genuinely present in the national character, and in particular to a deep and almost mystical sense of communion with nature that one can still recognize as peculiarly Finnish. (His father had been an enthusiastic collector of Finnish folk poetry, in which this animistic element is strong.) Topelius also played a major role as an educator, and wrote many stories and nature pieces for children. Although these are frankly didactic in intention they are charmingly written, and their author is still affectionately referred to as 'Uncle Topelius'.

Runeberg and Topelius had the advantage of writing in a literary language with its own classical tradition and a range of accepted models for prose and verse composition. It was by now the dream of many, and the conviction of some, that Finnish too might be successfully developed into a flexible literary language capable of serving all the cultural needs of a modern nation. The various dialects had begun to be the subject of serious study, grammars were being written and the language was even be-

FINLAND: AN INTRODUCTION

ginning to be taught in schools and at the University. Since 1831 the Finnish Literature Society had been stimulating public interest in the collection of Finnish folk poetry. This had been going on in a small way ever since the time of Porthan, but now it was eagerly taken up by a growing number of intellectuals; students gave up their vacations to long journeys in remote parts of Finland, hunting out the oldest 'runo-singers' and noting down long passages of verse. It had long been realized that many of these poems dealt with the same legendary heroes or demigods, the chief of whom was Väinämöinen; and from the material collected in many different districts something resembling a complete mythology began to emerge. One of the most ardent of the collectors was Elias Lönnrot, whose travels in search of folk material took him even beyond the political frontier of Finland, into eastern Karelia. It was he whose idea it was to weave a kind of national epic out of the thousands of lines of verse he had collected, much as he believed Homer to have acted in piecing together the legends of the Trojan War.

The first edition of *Kalevala* appeared in 1835; an expanded and rearranged version, containing much newly-collected material, followed in 1849. Out of some 23,000 lines of verse only a few hundred had been 'written in', mostly as connecting material, by Lönnrot himself. The rest was genuine folk poetry, collected over a wide area and consisting partly of narrative episodes, partly of spells and charms. Making his selection from an immense quantity of material, comparing variants and piecing together an 'ideal' version of each episode, Lönnrot arranged his poem so as to begin with the Creation of the world and the birth of Väinämöinen, and end with an allegory of the coming of Christianity. The intervening episodes, into which the spells and charms are woven at suitable points, deal with four principal themes: the rivalry between the heroes of Kaleva and the people of the Northland (Pohjola), the magical skill of Väinämöinen and the smith Ilmarinen, the amorous adventures of the reckless Lemminkäinen, and the tragic story of Kullervo.

The impact of *Kalevala* was tremendous: it was as though Finnish literature had suddenly sprung into being, fully grown. No work by a single individual, whether in prose or verse,

South Harbour waterfront, Helsinki

The morning market, Helsinki

could have had a comparable effect. Throughout the rest of the nineteenth century, and well into the twentieth, it remained the sacred book of the Finns and the inspiration not only of writers, artists and musicians, but also of politicians, educationists, and all who shared the growing faith in a Finland that might one day be fully independent.

Unfortunately *Kalevala* does not translate well: when imitated in English the metre becomes that of Longfellow's *Hiawatha* (which was itself inspired by a German translation of *Kalevala*) and lends itself only too easily to bathos or sheer monotony. The incredibly rich sound of the original, with its subtle stress-patterns, climaxes and cadences, its alliterations and emotional sound-effects, cannot be reproduced. The poem is largely about magic and in particular about the magical power of words; and the poetry is clearly recognizable as a kind of verbal sorcery, designed to spell-bind the listener. Even in translation, however, it is possible to appreciate the contrast between the mighty deeds and miraculous events recorded and the rustic simplicity of the setting: these iron-age heroes live, not in rich palaces, but in lowly farms, where their aged mothers lay down the law and make sure that they eat a good breakfast before setting out.

In 1840-1 Lönnrot brought out *Kanteletar* ('Muse of the Kantele'), an extensive anthology of folk poetry of a more lyrical type. His work as a whole gave Finns a sense not only of the richness of their own language but also of a tradition reaching far back into the past, and proving their possession, as a people, of a certain creative power. But it remained to be seen whether an individual Finnish writer would ever produce a work of genius, and most of the intellectuals were still sceptical.

When Aleksis Kivi, in 1860, published *Kullervo*, the first tragedy written in Finnish, he won a prize of 600 marks from the Finnish Literature Society, but no one realized the position he would come to hold in the history of Finnish literature. His path was not easy: dogged by poverty and ill-health, he met with little recognition until the last few years of his short life. At thirty-six he became incurably insane and he died, penniless, a couple of years later. He is now remembered as the author of the greatest play and the greatest novel in the Finnish language, and his statue stands in a conspicuous position in front of the National Theatre. The play, *Nummisuutarit* ('The Village Cobblers') is a comedy of country life. The influence of Holberg, and more strongly that of Shakespeare, can be seen in the writing, but the play is a highly personal and original creation. It is still frequently performed, and its principal characters, who are depicted realistically and in surprising depth, are so familiar to the Finns that they are often referred to almost as though they were real people.

The novel, *Seitsemän veljestä* ('Seven Brothers'), is of even greater originality. It tells of seven village boys who leave home, not for the great city as they would nowadays, but into the depths of the virgin forest, where they hope to fend for themselves, far from parental and parochial discipline. In their encounters with untamed nature they re-enact (in effect) the history of their earliest Finnish ancestors. After many adventures they return to their home parish, conscious at last of the need to civilize themselves. The characters of the seven brothers, their interaction on each other and the different processes by which each is led to his final decision, are brought out with astonishing skill. The story is told with great humour and great understanding; and in Kivi's prose, mingling the lively dialect of his native district with the dignity of the old Bible translations, Finnish springs to life as a fully-formed literary language. *Kalevala* is not an epic, but Kivi's novel is. Moreover, its utterly unromantic tone provided a necessary corrective to the somewhat idealized and conventionalized national image that had begun to form.

The work of J. V. Snellman, the cultural and political leader of the national movement, is mentioned elsewhere in these pages. During the last thirty years of the century it was clear that the movement was now the most powerful force in the country. Education in Finnish made rapid strides, Finnish newspapers proliferated, and the works of European philosophers, novelists, poets and dramatists became more widely known. Few of the Finnish authors of this period are much read nowadays, but many of them played an important part in the development of the art of writing and in the spread of ideas. Finnish critics attempt, in the German manner, to divide Finnish literature into clearly marked periods with tidy labels such as post-romantic, neo-romantic, early realistic, and so on. But the truth is that while a certain romantic idealism undoubtedly attached itself to the national movement as a whole, the Finns are not and never have been a romantic people.

An author whose work spanned the period from the eighties to the achievement of independence was Juhani Aho, whose early story *The Railway* was translated into English (but is no longer in print). His admirable prose is now, perhaps, a little old-fashioned in its cadences: there is a faint Ruskinian flavour about it. But his work will survive. His novels, particularly *Parson's Wife* (1893), *Spring and Backwater* (1906) and *Juha* (1911), were solid achievements and it is a pity that they are not available in an English translation. Thanks to the many translations of the Russian novels of this period we have a strong sense of the Russian background and the Russian character: of Finland we have no comparable picture, and this Aho could give. In his novels the national image is presented from many angles, quietly and perceptively: it is significant that Aho was also one of the first Finns to write books about travel abroad. He was a master in the evocation of the Finnish landscape and the reflection of its moods in those of his characters.

Among the few Finnish novels to have been translated into English is Linnankoski's *Song of the Blood-red Flower* (1905). This rather lyrically-written novel brings out the Lemminkäinen aspect of the Finnish character: its hero, Olavi, is a personable young lumberjack who finds success with the women almost too easy. He progresses through a series of amorous adventures to a sense of responsibility—it is interesting to see how even in this swashbuckling novel the didactic element makes its appearance, almost, it would seem, against the author's will. Once again we are reminded of the inescapable influence of the Lutheran Church, with its deep seriousness and its emphasis on self-discipline; an influence which has continually served to balance the passionate love of freedom and the deep need for self-assertion that might otherwise have led to an unfettered romanticism.

Social and political questions, during this period, were often aired in drama and fiction, and the 'Finnish image', set in its contemporary context, was seen more clearly but not basically altered. Minna Canth, in the nineties, dealt with such problems in her plays, which showed the influence of Ibsen and are still admired and performed. Among important novelists of the earlier part of this century were Joel Lehtonen and Ilmari Kianto, both of whom combined a romantic feeling for Finland and its people with a realistic psychological approach and a touch of satirical humour. In the plays and short stories of Maria Jotuni both the ideals and the failings of the characters were analysed with ruthless insight, but also with a warm humour born of true compassion. Her people were Finns in a Finnish setting, but first and foremost they were real people. Aino Kallas, married to an Estonian, could have romanticized her new compatriots (they are related to the Finns), but her novels and short stories (one collection has appeared in English under the title of *The White Ship*) became increasingly realistic in their delineation of character and situation.

The writing of fiction was still regarded primarily as a fine art (the purely commercial aspects of the novel had yet to be discovered), and great attention was accordingly paid to prose style. In the work of some writers it almost took precedence over plot. Volter Kilpi, whose elaborately aesthetic prose has remained obstinately untranslatable, might be classed with such writers as Pater or George Moore; yet in a curious way he also foreshadows the future, for he seems to have hit quite independently on the idea of the 'interior monologue'.

Finnish poetry, meanwhile, was less actively concerned with the national image, its business being with the human predicament and the expression of human experience at its deepest level. It would be rash as well as difficult to try to name the dominant themes of Finnish poetry: but certainly one can recognize the animistic approach to nature that has been inherited from the folk-poems; and if there is indeed a dominant image it is that of Kullervo—black, gloomy, defiant and at odds with the universe. During the latter part of the nineteenth century great strides had been made in the handling of metres and rhythms. In the work of Eino Leino craftsmanship was combined with a passionate and rather mystical strain of lyricism, and it is he who stands out as the most vivid personality of the period which followed.

With the achievement of independence in 1917 a great historical landmark had been reached, but it took some time for the effects to be seen in literature. The national image had been created, and it was natural that an independent Finland should wish to affirm and consolidate it rather than to start modifying it straight away. In the civil war the right wing had been overwhelmingly victorious, and the existence of the other side now tended to be glossed over, ignored, or forgotten. A sympathetic understanding of both sides can, however, be found in Sillanpää's novel *Meek Heritage* (1918), of which an English translation exists. Sillanpää was the outstanding Finnish novelist of the inter-war period (he won a Nobel prize in 1939). *Fallen Asleep While Young* (1931) is another of his novels that has been translated into English. On the whole, however, his rather poetical prose defies translation, and the rural settings present an unfamiliar background which it is not the author's concern to elucidate to foreigners. The influence of Maeterlinck can be seen in his work, and his approach to character has sometimes been described as biological rather than psychological.

In the late thirties, almost for the first time, the industrial population of the towns began to make its appearance in fiction, notably in the quiet and deeply sensitive novels of Toivo Pekkanen; but it was not until after the war, in the late forties, that more pronounced left-wing views began to get a hearing.

For English-speaking readers the most easily approachable writer of the post-independence period has been Mika Waltari, who strikes the outsider, at least, as more cosmopolitan in his style and choice of themes than most of his compatriots. His prose goes neatly and satisfactorily into English. *Sinuhe*, a tale of ancient Egypt, is well known in translation and has been filmed. But although the Finns have made him an academician there is sometimes a faintly grudging note in the praise he is given: he has not concerned himself primarily with the national image.

During the inter-war period there was a considerable revival of literature in Swedish, which had become somewhat swamped by the increasing flood of poetry and prose in Finnish. With independence achieved and the two languages firmly given equal official status, the language controversy lost a certain amount of its sting, though it cannot be said to have died down completely till after the Winter War of 1939–40. In lyric poetry, particularly, the importance of the work being done in Swedish came to be increasingly recognized. The poetry of Edith Södergran was discovered by the discriminating, and had an influence on the work of several Finnish poets. Diktonius and Enckell have found appreciative readers not only in their native Finland but also in Sweden. Walentin Chorell, writing in Swedish, is one of the few notable dramatists of the forties and fifties. In fiction, however, the 'Swedo-Finns' have until recently been heavily over-shadowed by their Finnish-speaking colleagues, though the work of Sally Salminen (whose *Katrina* appeared in English and won an international prize) did become fairly widely known abroad.

Since the end of the war, and particularly since about 1960, when the wartime generation came of age, there have been very noticeable changes in the intellectual climate of Finland. Between the wars the national image was touched up and broadened a good deal, but in itself it was sacrosanct and inviolable. From the outsider's point of view the effects on art and literature were sometimes disconcerting: culturally the country appeared to be lost in a kind of pre-Raphaelite mist and dominated by stereotyped Kalevala motifs. Now a new generation (containing a large proportion of war-orphans) has come on the scene and is proceeding, very vigorously, to sweep all this away. Rather suddenly, Finnish literature has become more diversified, more critical, more experimental, and in many ways more cosmopolitan. A national image, changing with the times yet retaining much of the old tradition, will of course continue to be reflected in the work of Finnish writers; but its presentation has ceased to be their primary concern.

NEW WRITERS

KAI LAITINEN

'THE Russians won, but brave little Finland came a good second.' Thus did an ex-soldier, Väinö Linna, a survivor of the Finnish-Russian war, describe its closing stages in his novel *Tuntematon sotilas* (*Unknown Soldier*), his acknowledgment of the incontrovertible fact of Soviet victory humorously depicted in the language of sport.

This sense of the ludicrous pervades all the writings of the self-educated former Tampere cottonmill workman, who served through the fighting as a non-commissioned officer and wrote his book at the age of 34, ten years after the end of the conflict. It described the doings of a small group of soldiers between 1941 and 1944. In it he poked fun at the vocabulary of patriotism and parodied wartime oratorical bombast; he sharply criticized the officer class and, as for the semi-official women's para-military organization, Lotta Svärd, he painted such a picture of it that he was accused of dishonouring Finnish womanhood. The story aroused a storm of discussion, argument and indignation. Admired by some, reviled by others, it broke up friendships and parted acquaintances; but it was read—everywhere, and to the tune of 400,000 copies. No other Finnish publication has ever approached such figures so quickly.

Linna did not rest on his oars, but continued with a second and longer novel, called *Täällä Pohjantähden alla* (*Under the Northern Star*), named after a melancholy century-old song. It appeared in three parts over the years 1959–62, and its theme is life in a small village, seen through the eyes of a poverty-stricken crofter family, between the end of the 1800s and the close of the Second World War. Its subject, so beloved of Finnish writers, is humanity, its treatment realistic and humorous as in Linna's earlier work and as in the classical fiction of Aleksis Kivi (*Seitsemän Veljestä, The Seven Brothers*) and Joel Lehtonen (*Putkinotko*). This tale was also a success, arousing the same wide attention because of the author's ability to make the reader see life through his eyes. Thus by describing the origin and growth of class hatred as seen from the Red side, culminating in the civil war and tragic defeat of 1918, Linna successfully modified hitherto widely-held prejudices and, as a reviewer expressed it, rehabilitated the Red soldier.

Linna was not alone in dealing with recent great wartime upheavals. They aroused the attention of a man eight years younger, a publisher's clerk, Veijo Meri, who himself had been too young to take part in hostilities. He had grown up in an n.c.o.'s family, had lived in garrison towns all over Finland and at the start of the Winter War of 1939-40 was quite near the Soviet frontier on the Karelian Isthmus. He knew both army and soldiers from the professional angle, as if himself a conscript. He wove the topics, anecdotes and events personally known to him into tales characterized by dead-pan humour. He made no attempt to use the artifice of traditional fiction as had Linna, but preferred by stylistic methods to portray war as at once hideous, grotesque and laughable. He is a kindred spirit to Charlie Chaplin and Jaroslav Hasek, creator of the Good Soldier Schweik. His characters are always on the move, always plagued by uncertainty. When they do the right thing it is by mistake, and when their intentions are good they make a hash of it. Mostly they survive, often fearfully battered, but still alive.

Veijo Meri's most famous novel, *Manillaköysi* (*The Manila Rope*) is about a soldier, Joose, who finds a length of fallen cord lying on a road and decides to smuggle it home from the front. To escape detection he winds it round his body, but during the long train journey it starts to chafe him and his leave becomes a nightmare. By the time he arrives, half dead, at his destination, he is so physically weak that the rope has to be cut free. But the description of Joose's vicissitudes is only half the story. Equally important is what he hears on the train—chronicles and anecdotes which, like the many-coloured pieces of a mosaic, Meri coalesces into an overall picture of war, with all its cruelty, tragi-comedy, blind chance and what quality you will but one: heroism. He has used this same narrative style in all his fifteen books, but has never quite been able to match the unique and original qualities of *Manillaköysi*.

The third key-figure of post-war Finnish literature is Paavo Haavikko, neither a Tolstoyan epic writer like Linna nor a master of the absurd such as Meri. He is a poet, and above all a creator of the language of verse. The manager of a large publishing house, he has to his credit economic achievements which many a businessman might envy, and bohemianism is quite alien to him. As a poet he is markedly intellectual, a man of acute and perceptive vision. Because his output covers a wide variety of themes, he is not easy to classify. He often displays a strong visionary streak combined with a wealth of whimsical poetic imagery and metaphor. Another talent is his knowledge of the world and awareness of life's complexities. In his enthusiasm for historical and political topics, he often manipulates them so as to dovetail past and present with surprising and ironical results. A dramatist and prose writer as well as a poet, one of his plays is *Agricola ja kettu* (*Agricola and the Fox*), in which the chief character, a sixteenth-century bishop and bible translator, becomes a pawn in the struggle between the King of Sweden and the Tsar of Russia. He uses this situation to examine and describe the plight of a small nation enmeshed in a great power conflict of interests. This at least is how the plot was interpreted by Kalle Holmberg, director of Helsingin Kaupunginteatteri (Helsinki Municipal Theatre), who disguised Stalin as Ivan the Terrible, while a peace delegate obviously represented former president Paasikivi. In his poem *Neljätoista hallitsijaa* (*Fourteen Rulers*), whose theme is the history of Byzantium and whose main protagonist is the servant of many emperors, a court historian, Michael Psellos, Haavikko deals once again with political realities. Power, says an abdicating monarch in his poem, is a maze where penetration is difficult and escape impossible; and in the description of such labyrinths lies Haavikko's special talent.

Linna, Meri and Haavikko all write in the majority language, Finnish, but many outstanding authors have Swedish as their mother tongue. In theory the entire Scandinavian reading public should be open to them, but this rarely happens. In outlook, choice of subject and delineation of character they belong to Finnish literature and their work reaches Finnish-language readers in translation. Among the important younger writers, a contemporary of Meri and Haavikko, is Christer Kihlman. This author made his name with a novel called *Se upp Salige* (*Watch Out, Blessed One*), in which he describes the struggle of an insignificant editorial assistant on a Swedish-language newspaper to reconcile a bourgeois scale of values with his innate personal honesty. In his next book, Kihlman deals with the situation of a cloistered family and the difficult progress of two brothers to maturity. The same search for truth displayed in his earlier fiction is once more clearly apparent. 'Writing is seeking', says one of the brothers; and in all his social and political essays Kihlman, a man of left-wing views and a relentless self-critic, has indeed continued and expanded his exploration.

The list of outstanding modern Finnish authors does not stop with Linna, Meri, Haavikko and Kihlman. A number of impressive newcomers can be named, among them a lyric-prose writer of the young generation called Pentti Saarikoski, and a leading prose writer of the 1960s, Hannu Salama, whose novel *Juhannustanssit* (*Midsummer Dance*) aroused wide discussion and caused a law suit. Other members of the Finnish literary new wave are Eila Pennanen, Eeva Joenpelto, Eeva-Liisa Manner, Tuomas Anhava and Antti Hyry. However, in one respect Linna, Meri, Haavikko and Kihlman are prototypes—they show the sort of problems post-war Finnish literature has examined and the types of artistic solutions it has adopted. As Linna wrote in 1964, 'Life and the world exist; and the role of art is not to take refuge in isolation and self-containment, but to fulfil its task as recorder and interpreter of the affairs of mankind.'

SIBELIUS IN AMERICA AND BRITAIN

ERIK TAWASTSTJERNA

'Well, we shall see how things go in America. There are many things against me but I am so much better equipped to deal with them.'

Sibelius was in good spirits when on 19 May, a Tuesday, he stepped on board the Norddeutscher Lloyds double-propeller mailboat Wilhelm II at Bremerhaven. The next day, at eight minutes past six in the evening, the steamship passed Cherbourg's breaker while Sibelius sat in his cabin and went through the orchestral parts of The Oceanides. During the rest of the journey he enjoyed the ocean waves and watched in vain for a whale, but he had to

FINLAND: AN INTRODUCTION

rest content with the sight of fifty-odd flying-fish who passed the ship. To pave the way for his arrival, the New York Tribune gave prominence to an illustrated article by Henry Krehbiel that Sunday under the headline 'Finland sends musical envoy'.

On arrival in New York the following Tuesday, the 26 May, he stayed in his cabin for an hour so as to avoid the horde of reporters that met the boat. Naturally they succeeded in getting hold of him but, with the help of his American host Carl Stoeckel, he managed eventually to get away. A suite had been reserved for him at the Essex Hotel where he was introduced to Mrs Ellen Battell-Stoeckel. Mr Stoeckel described their first encounter:

'He took her hand, and kissed it three times respectfully and graciously, following all the dictates of etiquette. As far as his outer appearance is concerned, I would imagine that he was about five foot ten or eleven in height with a well-built, well-proportioned frame. His forehead was handsomely-formed and he made a distinguished impression. He paid careful attention to his wardrobe. His suit, linen and shoes were all of the best quality and cut. His hair was very short and he was not at all like the picture one generally imagines of a foreign composer. If I had passed him in the street I would have taken him for a professional gentleman, possibly a doctor or a civil engineer.'

Stoeckel was a gourmet but in Sibelius he found his match:

'We went to Delmonico's for supper as this restaurant was famous for its fresh caviare. We ordered some of this delicacy which delighted Sibelius who was good enough to say that it was finer than anything that could be found in a Russian hotel. We ate grilled salmon since the composer liked fish in any form and followed this with fried chicken and potatoes à la Delmonico and for the composer a green salad with tomatoes.'

The rehearsals began on Thursday at Carnegie Hall. Dressed

in a brand-new white flannel suit he mounted the rostrum and was greeted with applause by the Festival Orchestra which numbered seventy-five musicians chosen from the Philharmonic Society and the Metropolitan Opera. Before him, Henry Hadley had rehearsed his new tone poem, Lucifer. Stoeckel watched how Sibelius with his professional eye,

> 'carefully studied the orchestra while he was waiting his turn to conduct, and it was remarkable how he singled out the best players among the violinists, violists, cellists, double-bass players, flautists, clarinettists and horn-players. He didn't make a single mistake. He began the rehearsal with Pohjola's Daughter. At first he was a trifle nervous but this soon passed and it became apparent that he had complete mastery over the players. Afterwards he went through the new work, The Oceanides, which was totally unlike anything the musicians had ever played before. I believe that at first they didn't understand it at all, to judge by their remarks. But the following morning having gone through it three times they were wholly enthusiastic: the music's beauty seemed to grow at each hearing.'

On Friday afternoon Sibelius and Stoeckel took the train to Norfolk. When Sibelius went through Grand Central Station he exclaimed 'What a concert hall this would make if only one had an orchestra of 200 or 300 men!' During the journey he was fascinated by the name of the Housatonic River and intoned the Indian-sounding syllables several times. They arrived in Norfolk that evening, and Sibelius was taken to the White House, the residence of the Stoeckels which had been built in 1798 by Mrs Stoeckel's grandfather, Joseph Battell. He was put in the old blue room, the former library on the first floor. Sibelius called the White House 'The Home of Poetry'. 'I'm enjoying myself. For once I am sufficiently well looked after. Negroes, whites, and maids of all colours.'

The 1914 Festival opened on the 2nd June in traditional fashion

FINLAND: AN INTRODUCTION

with a choral of Robbins Battell followed by Hadley's tone poem, Lucifer *and Bruch's Oratorio* Arminius. *Stoeckel noticed that Sibelius didn't care for* Arminius *but that* Lucifer *made a good impression on him. The next day, after a brilliant performance of Handel's* Messiah, *found Sibelius and Hadley in deep conversation.*

Sibelius made the most systematic use of his rehearsal time; Tuesday morning he devoted specially to Pohjola's Daughter *and* The Oceanides *which were new to the orchestra. The following day he devoted to more familiar pieces and paid special attention to the brass effects which he wanted to have rounded, polished and powerful without explosive impact. So came the day of the concert, the last day of the Festival, Thursday 4th June. As on every other morning at the White House, he rose early and was shaved by a barber who had been engaged at his express wish.*

When the evening came he set out for the concert hall; he felt nervous but assured Stoeckel that this usually went as soon as he had mounted the podium. The conductor's rostrum was decorated with the American and Finnish flags. 'The Lion [the Finnish emblem] was there', *noted Sibelius with satisfaction. The orchestra quietened and he raised his baton for* Pohjola's Daughter. 'As a conductor Sibelius was graceful but at the same time powerful; he didn't bother to beat time: one, two, three, four. His gestures reminded one rather of a man reciting a powerful poem,' *wrote one of the critics. The programme continued with the Suite from* King Christian II, The Swan of Tuonela, Finlandia, Valse Triste *and, as a final item,* The Oceanides. 'After the closing number the composer was greeted with an ovation the like of which I've never heard anywhere else', *wrote Stoeckel.* 'The least excited in the hall was presumably the composer himself. He bowed several times in the distinguished fashion that was typical of him and placed his laurels on the rostrum.' *Afterwards he sank exhausted into an armchair with tears in his eyes at the back of Stoeckel's box and listened to the second half of the programme. At the end of the concert he stood while the orchestra and choir sang* Our Country *the Finnish National Anthem, and* America

Forever. '*He was very moved and took my hand saying, "Finland thanks you and your wife, I take the performance of our national song as a mark of honour not for me but for my country."* '

The following Sunday he spent in New York and read with delight Krehbiel's article on the Norfolk Festival which concentrated on Sibelius. Krehbiel associated The Oceanides with Aeschylus' Prometheus Unbound. '*The Finnish composer stands before the world as a nationalist and enshrines the ideals of his country in the same way as Tchaikovsky represents Russia, Dvořák Bohemia, Saint-Saëns France, Elgar England and Richard Strauss Germany,*' he wrote of Pohjola's Daughter. This was probably the first and only occasion on which Sibelius was compared with Saint-Saëns!

Olin Downes wrote that over the last fifteen years he had only felt that he was in the presence of genius on three occasions: when Richard Strauss performed his own compositions in Philadelphia and Boston in 1904; when Toscanini conducted Tristan and Isolde in Boston in 1910, and now when Jean Sibelius conducted his own work in Norfolk. The only anti-Sibelian was presumably the composer Loeffler, known for his remark to Downes: 'Sibelius? Sibelius! My dear Downes, I must tell you the truth. I prefer music without cod-liver-oil.'

On the evening of 15th June Sibelius was the guest of the Stoeckels at Delmonico's for the last time, 'Liebe alte Heimat' as he dubbed the restaurant. The meal began with 'a healthy portion of the most delicious caviare that had just arrived from Russia via Paris' and ended with champagne which Sibelius mixed with sodawater. The next morning Sibelius went to the Hamburg-America line docks, where the President Grant was ready for departure. Through his connections Stoeckel had managed to secure Sibelius an officer's cabin to himself as accommodation on the boat was fully booked. As a final gesture he bought presents for Sibelius's family: a ring set with a jewel for Mrs Sibelius and toys for the children.

Sibelius seemed quiet and subdued, and Stoeckel tried in vain

FINLAND: AN INTRODUCTION

to cheer him up. They inspected the luxurious ocean liner together and when the time came to take their farewells, everyone felt terribly upset. Sibelius kissed Mrs Stoeckel's hand many times and hugged his host. From the President Grant, 'Finland's musical envoy' cabled his thanks to his host which Stoeckel answered. There had without any doubt been something of 'A Thousand and One Nights' about Stoeckel's hospitality and, like another Haroun-al-Raschid, he had fulfilled all Sibelius's wishes; all except one. He had not succeeded in conjuring forth a whale.

AN ENGLISH POSTSCRIPT

The description of Sibelius' journeys to England is spread over many chapters in the composer's biography which I am engaged in writing. His five concert tours in England in 1905, 1908, 1909, 1912 and 1921 offer an almost inexhaustible source of material, rich both in personal detail and in relation to the history of music. Critics and the general public took to him with sympathy and understanding right from the beginning. As early as 1905, Ernest Newman wrote of the First Symphony that 'Mr Sibelius in Finland' could succeed where Grieg had failed: in deriving from a national lyrical idiom 'the malleable foundations of greater and more highly organized forms of music.'

When Sibelius conducted the First Symphony in Birmingham in December, 1905, at the invitation of Granville Bantock, Newman felt himself 'transported into a quite new civilization'. Seven years later, Sibelius performed in Birmingham again, this time with his Fourth. This was a controversial piece at the time, which the Vienna Philharmonic refused to play that same autumn, although it had been included in the programme by none less than the famous conductor, Weingartner. But Newman understood this music, and he thought that the development of Sibelius' style towards simplicity and concentration was related to similar traits in some of the most imaginative composers of the day. By comparing Sibelius with Schönberg in this connection—to the latter's disadvan-

tage—Newman sowed the first seeds of one of the most bitter musical feuds of the century.

Sibelius' English friends give glimpses of his personality: 'An arresting, formidable-looking fellow, born of dark rock and Northern forest . . .'. Thus he is remembered by Arnold Bax during the London festival of 1909. Mrs Rosa Newmarch, his true friend and protagonist, got this impression of him in the midst of the social whirl: 'I know you are a bit emotional about life's trivia, but very confident about things that matter.' And after she had met Rachmaninov, she wrote to Sibelius: 'He is reserved . . . nearly as reserved as you are.'

BEFORE AND AFTER SIBELIUS

SEPPO HEIKINHEIMO

'I THOUGHT I was arriving in a remote provincial town in which I would find hardly any music of a very high standard. So it came as an even greater surprise that Helsinki is a lively musical city offering both variety and high standards.' These words, reputedly spoken by the Soviet conductor Kiril Kondrashin after his first visit to Helsinki in 1968, reflect what is undoubtedly a widely held view among those in the world's major musical centres. And the best remedy, as in Kondrashin's case, is a visit to the city itself.

But before setting off, the visitor would be well advised to find out some of the basic facts about the country he is going to visit. Finland's musical history is relatively short; it can thus be condensed in a few sentences before surveying the current musical scene, in many ways worth describing.

Early Finnish music was predominantly the realm of the lower classes. Subordinate first to Sweden and then to the Russian tsars, Finland had no court of her own to nurture a higher musical culture. Folk music was, however, extremely rich, and was complemented by the *piae cantiones* songs, especially popular among students. In 1790, the Turku Music Society was founded in what was then the capital, and from this event dates a developing interest in more sophisticated music. This society, in a small university town, had about 900 members, 70 of them active players. The society's music library contained about 2,000 works, and a close watch was kept on what was happening abroad. Many works of note in Western music were given in Turku only a year or two after their first performance. In the nineteenth century Turku's musical tradition was carried on in Helsinki, after it became the capital of the Grand Duchy of Finland under the Russian tsars. Finland's first leading musical figure was Fredrik Pacius, who led the society founded in Helsinki from 1835 onwards.

The real turning point in Finland's musical history, however, was 1882, which marked the opening of the Helsinki Music College (now the Sibelius Academy) by Jean Sibelius' first teacher, Martin Wegelius. It was also in this year that Robert Kajanus formed his symphony orchestra, now the Helsinki Philharmonic Orchestra. The founding of these two institutions provided the vital impulse for the development of music in Finland; without them Jean Sibelius could not have developed in such a favourable setting.

The creation of these cultural establishments came at a time of general national awakening, whose most important feature was the raising of the Finnish language to a status equal to Swedish, until then the only language spoken by the educated classes. This movement was lent further impetus by the flowering of Finnish folklore. The stimulus provided by *Kalevala*, the Finnish national epic, was tremendous; it left its mark on all branches of the arts and is also clearly reflected in the early works of Jean Sibelius, the bulk of which are directly or indirectly inspired by *Kalevala*.

The assertion of her own culture and national identity—crowned by independence in 1917—had such a strong influence on Finland that for many decades it led to an exaggerated sense of self-sufficiency. In the 1920s a group began to make its voice heard in the arts—especially literature—with the highly revealing catch-phrase 'windows open to Europe'. This relatively small group, calling itself the 'torch bearers', remained a minority however. Even further from the mainstream of public opinion were the few Finnish composers who tried to compose music in the spirit dictated by international trends during the period between the two world wars.

The composer to suffer most was Aarre Merikanto (1893–1958), son of the popular National-Romantic composer Oskar Merikanto, whose expressionist works got such a cold reception that he was compelled to adjust his style to suit the Finnish spirit of the times. Above all this spirit was marked by a disproportionate adoration of Sibelius. This giant so overshadowed his contemporaries that their merits have only begun to be noted since his death. Thus Merikanto's opera *Juha* had to wait over four decades for its first performance. Finally raised from oblivion, this drama set on the border between Finland and Russia, sometimes on one side, sometimes the other, and reflecting the tension at a personal level, has been recognized as one of the masterpieces of Finnish opera literature. The surging power of the music recalls Janáček in many places, yet it has a flavour that is genuinely Finnish. Merikanto's *Juha* has been a great success at the Savonlinna Opera Festivals, of which more will be said later.

The shadow of Sibelius not only had a detrimental effect on his contemporaries at home, but it restricted their chances of making their voices heard abroad. The person to suffer least from this was probably Yrjö Kilpinen (1892–1959), who concentrated almost exclusively on Lied and whose rugged and masculine songs have won their firmest foothold in German-speaking countries. In addition to Finnish, Kilpinen set a lot of Swedish and German texts to music. The composer to be overshadowed most, and unjustly, by Sibelius was Leevi Madetoja (1887–1947), whose brooding and introvert expression is a true reflection of one aspect of the Finnish character. In complete contrast to Madetoja is Uuno Klami (1900–61), representing the high-spiritedness of the Karelians and whose colourful orchestral works of French influence stand out among Finnish music.

Looking back on the period before the Second World War, Sibelius can also be used as a starting point in assessing musical life in general. To exaggerate slightly, though not without justification, one can say that the international reputation won for Finland helped those sitting on the national coffers and suffering from the general malady of all fund distributors: an unwillingness to devote money to the arts. Many of the basic investments vital to music were never made, under the facile pretext: 'after all, we *have* got Sibelius'. Musical training was to a large extent neglected throughout the country, as was the development of national publishing activities. But to be fair, Sibelius' period of active creativity did not extend very far into the years of Finnish independence. Thus the Finnish arts authorities cannot be blamed for the national misfortune that all Sibelius' major works have been published abroad. On the other hand an unforgivable oversight was committed when it comes to the rest of Finnish music, which, with very few exceptions, remained at the manuscript stage. The slow progress now being made in publishing cannot make up for past oversights, as a number of manuscripts have been irrevocably lost.

Broadly speaking music did not really begin to thrive in Finland until the early 1950s; the 1940s passed in war and repairing the damage wrought by it, leaving but meagre resources available for music and the arts. The situation came to a head in 1966 when the Sibelius Academy became an establishment supported entirely from state funds, in the same way as the universities. Formerly by statute a private enterprise, though in receipt of state aid, it is still the only university-level music college in the whole of Finland. A year later, in 1967, a law on music colleges came into force guaranteeing Finland's other music colleges much more secure government aid than was previously the case. Though proportionately small, this aid is a regular source of income for the 46 colleges serving a population of less than five million.

Another notable improvement was the law on grants to artists that came into force at the beginning of 1970. This law provides financial security for slightly more than one hundred Finnish artists a year in the form of one-, three- and five-year grants. About one fifth of these are awarded to musicians every year. The one-year grants are intended for young people, the three- and five-year grants for artists who have already demonstrated their 'creative ability'. This system, crowned by a number of artist-professorships awarded for a specific term, is a notable improvement, since the grants previously awarded were mainly in the hands of numerous private foundations of slender resources.

Despite these changes, the social standing of the musician in Finland has been relatively poor until very recently, as a result of which the most talented students have usually turned to other professions. In particular there has been a shortage of string players, as is the case all over Western Europe. There has also

FINLAND: AN INTRODUCTION

been some difficulty in recruiting music teachers for schools, though there have recently been some signs that the situation is improving.

The shortage of string players was particularly noticeable all over Finland in the 1960s, when existing orchestras expanded and many new ones were formed. The Finnish National Opera, for example, founded its own orchestra (admittedly only fifty strong), having formerly relied on the Helsinki Philharmonic. As the Helsinki Philharmonic also took on a further fifteen string players in the same decade (the orchestra at present has a total of ninety-five players) the country's small reserve of musicians was understandably put to the test. The provincial orchestras suffered most of all.

In other respects, too, Helsinki has come to play too dominant a role in Finnish musical activities. Finland's only professional opera company operates in the capital, as do the country's two full-sized symphony orchestras, the Helsinki Philharmonic already mentioned and the Finnish Radio Symphony Orchestra. Recitals, which here as elsewhere in Europe are losing ground to radio, television and the recording industry, are heard only sporadically outside Helsinki, mainly under the auspices of provincial summer festivals. Radio and television (likewise the Finnish art recording industry slowly getting off the ground at the beginning of the 1970s) are the very media on which most hopes are pinned as the promoters of musical understanding. Unfortunately, the use of these influential channels is by no means assured since transmission hours and the necessary funds are subjects of a bitter tug-of-war among those at the state radio company who decide on such matters.

The musical battle being waged on all fronts is divided into two opposed camps, one of which defends the conditions vital to classical music, while the other sees this as a bourgeois relic, music for an elite, hardly worthy of state support. The very expression 'bourgeois relic' reveals that the people who have adopted it are politically left wing, for the most part members of the younger generation. It would be in the interests of the whole nation if politics were removed from the battle and the two opposed factions came to terms. One factor that has proved a great aid in levelling out the musical habits of different social groups is the fast-developing popularity of summer music festivals. Two of these in particular, the Savonlinna Opera Festival and the Kaustinen Folk Music Festival, have attracted vast audiences. Thus, any claims that the Savonlinna festival appeals only to an opera-going elite, for example, have been totally disproved.

The Savonlinna Opera Festival in July, revived in 1967 and set in medieval Olavinlinna castle, draws people from all over Finland. The programme always includes two works, one a repeat from the year before and the other a new production. The most notable artistic performance at the Festival has been the opera *Juha* by Aarre Merikanto. The Kaustinen Folk Music Festival, also still in its youth, has outdone the Savonlinna Opera Festival ten times over in general popularity: as a rule more than fifty thousand people have crowded into this little Ostrobothnian village to listen to round-the-clock performances of folk music.

More 'normal' in character, yet nevertheless musically interesting, are the Helsinki Festival in August-Septemper and the Jyväskylä Festival in July. The Helsinki Festival provides a wide range of events in all branches of the arts, while Jyväskylä, a university town in Central Finland, features chamber music of the highest standard coupled with interesting congresses on topical themes. Other festival towns are Turku (which boasts both an 'ordinary' music festival and a mammoth rock festival) and Pori where, for one week in summer, the spotlight is on jazz.

These festivals, along with the normal season, provide visitors with a chance to get to know Finland's best musicians, though Finnish conductors in particular have already won themselves an international reputation. Without comparing figures for other countries I would go so far as to claim that Finland has acquitted herself extremely honourably in producing one top-rank conductor per million inhabitants. The best-known name is without doubt the brilliant winner of the first Herbert von Karajan competition in 1969, Okko Kamu—a self-taught conductor who has risen from first violin in a string quartet and leader of the National Opera Orchestra to international fame. In the summer of 1971, Kamu became chief conductor to the Finnish Radio

FINLAND: AN INTRODUCTION

Symphony Orchestra, replacing Paavo Berglund who, after moulding this orchestra into a first-rate group of players over the ten years he was with them, resigned in order to be able to concentrate on his growing international activities. Two other leading Finnish conductors are Jorma Panula, conductor of the Helsinki Philharmonic, and Leif Segerstam. The latter, like Kamu, represents the young generation of conductors and in a short time has risen to a position of honour at the Stockholm and West Berlin operas.

Apart from conductors Finland has found another important musical export in her opera singers, the best known being Martti Talvela and Tom Krause, now living in Hamburg, and Kim Borg, who has chosen Copenhagen as his base. When it comes to Finnish instrumentalists, however, the tale is not so glorious. The only Finnish player to aspire to an international career—yet one all the more promising—is the brilliant young 'cellist Arto Noras.

Although it is now more than a decade since the death of Sibelius and his radiance no longer has such a constricting effect on other Finnish composers, it has nevertheless been relatively difficult for them to gain international recognition. Most successful in this respect are the illustrious pair Erik Bergman (1911–) and Joonas Kokkonen (1921–). Bergman has been one of the major pioneers of serial music in Finland; one of Finland's leading choral conductors, he has produced a wealth of interesting choral music. In following modern trends Joonas Kokkonen has been more cautious than Bergman; starting from the 'conservative modernism' of Bartok he has developed a style of his own, the dominant features of which are the iron logic of his motif thinking and a translucent use of the orchestra that is skilful yet not forced for the sake of effect.

An equally illustrious pair are to be found in the next generation, too. Einojuhani Rautavaara (1928–) and Aulis Sallinen (1935–) both write in a distinctive style yet both are musicians in the good old sense of the word. Of the two Rautavaara is more passionate; his list of compositions includes works representing the most varied of styles, from the most highly theoretical serialism to the ultimate in Neo-romanticism. All his works are characterized by the richness of his musical invention and brilliant realization.

The qualities of Aulis Sallinen's music are more subtle: his trump cards are his uncompromising sincerity and his exceptionally firm grasp of formal logic—features that lead the listener to say 'here is a real composer', after hearing any of his works.

At the moment the youngest generation of composers is represented by Erkki Salmenhaara (1941–) and Pehr Henrik Nordgren (1944–), the former influenced by Ligeti, a brooding composer striving towards neo-simple grandeur, the latter given to a lush, harmonious style, a conservative modernist yet with an interesting style of his own.

In the early years of the 1970s future prospects for Finnish music look promising. Musical education is at last gathering impetus and beginning to bear fruit in all the various sectors. The activeness and independence of style of Finnish composers—and naturally there are many more than the few mentioned here—promise interesting results in the future. And perhaps the crowning of all this is that after a wait of more than fifty years, longer even than Finland has been independent, the capital at last has a concert hall worthy of Sibelius.

All that Finland and her capital lack at the beginning of the 1970s is a decent opera house, the building of which may well be in the hands of the political decision-makers in this decade. We can only believe and hope that the Finnish National Opera will finally be able to move out of the cramped quarters of a former garrison theatre—a relic of tsarist times—into something more fitting. It is what the Opera's excellent singers and, indeed, Finland's musical public as a whole deserve.

PAINTING AND SCULPTURE

JOHN BOULTON SMITH

THE Finns are an artistic people. The visitor walking round Helsinki will quickly be struck by this. He will see architecture of character and an abundance of twentieth-century sculpture. When he visits a Finnish home the walls will very likely be covered with original pictures and although many of these will not be masterpieces it will be at least evident that Finns like to have 'real' pictures round them. He will probably already have seen modern Finnish textiles and other crafts in his own country and he will see from the Finnish museums that these have old and strong roots. In the past Finnish art has nearly always been closely linked with the folk-crafts and, except perhaps for some centuries during the Middle Ages, it is only in comparatively modern times that the fine arts have really stood out on their own.

Strong artistic creativity in Finland goes back to prehistoric times and some beautiful animal sculptures from the Stone Age exist. Finnish folk-lore is very old indeed and in the *Kalevala*—the national epic assembled from old folk-ballads—figurative drawing and sculpture are described. Nothing quite like these pieces has survived but many other early articles have, notably woven or carved ones, often executed with real taste and skill.

The coming of Christianity in the twelfth century opened Finland up to cultural influences from outside and created a demand for an extensive new field of art. Early churches were built of wood and little remains of them. But in the next century the Catholic Church became stronger and stone churches started to appear. They were embellished with frescoes and gilded and painted wooden statues, giving the interiors a rich and colourful appearance. The style of this art came usually from north Germany, either directly or through Sweden. Work of the foreigners was copied by the local artists; usually the native product has less smooth sophistication than the import and instead a more rugged and primitive quality which can have great dignity and charm. In the treatment of the figures many naive and unselfconscious touches come out, particularly in the 'morality' subjects, where homely, grotesque devils carry out duties often attributed to them by folk-tales. The scenes with figures are usually framed by richly garlanded ornamentation.

Plate 52 shows the east wall of Rymättylä Church, near Turku. The paintings, executed around 1520, illustrate the Last Judgement and are based on a woodcut from Central Europe. Christ is shown enthroned on a rainbow, with the lily of mercy by His right hand and the sword of justice by His left. The Virgin and St John the Baptist kneel in intercession for humanity, while the dead rise from their graves to be taken to their ultimate destinations. Below are the twelve apostles. Woodcarving has traditionally been strong in the Baltic. Here again the Finnish artists interpreted the foreign examples with naive sincerity. The carving from Hollola Church, *c*. 1480 (Plate 51) demonstrates a sensitivity to decorative shapes, which are combined with the characterful local types of the figures in a way that is most appealing.

Soon after the date of these works, the Reformation came to Finland. Although the change-over to the new faith was a comparatively gentle one, church art ceased, except in the remoter, northerly parts of the country. But throughout the ensuing centuries folk-art continued to flourish.

With the beginning of the nineteenth century the position of art began to change radically. Throughout Europe it was to be a century of reawakened nationalism and patriotism, many artists and writers going for inspiration to the heroic legends of their countries' pasts. Finland was no exception. The writers were the first to do this, as in Lönnrot's collection of the *Kalevala*. Finnish painting and sculpture were slower in reawakening and for the first part of the century most of it remained rather provincial. In

FINLAND: AN INTRODUCTION

1846 the Finnish Arts Association was instituted; exhibitions were organized and a school and an art gallery founded. The most enterprising artists went abroad for their advanced training and, in mid-century, Düsseldorf, with its contemporary fame for romantic sentimental realism, was the favourite centre. By the 1870s this had shifted to Paris, the example being set by Albert Edelfelt. Edelfelt was an able painter of a variety of subjects, especially strong in his portraits, and his work put Finnish art on a respectable European level as never before. Perhaps it was necessary for his generation to achieve this standard of international proficiency on which the succeeding one could build more confident individual national expression. The sculptor Ville Vallgren, one year younger than Edelfelt, was also able to achieve a modest reputation abroad in an international idiom, with his art-nouveau statuettes.

With the last two decades of the century national romantic art blossomed. The most important painter was Akseli Gallen-Kallela (1865–1931), the contemporary and friend of Sibelius. Gallen-Kallela's art is completely concerned with Finland. Nevertheless, he spent some time in Paris, Berlin and London where he seems to have been more interested in the contemporary developments of symbolism, art-nouveau and the arts and crafts revival than in the Impressionists and their followers. The 'Great black woodpecker' of 1893 (Plate 57) seems near the heart of his work. It was painted when he was starting to leave the straightforward realism of his early works for something more simplified and stylized, and it vividly expresses the loneliness and vastness of the Finnish landscape. The artist has described the red of the bird's head as crying out as a symbol of a living being in the wilderness. It is interesting that he has enclosed the picture in a frame painted with decorative ornamentation based on forms from nature and it underlines his growing interest in craft work. Gallen-Kallela's love for the Finnish spirit comes out too in his many pictures based on the *Kalevala*, a theme which was to absorb him for most of his life. Among the most impressive are 'Joukahainen's Revenge', 'The Defence of the Sampo' and 'Kullervo's Departure for the Wars'.

Other artists were also occupying themselves with national

and folk subjects as, for example, the painters Hugo Simberg, Juho Rissanen and Pekka Halonen. Hugo Simberg (1873–1917) is principally a master on a small scale (although he also painted some frescoes). Probably his best-known pictures are of Death and small devils; they suggest a connection with medieval Finnish church paintings, (many of which were being restored during this era) and also contemporary international symbolist subjects. But Simberg saw them in an utterly personal way; they can have a whimsical poetry, as in 'Death on Skates' (Plate 58), or humour, as when Death asks the artist to draw pictures on his scythe. He also has a real lyric talent for landscape and made some very evocative drawings of the Finnish scene.

Another of Finland's most original artists was Helena Schjerfbeck (1862–1946). Schjerfbeck's originality is not connected with any obviously national Finnish spirit—most of her paintings are of figures, domestic interiors or still-lifes—but is in the personal poetry with which she sees her subject and her sensitive and individual technique. Recognized as brilliantly talented in her youth, then forced by ill-health to lead a retiring existence in middle age, she was 'rediscovered' in the 1930s as one of the best modern Scandinavian painters. Her paintings, usually on an intimate scale, concentrate on increasing simplification as she gets older. 'Girls Reading', of 1907 (Plate 54), is typical of her middle period, with its crisp, clipped drawing, precise disposition of shapes on the canvas and subtle colour relationships.

At the turn of the century Finnish art had much to be self-confident about. A number of talented artists were working in individual styles and an image of Finland was starting to emerge. At the Paris World Exhibition of 1900 the contribution by Finnish artists was well received. But only eight years later there was a change and when the best Finnish work was again sent to Paris it severely criticized for being cold and colourless. The artists were shocked by this criticism and seven of them banded together in a group, later called the Septem, with the intention of reforming Finnish art on the basis of the brilliant colour of the French Impressionists and their successors. The leaders were Magnus Enckell and A. W. Finch. By brightening their colours and abandoning most national romantic subjects the Septem gave a new direction to Finnish art at the beginning of the century.

Only a few years later another group was formed which was to prove even more dominant than the Septem. This was the November group. The work of the different members was in fact very varied, but it is possible to summarize some general characteristics. The November group generally accepted the brighter colours introduced by the Septem, but added to this some of the formal qualities of Cézanne and even a little from the Cubists. But, still more important, some of them carried on the earlier interest in national 'primitive' subjects, now treating them with the aggressive accents of modern Expressionism. Outstanding among these artists was Tyko Sallinen (1879–1955). Sallinen came from a humble, fanatically puritan home. After some years travelling abroad he made his first big impact at home with his 'Washerwomen', a painting of robust and earthy Finnish women in brilliant colours and violent, bold drawing. His colour gradually became more restrained and in 1918 he painted what is probably his best-known picture, the 'Hihhulit' (Plate 53). The Hihhulit were the fanatically religious sect which he had known from his childhood, and he shows them in their ecstatic worship. Sallinen's violent expressionistic way of painting communicates all their excitement and fervour; it is thoroughly modern and yet, at the same time, suggests something of old Finnish art.

The Septem and the November groups were the most powerful new forces up to at least 1930, and after them Finnish art turned away from international modern idioms for some years; there is, for example, no hint of abstract or surrealist art. Artists continued to use styles to which they were now accustomed; sometimes the older artists were still able to surprise, as did Helena Schjerfbeck. Graphic art, which had previously occupied a subsidiary place, save for a few notable exceptions like Gallen-Kallela and Simberg, came into its own with the foundation of the Society of Finnish Graphic Artists in 1931. But sculpture was the art which now came increasingly to the front.

We have already seen the Finnish fondness for carving in early times. During the nineteenth century, although technically accomplished, it was generally less individual than the best painting. With the twentieth century it became increasingly important and in contemporary Finland, with its imaginative architecture and planning, public sculpture plays a major part. The leading sculptor of the first half of this century was Wäinö Aaltonen (1894-1966). Aaltonen was impressed with the qualities of the local granite and some of his best early works, like the 'Granite Boy', are in this medium, simplified, weighty and rhythmic. As he became older this heavy, primitive feeling became less apparent and his style matured into a modern classicism. Bronze became one of his best media, as in the well-known figure of the runner, Paavo Nurmi of 1924-5 (Plate 60). But there have been other good sculptors. Very different from Aaltonen is Hannes Autere (1888-1967) who followed the folk tradition of woodcarving, especially church sculpture, living a rural life in his home district. His 'Country Dance' (Plate 55) has something in common with Sallinen, but its good-tempered rustic vitality is more completely in the country tradition.

During the Second World War and the years immediately following, the forms of Finnish art changed little. Patriotic enthusiasm encouraged such traditionally favourite subjects as the Finnish countryside. Art remained firmly figurative and even those who followed Parisian rather than more national traditions kept to representational subjects.

Abstract art finally began to appear during the 1950s with Sam Vanni (b. 1908), one of the founders of the Prisma group, as its senior exponent. In 1960 Vanni created the first completely abstract mural in Finland and followed it five years later with the notable 'Work and Leisure' in the Post Office Savings Bank, Helsinki. He has become increasingly interested in dynamic, hard-edge abstract and kinetic art and has had much influence on younger artists both by his example and his teaching. A good example of his work is 'Contrapunctus', 1959-60, (Plate 56). In recent years several of the best new painters have been absorbed in more romantic imaginative art, sometimes of a personal or surrealistic fantasy. A compelling example is the work of Kauko Lehtinen (b. 1925). His world is figurative, but inhabited by strange, eerie personages from his own imagination, partly menacing, though sometimes this is tempered by a whimsical wit. The deceptively scratchy lines and blotches are in fact used with a sophisticated technical assurance to convey the mysterious atmosphere, as in 'Head on Black Background' (Plate 59).

Sculpture has continued strong, also remaining figurative until the mid-1950s. Aimo Tukiainen (b. 1917) is one of the most important sculptors. For some years his major works were realistic, as with the bronze equestrian statue of Marshal Mannerheim in Helsinki, with its elegance and springy strength. At the same time his sculpture was also starting to move in a different direction and his later work is mainly abstract. Nearly always, though, this has a clear meaning behind it, as when he depicts the idea of strong forces struggling and crushing in his war memorial at Hämeenlinna. One of the most interesting of the younger men is Kain Tapper (b. 1930), an artist of real sensitivity. In his statue of the young Sibelius at Hämeenlinna, he shows that a full-length portrait can still appear fresh and new, but his most typical work is abstract. He seems to see that a piece of stone or wood has a life of its own and then, by slightly moulding or shaping it, he reveals this life to us, as in 'Wood', 1962–6 (Plate 61).

There is much vitality in Finnish art today. But there could be a real or potential problem. To the sympathetic foreigner, the Finns appear a creative people with genuine artistic roots. It has in the past seemed possible to pick out intrinsically Finnish characteristics; identification with nature, both lyrical and in a particular kind of rough humour; strength of folk traditions, with certain crafts particularly characterful as in carving and textiles. But today, things militate against this. With the assistance of modern communications, art is growing increasingly international and it can be difficult for an artist from a small country to develop in a personal or national way without seeming provincial or old-fashioned. So far Finns have been particularly successful, in several branches of their artistic culture, in making modern idioms individual and meaningful. Let us hope they can continue to do so.

43. Reindeer owners keep an annual check on their herds at the winter round-ups.

44. Most towns and many villages have their own ski jump

45. Swimming in a clearing in the ice: a minority sport, but a speciality of Finland

46. Serious matters in an elementary school
47. Some younger citizens of the nation on skis

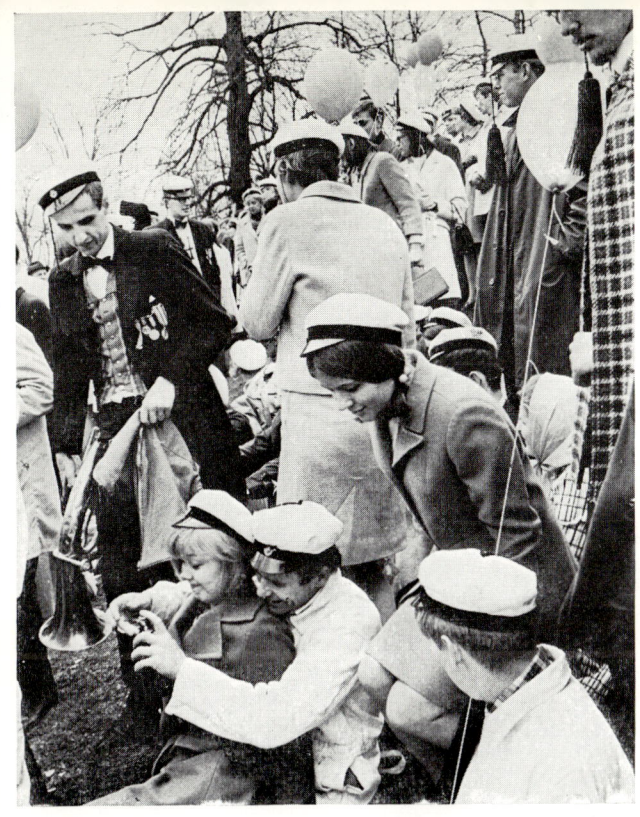

48. *Vappu* celebrations on May 1st: a nation-wide welcome for the spring

49. Carpet washing, Finnish style

50. Christmas Eve at Hietaniemi Cemetery, Helsinki: a light is placed by every grave

51. Wood-carving from Hollola Church, 1480 (p. 251)

52. Rymättylä church: east wall (p. 251)
53. 'Hihhulit': a Finnish religious sect, by T. K. Sallinen, 1918 (p. 254)

54. 'Girls Reading' by Helene Schjerfbeck. Water-colour, 1907 (p. 253)
55. 'Country Dance' by Hannes Autere. Relief in wood, 1923–5 (p. 255)

56. 'Contrapunctus' by Sam Vanni, Collage, 1959–60 (p. 255)

57. 'Great Black Woodpecker' by Akseli Gallen-Kallela, 1893 (p. 252)

8. 'Death on Skates' by Hugo Simberg. Etching (p. 253)

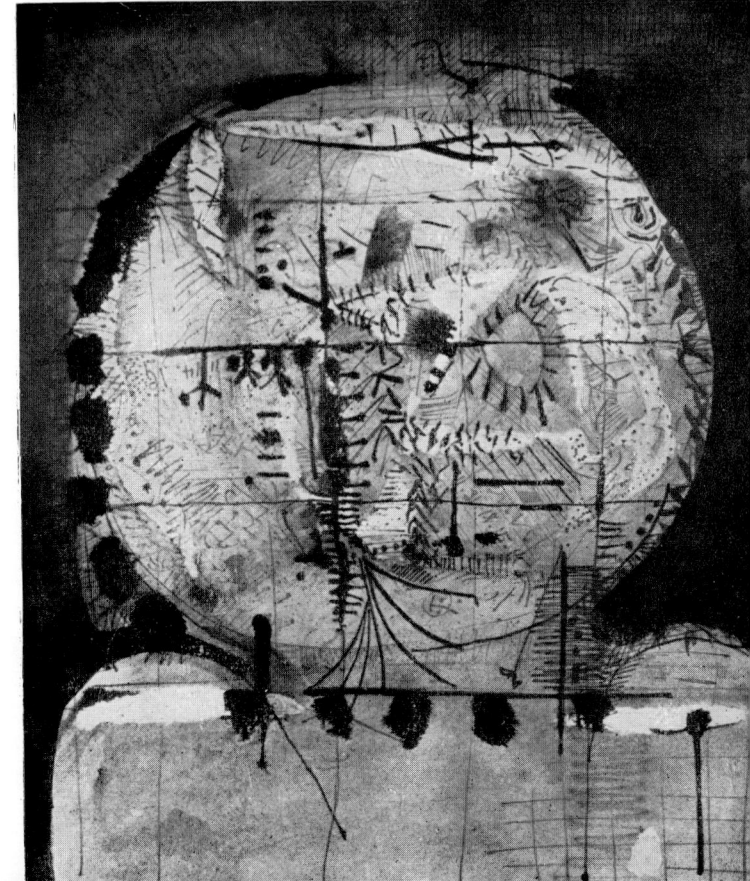

9. 'Head on Black Background' by Kauko Lehtinen. 1962 (p. 256)

60. 'Paavo Nurmi' by Wäinö Aaltonen. In bronze, 1924–5 (p. 255)   61. 'Wood' by Kain Tapper, 1962–6 (p. 256)

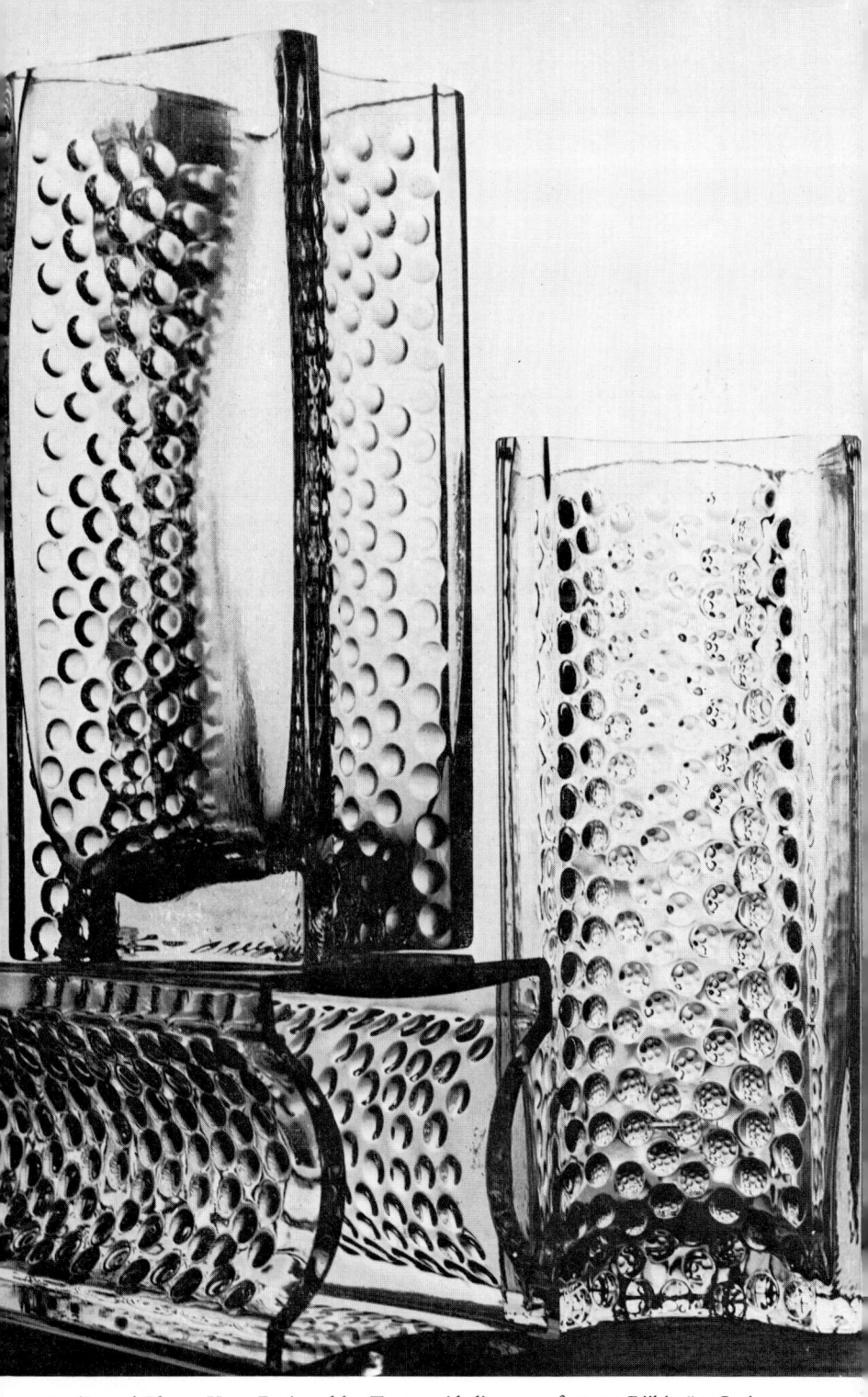

62. 'Largo' Blown Vase. Designed by Tamara Aladin, manufacturer Riihimäen Lasi

63. Ceramic plate by Birger Kaipiainen: fruit and flower motif, partly in relief (manufacturer, Wärtsilä/Arabia)
64. Bowl with 'Flora' design, by Oiva Toikka

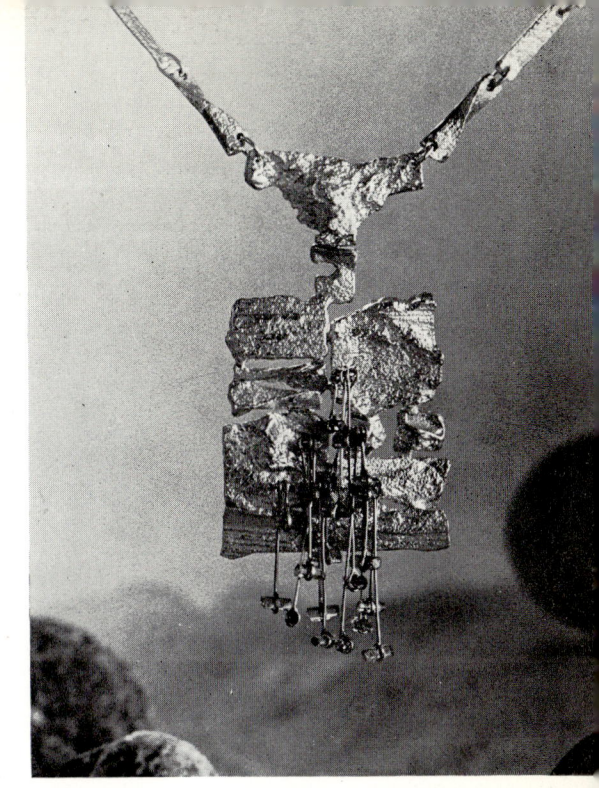

65. Pendant 'Flowering Wall', 18 carat gold, stones green tourmalines. Design by Björn Weckström, made by Lapponia Jewelry

66. Stainless steel cutlery 'Finnline'. Designed by Bertel Gardberg, manufacturer Hackman

67. Printed cotton sateen 'Paratiisi'. Designed by Marjatta Metsovaara, manufacturer Tampella

THE THEATRE

RITVA HEIKKILÄ

'Most of my cabinet', a Finnish Prime Minister once remarked, 'have been on the stage'; nor is there any reason to doubt his assertion. For a nation popularly considered phlegmatic, its citizens display a phenomenal taste for histrionic performance. So much so, that it is difficult to find anyone in the whole country who has not at some time taken part in theatricals in one form or another.

Add to this two other striking facts: first, that about half the entire population goes to the theatre at least once a year; and, secondly, that the state and municipal authorities subsidize drama to the extent of no less than £1 sterling per ticket sold. Small wonder that audiences are both growing and getting cheaper live entertainment than in most other countries.

The obvious starting point for the overseas visitor is Helsinki which, with twelve theatres, has comparatively more playhouses than any other northern city. Indeed, the tourist could go to the theatre every evening for a whole month without seeing the same play twice, since all are organized on the repertory system, from the largest with ten to twenty productions down to the smallest with only two or three. The two major enterprises are the Kansallisteatteri (the National Theatre) and the Kansallisooppera (the State Opera House). The former has two stages, concentrates on the Finnish spoken word and has an illustrious history of classical productions; these include twenty-two Shakespeare plays, sixteen Molière comedies and a host of works by major Scandinavian, British, American and Slav dramatists, as well as numerous more modern pieces by both foreign and domestic playwrights. The State Opera has a continuous output not only of classical operatic productions but increasingly of today's outstanding composers as well. A number of its former artistes have made international reputations in the great opera companies of the world. The Opera also maintains a ballet company which has numerous foreign tours to its credit.

Somewhat lighter material is offered by a second pair of institutions, one of them in Swedish. The Helsingin Kaupunginteatteri (Helsinki Municipal Theatre) was re-established in 1967 in a fine new theatre building of internationally recognised architectural merit. It concentrates mainly on modern plays, musical comedy, light opera, operetta and American-type musicals—its *Fiddler on the Roof* ran for nearly 500 performances. The Swedish house, Svenska Teatern, the oldest in the country, with two stages, has a similar theatrical policy and for linguistic reasons has been able to attract notable performers from all over Scandinavia.

Among the remainder, three are especially worth a visit—Lilla Teatern (Little Theatre), the Jurkka and the Intimi. Lilla Teatern has two stages and maintains a most interesting repertoire of traditional and experimental plays. Its small but highly-skilled ensemble is very popular both in Finland and Sweden, where the company performs for several weeks in every year. The Jurkka, named after a well-known Finnish theatrical family, is the smallest in the city and popular because of its intimate atmosphere. The Intimi specializes in boulevard comedies interspersed with serious drama.

Thus Helsinki has a surprisingly wide theatrical range. This explains why, although the city has a population of only half a million, its audiences total nearly 800,000 annually, many of them swollen of course by drama fans from the countryside.

The capital, however, has no monopoly of good theatre. Two houses in Tampere, Finland's largest industrial city—Tampereen Teatteri and Tampereen Työväen Teatteri—have been in business since the turn of the century and have many excellent productions to their credit. Each has two stages. Additionally, there is a theatre in nearly every Finnish town, down to the very smallest, and of these nine are municipally-owned. This means that the urban authorities meet running costs in the same way as for local schools, libraries, hospitals and museums. Professional theatres number thirty-four in all, eight of them built since the war and three—in Helsinki, Turku and Kuopio—being considered of high architectural standard. Registered amateur societies putting on their own regular productions total nearly 900. Add to these innumerable unregistered groups of enthusiasts all over Finland and the figures become very large indeed.

But in addition to these year-round enterprises Finland, in spite of its brief summer, has various summer stock theatres, some professional, some amateur. One is outstanding and deserves a paragraph to itself

This is the Pyynikki in Tampere; and its revolutionary design has earned it worldwide professional and public acclaim. The circular open auditorium, holding 800, is steeply banked and revolves through the whole 360 degrees. Encircling it and forming a complete outer ring, is a wide stage which at certain points reveals the surrounding parkland as a backdrop. The whole setting is superbly enhanced by lake shores and islands in the middle and far distance.

Although Finland certainly does not lack theatres, some of the remoter and more sparsely inhabited regions do present a cultural problem, especially in the north and east. To overcome this, established companies are being sent out on regional tours and first results of the scheme are encouraging.

Such are the theatres. What of the entertainment provided? It must be remembered first that Finland is a bilingual country, in which seven per cent of the population speaks Swedish as its mother tongue; and this is reflected in the theatre. As we have seen, the two Swedish-language houses have four separate stages between them. There are two more in Turku and Vaasa. The remainder perform in Finnish.

Over the years the list of productions in one or other language has covered an impressively wide field. In addition to Shakespeare and Molière, nearly all the outstanding dramatists of the world have been presented: Ibsen, Strindberg, Gorki, Chekov, Lope de Vega, Schiller, Goethe, Hauptmann, Sheridan, Bernard Shaw, Wilde, T. S. Eliot, Osborne, Wesker, Arden, Pinter, O'Neill, Arthur Miller, Tennessee Williams, Albee, Sartre, Anouilh, Giraudoux, Beckett, Ionesco, Genet and many others. Guest

FINLAND: AN INTRODUCTION

companies have included the Royal Shakespeare, Comédie Française, Berliner Ensemble, Burg Theater, Schiller Theater, Gorki Theatre and Piccolo Teatro.

However, despite the apparent preponderance of plays by foreign writers, at least fifty per cent of productions are the output of Finnish talent. Managements, in fact, feel a moral obligation to support the country's own dramatists, both classical and modern. First place is by common consent given to Aleksis Kivi, a playwright of the last century, whose best known works are *Nummisuutarit* ('The Village Cobblers') a tale of a village cobbler, and *Seitsemän Veljestä* ('Seven Brothers') which tells of the seven sons of a backwoodsman. Another classical author is Minna Canth, strongly influenced by Ibsen, who depicted social inequalities at the turn of the century, in particular the inferior status of women. Among the moderns, a resounding success has been attained by a dramatized version of a war novel, *Tuntematon Sotilas* ('Unknown soldier') by Väinö Linna. This book is certainly among the finest ever written in the genre. Coming to the present generation, the foremost new names are Eeva-Liisa Manner, Inkeri Kilpinen, Paavo Haavikko and Veijo Meri.

Finally, the guest system has not been exclusively one way. Many Finnish companies, headed by Kansallis Theatre, have toured abroad, principally in Sweden where there is an expatriate population of 300,000 Finns, but also in Denmark, France, Norway, Germany, Austria and the USSR.

Some words should be said about the stage as a profession. In Finland, the repertory system is the rule, and this has facilitated the formation and growth of societies by all those associated with it, including not only performers but also directors, managers, designers and writers. The oldest of these has already been in existence for more than fifty years. The best known is Suomen Näyttelijäliitto, the nearest equivalent to Equity in the West, which has some 800 members. Together with the allied craft unions, its influence over the years has achieved notable improvements not only in artistic standards but also in working conditions. Thus, actors are entitled to two-year contracts, a minimum wage scale and two-months' paid annual holiday. A pension scheme is also in operation.

Links with colleagues abroad have not been neglected. Finland in 1950 joined UNESCO's International Theatre Institute on which the Director of Kansallis Theatre, Professor Arvi Kivimaa, served as vice-president for several years.

It has been shown that the theatre in Finland enjoys wide public and civic support. Yet progress is still impeded by serious handicaps. The first is lack of funds, in which respect Finland lags behind many other countries, notably Sweden where the state contribution is five times larger. The unwillingness of Finnish managements to raise seat prices also adds to this economic problem which, in turn, limits resources for technical facilities, especially in the smaller houses. The second difficulty is the insuperable and unalterable fact that Finnish is understood by only five million people.

On the artistic side the strength of the average Finnish production rests on robust, fresh and light-hearted performance, the weakness a tendency to deficient vocal technique, attributable perhaps to the brevity of the country's theatrical tradition. There is also the same shortage of good plays and directors experienced in most countries. An effort is being made to overcome this by travelling scholarships and monetary grants for study abroad; but much benefit is often lost because the recipients have poor linguistic standards. Nevertheless, gifted writers are now starting to appear in encouraging numbers, while the expansion of training facilities should result in greater competence. Indeed, over the past few years, a number of theatre groups of young actors seeking new forms and audiences has appeared, concentrating on documentary, political satire and experimental programmes. The government has in fact given assistance to several left-wing companies presenting material sharply critical both of the traditional theatre and the Establishment.

Fittingly, the final word is with history. Drama in Finland sprang from grass roots. Unlike many other nations, the country never had anything remotely resembling a court theatre. It emerged spontaneously during the nineteenth century, the offspring of countless enthusiastic amateur societies and cultural groups in the agricultural and urban communities, inspired by genuine love of the theatre to found centres where plays could be performed everywhere. The movement's basis was romantic and nationalistic: it brought a deep, determination that, in the words of the father of the Finnish theatre, Dr Kaarlo Bergbom, '... all Finns, even the humblest, might participate in one of mankind's greatest intellectual experiences, the world's finest plays, performed in their own Finnish language.'

THE YEAR IN FINLAND

PHYLLIS CHAPMAN

JANUARY
1   *New Year's Day, public holiday*

DECEMBER–
MARCH

Reindeer round-ups take place in various parts of Lapland, between Christmas and the end of March. They are intensely lively affairs, and for many Lapps they are also social occasions when they meet relatives and friends. The round-ups may last several days for often there are thousands of reindeer to be sorted and marked.

FEBRUARY

5 — Runeberg Day, commemorating the Finnish National poet, Johan Ludvig Runeberg. *Flags fly everywhere and schoolchildren are given the day off. Special celebrations take place all over the country, especially in Helsinki, where Runeberg's statue in the middle of the city is lit up with torches and decorated with garlands of spruce and flowers. Students pay homage here and at the statue in Porvoo where the poet lived many years.. Special 'Runeberg cakes' are sold throughout the country in memory of those his wife used to bake for him.*

28 — Kalevala Day, commemorating the day in 1835 when Elias Lönnrot completed his manuscript of Kalevala, *the Finnish national epic. The celebrations are similar to those on Runeberg Day.*

MARCH

Nine days — *Helsinki Boat Show, international exhibition.*
Two days — *Salpausselkä International Winter Games at Lahti.*
Two days — *Puijo International Winter Games at Kuopio.*
Two days — *Ounasvaara International Winter Games at Rovaniemi.*

APRIL

Easter — *Church Festivals in Lapland are celebrated on Lady Day, at Easter and early in September. Lapps in their brilliant costumes gather in some of the big villages to attend special church services followed by a programme of events such as lasso-throwing competitions and ski-racing behind reindeer on a frozen lake. Colourful Lapp weddings are often held on these occasions.*

Two days — *Rukatunturi International Winter Games at Kuusamo.*

THE YEAR IN FINLAND

APRIL
30
May Day Eve (Vappu), the gayest night of the year, celebrated much in the style of a carnival, especially by students. Balloons, paper streamers and bright paper decorations and hats abound. In Helsinki the great moment is at midnight when students mass in the Market Square and one of them climbs the statue of Havis Amanda to crown her with a student cap. Havis Amanda symbolizes Helsinki rising out of the sea.

MAY
1
May Day continues 'Vappu'. Students inevitably take things easy after the exertions of the previous night, but for organized workers it is the big day of the year. However, for everyone, young and old, the first of May is the herald of spring to come.

Whit Sunday
Ritvala Helka Folklore Festival (Ritvalan Helkajuhlat) at Sääksmäki, north of Hämeenlinna. An age-old celebration of early summer. The maidens of Sääksmäki village, in picturesque national dress, gather at the 'Raitinmäki' crossroads, and then walk in procession to 'Helka' hill, singing ancient folksongs. Later there is an open-air programme of folk dances and music, and the singing of Kalevala *and* Kanteletar *poems. Bonfires are lit in the evening.*

JUNE
4
Flag Day of the Finnish Armed Forces, in commemoration of Marshal Mannerheim's birthday. Throughout the country it is a special day for the army. The main event is a march past at one of the principal garrison centres.

12
Helsinki Day, to mark the founding of the city in 1550, has been celebrated since 1959 and its purpose

265

FINLAND: AN INTRODUCTION

is to give citizens an opportunity to get to know their home town. Free guided visits to historical sites as well as municipal offices and institutes, and special programmes for young and old. Each Helsinki Day has a special theme around which the programmes are arranged.

About 24th Midsummer, celebrated during the weekend closest to June 24th, is the festival of the long light days of the northern summer and of the midnight sun in Lapland. According to ancient Scandinavian tradition, bonfires are lit all over the country by the innumerable lakes and on the countless islands. Midsummer Eve is also Finnish Flag Day. Music, dancing, and folklore are all part of the festivities. In Åland, Midsummer maypoles are erected.

The Sampo Festival is usually held on the first Sunday after Midsummer, at Paikkari cottage in Sammatti, home of Elias Lönnrot, compiler of the national epic Kalevala. The festival revives the ancient traditions of Kalevala, and includes recitals from the epic, and plays.

Three days Strawberry Carnival at Suonenjoki, near Kuopio. Strawberry auction, processions through the town, plays and Miss Strawberry election.

JUNE
One week Kuopio Dances. Folk dance, ballet, music.
One week Vaasa Festival. Jazz, pop and cultural seminars.

JUNE–
JULY–
AUGUST

There are an increasing number of informal summer art exhibitions. One of the best known is at Purnu, near Tampere, in a beautiful lake landscape. Modern Finnish art is well represented by young painters, sculptors and graphic artists. At the Suvi-Pinx *exhibition, Sysmä, Suopelto near Heinola, paintings, sculpture and graphics.*

When ordinary theatres close for the summer, the many summer theatres begin all over the country. Some are set in historical surroundings, like the castle ruins at Raasepori near Tammisaari, and Kastelholm in the Åland Islands, as well as at Suomenlinna fortress on an island just outside Helsinki.

JUNE–
JULY–
AUGUST–
SEPTEMBER
The Greek Orthodox Pradznik festivals are of medieval origin, and celebrated only in Karelia, mostly in the vicinity of Ilomantsi near Joensuu. The Pradznik starts with a vigil, followed by a morning service. The participants are offered refreshments, and festivities continue with dancing, games and merrymaking. The best known pradzniks are Petru Pradznik at Hattuvaara in June, Ilja Pradznik in July, Squasa Pradznik, Lieksa in August and Melaselkä Pradznik in September, all near Ilomantsi.

JULY
Two weeks
Jyväskylä Arts Festival, the biggest cultural event in Finland. The programme includes lectures, courses, seminars on a serious topic of universal interest, and exhibitions of all kinds, as well as concerts, films and plays.

About two weeks
Savonlinna Music Festival. Summer music courses and Lied and opera singing with Finnish and international teachers.

Two weeks
Savonlinna Opera Festival at Olavinlinna Castle, as well as concerts, folk dancing, plays, design and art exhibitions and other entertainment.

Three days
Pori Jazz Festival on an island near the town. International performers at concerts, jam sessions, final picnic concert.

One week	*Kaustinen Folk Music Festival.* Folk music, old and new, from Finland and abroad.
21	*Crayfish season begins.* This means lots of gay parties for those who are crazy about this delicacy. Restaurants are often decorated with pictures of crayfish, and visitors can order big plates with huge piles of them decorated with fresh green dill. Traditionally Finnish aquavit or vodka helps to wash them down, and there are people who easily get through forty or more at a sitting. But even more delightful are the parties in the summer cottages by the lakeside. The crayfish are often caught from some nearby lake on the previous or even the same night.

JULY

Yachting Regatta at Helsinki

Yachting Regatta at Hanko

Outdoor Drama Festival (Kivi-juhlat) at Nurmijärvi. Performances of Nummisuutarit *and* Seven Brothers *by the great Finnish nineteenth-century writer, Aleksis Kivi.* The theatre is on the Taaborinvuori hill, near the birthplace of the author in Nurmijärvi, about twenty-five miles from Helsinki.

27   *Lay-a-Bed Day at Hanko and Naantali.* Based on the old legend of the Seven Sleepers. Everyone is woken up at 6 a.m. and whoever oversleeps is given a ducking in the sea. There is a procession through the streets, and prizes are given for the best 'dressed' participants. Dancing from early morning till late at night. Prize also for 'Sleepy Queen'.

AUGUST

One week   *Tampere Theatre Summer drama festival.* A survey of modern Finnish theatre and foreign plays. Performances of famous Finnish plays e.g. Seven Brothers at Pyynikki Open Air Theatre with revolving auditorium start mid-June.

One week Turku Music Festival. Chamber music, performances in old historical settings like the Cathedral and Castle, nearby manor houses and medieval churches. Folk music at Luostarinmäki Handicrafts Museum. Three-day Rock and Pop Festival at Ruissalo Camping Site.

Three days Europe Motor Rally at Jyväskylä

Two weeks Cultural Seminars at Joensuu open-air theatre, including concerts, art exhibitions and plays.

Three days Mikkeli Fish Feast, festival with street dancing, night market and arts events.

AUGUST–SEPTEMBER

Three weeks Helsinki Festival. Opera, ballet, concerts, drama, films, art, jazz, pop, seminars, exhibitions and happenings throughout the town.

SEPTEMBER

Two days Turku Handicrafts Days at Luostarinmäki Handicrafts Museum housed in authentic dwellings of bygone craftsmen.

Helsinki Trade Fairs, in alternate years technical and consumer goods.

OCTOBER

10 Aleksis Kivi Day, commemorating his birthday. In Helsinki, students pay homage at his statue outside the National Theatre, and schools all over the country have a holiday.

FINLAND: AN INTRODUCTION

DECEMBER

'Pikkujoulu', Little Christmas. For Finns, Christmas time starts on the Eve of Advent. It is celebrated much in the same way as 'real' Christmas, only on a smaller scale. In many homes there are little trees with candles, small presents are exchanged, and Christmas songs are sung and even some traditional Christmas dishes are served. The shopping season opens officially.

6   *Independence Day. Special festivities and military parades all over the country. In Helsinki, students take part in a memorable torchlight parade in the evening. Candles glow in the windows of every home and official building. The President of the Republic holds a big reception in his Palace, to which leaders of every section of the community are invited, as well as the diplomatic corps.*

24   *Christmas Eve, main celebration of Christmas. Shops close early, and no traffic after 6 p.m. Christmas in Finland is a family celebration, and Christmas Eve is particularly popular with children, as Father Christmas visits most families in person. Christmas trees are brought into every home and decorated gaily. In the evening, the traditional Christmas meal, invariably a ham and rice porridge, is eaten, and the children dance round the tree. Candles and flowers are taken to the graves of relations and the dead of World War II. On Boxing Day morning a visit to church, in the countryside often by horse-sleigh.*

31   *New Year's Eve, celebrated throughout the country. Tin is melted and thrown into cold water to tell fortunes for the coming year. Crowds gather at the Senate Square outside Helsinki Cathedral to listen to the Prime Minister's New Year Speech.*

THE PRESS

LANCE KEYWORTH

THE Finns are voracious readers, for many reasons. The nation is 100 per cent literate. The long and dark winters leave plenty of time for reading. They have a healthy curiosity about the world beneath their windows and beyond their frontiers. Virtually every home, every farmstead has a well-stocked bookshelf, and it is even more certain that every family subscribes to at least one newspaper. One Finnish editor says: 'Newspaper reading is an old habit; what is more a natural one to a nation which procures from its own forests the raw materials to satisfy its desire to read.'

The first Finnish newspaper appeared when the country was under Swedish rule, in 1771. Thus the Finnish press has already celebrated its bicentenary. Its development has been remarkable. Both under Sweden and when Finland was an autonomous Grand Duchy of the Tsarist Empire, newspapers and periodicals had a very chequered career, were constantly being banned, and were always subject to censorship.

Not until Finland gained its political independence over fifty years ago did the free, modern press of Finland really have a chance to develop. In 1915, there were 99 newspapers published at least three days a week, and taking in periodicals as well the total was 445 publications. Today, there are 88 newspapers and about 1,500 periodicals. In 1905, the postal services handled 20·5 million papers, in 1969 the total was 636·7 million. The population of Finland is 4·7 million.

Using the UNESCO definition, there are sixty-five dailies with a combined circulation of 1,870,000. More seven-day newspapers are published in Finland than anywhere else in Scandinavia, and in the last fifteen years their number has increased from sixteen to twenty-two. Incidentally, there are no special Sunday papers like *The Observer* and *Sunday Times*. The fact that each of the 1·4 million households in Finland own at least one radio and two-thirds of them both a radio and a TV set lends emphasis to these statistics.

Given the sparse population and the intense competition among so many papers, some of them have a very small circulation. In fact, there is really only one newspaper in Finland which has a 'national' character. That is *Helsingin Sanomat* with the extraordinarily high circulation for Finnish conditions of more than 250,000. Some of the 'throw-aways', part of the customer service of co-operatives and banks, reach circulations on both sides of 400,000, but these are periodicals. Most have little or no political influence, but their importance in commerce is considerable. Over 90 per cent of the newspaper edition is sold by subscription; bookstand sales are unimportant. Evening papers are only published in Helsinki (three) and Jyväskylä (one).

In the broad view, Finnish newspapers have moved through the cycle from idealism through party support to the present-day trend towards no party affiliation. Papers that can manage without party aid tend to proclaim themselves independent today—competition and business aspects have forced at least the major publishers to take the practical view to increase circulation. Between 1964 when there were 104 papers published at least three times a week, and 1971, 33 papers folded. Most of the casualties occurred among papers of a local character that were founded for purely party reasons and had little real viability. Air transport and improved postal facilities also helped to kill off the weaker papers, for now Helsinki papers can reach virtually every part of Finland the same morning. While the demise of a newspaper is always a matter for regret, free competition has led to higher standards among the survivors.

Every Finn—except perhaps the founder of a new party—admits that Finland has too many political parties. No less than eight parties are represented today in the 200-seat parliament. Of the 88 papers published at least three times weekly, 38 own to no party affiliation, 50 are party organs. In my personal opinion, the least readable papers, those with the poorest standards, are nearly always the party organs, with exceptions such as *Aamulehti*, *Karjalainen* and *Savon Sanomat*. They indulge in endless polemics, and this is not confined to the editorial columns. A Finnish authoress interviewed in a Helsinki daily said: 'Lack of objectivity is notable in Finnish discussions. Instead of getting to the point, we start on personalities; sensitive questions are avoided by explaining things away.'

Yet the Finnish press has one unique feature lacked by the Anglo-Saxon newspapers as a whole. Irrespective of party colour, papers summarize daily the editorial comment of interest that has appeared in the competition. The Helsinki dailies even summarize editorial comment appearing in the more important provincials. This is a valuable service both for observers of the Finnish scene and for subscribers with questing minds.

If party polemics spoil the pages of some of the major dailies, full and relatively objective coverage of foreign news is a counterbalancing feature of the foreign pages. The 'average' Finn probably takes more interest than his British counterpart in foreign news, and in my opinion is better-informed about world affairs. It is very natural that he should be, exposed as he is to the repercussions of decisions beyond his country's control made by the big powers. Editorial comment on foreign affairs is, of course, coloured by the paper's interests, whether it is a political organ or non-party. Latterly, there has been less restraint about distant events of which the writers have no personal experience, like apartheid in South Africa, race relations in America. The Communist press, of course, has never pretended to show this caution, but certain distant events, such as Vietnam, have been just as hotly debated in the Liberal and Social-Democratic papers.

This is probably a good place to say a few words about freedom of the press in Finland. This freedom is written into Article 10 of the Constitution which reads: 'Finnish citizens shall enjoy freedom of speech and the right of printing and publishing written or pictorial representations without any previous authorization.' There are certain natural limitations written into the Criminal Code. The press may not pronounce on the innocence or guilt of a person on trial, and may not publish anything treasonable or actively furthering high treason. A more controversial law was passed in 1948, making it a criminal offence to damage Finland's relations with a foreign state by publicly and intentionally abusing that country. This has been interpreted by some as limiting editorial comment on foreign events. In fact, however, while editors usually exercise self-restraint in this matter, they can and do write strongly on occasion. Two examples are the Hungarian crisis in 1956 and the Czechoslovakian invasion in 1968.

For financial reasons alone, few Finnish papers can maintain foreign correspondents abroad. These are based in the major news centres—London, Paris, Washington, Moscow, Bonn and Stockholm. The main source of foreign news is the international wire services. Most of them work through the Finnish News Agency (STT-FNB), the only national news agency, which serves all the papers of Finland and the Finnish Broadcasting and Television Corporation. It has a direct teleprinter service from Reuters, Agence France Presse, the Soviet APN and TASS, and the Scandinavian national news agencies. In STT, the foreign desk editor selects the dispatches he considers of most interest to Finnish readers. These are translated into Finnish and Swedish—not edited—and sent on to every paper in Finland. Some of the bigger dailies are direct subscribers to the AP and UPI services, and others again take the *New York Times*, *The Times*, *The Observer* and similar services. Many of the bigger papers also buy syndicated columns, especially the big names from the United States.

Turning to less weighty matters, the Finnish press has features which the reader of English papers can find amusing or irritating. Layout often leaves a lot to be desired. Too many stories are crammed on to the main news page, and after a few sentences continued elsewhere inside. This is irritating for the man who reads his morning news in bed, at the breakfast table or in the tram. The letters to the editor column is boring beyond belief—not least because very few correspondents dare to sign their own names to the letters. But one or two papers have improved their letters columns recently. An amusing feature is the birthday list. The birth date and a brief biography of everyone who is anyone and many who are not are noted in the papers at the half-century, and thereafter every ten years. The only way to avoid this is to pay STT the equivalent of £3 and have the agency instruct all newspapers that you do not wish to have your birthday announced.

A very positive feature is the virtual absence of sensationalism, although it is a little startling for an English correspondent to read a headline like: 'The police have arrested the murderer, but he hasn't confessed yet.' Sex, murder and crime in general are played down consistently. Most papers in the world are devoting more and more space to sport, but Finland must be leading the field. The cultural pages, too, are fat.

Writing and editing sometimes leave something to be desired in most papers. Even the Finns find it difficult to write really good Finnish, I am told, so that may be one reason for the problem. Another is probably the low rates of pay for junior reporters and, indeed, many senior editors do not do well. The consequence is a tendency to use hand-outs from press conferences and avoid doing any 'homework' before going out on a story. Copy from outside contributors is usually too long and badly needs subbing. There seems to be no premium on space. In short, more and better journalist training seems to be indicated. Four-fifths of all journalists in Finland have no training at all in their trade. Yet it is amazing that these same reporters can cover press conferences and conduct interviews in one or more foreign languages as well as the two official languages (Finnish and Swedish) of the country.

The government appointed a committee in 1967 to investigate the training requirements in journalism. Its fairly detailed report was handed to a small working group for consideration of the practical aspects. This group has now recommended to the Ministry of Education a series of graded courses at Tampere University, with most of the bill being paid by the State. The courses will begin in 1972 if all goes according to plan.

Another question that is under active consideration just now is journalistic ethics. Finland has a Council for Mass Media, equivalent to the Press Council for Britain. But lack of funds, premises and permanent staff have prevented it from working really effectively. Four of its twelve members are nominated by the publishers and four by the unions of journalists, and they elect the chairman. These nine, in turn, elect four representatives of the public. A state grant is being sought to put the council on a more regular working basis.

There was an interesting court case in 1965 in which a Helsinki reporter was fined for refusing to reveal her source of information. The ensuing protest led to the appointment of a state committee and its recommendations were embodied in a new law on the subject in 1966. This acknowledges that a newspaper or magazine reporter (radio and television reporters will be covered in a new law now under preparation) has the right—but no obligation—to refuse to reveal his source. There are two exceptions: if, in a court case, the sentence foreseen for the crime is six years' hard labour or more, the journalist must, if the court so orders, reveal his source (crimes of murder, manslaughter, high treason, etc.); the same applies if the accused has broken his oath of secrecy (e.g. a doctor or an official). In both cases, the journalist can appeal to a higher court before complying with the order of the lower instance, and in any case the court must sit in camera to hear the name of the source.

Partly because of the casualties among party organs, partly because of the debate on the same subject in Sweden, the question of subsidizing party papers was raised in 1965. Three parties supported the idea, maintaining that they could not air their views in the independent press. The rest of the press went to battle on the claim that such subsidies would endanger the freedom of the press. *Kouvolan Sanomat*, an independent provincial which claims a readership of 100,000, actually offered every democratic party half a page once weekly. To make the proponents of subsidization accept the offer, it also announced that any party which left its space unused would be denounced as having nothing to say and therefore undeserving of a subsidy anyway. A bill was introduced, but defeated in Parliament early in 1966. The outcome was that parties, and not their papers, are now paid a subsidy to use as they think fit. Some papers have benefited, but no statistics are available. In 1971, for the first time, the state subsidized papers in economic difficulties by giving them reduced telex and postage facilities.

To conclude, Finland has a free press of high European standard. It is very jealous of its privileges and some of its most effective campaigns since the war have been in defence of its own rights when these seemed to be threatened.

FINNISH FOOD

J. AUDREY ELLISON

Finnish Food could perhaps be described as the food of our time. Finns appreciate basic, natural food-flavours and there seems to be a strong trend in certain market sectors for foods of this kind—hence the willingness of many shoppers to pay higher prices for 'natural' products, naturally grown and bred foods as opposed to the factory farmed, the synthetically coloured and flavoured, and those 'enriched' with added vitamins, emulsifying, stabilizing and anti-oxidant agents.

Finns, however, have a special taste for wild-gamey flavours. Finnish food, like that of most nations in Europe, is a blend of *traditional and new dishes. The main basic themes—local and national food resources prepared according to older methods of food preparation—are there; but so, too, are the results of modern food technology—products and ready meals made to high quality standards in food factories. Many Finnish homes are equipped with home freezers and this also has an influence on eating patterns.*

The mention of the words 'Finnish food' conjures up a varied gastronomic picture. There are sour rye breads, soft and hard; velvety viili— *a thick, summer-milk product;* piimä, *another cultured milk, but slightly effervescent and meant to be drunk from a glass rather than eaten with a spoon like* viili. *There are gleaming smoked whitefish, berries and fungi of many kinds, crayfish, salmon and dill, soups made from delicate young summer vegetables* (kesäkeitto), *from peas and cabbage; salmon* seljanka *soup; burbot-soup—highlight of the winter soups garnished with potato slices and lightly cooked burbot liver;* Kainuu *fish soup; broths of game and beef; even* Aura *blue-cheese soup.*

Other fare includes cabbage rolls, home-made cheeses and coffee breads, home-brewed beer, creamed morels and chanterelles, rowanberry jelly, ptarmigan, pheasant, elk, hare and many reindeer delicacies. Among these are reindeer tongues (both fresh and smoked), marrow-bone soup, smoked reindeer with pumpkin chutney and scrambled eggs, and slivers of frozen reindeer meat fried with bacon (poronkäristys) *and crushed red whortleberries. Cardamom, juniper, dill and allspice are among the flavourings closely linked with Finnish food.*

Such is the visitors' range of choice. Many dishes can be made at home and a list of reference books describing some traditional recipes is given on page 341–2. Some of these recipes could be included when preparing a buffet table for a party. Such a table is known in Finland as voileipäpöytä *and both Jorma Soiro and Beatrice Ojakangas describe the array of dishes which can make up a well-laden buffet table. Useful glossaries of Finnish food terms are to be found in Jorma Soiro's* Finnish Cookery *and a culinary glossary is included in Time-Life's:* Cooking of Scandinavia.

FINLAND: AN INTRODUCTION

Karelian cooking more than any other Finnish provincial cooking shows the influence of Russia, with its blend of Eastern and Western traditions. For instance, there is the sweet-sour borscht made with beetroots and red cabbage served with soured cream and lemon; and the open rye-dough pasties filled with rice, brushed after baking with a glaze of melted butter and boiling water and served with egg-butter, a mixture of finely chopped hard-boiled eggs and butter.

Similar pasties of the basic rye-dough may be stuffed with potato, carrot or cheese fillings. Other dishes include deep-fried, rice-filled pasties made with rye dough, Shrove Tuesday blinis served with roe, and baked rahka (based on the Russian pasha of Eastertide), wheaten pasties containing vanilla-flavoured soured milk, eggs, raisins and sugar. The traditional Finnish Easter dish is mämmi, a baked rye pudding flavoured with orange peel and raisins. Karelian hot pot made with pork, beef and mutton is cooked in an earthenware pot. Then there are the 'hearty' baked casseroles of swedes, carrots and potatoes. Another link with Russian cuisine is lohipiiras or salmon pasty known in Russia as koulibiac.

Other regions with characteristic cooking include the provinces of Savo and Häme and, of course, Lapland. Savo's outsize rye-dough pasties, kalakukko, are often baked for more than 5 or 6 hours. Such pasties are filled with freshwater fish and pork. Freshwater fish abound in the Savo lake district and there are many delicious dishes prepared from one of the smallest of them, the muikku or vendace, a whitefish species rarely found in British lakes. Vendace roe, like that of the burbot, is used as a substitute for caviar. Other Savo specialities include lightly salted whitefish (eaten raw), midsummer's day barley pancakes, pit-baked turnips and baked red-whortleberry pudding.

Häme, a wealthy fertile province famous for its large-scale, magnificent feasts, has a few culinary specialities, notably soft, mild-flavoured egg cheeses made from full-cream milk. Sweetened potato pudding, baked in a mould, is also a Häme speciality but adopted on a national scale at Christmas time. Another traditional *potato dish comes from Satakunta, a western province. It is a casserole of grated potatoes baked with eggs, milk, butter, flour and seasoning.*

Native wild berries are the basis for the most popular sweet dishes. The berries include cranberries, red whortleberries, cloudberries and the arctic bramble. Arctic brambles are so rare that they are only used in the form of preserves or the liqueur distilled from them. Cranberries and red whortleberries are available in various forms including fresh, deep frozen, and bottled in syrup. Cloudberries are available fresh, deep frozen, canned in syrup, as a preserve and a liqueur. The berries are used to make parfaits, crème bavaroise, *and* kiisseli (*a starch-thickened, cold sweet often made from cranberries*). *Cloudberries may be served on their own, or with whipped cream and sugar, or with almond cake and ice-cream.*

The Finnish cheese board can offer a wide selection. Several are variants of cheeses originally produced elsewhere, for example Cheddar, Emmenthal, Edam, Camembert and Tilsit, whilst others are original Finnish cheeses. Turunmaa, *for example, is a mild, full-flavoured cheese containing 50 per cent butterfat. Some of the local fresh cheeses are made from fresh milk or beestings or from a mixture of soured and fresh milks and possibly eggs. The fresh cheeses may seem bland to British palates but the textures are usually very pleasant.*

Opportunities for training in food science at the University of Helsinki continue to widen. Dairy science has been an established part of the curriculum at the University of Helsinki's Department of Agriculture for over sixty years. Nutritional chemistry, microbiology of foods and agricultural economics have for many years been subjects of study in the department and in 1961 the Institute of Meat Technology was founded as part of the agricultural faculty.

In 1965, assistant professorships in food chemistry and technology were founded. The young Institute of Food Chemistry and Technology can make a major contribution to the future of the food industries in Finland both by the original research programme being carried out there and by the sound training given to those who study there—the future chemists and technologists of Finland's food industries.

The training of home economists in Finland is carried out at several colleges, including Helsingin Kotitalousopettajaopisto (Helsinki School of Domestic Science) and at the University of Helsinki at Viikki. A number of home economists are employed in test and development kitchens of large food manufacturers in Finland. A small number with training in nutritional chemistry are entering the field of dietetics.

Students wishing to enter the hotel and catering industries are indeed fortunate to have an establishment like the Hotel and Restaurant Institute in Helsinki. Hotel Haaga, which opened in 1970, is run in close co-operation with this institute. There is also an older-established hotel and restaurant school in Helsinki, founded in 1935, for training entrants to the hotel and catering trades.

Packaging and presentation of food are important sales factors and a good example of this is the Finlandia dry-vodka packaging. For this product a beautiful bottle was designed by Tapio Wirkkala. The vodka is prepared from Finnish grain and clear water from a deep well. Arctic berry liqueurs are a group of products with a special gourmet appeal and the perfect finale to a Finnish menu in any part of the world.

A number of Finnish foods and beverages are exported to Britain and some of these can help in making up a buffet table. They include Valio dairy produce: Midnight Sun butter, cheeses—notably Finnish Emmenthal and Finnish Edam, eggs, Scandacrisp—a dark, thin, sour-dough crispbread, My Crisp rye crispbread, Canelo cinnamon rusks, Koff lager, Finnish vodka, and a limited supply of three arctic berry liqueurs: Suomuurain, Mesimarja and Karpi (prepared from cloudberries, arctic brambles and cranberries respectively).

What does the future hold for exports of Finnish foods? Canned (and possibly deep-frozen) ready meals, soups and pâtés based on wild-flavoured game fare should find a potential market in the gourmet and delicatessen sections of the food trade as should the traditional accompaniments to many of these dishes, namely jellies and preserves from wild berries. Finland's new fructose sugar plant—the largest in the world—will no doubt increase the exportability of this commodity. Confectionery (notably chocolates, fruit jellies and liquorice goods) and dairy products (particularly Finnish Emmenthal) are in steady demand. The crispbreads and sauna-smoked meat products could be promoted more intensively.

The subject of environmental pollution is becoming increasingly important in the attitude of the discriminating and health-conscious consumer. Natural products of the Finnish woods and rivers should be in a strong market position in this context: for example, rainbow trout from unpolluted waters, game, game birds, mushrooms and berries from the forests.

HOLIDAYS IN FINLAND

BENGT PIHLSTRÖM

Take a tourist catchword based on reality, like 'Land of a Thousand Lakes' and the epithet may stick. Finns find the slogan wearisome and trite; but the fact remains that Finland does have over sixty thousand lakes, one system in the east being the largest in Europe, and the accuracy of the picture conjured up cannot be gainsaid. A claim by a neighbour country to an even larger total is laughed off by the counter-assertion—self-evidently true to any patriotic Finn—that they can't be bothered to count the small ones!

In a progressively urbanizing Europe, Finland's greatest wealth is her natural resources. These comprise not only the superb inland waterways, but also the virgin forests and barren fells of Lapland, where the sun shines round the clock for two whole months, and a coastal archipelago second in size only to that of Greece. In relation to population (barely five million) and area (larger than Britain or Italy), the country has therefore one of the last remaining reserves of scenery, clear water and fresh air.

The identity of her second major asset surprised the entire nation. After an American Travel Writers' convention held in 1970, a poll of the participants revealed the country's greatest attraction to be the Finns themselves. Research among British tourists gave the same result.

For a people which had pictured itself as taciturn and introvert, this was a startling conclusion. In fact, of course, townspeople, countryfolk and backwoods dwellers alike are all pleased to meet foreigners and—language difficulties notwithstanding—break down what they feel as isolation. Large-scale tourism is still unknown and a foreigner is not only a visitor but a guest. This compulsive urge to promote contacts is being satisfied by a

HOLIDAYS IN FINLAND

programme known as 'Find the Finns', enabling natives and foreigners to meet in a domestic setting, and the scheme has now been extended from Helsinki to other towns.

Human friendliness and superb natural amenities are invaluable constituents for a developing tourist industry, but merchandizing requires concrete products. For this reason accommodation has been rapidly expanded. Helsinki has now acquired its first really large hotels, the Intercontinental and the neighbouring Hesperia, with a combined total of nearly 600 rooms. Facilities have been brought up to a high standard and noteworthy newcomers in this respect have been the holiday centres using the hotel-cum-bungalow system. A start has also been made in central Finland, where Sandpiper Hotels (called in Finnish 'Rantaloma'), near Jyväskylä, have adopted the principle of the individual chalet, each containing bedroom, kitchen, all modern conveniences and, in some cases, its own sauna. A private beach and a boat are also included, while a central complex houses a hotel, restaurant and discothéque.

Another notable addition has been the conversion to hotels of several manor houses, the country's 'stately homes', some in the luxury class, such as Haikko, near Porvoo, where visitors may enjoy the grace and style of the rooms where the Russian Royal family once spent their summers; others are in a more rustic milieu such as Ilola, north of Lahti, with bedrooms in romantic lake-shore outhouses and ballroom dancing in an old barn.

The tourist drive has now penetrated every region, including the Åland Archipelago and the islands off Turku to the southwest, some thirty thousand in all, with cottages for hire, excellent fishing and wonderful scenery for yachting enthusiasts; and the lake district, where there are angling, canoeing, water ski-ing, golf, tennis and riding facilities, such as at Aulanko Hotel, outside Hämeenlinna, birthplace of Sibelius. Other attractions are the fantastic lake trips, such as by The Finnish Silverline from Hämeenlinna to the second largest city, Tampere, or by the hydrofoil *Tehi* from modern Lahti to Jyväskylä and some of Alvar Aalto's finest architecture. Travellers seeking the exotic will find it in the east, among the delightful open-hearted Karelians with their especially succulent cuisine and Greek

FINLAND: AN INTRODUCTION

Orthodox religious services and churches, including a pair of monasteries. Two cultures made their way into Finland, from West and East, and this is their meeting place.

The west coast has hitherto contributed little to the holiday traffic, but the charming small towns and fine beaches of the region are starting to attract attention. To the north lies Lapland, covering one-third of the whole country. Rovaniemi, administrative capital of the province, lying just outside the Arctic Circle, has an excellent jet plane service which puts it within two hours' of Helsinki for the tourist; and along the main roads up towards the Arctic Ocean are a number of first-class hotels lying at the feet of majestic, rugged fells. The most popular include those at Pallastunturi and Kilpisjärvi, the latter near Saana, the former holy mountain of the Lapps in the north-west arm of Finland. A whole new Alpine hotel network, with modern restaurants, swimming pools and ski-lifts, has grown up east of Rovaniemi, the so-called North-east Fell district of which Pyhä, Suomu and Ruka fells are the best known. In Lapland the visitor can enjoy successively the warm summer midnight sun, the flaming autumn vegetation hues, the Northern Lights and reindeer round-ups of Christmastime, and the brilliant early spring sunshine of the ski-ing season stretching into May.

The tourist season is thus becoming year-long. Cross-country ski-ing is achieving increasing popularity in both Europe and North America, and in Finland this traffic is stimulated by the additional enticements of cultural events, shopping sprees and special interest programmes covering such features as architecture and industrial design. The country is, in fact, liveliest in the inaptly named off-season; but an impressive series of summer attractions, known as 'Finland Festivals', has now been organized, embracing all aspects of modern cultural life from symphony concerts and church music to rock-and-roll and underground films. These start with a ballet season at the beginning of June in Kuopio (where the revolving restaurant at the top of Puijo Tower is worth a visit), continues in Vaasa with pop art, and on to a theatre, concert and film festival in Jyväskylä. The outstanding July event is the traditional programme of opera in Savonlinna, staged in the majestic 500-year-old Olavinlinna Castle. Jazz enthusiasts foregather in Pori, on the west coast, and others head for Kaustinen, in Ostrobothnia, to hear folk music. Elsewhere country dance displays attract audiences of thousands to prove that folklore is experiencing a renaissance.

The summer festivals culminate in the three major cities. In Tampere, a leading theatre town, visiting theatrical companies from all over Europe perform, attracted by the world's first revolving auditorium. In Turku, the entertainment ranges from church and chamber music in the cathedral to a rock-and-roll happening on offshore Ruissalo Island near the archipelago's most modern hotel. The season closes with a three-week programme of symphony concerts, opera, ballet, jazz, films and exhibitions in the capital, from the end of August to mid-September. The culturally-minded visitor who can take everything on offer may then 'get away from it all' in a holiday village.

The 'Finland Festivals' events do not exhaust the list. Log-floating championships, regattas, shooting the rapids, lacemaking weeks, arts and crafts competitions and strawberry carnivals fill out the remainder of the long summer days and short nights.

There is no difficulty about access. Air and train travel are among the cheapest in Europe and Finnair, the national airline, covers the whole country including Ivalo, nearly 200 miles into the Arctic Circle. For eighty dollars (thirty-three pounds) the company's Holiday Ticket entitles the holder to travel at will on the domestic network for fifteen days. There are also cheap rail tickets, combining with air, bus and steamer travel.

Finland is, incidentally, a useful take-off point for travel to the USSR. Bus services start from Helsinki and Lappeenranta; a few hours sailing by Soviet ship from Helsinki takes one to Tallinn, the Estonian capital on the south coast of the Gulf of Finland, and the trips by modern Finnish vessels to Leningrad, for which no visas are required, are especially popular. Passengers live on board during the stay in the city.

In the past decade Finland's income from tourism has increased tenfold, a growth rate few West European countries can match. Nevertheless, tourism is not a complete novelty. The Finnish Travel Association was started as far back as 1887, with the idealist aim of enabling Finns to discover their own land. By the

FINLAND: AN INTRODUCTION

1920s various hotels had already been built, including some in Lapland. However, the leap forward came after the last war. Whereas a bare 150,000 foreign visitors came in 1952, the year of the Helsinki Olympic Games, by 1970 the figure had risen to no less than 1·5 million, chiefly from Sweden, followed by West Germany, Norway, the USA and Britain.

This massive development has forced the authorities to take action. In 1971 a tourist department was established in the Ministry of Commerce and Industry and, in fact, several years previously the state had assumed financial responsibility for ten tourist information offices set up abroad, headed by New York and London, now run by a Ministry subsidiary, the Finnish Tourist Board. At the same time Finnair has extended its routes as far as New York, with a further planned advance to Tokyo. For sea travel, the largest car ferries to both Sweden and West Germany are Finnish-operated. At home a genuine tourist industry has come into existence.

As a foreign currency earner tourism has leapt into fourth place, exceeded only by the timber, paper and allied industries, metals and textiles, and continued development seems assured. With the certain growth of world demand for rural amenities and leisure pursuits, Finland will increasingly have something to offer.

The coming of autumn in Lapland

On a frozen lake, Finnish Lapland

THE SAUNA CULT

MARJATTA HERVA

Sauna—a familiar word? Well, you know one word of Finnish at least, and one that has already found its way into the dictionaries of some languages. For the Finn, though, it means much more than just a bath-house. It evokes a host of ideas and feelings that are all part and parcel of the traditional Finnish bathing ritual.

Sauna is an inescapable part of Finnish life. You could no more deprive a Finn of it than the Englishman of his hot-water bottle. The Finn goes to sauna with no more ado than people in other countries go to work, and he need go no further than round the next corner to find one. It costs next to nothing and brings the joy back to living. In Finland the sauna is not the status symbol that it has become in many countries where it has won popularity. Everyone, from babes in arms to the very old, from the penniless dreamer to the disgustingly rich, pays it a regular visit.

FINLAND: AN INTRODUCTION

Nowadays the sauna comes in many shapes and sizes. In the towns you can go to a public sauna. Some have separate baths for men and women, others allow men and women in on different days. The public sauna, however, is ceasing to play so important a role as new blocks of flats are built. These almost always have their own sauna which each family can hire for an hour or two at least once a week. In some blocks it is in the basement, in others you find it on the top floor, perhaps even in an adjacent building or in the proximity of the heating plant. In older houses the bathroom may be large enough to divide in two so that one half can be converted into a sauna. The equipment and fittings for this kind of conversion are mass produced.

Wherever possible the farmer builds his sauna hut—usually recognizable by its distinctive coat of red paint—by the sea or at the edge of a lake. For most of the year Saturday is, by tradition, the day when the sauna is heated, but during the short summer it will be in use almost daily. The town dweller too prefers to build his summer cottage by the water's edge. His sauna is never far away and may nowadays have been built as part of the cottage. The Finns make the most of their summer. It is an enchanting, almost magical season, but short. Every moment must be enjoyed to the full. The fragrant, pungent steam—the Finns even have a special word, löyly, for it—the aroma of the freshly-cut birch whisk and the plunge into the lake are what the Finn needs to revitalize him and to restore his spirits for the long, dark winter.

The sauna is an essential part of the treatment of certain disablements. Sports grounds provide saunas in which the athletes can relax their tensed muscles. You find them at swimming pools. Many clubs have their own. Nor is the tourist forgotten. You will find a sauna in the largest hotel and on the most remote camping site. Boy scouts have perfected the tent sauna and the Finnish soldier can turn a dug-out into one. The Finn who seeks solitude deep in the forest or out on the fells builds himself one and uses it at night as his bedroom. Many factories and offices have their prestige saunas, and the Finnish President offers his guests a selection designed to suit every taste. Politicians and businessmen will go to the sauna before negotiations begin; afterwards, problems seem smaller and everyone is co-operative.

Between them the nearly five million Finns have almost a million saunas. During the 1930s many thought that the institution would fall out of use and be forgotten as the bathroom became a standard fitting in new flats and houses. Things turned out differently. The popularity of the sauna has increased enormously since the war and nowadays no one would ever dare suggest that a Finn could go through life without it.

The sauna ritual has three distinct stages: perspiration, washing, cooling. For the Finn, the whole process follows a set of unwritten rules which are learnt in childhood. Whether you have a 'dry' or 'damp' sauna (which depends on the construction of the stove) and how long you spend in the steam room are matters of personal choice. For the connoisseur only the 'smoke' sauna will do. In this, the smoke from the stove is allowed to circulate inside and expelled from the sauna just before it is used. The result is a marvellous woody tang. The over-vigorous use of the whisk and the roll in the snow are aspects of the ritual urged on the unsuspecting foreigner but not always practised so devotedly by Finns themselves.

A temperature of 194°F (90°C) is enough to open the pores of the skin, essential function of the sauna. After perspiring enough you wash and allow the body to cool. Ideally, this is helped by a plunge in the sea or lake, but where this is not possible a bath, shower, a bucket of water poured over your head or even sitting quietly in a cool place is adequate. Remember to take certain simple precautions before you go to sauna. Do not eat or drink nor do anything else likely to increase the work load on the heart immediately beforehand. Physiological research has shown that the sauna increases the circulation and thus adds to the load on the heart. Provided you have a healthy heart, it is perfectly safe. Sufferers from any kind of cardiac complaint, however, should not go without first seeking medical advice.

Time stands still in the sauna. The whole ritual including

several visits to the steam room and a cold plunge after each visit can last several hours. Many Finns regard this as a pleasant way of spending an evening and invite friends over 'to sauna'. All sense of hurry is left in the changing room with your clothes. Finnish physiologists have tried to discover the secret of the sense of well-being that follows. Their research has led them to the conclusion that it results from stimulation of the circulation and of other vital bodily functions. A recent examination of the psychological effects has given a scientific basis to what every sauna fanatic knew already: anxiety, depression, bad temper, all give way to a sense of general relaxation in the heat of the sauna.

The world over, the sauna is regarded as a Finnish institution. Although the Finns have undeniably done more than any other nation to perfect it, they cannot claim the honour of having invented it. Ethnographers all agree that it originated many thousands of years ago in the primitive conditions of Arctic Eurasia. The etymologies of words connected with the sauna ritual—including the word sauna—all indicate that the ancient Finns first became acquainted with this form of bathing some two thousand years ago, before they had even set foot in their present homeland. They were still living in areas south and east of the Gulf of Finland where they formed the western end of a chain of Finno-Ugrian peoples extending across Northern Russia.

The ancient Finns took the sauna with them as they carved homes out of the primeval wilderness. The bath-house was a central feature in their isolated lives and witnessed all their joys and sorrows. It was the place where the old were taken to die and where mothers gave birth. The quack applied his blood-letting cups there. It was the place where flax was prepared for spinning, the smoke from the stove cured the family's meat and the malt for beer was soaked there. The girl about to be married bathed in her parents' sauna before setting off for her new home. Each had its own resident tutelary spirit and until recent times no one would have thought of heating the sauna without first making an appropriate offering. No festival or celebration could start without a visit to the sauna. And even nowadays the Saturday visit marks the end of the week's work and the beginning of the day of rest.

Against this background of history and tradition it is not surprising that the Finn looks askance at the more bizarre characteristics associated with the sauna abroad. Salesmen in some countries have ascribed functions to it that the Finn has never even thought of. It is not a private brothel, it is not a nudist colony, nor is it a slimming machine. It was never intended as an extension to a bar. The reasons for removing your clothes are strictly practical: you cannot enjoy the sauna with clothing soaked in perspiration sticking to you—and the whole object is to enjoy the experience. The Finns could not care less what kind of steam boxes people choose to sit in nor what kind of slimming gadgets they devise provided the sauna's name is not used to promote their sales.

The Finns treat the sauna with great respect. From ancient times behaviour in it has been regulated by a code of unwritten rules. An old proverb states that you should behave in the sauna as you would in church. Do not make unnecessary noise, do not shout, do not swear and do nothing to disturb others. The sauna is not just a place to wash in. If it were, it would never have survived for almost two thousand years as the tradition of a whole nation and spread far and wide all over the world.

FINNS ABROAD

ERKKI SAVOLAINEN

For the past hundred years or more Finns, for a variety of motives, have been quitting their native land permanently or temporarily. The departing groups have varied widely in composition and size, ranging from the comparatively affluent educated to the poor and unskilled, and quantitatively from the temporary transfer of small numbers to mass permanent exodus on a scale sufficient to modify the national demography.

These movements have been additionally stimulated by the esteem earned by the emigrants in their new homelands: the professional men as highly trained, industrious and competent, the artisans, semi-skilled and farmworkers as energetic pioneers and trail-blazers, prepared to face and overcome hardships in establishing themselves overseas. In brief, host governments have found them good potential citizens and desirable immigrant material.

In earlier centuries, war or religion accounted for a certain movement of population, either west to Sweden or east to Russia. But apart from a small body of peasants, brought over in the sixteenth century to Värmland by the Swedish government, some of whom later settled in the present State of Delaware, USA, emigration proper started in the mid-nineteenth century. It consisted of two streams heading in diametrically opposite directions, east and west, the flow checked only by the First World War.

To the east lay the overlord, Tsarist Russia, ruling the then autonomous Grand Duchy of Finland. In this huge empire, and particularly in St Petersburg (Leningrad), Finns found that they could successfully compete for much attractive and lucrative employment; and over the decades a steady flow of officials,

professional soldiers and sailors, businessmen and skilled craftsmen took up posts in the Russian establishment and economy.
General (later Marshal and finally President) Mannerheim, for instance, had a distinguished career in the Russian army from 1887 to 1917. Casimir Ehrnrooth fought with distinction in the Russian-Turkish war (in which incidentally an entire Finnish battalion also took part), and sponsored by the Russians he later even became a minister in the Bulgarian government. In the Russian navy no less than seventy-one admirals came over the years from Finland, among them Vice-Admiral Etholen, Admiral Furujhelm, Admiral von Kramer, at one time Chief of the General Staff and Minister of the Navy, and Admiral Avellan, likewise Minister of the Navy. At the disastrous battle of Tsushima, in the Russian-Japanese war, Vice-Admiral Enqvist managed to extract three ships of his command and bring them safely to Manila.
This outlet was abruptly closed by the Russian October Revolution of 1917. Indeed, for some years prior to and during the First World War, when Finnish aspirations for independence from Russia were at their keenest, a kind of counter-movement in the shape of Finnish enlistment for training in the German army had been taking place. The collapse of both Tsarist Russia and the Kaiser's Germany, however, put an end to both traffics. After the tragic Finnish civil war which ensued, the only fresh arrivals in the Soviet Union were a small band of left-wing refugees from the losing side, who settled in eastern Karelia and the Leningrad area, where part of the population was Finnish-speaking. One of them nevertheless rose to eminence: O. W. Kuusinen, first as member and later as a Presidium secretary of the Central Committee of the Communist Party. Earlier he held a high post in the Comintern. Kuusinen, who died in 1964, therefore reached a higher postwar expatriate status than any other Finn.
Contemporaneously with the movement eastwards, another was in progress to the west: to the USA and Canada. However, it was sustained for different reasons and mostly involved a dissimilar type of emigrant—the poor and unskilled, the proletariat of the towns and countryside. The basic cause was that the landless peasants grew from being in a minority to outnumber the farm-owners. Forced into the cities and industrial centres in search of

work, they fell victims to the depression years of the 1860s and 1870s, generating in turn a steady exodus to the New World which lasted up to the First World War and totalled some 300,000. Approximately 10 per cent of them admittedly returned eventually, but even today there are an estimated 100,000 native-born Finns still living in the two countries, and many towns and even whole districts are predominantly Finnish. The rate of emigration dropped between the two world wars, when the US Government reduced the immigration quota, though in this period a further 10,000 went to Canada of whom a part once again returned. After the Second World War the US Government reduced the quota still further and the annual intake has now dwindled to a few hundred.

Although the local American-Finnish societies and the Finnish-language newspapers are disappearing among an ageing expatriate population, love of the 'Old Country' has persisted and large numbers, many to be sure old-timers and pensioners, take holidays in Finland. When in 1970 President Kekkonen visited the USA, thousands of the population of Fitchburg, Mass, turned out to greet him; and in a speech he expressed his pleasure at the extent to which even second- and third-generation Finns, although now only English-speaking, still cherished affection for the land of their ancestors.

These two outflows, though important and extensive, were to be dwarfed in volume and intensity by the migratory events of the post-war period, the combined result of two powerful and complementary pressures. In Finland industrial and agricultural mechanization was exceptionally rapid; and once more, as in the previous century, a formidable volume of displaced rural workers in vain sought work in the towns and industrial centres. Neighbouring Sweden, on the other hand, more highly industrialized than Finland, had for years been suffering from an acute labour shortage. Inevitably a willing supply moved in to meet an unsatisfied demand; large numbers of immigrants, the Finns in the van, flowed in to Sweden from all over Europe. So intense was the Finnish influx that in the space of two decades it reached 300,000, or as much as over the whole seventy-year cycle of the outflow to North America.

This phenomenal manpower loss has had political consequences. In 1969, for instance, Finland's population actually declined for nearly the first time in her history. Again, the majority of the departing citizens were in their most productive working years. Most seriously, they had received their education and skills in Finnish schools and training establishments. Statesmen have therefore had to consider whether the country could afford a continuing brain-drain of this magnitude. As a result, by organizing technical educational facilities in areas where manpower is still in demand, and by the expansion of grants to domestic industry itself, a start has already been made to halt the trend. Such measures, nevertheless, take time to show results and, while Sweden's wave of prosperity lasts, the drift westwards may persist.

There are some interesting social contrasts between the Swedish and New World communities. In Sweden over 90 per cent of the new arrivals have become town dwellers, whereas in America and Finland itself more than one half live in rural areas. In Sweden again the Finns tend to congregate in colonies and appear slow to learn the host language. Across the Atlantic, on the other hand, the urge to assimilate linguistically as quickly as possible is very noticeable. A possible reason for the phenomenon is the proximity of Finland to the groups in Sweden and the ease of return if desired. Under questioning most expatriates claim that they intend eventually to go back.

Compared with what has been described, other movements of Finns abroad are less important if sometimes unusual and intriguing. Most interesting has been the army's United Nations peace-keeping activities, in Suez, Kashmir, Jerusalem (where General Siilasvuo is a senior officer) and Cyprus, whose international force was commanded by General Martola. Dotted round the world are smaller but still sizeable Finnish emigrant communities, in Australia, South Africa, New Zealand and the South American countries. In Europe, Sweden of course apart, the only significant groups are in Germany and the United Kingdom. Over the years there have been attempts, all unsuccessful, by dissident idealist factions to found more or less utopian settlements in Penedo (Brazil), Misiones (Argentina) and Malcolm Island (Canada). Many children were evacuated during the Second World War to Sweden and Denmark, some of whom married locally and did not return. The *au pair* girls, mainly students travelling abroad to study foreign languages, penetrate many European households, principally in West Germany and Great Britain.

The real ambassador of Finland, however, is typically the expatriate professional man, official, engineer or sales representative, often associated with some local cultural institution or Finnish-owned factory sales organization, resident in substantial numbers not only all over Europe but also in the Americas North and South, the Middle and Far East, Africa and the Antipodes. He and his compatriots bear the major responsibility for perpetuating status, goodwill and respect for Finland among the nations of the world.

THE FINNS AND THE BRITISH

PHYLLIS CHAPMAN

The Finns and the British have rarely been enemies (except technically during the Second World War). But today they are waging a battle of a different kind: in your home, although you may hardly have noticed it. Look at the wrapping on your packet of butter, the label on your wife's tights or your husband's suit. Where did that wineglass or coffee cup come from, or the pulp from which your newspaper was made? Friends of Finland will have made many such purchases consciously, especially if they admire Finnish design. Famous stores in Britain have enthusiastically taken up the promotion of goods from Finland. But the Finns are not having it all their own way. In 1970 the British launched an export drive themselves, culminating in a massive appearance at the Helsinki International Trade Fair and now the most popular British products are entrenched in Finland's department stores.

FINLAND: AN INTRODUCTION

The arrival of the Finnish car ferry Finnpartner at London's Tower Bridge in autumn 1968, with the imaginative floating exhibition staged by the students of Helsinki Technical University, was the powerful opening shot in the export campaign. At the time, those connected with tourism could not help regretting that the Finnlines ship did not ply regularly between the two countries as had the vessels of the Finland Steamship Co. from as early as 1884. History will repeat itself when, in 1973, a new cargo vessel with cabins for thirty passengers operates a year-round service, taking only $2\frac{1}{2}$ days between Helsinki and London. Meanwhile the air services maintained by Finnair and BEA continue to increase and the number of tours to Finland grows each year.

Visitors to Finland today are delighted at their friendly reception by a nation whose genuine hospitality is quite free of commercialism, though some may admit that the healthy Finnish beds are too hard for them! But centuries before, contacts were less warm and often resulted from volunteers joining in whatever war prevailed at the time. Thus many Scots fought for King Gustavus II Adolphus in such conflicts as the Thirty Years' War when Sweden-Finland was a great power. Many of these soldiers subsequently settled in Finland and descendants of such families as the Ramsays and the von Wrights have played a prominent part in Finnish affairs. But if the British were not participating in a war they were even then engaged in contemporary export drives, so that contacts continued to be a curious mixture of conflict and commerce. A variety of goods, including Gloucester cheese, brown ale and clothes for the ladies of the Ostrobothnian ports, were being sent from Britain and considerable quantities of tar left Oulu for use by the Navy in the eighteenth century. During the Great Northern War of 1700–31 traders were in constant danger from interference by the warring navies of Sweden and Russia. Sir John Norris was sent to convoy merchantmen round the coasts of Finland which were, in any case, dreaded for their vast number of rocks and the severity of the climate for a great part of the year. His logbooks charted these shores more accurately than ever before. Because the

British feared local conditions, most of the trade was carried on in Finnish ships and, by the 1850s, forty to fifty a year visited London. Pehr Malm is typical of these merchants who often came to England and, in 1856, he sent his son Otto to John Good in Hull where Malm was honoured by having a street named after him. John Good had founded his shipping firm in 1835 after twenty-two years at sea, mainly in Baltic waters, and the firm still flourishes.

By the time of the Crimean War, Britain and Finland were on opposite sides since Sweden had surrendered Finland to Russia in 1809. An English squadron attacked or landed at various Finnish harbours such as Oulu, where the tar stocks and boats were destroyed, and at Kokkola (Gamlakarleby) where the Finns captured a boat which is still on view in the 'English Park'. Combined British and French squadrons landed on Åland in 1854, attacked the fortress of Bomarsund and the ruins remain a tourist attraction. The most spectacular, if least successful, of these enterprises was undertaken the following year when the fleets bombarded the fortress of Sveaborg (now Suomenlinna) just off Helsinki. The inhabitants of the town went up to the aptly named Observatory Hill and watched the 'performance'.

Hundreds of Finnish prisoners taken at Bomarsund, including women and children, were eventually held in Lewes Jail, Sussex. The conditions were not unduly harsh, for the prisoners received gifts, were able to make purchases in the town, and the officers were invited out socially. Twenty-eight of the prisoners died before release came in 1856 and they were buried in the cemetery of St John sub Castro where a stone monument was erected to them by order of Tsar Alexander II in 1877.

It was always obvious that Britain had great sympathy for Finland and this was most outspoken after the February Manifesto of 1899 brought in the period of Russification. The resulting international petition contained the names of such illustrious Britons as Lord Lister, Florence Nightingale, Thomas Hardy and George Meredith.

FINLAND: AN INTRODUCTION

Peaceful, industrial development in Finland was profoundly influenced by Britain, and notably by Scotland. James Finlayson was an engineer working in Russia when he was persuaded by a friend to go to Finland in 1819. The following year he set up a small enterprise in Tampere which in 1828 developed into the first spinning mill in Finland, with cotton imported from England. Today bright material from Finlayson-Forssa is an export success in Britain. Another Scot, William Crichton, bought a mechanical workshop from a compatriot in Turku in 1863 and this became one of Finland's biggest industrial enterprises, now owned by the Wärtsilä concern which also controls the Arabia porcelain factory whose products are popular in Great Britain. The wheel has once more come full circle.

Among the travellers in the opposite direction at this time was Johan Jacob von Julin, the first of whose many visits was in 1815. He married a Scotswoman and his home in Fiskars became a centre for the diffusion of English ideas and techniques. Thus he established the first steam navigation company in 1819, the first savings bank in 1820 and the first Lancaster Bell school two years later. He imported the first English cattle stock, introducing the all-important Ayrshire cow in 1845.

Although there had been these fruitful contacts between the two countries for many years, rather little was generally known about Finland in Britain. The country had literally been put on an English map as early as 1680 in Moses Pitt's Atlas *which remarked:* 'The ancient inhabitants of Finland were the most hospitable and least barbarous of any of the Scandinavians, but at present they are of all (the Lapps only excepted) the most fierce and uncivilized.' But the first book of any consequence for travellers was that of Edward Clarke whose Travels in Various Countries of Scandinavia; Including Denmark, Sweden, Norway, Lapland and Finland, Undertaken in 1799, *appeared in 1819. His picture of the Finns is hardly flattering. Twenty years later John Murray published the* Handbook for Travellers in Denmark, Norway and Sweden. *By 1861* The Popular Encyclopaedia *had the* following entry: 'The Finns are of small size but robust... are principally Christians... in the narrower sense, are grave, laborious, industrious people, inured to every hardship, fearless, brave, firm, but self-willed and obstinate, but they are withal, very kind and hospitable. They are not wanting in intelligence and are very fond of poetry and music.' In a more illustrious publication the description of physical characteristics still contained phrases like 'low forehead, flat features... protruding mouth, thick lips' etc. It did not help either that representation of the country in the London Exhibition of 1862 was poor, as Topelius found when he visited the city, which incidentally did not much impress him other than by its crowds and general dinginess.

However, interest in Finland grew sufficiently for an Anglo-Finnish Society to be founded in London in 1911. The society's existence was interrupted soon after by the First World War, but when it resumed activity dinners were held annually to celebrate Finland's Independence Day on December 6, as they still are. Although the Second World War forced another interruption, members played an active part by collecting funds and comforts for the Finnish Red Cross, and the Society was reborn in 1954. Its programme of cultural events and social activities attracts friends of Finland and Finns resident in Britain. It maintains contact with the Finnish Church in Rotherhithe and its lively Church Guild. Among the members of both associations many 'mixed' marriages are proof of one of the most successful forms of Anglo-Finnish co-operation. The Church's annual bazaar is besieged by buyers eager for Finnish food and design products. The Church is one of the oldest Finnish institutions in Britain, having been opened in 1857. The present building, designed by Cyril Mardall, himself half Finnish, was finished in 1958. The Anglo-Finnish Society also co-operates with similar associations and belongs to the Confederation of Scandinavian Societies in Great Britain.

Over in Finland the Finnish-British Society of Helsinki was founded in 1926. There are now about sixty similar Societies and the British Council annually selects thirty teachers of English *required by them. Some of the teachers pay their hosts the compliment of marrying and settling down in Finland. Other links have been formed by the scholarships awarded by the British and Finnish Governments for study in the other country.*

Although the first English lecturer was appointed to a Finnish University in 1879, it was not until the late 1940s that a lectureship in Finnish was established in Britain at Hull University. This terminated about ten years later and only in 1968 was an assistant lecturer appointed to the School of Slavonic and East European Studies in the University of London. The subsequent spread of Finnish studies in Britain is discussed elsewhere.

It is inevitable that British culture should be well known in Finland though it is perhaps remarkable that Shakespeare continues to be the foreign playwright whose works are most often performed there. Thus the Royal Shakespeare Company's visits are always welcome. So are the almost annual performances by the Royal Ballet, with Margot Fonteyn the favourite ballerina. British musicians and conductors are frequent visitors and Benjamin Britten received the Sibelius Prize in 1965.

Sibelius has for long been the best known of Finnish composers in Britain. In 1965 the Memorial Concert was performed by the Helsinki City Orchestra at the Royal Festival Hall where an exhibition was also held featuring a model of Eila Hiltunen's Sibelius monument. Among the many famous conductors at concerts all over Britain have been Jussi Jalas and Paavo Berglund. The latter is particularly associated with the Bournemouth Municipal Orchestra and a performance of the Kullervo Symphony with this orchestra and the University Student Choir in November 1970 at the Royal Festival Hall was a real triumph. The young Okko Kamu shot into prominence when conducting the New Philharmonia Orchestra only a few weeks earlier in the same hall. Singers such as Anita Välkki, Kim Borg and Tom Krause have long been familiar to opera and concertgoers.

In 1967 the public had the opportunity of getting to know the work of younger composers during the Camden Festival. But it was also the occasion of two exhibitions, one of Helsinki and another of books, both designed by Tapio Wirkkala. Ten years earlier Alvar Aalto received the Royal Gold Medal from the Royal Institute of British Architects about the time of an exhibition of Finnish architecture there. Major design exhibitions have been held, one in 1961 at the Victoria and Albert Museum (designed by Timo Sarpaneva who became an honorary member of the Royal Society of Arts in 1963) and another in 1965 at the Building Centre in London. Plans to familiarize the public with other aspects of Finnish culture include an exhibition of Finnish prints.

The sauna is one manifestation of Finnish culture which has met with very rapid public approval. Comment on what was long regarded as a curious custom has featured prominently in travel books from earliest times. Among their authors at the end of the last century were some of those typically adventurous Englishwomen often found in remoter parts of the world. Their picturesquely entitled works include Miss Clive-Bayley's Vignettes from Finland or Twelve Months in Strawberry Land *in 1895 and Mrs Alec Tweedie's* Through Finland in Carts *in 1897, while Miss Rosalind Travers' authoritative* Letters from Finland *appeared in 1911.*

Today, the need for information by the tourist is catered for by the Finnish Tourist Board's office in London, opened in 1958. It is responsible for enlightening the travel trade and the public about the attractions of Finland and although it now has at its disposal many more brochures than the one produced by the Finnish Travel Association in 1894, the charm of the country cannot be better described than it was then. 'For those coming from places where culture and manufactures have cleared away most of the original charm of nature, the virgin state of the northern landscape, the forest . . . the beautiful lakes, the fast-flowing rapids . . . needs must afford a peculiar delight, and a sojourn there will certainly be a good change for a man, bored with the worries of over-cultured life!'

REFERENCE SECTION
USEFUL ADDRESSES

Compiled by
RIITTA KALLAS

The English translations of organizations listed here are not necessarily the official English names used in Finland. In some instances Finnish or Swedish titles have been retained for the sake of clarity.

ADVERTISING
Association of Finnish Advertisers, Mechelininkatu 21A, Helsinki 10.
Association of Advertising Agencies, Pieni Roobertinkatu 13B, Helsinki 13.
The Public Relations Society of Finland, Kalevankatu 30, Helsinki 10.

AGRICULTURE
National Board of Agriculture, Mariankatu 23, Helsinki 17.
Finnish Agricultural Council for Public Relations and Information, Simonkatu 6, Helsinki 10.
National Association of Agricultural Societies, Lönnrotinkatu 11, Helsinki 12.

AIR LINES
Finnair Oy, Töölönkatu 4, Helsinki 10.
Kar-Air Oy, Lönnrotinkatu 3, Helsinki 12.

AMERICAN-FINNISH ORGANIZATIONS
Finnish-American Society, Mechelininkatu 10, Helsinki 10.
Finnish-American Chamber of Commerce, Eteläinen Esplanadikatu 18, Helsinki 13.
Finnish Committee on Study and Training in USA, Mechelininkatu 10, Helsinki 10.

ANGLO-FINNISH ORGANIZATIONS
British Council, Eteläinen Esplanadikatu 22, Helsinki 13.
Finnish-British Society, Puistokatu 1b A, Helsinki 16.
Finnish-British Trade Association, Eteläinen Esplanadikatu 2, Helsinki 13.

USEFUL ADDRESSES

ARCHAEOLOGY
Finnish Archaeological Society, National Museum, Mannerheimintie 34, Helsinki 10.

ARCHITECTURE
Association of Finnish Architects, Unioninkatu 30A, Helsinki 10.
Museum of Finnish Architecture, Puistokatu 4, Helsinki 14.
Department of Architecture, Institute of Technology, Otaniemi.

ARMY AND AIR-FORCE
General Staff, Information Section, Eteläinen Makasiinikatu 8, Helsinki 13.

ART
Ateneum, Art Academy of Finland, Kaivokatu 2-4, Helsinki 10.
Forum Artis, c/o Jukka Kemppinen, Mikonkatu 6C, Helsinki 10.
Society of Finnish Artists, Ainonkatu 3, Helsinki 10.

ASTRONOMY
The Observatory, Tähtitorninmäki, Helsinki 14.

AUTHORS
Association of Finnish Authors (Suomen Kirjailijaliitto), Runeberginkatu 32C, Helsinki 10.
Association of Finnish Critics (Suomen Arvostelijain Liitto), Fredrikinkatu 62A6, Helsinki 10.
Association of Finnish Dramatists (Suomen Näytelmäkirjailijain Liitto—Finlands Svenska Dramatikerförbund), Vironkatu 12B, Helsinki 17.
Association of Swedo-Finnish Authors (Finlands Svenska Författareförening), Runebergsgatan 32C, Helsingfors 10.
Union of Finnish Translators (Suomen Kääntäjäin Yhdistys), Fredrikinkatu 62A6, Helsinki 10.

BALLET AND OPERA
Association of Finnish Dancers, Lönnrotinkatu 29E, Helsinki 18.
Finnish National Opera, Bulevardi 23-27, Helsinki 18.

BANKING
Bank of Finland, Snellmaninkatu 8, Helsinki 17.
Central Bank of the Savings Banks (Säästöpankkien Keskus-Osake-Pankki), Aleksanterinkatu 46, Helsinki 10.
Central Bank of the Co-operative Credit Societies (Osuuskassojen Keskus Oy), Arkadiankatu 23, Helsinki 10.
Finnish Bankers Association, Aleksanterinkatu 36A, Helsinki 10.

FINLAND: AN INTRODUCTION

Finnish Export Credit, Inc., Eteläranta 6, Helsinki 13.
Industrialization Fund, Inc., Lönnrotinkatu 13, Helsinki 12.

BLIND PEOPLE

Association for the Blind, Mäkelänkatu 52, Helsinki 51.

BOY SCOUTS

Finnish Boy Scouts Association, Heikkiläntie 10, Helsinki 20.

CAMPING

Finnish Travel Association, Camping Section, Uudenmaankatu 16A, Helsinki 12.

CHEMISTRY

Chemical Association, Fabianinkatu 7B, Helsinki 13.

CHESS

Finnish Chess Association (Suomen Keskusshakkiliitto), Relanderinaukio 2D28, Helsinki 57.

CHILD WELFARE

Helsinki Child Welfare Office, Toinen linja 4, Helsinki 53.
Mannerheim League for the Protection of Children, Toinen linja 17, Helsinki 53.

CHORAL SOCIETIES

Association of Finnish Singers and Instrumentalists (Sulasol), Kluuvikatu 8, Helsinki 10.
Finnish Association of Church Choirs (Suomen Kirkkokuoroliitto), Karhulantie 62, Karhula.
Swedo-Finnish Association of Church Choirs (Finlands Svenska Kyrkosångförbund), Kantelevägen 13D, Helsingfors 42.
Swedo-Finnish Union of Singers and Musicians (Finlands Svenska Sång-och Musikförbund), Annegatan 12, Helsingfors 12.
Finnish Workers Musical Association (Suomen Työväen Musiikkiliitto), Hallituskatu 19, Tampere 20.

CINEMA

Association of Finnish Film Producers, Kluuvikatu 3A57, Helsinki 10.
Chamber of Finnish Film Industry (Suomen Filmikamari), Kaisaniemenkatu 3B, Helsinki 10.
Finnish Film Foundation, Kaisaniemenkatu 3B, Helsinki 10.
Finnish Film Archives, Eteläranta 4B, Helsinki 13.

CO-OPERATIVE ORGANIZATIONS

Central Co-operative Hankkija, Salomonkatu 1, Helsinki 10.
Central Co-operative Karjakunta, Lautatarhankatu 4, Helsinki 50.

USEFUL ADDRESSES

Central Co-operative SOK, Vilhonkatu 7, Helsinki 10.
Co-operative Wholesale Society OTK, Hämeentie 19, Helsinki 50.
Pellervo Society, Simonkatu 6, Helsinki 10.
Valio, Co-operative Dairies Association, Kalevankatu 61, Helsinki 18.

DEAF PEOPLE
Finnish Association for the Deaf, Liisankatu 27E, Helsinki 17.

DESIGN
Finnish Design Center Oy, Kasarminkatu 19, Helsinki 13.
Society of Arts and Crafts, Unioninkatu 30A, Helsinki 10.
Finnish Association of Designers ORNAMO, Unioninkatu 30A, Helsinki 10.
Institute of Industrial Art (Taideteollinen Oppilaitos), Kaivokatu 2-4, Helsinki 10.

DISABLED PEOPLE
Finnish Association of Disabled Civilians and Ex-Servicemen (Suomen Siviili- ja Asevelvollisuusinvalidien Liitto), Mannerheimintie 44A, Helsinki 26.
Association of Disabled Ex-Servicemen (Sotainvalidien Veljesliitto), Kasarminkatu 34, Helsinki 13.
Foundation for the Disabled (Invalidisäätiö), Tenholantie 10, Helsinki 28.

ECONOMY
Department of National Economy, Ministry of Finance, Kirkkokatu 14, Helsinki 17.
Finnish Market Facts Ltd, Topeliuksenkatu 17C, Helsinki 25.
Institute for Economic Research, Bank of Finland, Snellmaninkatu 8, Helsinki 17.
Commission for Foreign Investments, Ministry of Commerce and Industry, Aleksanterinkatu 10, Helsinki 17.
Society for Political Economy (Kansantaloudellinen Yhdistys), Kirkkokatu 14, Helsinki 17.
Swedo-Finnish Economic Society (Ekonomiska Samfundet i Finland), Sportsvägen 12, Grankulla.

EDUCATION
Ministry of Education:
  General Department,
  Schools Department,
  Department of Higher Education and Science,

FINLAND: AN INTRODUCTION

Department for International Relations,
Commission for International Scholarships,
Rauhankatu 4, Helsinki 17.
National Board of Schools, Eteläinen Esplanadikatu 16, Helsinki 13.
Centre for Civic Education (Kansalaiskasvatuksen Keskus), Kasarmikatu 23A, Helsinki 13.

EMBASSIES
Foreign Embassies and Consulates in Finland
Australia
Sergelstorg 12, Stockholm, Sweden (Embassy).
Canada
Pohjoinen Esplanadikatu 25B, Helsinki 10 (Embassy).
Great Britain
Uudenmaankatu 16-20, Helsinki 12 (Embassy).
Ireland
Östermalmsgatan 97, Stockholm, Sweden (Embassy).
USA
Itäinen Puistotie 21, Helsinki 14 (Embassy).
Finnish Embassies and Consulates Abroad
Australia
83, Endeavour Street, Red Hill, Canberra (Embassy).
Canada
85, Range Road, Ottawa 2, Ont. (Embassy).
Dominion Square Building, 1010 St Catherine Street, Montreal 2, Quebec (Consulate).
Great Britain
66, Chester Square, London S.W.1 (Embassy).
Ireland
8, Groot Herrtoginnelaan, Den Haag, Netherlands (Embassy).
19, Lower Pembroke Street, Dublin 2 (Consulate General).
United Nations
866, United Nations Plaza, New York 17, N.Y. 10017 (Permanent Mission).
149 A, route de Ferney, 1218 Le Grand-Saconnex, Genève.
USA
1900, 24th Street, N.W., Washington D.C. 20008 (Embassy).
Finland House, 540, Maddison Avenue, New York, N.Y. 10022 (Consulate General).

USEFUL ADDRESSES

120, Montgomery Street, San Francisco, California 94104 (Consulate General).
3600, Wilshire Bulevard, Los Angeles, California 90005 (Consulate).
1111, Church Street, Evanston, Illinois, 60201 (Consulate).

ENGINEERING
Engineering Society of Finland (STS) (Finnish), Yrjönkatu 30, Helsinki 10.
Engineering Society of Finland (TFIF) (Swedo-Finnish), Georgsgatan 30, Helsingfors 10.
Association of Engineers, Yrjönkatu 30, Helsinki 10.
National Board of Building, Siltasaarenkatu 18-20, Helsinki 53.
National Board of Public Roads and Waterways, Eteläinen Esplanadikatu 4, Helsinki 13.

ESPERANTO
Esperanto Foundation, Iirislahti, Esperantotie 4.

EXHIBITIONS
Department for Trade Fairs Abroad, Finnish Foreign Trade Association, Eteläinen Esplanadikatu 18, Helsinki 13.
Commission for Trade Fairs, Central Chamber of Commerce, c/o Association of Finnish Advertisers, Mechelininkatu 21A, Helsinki 10.
Commission for Cultural Exhibitions, Ministry of Education, Rauhankatu 4, Helsinki 17.

FASHION
Finn-Flare Team Oy, Turuntie 20, Salo.
Kalevala Koru, Fredrikinkatu 41C, Helsinki 12.
Marimekko Oy, Vanha talvitie 3, Helsinki 50.
Studio Nurmesniemi, Merikatu 1, Helsinki 14.

FLORA AND FAUNA
Botanical Garden, Kaisaniemi, Helsinki 17.
Finnish Society for Nature Protection, Fredrikinkatu 77A, Helsinki 10.
Finnish Society for Protection of Animals, Lutherinkatu 8C, Helsinki 10.
Societas pro Fauna et Flora Fennica, Storsvängen 15bB, Helsingfors 20.
Finnish Biological Society Vanamo, Snellmaninkatu 9-11, Helsinki 17.
Zoological Museum, Pohjoinen Rautatiekatu 13, Helsinki 10.

FINLAND: AN INTRODUCTION

FOREIGN CITIZENS
Ministry of the Interior, Aliens Section, Fredrikinkatu 21, Helsinki 12.
FORESTRY
National Board of Forestry, Erottajankatu 2, Helsinki 12.
Forestry Department, Ministry of Agriculture, Ritarikatu 2B, Helsinki 17.
Finnish Forestry Association, Snellmaninkatu 13, Helsinki 17.
Finnish Society of Forestry, Unioninkatu 40B, Helsinki 17.
GENEALOGY
Genealogical Society of Finland (Suomen Sukututkimusseura), Snellmaninkatu 9–11, Helsinki 17.
GENERAL INFORMATION
Press Bureau, Ministry for Foreign Affairs, Ritarikatu 2, Helsinki 17.
Finn Facts Institute, Unioninkatu 14A, Helsinki 13.
GEOGRAPHY
Geographical Society of Finland, Snellmaninkatu 9–11, Helsinki 17.
Land Survey Board, Kirkkokatu 3, Helsinki 17.
GEOLOGY
Finnish Geological Society, c/o Geologinen tutkimuslaitos, Otaniemi.
GIRL GUIDES
Finnish Girl Guides Association, Heikkiläntie 10, Helsinki 20.
GLIDING
Aeronautical Association of Finland (Suomen Ilmailuliitto), Malmi Airport, Helsinki 70.
HANDICRAFTS
Finnish Friends of Handicrafts (Suomen Käsityön Ystävät Oy), Yrjönkatu 13, Helsinki 12.
Federation of Handicrafts and Light Industry, Kansakoulukatu 10A, Helsinki 10.
HISTORY
Finnish Historical Society, Soukankuja 7D78, Soukka.
National Museum, Mannerheimintie 34, Helsinki 10.
Association of Friends of History (Historian Ystäväin Liitto), Rauhankatu 17, Helsinki 17.
HORTICULTURE
National Board of Agriculture, Mariankatu 23, Helsinki 17.
Horticulturalists Association, Lönnrotinkatu 22A, Helsinki 12.
Market Gardeners Association, Temppelikatu 3–5, Helsinki 10.

USEFUL ADDRESSES

HOTELS
Finnish Hotels Federation, Pohjoisranta 20A, Helsinki 20.
Finnish Hotels and Restaurants Association, Eerikinkatu 16A, Helsinki 10.

HUNTING
Finnish Hunting Federation (Suomen Metsästysyhdistys), Viikinmäki, Helsinki 56.
Finnish Hunters Association (Suomen Metsästäjäliitto), Vänrikki Stoolinkatu 8A, Helsinki 10.
Department of Fisheries and Hunting, Ministry of Agriculture, Hallituskatu 4, Helsinki 17.

HYDRO-ELECTRICITY
Imatran Voima Oy, Consulting and Foreign Department, P.O. Box 138, 00101, Helsinki 10 (Malminkatu 16, Helsinki 10).
Consulting Engineers Office, Eteläinen Esplanadikatu 14, Helsinki 13.
International Commission on Large Dams: Finnish Committee, P.O. Box 138, 00101, Helsinki 10.

INDUSTRY
Federation of Finnish Industries, Eteläranta 10, Helsinki 13.
Union of Manufacturers, Mariankatu 26B9, Helsinki 17.

INSURANCE
Association of Finnish Insurance Companies, Bulevardi 28, Helsinki 12.

JEWISH ORGANIZATIONS
Central Council of Jewish Communities in Finland, Malminkatu 26, Helsinki 10.

JOURNALISM
Association of Finnish Journalists, Yrjönkatu 11A2, Helsinki 12.
Association of Finnish Magazine Editors, Vuorimiehenkatu 14C, Helsinki 14.

LAPLAND
Educational Society for Lapland, Kimmeltie 11C, Tapiola.
Research Society for Lapland, Rovaniemi.

LAW
Association of Finnish Lawyers, Runeberginkatu 39, Helsinki 10.
Finnish Society of Jurisprudence, c/o Asianajotoimisto Hannes Snellman, Aleksanterinkatu 48A, Helsinki 10.

LIBRARIES AND ARCHIVES
Library Society of Finland, Museokatu 18A, Helsinki 10.

FINLAND: AN INTRODUCTION

Finnish Research Library Association, c/o Box 503, Finnish Meteorological Institute, Vuorikatu 24, Helsinki 10.
University Library, Unioninkatu 36, Helsinki 17.
Parliamentary Library, Eduskuntakatu, Helsinki 17.
Library of Learned Societies, Snellmaninkatu 9–11, Helsinki 17.
National Archives, Rauhankatu 17, Helsinki 17.
Finnish War Archives, Siltavuorenranta 16, Helsinki 17.
Helsinki City Library, Richardinkatu 1, Helsinki 13.
Turku University Library, Turku.
Åbo Academy Library, Åbo.
Turku City Library, Turku.

LITERATURE

Finnish Literature Society (Suomalaisen Kirjallisuuden Seura), Hallituskatu 1, Helsinki 17.
Swedo-Finnish Literature Society (Svenska Litteratursällskapet i Finland), Snellmansgatan 9–11, Helsingfors 17.

LOCAL GOVERNMENT

Union of Finnish Towns, Eduskuntakatu 4, Helsinki 10.
Union of Finnish Local Authorities, Albertinkatu 34, Helsinki 18.
Union of Swedo-Finnish Local Authorities, Albertsgatan 34C, Helsingfors 18.
Local Government Department, Ministry of the Interior, Hallituskatu 4E, Helsinki 17.

LUTHERAN CHURCH

Finnish Committee of the Lutheran World Federation, Vuorikatu 22A, Helsinki 10.
Association of Parish Workers in the Finnish Church, Vuorikatu 22A, Helsinki 10.

MEDICINE

Finnish Medical Association, Ruoholahdenkatu 4, Helsinki 18.
Finnish Dentists Society, Bulevardi 30B, Helsinki 12.
Finnish Medical Society Duodecim, Runeberginkatu 47A, Helsinki 26.
Swedo-Finnish Medical Society, Snellmansgatan 9–11, Helsingfors 17.
National Medical Board, Siltasaarenkatu 18A, Helsinki 53.

MENTAL HEALTH

Finnish Psychological Society, Ilmarinkatu 2C40, Helsinki 10.
Institute for Occupational Therapy, Haartmaninkatu 1, Helsinki 25.

USEFUL ADDRESSES

METAL INDUSTRY
Association of Finnish Metal and Engineering Industries, Eteläranta 10, Helsinki 13.
Metex Corporation, Ruoholahdenkatu 4, Helsinki 18.

METEOROLOGY
Central Office of Meteorology, Box 503, Vuorikatu 24, Helsinki 10.

MINISTRIES
Ministry for Foreign Affairs, Ritarikatu 2, Helsinki 17.
Ministry of Justice, Ritarikatu 2, Helsinki 17.
Ministry of the Interior, Hallituskatu 4E, Helsinki 17.
Ministry of Finance, Aleksanterinkatu 3D, Helsinki 17.
Ministry of Defence, Eteläinen Makasiinikatu 8, Helsinki 13.
Ministry of Education, Rauhankatu 4, Helsinki 17.
Ministry of Agriculture, Ritarikatu 2, Helsinki 17.
Ministry of Communications, Aleksanterinkatu 3D, Helsinki 17.
Ministry of Commerce and Industry, Aleksanterinkatu 10, Helsinki 17.
Ministry of Social Affairs and Health, Snellmaninkatu 4-6, Helsinki 17.

MISSIONARIES
Finnish Missionary Society (Suomen Lähetysseura), Tähtitorninkatu 16-18, Helsinki 14.
Finnish Society of Seamen's Missions, Albertinkatu 2, Helsinki 15.
Church of Finland Society for Home Missions, Töölönkatu 55, Helsinki 25.

MOTORING
Finnish Automobile Club, Fabianinkatu 14, Helsinki 10.

MUSEUMS
Finnish Museums Association, Museokatu 5A, Helsinki 10.
National Museum, Mannerheimintie 34, Helsinki 10.
Ateneum Art Gallery, Kaivokatu 2-4, Helsinki 10.

MUSIC
Sibelius Academy, Pohjoinen Rautatiekatu 9, Helsinki 10.
Composers Copyright Office Teosto, Hietaniemenkatu 2, Helsinki 10.
Music Information Centre, Runeberginkatu 15A, Helsinki 10.
Sibelius Society, Pohjoinen Rautatiekatu 9, Helsinki 10.
Turku Music Society, Piispankatu 15, Turku.

NUCLEAR PHYSICS
Finnish Nuclear Society, Malminkatu 16, Helsinki 10.

FINLAND: AN INTRODUCTION

Atomic Energy Commission, Aleksanterinkatu 10, Helsinki 17.

NURSING

Helsinki Nurses Training College, Tukholmankatu 10, Helsinki 29.
Finnish Nursing Association, Töölöntullinkatu 8, Helsinki 25.

ORNITHOLOGY

Finnish Ornithological Union, Pohjoinen Rautatiekatu 13, Helsinki 10.

ORTHODOX CHURCH

Helsinki Orthodox Congregation, Liisankatu 29, Helsinki 17.
Finnish Orthodox Church Assembly, Kuopio.
Orthodox Institute of the University of Helsinki, Vuorikatu 3, Helsinki 10.

PHILATELY

Philatelic Section, The General Post Office, Simonkatu 12A, Helsinki 10.

PHOTOGRAPHY

Finnish Photographers Association, Korkeavuorenkatu 2b F72, Helsinki 14.
Finnfoto (Suomen Valokuvajärjestöjen Keskusliitto), Korkeavuorenkatu 2b F72, Helsinki 14.

PHYSICS

Institute of Technology, Otaniemi.
Finnish Physicist Society (Suomen Fyysikkoseura), Mariankatu 14, Helsinki 17.
Swedo-Finnish Physicist Society (Fysiker Samfundet i Finland), Siltavuorenpenger 20, Helsinki 17.

POLICE

Police Force, Ratakatu 12, Helsinki 12
Criminal Investigation Department, Ratakatu 12, Helsinki 12.
State Police College, Otaniemi.
Police Department, Ministry of the Interior, Hallituskatu 4E, Helsinki 17.

POLITICAL PARTY ORGANIZATIONS

Centre Party (Keskustapuolue), Pursimiehenkatu 15, Helsinki 15.
Finnish People's Democratic Union (Suomen Kansan Demokraattinen Liitto), Simonkatu 8B, Helsinki 10.
Finnish Rural Party (Suomen Maaseudun Puolue), Pohjoinen Rautatiekatu 15B15, Helsinki 10.

Finnish Social-democratic Party (Suomen Sosiaalidemokraattinen Puolue), Paasivuorenkatu 3, Helsinki 53.
Liberal People's Party (Liberaalinen Kansanpuolue), Fredrikinkatu 58A, Helsinki 10.
National Coalition Party (Kansallinen Kokoomus), Iso Roobertinkatu 21, Helsinki 12.
Swedo-Finnish People's Party (Svenska Folkpartiet), Bulevarden 7A, Helsingfors 12.
Social-democratic League (Sosialidemokraattinen Liitto), Vironkatu 6A, Helsinki 17.

PRESS

Newspaper Association (Sanomalehtien Liitto), Mannerheimintie 18, Helsinki 10.
Magazine Association (Aikakauslehtien Liitto), Mannerheimintie 18, Helsinki 10.
Finnish News Agency (Suomen Tietotoimisto), Mannerheimintie 18, Helsinki 10.

Newspapers:
Aamulehti (National Coalition Party), Tampere.
Helsingin Sanomat (Independent), Ludviginkatu 6–8, Helsinki 13.
Hufvudstadsbladet (Independent, in Swedish), Mannerheimvägen 18, Helsingfors 10.
Kansan Uutiset (People's Democratic Union), Kotkankatu 9, Helsinki 51.
Suomenmaa (Centre Party), Kansakoulukatu 8A, Helsinki 10.
Suomen Sosialidemokraatti (Social-democratic Party), Paasivuorenkatu 3, Helsinki 53.
Turun Sanomat (Liberal People's Party), Turku.
Uusi Suomi (National Coalition Party), Lönnrotinkatu 4, Helsinki 12.

PRISONS

Prison Association (Kriminaalihuolto), Pengerkatu 30C–D, Helsinki 50.
Criminological Research Institute, Pengerkatu 30A, Helsinki 50.
Prisons Administration, Ministry of Justice, Fredrikinkatu 48A, Helsinki 10.

PUBLIC HEALTH

Hospitals Association, Pitkänsillanranta 1, Helsinki 53.
Institute for Occupational Therapy, Haartmaninkatu 1, Helsinki 25.

FINLAND: AN INTRODUCTION

National Medical Board, Siltasaarenkatu 18A, Helsinki 53.
Swedo-Finnish Society for National Health (Samfundet Folkhälsan), Topeliusgatan 20, Helsingfors 25.

PUBLISHERS

Finnish Publishers Association, Kalevankatu 16, Helsinki 10.
Werner Söderström Oy (WSOY), Bulevardi 12, Helsinki 12.
Kustannusosakeyhtiö Otava, Uudenmaankatu 8–12, Helsinki 12.
Kustannusosakeyhtiö Tammi, Hämeentie 15, Helsinki 50.
Kirjayhtymä, Simonkatu 6, Helsinki 10.
Weilin & Göös, Mannerheimintie 40, Helsinki 10.
Kustannusosakeyhtiö Gummerus, Jyväskylä.
Holger Schildts Förlags Ab (Swedo-Finnish), Annegatan 16, Helsingfors 12.
Söderström & Co. Förlags Ab (Swedo-Finnish), Bangatan 3, Helsingfors 12.

RADIO AND TELEVISION

Finnish Broadcasting Corporation, Kesäkatu 2, Helsinki 26.

RAILWAYS

Finnish State Railways, Vilhonkatu 13, Helsinki 10.

RED CROSS

Finnish Red Cross, Tehtaankatu 1a, Helsinki 14.

ROMAN CATHOLIC CHURCH

Catholic Information Centre, Puistokatu 1a, Helsinki 14.

SAUNA

Sauna Society, Vaskiniemi, Helsinki 20.

SCIENCE

Societas Scientiarum Fennica, Snellmaninkatu 9–11, Helsinki 17.
Academia Scientiarum Fennica, Snellmaninkatu 9–11, Helsinki 17.

SHIPPING

Central Board of Navigation, P.O. Box 158, Vuorimiehenkatu 1, Helsinki 14.
Finnish Shipowners Association, Eteläranta 10A, Helsinki 13.

SHIPBUILDING

Wärtsilä Concern Oy, Sörnäisten Rantatie 9–11, Helsinki 53.
Valmet Oy, Punanotkonkatu 2, Helsinki 13.
Rauma-Repola Oy, Snellmaninkatu 13, Helsinki 17.

USEFUL ADDRESSES

SPORT
Finnish Central Sports Federation (SVUL), Topeliuksenkatu 41a, Helsinki 25.
Workers Sports Federation (TUL), P.O. Box 9, Kauppamiehentie 6, Tapiola.
National Federation of Workers Sports Clubs (TUK), Läntinen Brahenkatu 2, Helsinki 51.
Swedish Central Sports Federation in Finland (CIF), Tempelgatan 19D, Helsingfors 10.
Finnish Football Association (Suomen Palloliitto), Bulevardi 28, Helsinki 12.
Finnish Olympic Committee, Topeliuksenkatu 41a A, Helsinki 25.

STATISTICS
Central Statistical Office, Annankatu 44, Helsinki 10.

STUDENTS
Finnish Association of Students Unions, Mannerheimintie 5C, Helsinki 10.
Student Service, Kampinkatu 4, Helsinki 10.
Trainees Exchange Office, Siltasaarenkatu 3, Helsinki 53.

TECHNOLOGY
Engineering Society of Finland (STS) (Finnish), Yrjönkatu 30, Helsinki 10.
Engineering Society of Finland (TFIF) (Swedo-Finnish), Georgsgatan 30, Helsingfors 10.
Academy of Technical Sciences, Lönnrotinkatu 37, Helsinki 18.
Swedo-Finnish Academy of Technical Sciences, Apollogatan 8, Helsingfors 10.

TEXTILES
Association of Finnish Textile Industries, Eteläranta 10, Helsinki 13.

THEATRE
Finnish Association of Theatrical Organizations, Vuorikatu 6A, Helsinki 10.
Swedo-Finnish Association of Theatrical Organizations, Svenska Teatern i Helsingfors, Helsingfors 13.
Finnish School of Drama, Itäinen Teatterikuja 2, Helsinki 10.

TOURISM
Finnish Travel Association, Uudenmaankatu 16A, Helsinki 12.
Tourist Board, Mikonkatu 13A, Helsinki 10.

FINLAND: AN INTRODUCTION

Finnish National Tourist Office, Scandinavia House, 505 Fifth Avenue, New York, N.Y. 10017.
Finnish Tourist Board, UK Office, Finland House, 56 Haymarket, London S.W.1.

TOWN PLANNING

Museum of Finnish Architecture, Puistokatu 4, Helsinki 14.
Department of Architecture, Institute of Technology, Otaniemi.
SAFA Planning and Building Standards Institute, Bulevardi 1, Helsinki 10.
Union of Finnish Towns, Eduskuntakatu 4, Helsinki 10.
Helsinki Regional Planning Authority, Aleksanterinkatu 15, Helsinki 10.

TRADE

Commercial Department, Ministry of Commerce and Industry, Snellmaninkatu 4-6, Helsinki 17.
Finnish Foreign Trade Association, Eteläinen Esplanadikatu 18, Helsinki 13.
Central Chamber of Commerce, Fabianinkatu 14, Helsinki 10.

TRADE UNIONS AND EMPLOYERS

Confederation of Commerce Employers (LK), Eteläranta 10, Helsinki 13.
Confederation of Finnish Trade Unions (SAK), Paasivuorenkatu 5B, Helsinki 53.
Confederation of Salaried Employees (TVK), Töölöntullinkatu 8, Helsinki 25.
National Federation of Finnish Employers (STK), Eteläranta 10, Helsinki 13.

TRANSPORT

Finnish Association for Transport Economics (Suomen Kuljetustaloudellinen Yhdistys), Fredrikinkatu 36B, Helsinki 10.
Finnish State Railways, Vilhonkatu 13, Helsinki 10.

UNITED NATIONS

Finnish United Nations Association, Unioninkatu 45B, Helsinki 17.

UNIVERSITIES AND COLLEGES

University of Helsinki, Fabianinkatu 33, Helsinki 17.
University of Turku, Turku.
Åbo Academy (Swedo-Finnish), Åbo.
University of Tampere, Tampere.

USEFUL ADDRESSES

University of Jyväskylä, Jyväskylä.
University of Oulu, Oulu.
Institute of Technology, Otaniemi.
Sibelius Academy, Pohjoinen Rautatiekatu 9, Helsinki 10.
Helsinki School of Economics, Runeberginkatu 14–16, Helsinki 10.
Swedo-Finnish School of Economics, Arkadiagatan 22, Helsingfors 10.
Turku School of Economics, Turku.
Swedo-Finnish School of Economics, Åbo Academy, Åbo.
Veterinary College, Hämeentie 57, Helsinki 55.

VETERINARY
Finnish Veterinary Association, Hämeentie 78A, Helsinki 55.
State Veterinary Institute, Hämeentie 57, Helsinki 55.

WELFARE
Family Welfare League (Väestöliitto), Bulevardi 28, Helsinki 12.
Ministry of Social Affairs and Health, Snellmaninkatu 4–6, Helsinki 17.
National Pensions Institute, Nordenskiöldinkatu 12, Helsinki 25.
Central Union of Social Welfare (Sosiaalihuollon Keskusliitto), Mariankatu 26B, Helsinki 17.
National Board of Social Welfare, Siltasaarenkatu 18C, Helsinki 53.

WOODWORKING INDUSTRIES
Central Association of Finnish Woodworking Industries, Eteläinen Esplanadikatu 2, Helsinki 13.
Association of Finnish Plywood Industry, Lönnrotinkatu 25A, Helsinki 18.
Finncell, Eteläinen Esplanadikatu 2, Helsinki 13.
Finnish Board Mills Association, Eteläinen Esplanadikatu 2, Helsinki 13.
Finnish Paper Mills Association, Eteläinen Esplanadikatu 2, Helsinki 13.
Finnish Paper and Board Converters Association—Converta, Unioninkatu 14, Helsinki 13.
Finnish Sawmill Owners Association, Fabianinkatu 29C, Helsinki 10.

YOUTH
State Commission for Youth Activities, Ministry of Education, Rauhankatu 9B, Helsinki 17.
Young Liberals Association (Liberaalinen nuorisoliitto), Fredrikinkatu 60A, Helsinki 10.
Finnish Youth Association (Suomen Nuorison Liitto), Simonkatu 12B, Helsinki 10.

Association of Finnish High School Pupils (Suomen Teiniliitto), Vironkatu 6A, Helsinki 17.

YMCA (Nuorten Miesten Kristillinen Yhdistys), Vuorikatu 17, Helsinki 10.

YWCA (Nuorten Naisten Kristillinen Yhdistys), Pohjoinen Rautatiekatu 23B, Helsinki 10.

Finnish Youth Hostels Association (Suomen Retkeilymajajärjestö), Yrjönkatu 38B, Helsinki 10.

SELECTED BOOKS

YRJÖ AAV

General works and geography
AALTONEN, H. *Books in English on Finland.* Turku 1964. 276 pp. Turku University Library, 8.
Atlas of Finland. 1–2. Ed.: L. Aario. Helsinki, Suomen maantieteellinen seura, 1960–1. 12 pp., 39 maps, 123 pp.
BACON, W. *Finland.* London, Robert Hale, 1970. 304 pp., ill.
BERRY E. *The Land and People of Finland.* Philadelphia, J. B. Lippincott, 1959, 126 pp., ill.
CONNERY, D. S. *The Scandinavians.* London, Eyre and Spottiswoode and New York, Simon and Schuster, 1966. xvl, 590 pp., ill.
DE BIASI, M. *Meet the Finns.* Helsinki, Tammi, 1969. 32, 96 pp. ill.
DE BIASI, M. and STENIUS, G. *Finlandia—Profile of a Country.* London, Hugh Evelyn, 1967. 155 pp., ill.
DESNEIGES, G. *Finland.* Transl. by S. Nickels. London, Vista Books, 1963; New York, Viking Press, 1964. 192 pp.
Facts about Finland. 12th edn, Helsinki, Otava, 1970. 64 pp., ill.
Finland. Creation and Construction. Ed. by H. Kallas and S. Nickels. London, Allen and Unwin; New York, Praeger; Helsinki, WSOY, 1968. 366 pp., ill.
Finland. Official Standard Names approved by the United States Board on Geographical Names. Washington, 1962. 556 pp., maps. Gazetteer no. 62.
Finland and its Geography. An American Geographical Society Handbook. Ed. R. R. Platt. New York, Duell, Sloan and Pearce; London, Methuen, 1955. xxv, 510 pp., ill.
Finland at Work. Helsinki, Otava, 1967. 128 pp., ill.
Finland Grows. Fifty Years of Independence 1917–1967. Ed. by J. Sipilä. Sales and Advertising Association of Finland, Helsinki, 1967. 77 pp., ill.

FINLAND: AN INTRODUCTION

Finland Handbook. 6th edn, Finnair (Aero oy) and Finnish Travel Association, Helsinki 1971. 439 pp.

HALL, W. *Green Gold and Granite. A Background to Finland.* 2nd edn, London, Max Parrish, 1957. 190 pp., ill.

—— *The Finns and their Country.* London, Max Parrish, 1967. 224 pp., ill.

HATZFELD-REA, M. E. *Finland Fantasies.* London, Stockwell, 1969. 126 pp., ill.

HIRN, M. *Kuvia katoavasta Suomesta . . . Pictures of Vanishing Finland.* (Drawings and Watercolours from the Finnish Archaeological Society's Art History Expeditions 1871-1902.) Helsinki, Weilin & Göös, 1970. 145 pp., ill.

Introduction to Finland, 1960. Edited in collaboration with the Ministry for Foreign Affairs. Porvoo, WSOY.

Introduction to Finland, 1963. Edited in collaboration with the Ministry for Foreign Affairs. Porvoo, WSOY.

JAATINEN, M. *Road in Finnish Landscape.* Porvoo, WSOY, 1967. 120 pp., ill.

MEAD, W. R. *Finland.* London, Ernest Benn, 1968. 256 pp., ill.

—— *How People live in Finland.* London, Ward Lock Educational Co., 1965. 112 pp., ill.

MEAD, W. R. and SMEDS, H. *Winter in Finland.* London, Hugh Evelyn and New York, Frederick A. Praeger, 1967. 144 pp., ill.

SIMPSON, C. *The Viking Circle.* London, Hodder and Stoughton, 1967. xv, 366 pp., ill.

Suomi. A General Handbook on the Geography of Finland. Geographical Society of Finland. Helsinki, 1952. x, 626 pp., ill. Fennia, 72.

THIEL, O. *Days in Finland.* Helsinki, Otava, 1971. 125 pp., ill.

Vanhoja Suomen karttoja. Old Maps of Finland. Introduction and text by I. Gordin. Transl. by E. Pennanen. Helsinki 1967. 111 pp., maps.

VILLANEN, N., VUOKONEN, A. and YRJÄNÄ, A. *A Finnish Melody of Landscape.* Porvoo, WSOY, 1965. 103 pp., ill.

VUOKOLA, A. and YRJÄNÄ, A. *Life in Finland.* Introduction by H. Waris. Porvoo, WSOY, 1966. 36 pp., 91 pl.

VUORELA, T. *The Finno-Ugric Peoples.* Transl. by J. Atkinson. Bloomington, Indiana Univ. Press, 1964. v, 392 pp., ill. Uralic and Altaic series, 39.

SELECTED BOOKS

Travel guides
Helsinki à la carte. By Western Foreign Press Club. Ed.: J. Suter. ed. Helsinki 1971. 96 pp., ill.
Institute of Directors' Guides to Europe. Sweden. Finland. London, Thornton Cox, 1970. 86 pp.
Nagel's Travel Guide to Finland. London, Frederick Muller and New York, McGraw-Hill, 1964.
NICKELS, S. *Travellers' Guide to Finland.* London, Jonathan Cape, 1965; New York, Harper and Row, 1966. 232 pp., ill., maps.
—— *The Young Traveller in Finland.* London, Phoenix House and Newton Centre, Mass, Charles T. Branford, 1962. 127 pp., ill.
PIHLSTRÖM, B. *Finland. Traveller's Guide.* Helsinki, Otava, 1971. 130 pp., ill.
Tourist Guide Finland. Helsinki 1961. 296 pp., XXXII, 24 pl., maps. Suomen kumitehdas.
Tourist Guide Finland. Helsinki 1968. 88 pp., ill., maps. Finnish Touristadvising–Suomen Turistineuvonta.

Travels in Finland (modern)
ASHCROFT, D. *Journey to Finland.* London, Frederick Muller, 1952. 292 pp., ill.
BACON, W. *Highway to the Wilderness.* London, Robert Hale, 1961. 189 pp., ill.
BELL, H. M. *Land of Lakes. Memories Keep Me Company.* London, Robert Hale, 1950. 246 pp., ill.
BLAKESTON, O. *Sun at Midnight.* London, Anthony Blond, 1958. 208 pp., ill.
BRADLEY, D. *Lion among Roses. A Memoir of Finland.* New York, Holt, Rinehart and Winston, 1965. x, 278 pp.
CITRINE, SIR WALTER. *My Finnish Diary.* London, Penguin Books, 1940. 191 pp., ill., maps.
GOURLIE, N. *A Winter with Finnish Lapps.* London, Blackie and Son, 1939. 243 pp., ill., maps.
HINSHAW, D. *Heroic Finland.* New York, G. P. Putnam's Sons, 1952. XXII, 306 pp., ill.
PYE, P. *A Sail in a Forest. Moonraker in the Baltic.* London, Rupert Hart-Davies, 1961. 174 pp., ill.

FINLAND: AN INTRODUCTION

SANSOM, W. *The Icicle and the Sun*. London, The Hogarth Press, 1958; and New York, Reynal, 1959. 159 pp., ill.
SUTHERLAND, H. *Lapland Journey*. London, Geoffrey Bles, 1946. VIII, 295 pp.
SYKES, J. *Direction North. A View of Finland*. London, Hutchinson and Philadelphia, Chilton Book Co., 1967. 191 pp., ill.
VYVYAN, C. C. *Random Journeys*. London, Peter Owen, 1960. 192 pp., ill.
WARNER, O. *A Journey to the Northern Capitals. Copenhagen, Oslo, Stockholm, Helsinki*. London, George Allen & Unwin, 1968. 157 pp., ill.

Travels in the past: a selection
ACERBI, JOSEPH. *Travels to the North Cape*. London, 1802.
BUNBURY, SELINA. *A Summer in Northern Europe*. Vol. 1. London, 1856.
CLARKE, E. D. *Travels in Various Countries of Europe, Asia and Africa*. Vol. 3. London, 1823.
CLIVE-BAYLEY, A. M. *Vignettes from Finland*. London, 1895.
KER PORTER, SIR ROBERT. *Travelling Sketches in Russia and Sweden 1805–8*. London, 1809.
MARSHALL, JOSEPH. *Travels in 1768, 1769 and 1770*. London, 1772.
MURRAY, JOHN. *Handbook for Northern Europe*. Part II. London, 1848.
PATERSON, JOHN. *A Book for every Land*. London, 1858.
TRAVERS, ROSALIND. *Letters from Finland*. London, 1911.
TWEEDIE, MRS ALEC. *Through Finland in Carts*. London, 1897.
WAINEMAN, P. *A Summer Tour in Finland*. London, 1908.

English novels with a Finnish background
DWYER, W. *The Laplanders*. London, Almorris Press, 1969. 80 pp.
ELLIOTT, R. *Kirsti and Ruski*. London, Macmillan, 1965. 128 pp., ill. A story for children.
GAVIN, C. *The Fortress*. London, Hodder and Stoughton, 1964; Hodder Paperbacks, 1969. A historical novel of Suomenlinna during the Crimean War.
JENKINS, A. *The Twins of Lapland*. London, 1960. 144 pp., ill.
——*Wild Swans at Suvanto*. London, Rupert Hart Davis, 1965. 190 pp., ill.

SELECTED BOOKS

KIRKBRIDE, R. *The Short Night.* London, Pan Books, 1971. 175 pp.
LYALL, G. *The Most Dangerous Game.* London, Hodder & Stoughton; and New York, Macfadden Bartell Corp., 1964. A mystery set in Finnish Lapland.
SOUTHALL, I. *Finn's Folly.* London, Angus and Robertson, 1969. 158 pp.
TAYLOR, G. *Mortlake.* Boston, Houghton Mifflin, 1960; London, Hamish Hamilton, 1961.

History
Atlas of Finnish History. Ed. by E. Jutikkala. 2nd edn, Porvoo, WSOY, 1959. 83 pp. Suomen tiedettä, 2.
BARROS, J. *The Åland Island Question: Its Settlement by the League of Nations.* New Haven, Yale Univ. Press, 1968. 384 pp., maps.
CLARK, D. *Three Days to Catastrophe.* London, Hammond, Hammond & Co., 1966. 228 pp.
ERIKSSON, P. *The Duchess. The Life and Death of the Herzogin Cecilie.* London, Secker and Warburg, 1958. 247 pp., ill.
Essays on Finnish Foreign Policy. Finnish Political Science Association. Vammala, 1969. 113 pp.
Finland 1917-1967. An assessment of independence. Helsinki, Kirjayhtymä, 1967. 170 pp., ill.
Five Northern Countries Pull Together. Sponsored by the Nordic Council and published under the auspices of the Ministries for Foreign Affairs of the five Northern Countries. 1967. 92 pp., ill.
GRIPENBERG, G. A. *Finland and the Great Powers. Memoirs of a Diplomat.* Transl. with an introduction by A. T. Anderson. Lincoln, Univ. of Nebraska Press, 1965. xx, 380 pp.
HANNULA, J. O. *Finland's War of Independence.* With an introduction by W. M. St.G Kirke. 2nd edn, London, Faber and Faber, 1939. 229 pp., ill.
HODGSON, J. H. *Communism in Finland. A History and Interpretation.* Princeton, New Jersey, 1967. 261 pp.
JAKOBSON, M. *The Diplomacy of the Winter War. An Account of the Russo-Finnish War, 1939-40.* Cambridge, Mass., Harvard Univ. Press, 1961. 281 pp.
—— *Finnish Neutrality. A Study of Finnish Foreign Policy since the Second World War.* London, Hugh Evelyn, 1968; New York, Praeger, 1969. 116 pp., ill.

JULKUNEN, M. and LEHIKOINEN, A. *A Selected List of Books and Articles in English, French and German on Finnish Politics in the 19th and 20th Century.* Turku, Institute of Political History, 1967. 125 pp.

JUTIKKALA, E. and PIRINEN, K. *A History of Finland.* New York, Frederick A. Praeger, 1962. XII, 291 pp.

KARLSSON, E. *Mother Sea.* London, Oxford Univ. Press, 1964. 264 pp., ill.

KEKKONEN, U. *Neutrality: The Finnish Position.* Transl. by P. Ojansuu and L. E. Keyworth. London, Heinemann, 1970. 235 pp.

KIVIKOSKI, E. *Finland. Ancient People and Places.* London, Thames and Hudson and New York, Frederick A. Praeger, 1967. 204 pp., ill.

KROSBY, H. P. *Finland, Germany and the Soviet Union, 1940–1941. The Petsamo Dispute.* Madison, Wisconsin, The Univ. of Wisconsin Press, 1968. XIII, 276 pp., ill.

LUNDIN, C. L. *Finland in the Second World War.* Bloomington, Indiana Univ. Press, 1957. XII, 303 pp.

LUUKKANEN, E. *Fighter over Finland. The Memoirs of a Fighter Pilot.* Ed. by W. Green. London, MacDonald; New Rochelle, N.Y., Sportshelf and Soccer Associates, 1963. 254 pp., ill.

MANNERHEIM, C. G. *The Memoirs of Marshal Mannerheim.* London, Cassell and Co., 1953; New York, E. P. Dutton, 1954. XII, 540 pp., ill.

MAZOUR, A. *Finland between East and West.* New York, D. van Nostrand, 1956. 290 pp., ill.

MIELONEN, M. *Geography of Internal Politics in Finland.* Turku, 1969. 60 pp., ill. Turun yliopiston julkaisuja A 2:41.

OLIN, S. C. *Finlandia. The Racial Composition, the Language, and a Brief History of the Finnish People.* Hancock, Mich., The Book Concern, 1957. XXI, 198 pp., ill.

PALM, T. *The Finnish-Soviet Armistice Negotiations of 1944.* Uppsala, 1971. 160 pp.

PALOHEIMO, L. and WATSON, J. W. *Finland: Champion of Independence.* St Champaign, Ill., Garrard, 1969. 112 pp., ill.

RINTALA, M. *Four Finns. Political Profiles.* Berkeley and Los Angeles, Univ. of California Press, 1969. 130 pp., ill.

—— *Three Generations: The Extreme Right Wing in Finnish Politics.* Bloomington, Indiana Univ. Press, 1962. 281 pp. Indiana Univ. Russian and East European series, 22.

SCREEN, J. E. O. *Mannerheim. The Years of Preparation.* London, C. Hurst & Co., 1970. 158 pp., ill.
—— *A Select Bibliography of Marshal Mannerheim. 1906–1967.* Helsinki, Otava, 1967. 27 pp.
SMITH, C. J. *Finland and the Russian Revolution 1917–1922.* Athens, Univ. of Georgia Press, 1958. 251 pp.
SOBEL, R. *The Origins of Interventionism. The United States and the Russo-Finnish War.* New York, Bookman Associates, 1960. 204 pp.
TANNER, V. *The Winter War. Finland against Russia 1939–40.* Stanford, Stanford Univ. Press, 1957. x, 274 pp.
TOKOI, O. *Sisu. Even through a Stone Wall.* New York, Robert Speller & Sons, 1957. 252 pp., ill.
TUOMINEN, U. *J. K. Paasikivi. A Pictorial Biography.* Transl. by D. Tullberg, Helsinki, Otava, 1970. 100 pp., ill.
UPTON, A. F. *Finland in Crisis 1940–41. A Study in Small-Power Politics.* London, Faber and Faber, 1964; Ithaca, New York, Cornell Univ. Press, 1965. 318 pp.
WARNER, O. *Marshal Mannerheim and the Finns.* London, Weidenfeld and Nicolson, 1967. 256 pp., ill.
—— *The Sea and the Sword. The Baltic 1630–1945.* London, Jonathan Cape, 1965. 320 pp., ill.
Wuorinen, J. H. *A History of Finland.* New York, Columbia Univ. Press, 1965. xv, 548 pp., ill.

Religion, education, the Press
Finnish Theology, Past and Present. Helsinki, Finnish Theological Literature Society, 1963. 168 pp.
Finland and its Students. Helsinki, The National Union of Students of Finland, 1970. 56 pp., ill.
GRÖNROOS, H. and MYLLYNIEMI, K. *Helsinki University Library.* Helsinki, 1965. 36 pp., ill.
GUSTAFSON, M. *Education in Finland.* Helsinki, Ministry for Foreign Affairs, 1968. 99 pp. Reference Publications, 2.
Higher Education and Research in Finland. Helsinki, Ministry of Education, 1968. 30 pp. Reference Publications, 3.
Libraries in Finland. Ed.: H. Kauppi. Helsinki, The Finnish Library Association, 1971. 62 pp., ill.

NIINI, A. *Vocational Education*. Helsinki, 1968. 82 pp.
NYBERG, R. *Educational Reform in Finland in the 1970s*. Helsinki, 1970. 118 pp. Reference Publications, 4.
OJANSUU, R. *Comprehensive School in Finland*, Helsinki, 1971. 123 pp. Reference Publications, 5.
SENTZKE, G. *Finland, its Church and its People*. Helsinki, 1963. 212 pp. Luther-Agricola Society B:3.
STEINBY, TORSTEN. *In Quest of Freedom: Finland's Press 1771–1971*, Helsinki, 1971. 163 pp., ill.

Administration
Constitution Act and Parliament Act of Finland. Helsinki, 1967. 85 pp.
ESKOLA, A. *Local Self-Government in Finland and the Finnish Municipal Law*, 3rd edn, Helsinki, 1968. 79 pp.
Essays on Finnish Foreign Policy. Finnish Political Science Association, Vammala, 1969, 113 pp.
Finnish Foreign Policy. Studies in foreign politics. Finnish Political Science Association, Helsinki, 1963. 232 pp.
The Finnish Legal System. Ed. by J. Uotila. Helsinki, 1966. 263 pp. Union of Finnish Lawyers, 26.
The Finnish Parliament. Helsinki, 1969. 86 pp., ill.
Law and Lawyers in Finland. Helsinki, The Union of Finnish Lawyers, 1971. 16 pp.
NOUSIAINEN, J. *The Finnish Political System*. Transl. by J. H. Hodgson. Cambridge, Mass., Harvard Univ. Press, 1971. x, 454 pp.
PESONEN, P. *An Election in Finland. Party Activities and Voter Reactions*. New Haven & London, Yale Univ. Press, 1968. XVIII, 416 pp., ill.
The Position and Functions of the Finnish Parliamentary Ombudsman. Helsinki, 1967. 24 pp.
REINIKAINEN, V. *English, French and German Literature on Finnish Law in 1860–1956*. Helsinki, 1957. 179 pp. Eduskunnan kirjaston julkaisuja, 2.
TÖRNUDD, K. *The Electoral System of Finland*. London, Hugh Evelyn, 1968. 160 pp.

Economics
Advertising Conditions in Finland. Institute of Practitioners in Advertising. London, 1970. 26 pp.
AUTIO, M. and LODENIUS, E. *The Finnish Paper Mills' Association*

SELECTED BOOKS

1918–1968. Creation and Stages of Development. Transl. by F. A. Fewster. Helsinki, Frenckell, 1968. VII, 279 pp., ill.

Economic Survey 1970. Helsinki, 1970. 120 pp. Valtiovarainministeriön kansantalousosasto.

The Forest Industry in Independent Finland 1918–1968. Helsinki, Central Association of Finnish Woodworking Industries, 1968. 198 pp.

Finland in Focus. Helsinki, The Finnish Foreign Trade Foundation, 1968. 48 pp.

Finnish Foreign Trade Directory 1971. The Finnish Foreign Trade Association. Helsinki, 1971. 587 pp.

Finnish Forest Improvement—Technics and Machinery. Transl. by V. Vainonen. Helsinki, Otava, 1970. 131 pp.

Finnish Forest Trade Directory 1969. A Commercial Reference Book. Helsinki, 1969. 536 pp.

The Finnish Timber and Paper Calendar 1970/71. Helsinki, 1970.

The Finnish Co-operative Societies Act. Helsinki, Pellervo-seura and Kulutusosuuskuntien keskusliitto, 1955. 126 pp.

HEIKKILÄ, R. *Finland, Land of Co-operatives.* Helsinki, Helsingin yliopiston osuustoimintainstituutti, 1963. 64 pp.

HELIN, R. A. *Economic Geographic Reorientation in Western Finnish Karelia.* Washington, D.C. 1961. 311 pp. National Academy of Sciences National Research Council. Publ. 909.

JENSEN, B. C. *The Impact of Reparations on the Post-War Finnish Economy. An Input-Output Study.* Homewood, Ill., Richard D. Irwin, 1966. VIII, 179 pp. Krannert Graduate School, Purdue University. Monograph Series, 2.

KNOELLINGER, C. E. *Labour in Finland.* Cambridge, Mass, Harvard Univ. Press, 1960. XII, 300 pp.

LINNAMO, J. *Finland, a Growing Economy.* Helsinki, Ministry for Foreign Affairs, 1967. 98 pp. Reference Publications, 1.

MAIJALA, K. *Finnish Animal Husbandry.* Helsinki, Representatives of Finnish Animal Breeding Associations, 1969. 102 pp., ill.

MEAD, W. R. *An Economic Geography of the Scandinavian States and Finland.* London, Univ. of London Press, 1958. XVI, 302 pp., ill.

—— *Farming in Finland.* London, Univ. of London, The Athlone Press and New York, Oxford Univ. Press, 1953. 248 pp., ill.

OECD Economic Surveys. Finland. May 1971. Paris, 1971. 59 pp.

Outlook for Growth in the Finnish Economy 1969–1973. The Secretariat of the Economic Council. Helsinki, 1969. 128 pp.

Waterpower in Finland. Ed. R. Salokangas etc. Transl. by E. Arhippainen. Tampere, Finnish Water Power Association, 1968. 135 pp., ill.

WESTERMARCK, N. *Finnish Agriculture*. 4th edn, Helsinki, Kirjayhtymä, 1969. 90 pp., ill.

Sociology

ESKOLA, A. *The Social Welfare Administration in Finnish Municipalities*. Helsinki, Suomen maalaiskuntien liitto, 1954. 20 pp.

Freedom and Welfare. Social patterns in the Northern countries of Europe. Ed. by G. R. Nelson. Copenhagen, The Ministries of Social Affairs of Denmark, Finland, Iceland, Norway, Sweden, 1953. 540 pp., ill.

The Lapps today in Finland, Norway and Sweden. 1. Ed. by R. G. P. Hill. Paris, 1960. Bibliothèque arctique et antarctique, 1.

KUUSI, P. *Social Policy for the Sixties. A Plan for Finland*. Helsinki, Finnish Social Policy Association, 1964. 295 pp.

Social Services in Finland. Ministry of Social Affairs and Health. 1–4. Helsinki, 1969–70. 28–40 pp.

TOLSA, H. (ed.) *Child Welfare in Finland*. Transl. by R. J. Milton. Helsinki, 1968. 80 pp., ill. Central Union for Child Welfare in Finland. Publ. 44.

Finnish language

AALTIO, M.-H. *Finnish for Foreigners*. 5th edn, Helsinki, Otava, 1971. 318 pp., ill.

——*Essential Finnish*. London, Univ. of London Press, 1964. 315 pp., ill.

ATKINSON, J. *A Finnish Grammar*. 3rd edn, Helsinki, Finnish Literature Society, 1969. 131 pp.

AUSTERLITZ, R. *Finnish Grammar*. Cleveland, Ohio, Bell & Howell, 1963. 591 pp. Research and Studies in Uralic and Altaic Languages, Project no. 36.

DENISON, N. *The Partitive in Finnish*. Helsinki, Finnish Academy of Sciences, 1957. 262 pp. Series B, Vol. 108.

Finnish for Travellers. By the staff of Editions Berlitz. Geneva, Editions Berlitz S.A., 1970. 177 pp., ill.

Finnish Graded Reader. Compiled and ed. by A. R. Bell and A. A.

Koski. Washington D.C., Foreign Service Institute, 1968. VII, 751 pp. Tapes.

Finnish Literary Reader. With notes by P. Ravila. Bloomington, Indiana Univ. Press, 1965. IX, 186 pp. Uralic and Altaic Series, 44.

Finnish Reader. Extracts from modern Finnish Literature selected, translated and decorated by A. H. Whitney. London, English Universities Press, 1971. 191 pp., ill.

Finnish Reader and Glossary. Compiled and ed. by R. Austerlitz. 2nd edn, Bloomington, Indiana Univ. Press, 1967. 294 pp. Uralic and Altaic Series, 15.

Graded Finnish Readers, Nos 1–3. Ed. by T. Heiskanen and Fr. P. Magoun, Jr. Helsinki, Finnish Literature Society, 1957. 102, 67, 76 pp.

HAKULINEN, L. *The Structure and Development of the Finnish Language*. Bloomington, Indiana Univ. Press, 1961. XII, 383 pp. Uralic and Altaic Series, 3.

HARMS, R. T. *Finnish Structural Sketch*. Bloomington, Indiana Univ. Press, 1964. VII, 105 pp. Uralic and Altaic Series, 42.

LEHTINEN, M. *Basic Course in Finnish*. Supervised and ed. by T. A. Sebeok. Bloomington, Indiana Univ. Press, 1963. XXXIII, 657 pp. Uralic and Altaic Series, 27.

LEHTONEN, J. *Aspects of Quantity in Standard Finnish*. (Diss. Jyväskylä). Jyväskylä, 1970. 199 pp. Studia philologica Jyväskäensia, 6.

SEBEOK, T. A. *Spoken Finnish*. New York, Henry Holt, 1968. 487 pp.

TUOMIKOSKI, A. and DEANS, H. *Elementary Finnish. Texts, Grammar, Glossary*. 2nd edn, Helsinki, Finnish Literature Society, 1969. 85 pp.

WHITNEY, A. H. *Teach yourself Finnish*. 7th edn, London, English Universities Press and New York, David McKay, 1971. 301 pp.

Dictionaries

ALANNE, V. S. *Finnish-English General Dictionary*. 3rd edn. Porvoo, WSOY, 1968. XXXVI, 1,111 pp.

HALME, P. E. *Finnish-English Dictionary*. Helsinki, Finnish Literature Society, 1957. 632 pp.

HART, K. A. and LAHTINEN, A. T. K. *English-Finnish Dictionary of Idioms*. 1. Helsinki, Otava, 1965. 340 pp.

RIIKONEN, E. and TUOMIKOSKI, A. *Englantilais-suomalainen sanakirja*. 5th edn, Helsinki, Otava, 1970. 835 pp.

TALVITIE, Y. *Englantilais-suomalainen tekniikan ja kaupan sanakirja.* 3rd edn, Helsinki, 1965. Täydennysosa. Helsinki, 1966. 1507 + 345 columns.

TUOMIKOSKI, A. and SLÖÖR, A. *English-Finnish Dictionary.* 5th edn, Helsinki, Finnish Literature Society, 1969. XIV, 1,100 pp.

WUOLLE, A. *English-Finnish School Dictionary.* 11th edn, Porvoo, WSOY, 1969. X, 536 pp.

—— *Finnish-English School Dictionary.* 10th edn, Porvoo, WSOY, 1966. 448 pp.

—— *Finnish-English-Finnish Red Dictionary.* 8th edn, Porvoo, WSOY 1969. 176, 181 pp.

Kalevala, Folklore

BOSLEY, K. *Tales from the long Lakes.* London, Victor Gollancz, 1966. 144 pp., ill.

BOWMAN, J. C. and BIANCO, M. *Tales from a Finnish Tupa. Folklore.* 5th print. Chicago, Albert Whitman, 1958. 273 pp., ill.

COLLINDER, B. *The Kalevala and its Background.* Stockholm, Almqvist & Wiksell, 1964. 112 pp.

DEUTSCH, B. *Heroes of the Kalevala, Finland's Saga.* New York, Julian Messner, 1971. 238 pp., ill.

HAAVIO, M. *Väinämöinen, Eternal Sage.* Porvoo, WSOY, 1952. 276 pp., ill.

HAUTALA, J. *Finnish Folklore Research 1828–1918.* Helsinki, Societas scientiarum Fennica, 1969. 197 pp. The History of Learning and Science in Finland 1828–1918, 12.

Kalevala, or Poems of the Kaleva District. Compiled by E. Lönnrot. A prose transl. with foreword and appendices by Fr. P. Magoun Jr., Cambridge, Mass, Harvard Univ. Press, 1963. XXIV, 410 pp.

Kalevala, The Land of Heroes. Transl. by W. F. Kirby. Introduction by J. B. Grundy. 1–2. London, Dent and New York, Dulton, 1961–6. VIII, 328 + VI, 285 pp. Everyman's library, 259–60.

KOMULAINEN, O. (ed.) *Old Finnish Folk Dances.* Kokkola, Suomalaisen kansantanssin ystävät, 1965. 43 pp.

MARANDA, E. *Finnish Folklore Reader and Glossary.* Bloomington, Indiana Univ. Press, Haag, Mouton & Co., 1968. XXII, 340 pp. Uralic and Altaic Series, 71.

The Old Kalevala and Certain Antecedents. Compiled by E. Lönnrot. Prose transl. with Foreword and Appendices by Fr. P. Magoun, Jr. Cambridge, Mass, Harvard Univ. Press, 1969. 312 pp.

Classical and modern authors
ANHAVA, T. *In the Dark Move Slowly.* London, Cape Goliard, 1969. 48 pp.
HAAVIKKO, P. *Selected Poems.* Ed. and transl. by A. Hollo. London, Cape Goliard, 1968. 72 pp.
HOLLO, A. *The Coherences.* London, Turret Books, 1968. 56 pp., ill.
—— *Faces and Forms.* London, Ambit, 1965. 72 pp.
—— *It is a Song. Poems.* Birmingham, Migrant Press, 1965. 49 pp., ill.
—— *The Man in the Treetop Hat.* London, Trigram Press, 1968. 42 pp., ill.
—— *Poems. Runoja.* Helsinki, Otava, 1967. 139 pp.
JANSSON, T. *Comet in Moominland.* Transl. by E. Portch. 5th impr. London, Ernest Benn, 1970. 192 pp., ill. Penguin Books, London, 1970. 158 pp., ill.
—— *The Exploits of Moominpappa. Described by Himself.* Transl. by T. Warburton. 3rd impr. London, Ernest Benn; New York, Henry Z. Walck, 1970. 160 pp., ill.; Harmondsworth, Middlesex, Penguin Books, 1969. 135 pp., ill.
—— *Finn Family Moomintroll.* Transl. by E. Portch. 5th impr. London, Ernest Benn; New York, Henry Z. Walck, 1970. 174 pp., ill.; Penguin Books, 1970. 156 pp., ill.
—— *Moomin, Mymble and little My.* London, Ernest Benn, 1965. 24 pp., ill.
—— *Moominland Midwinter.* Transl. by T. Warburton. 3rd impr. London, Ernest Benn; New York, Henry Z. Walck, 1967. 165 pp., ill.; Penguin Books, 1971. 139 pp., ill.
—— *Moominpappa at Sea.* Transl. by K. Hart. London, Ernest Benn, 1966; New York, Henry Z. Walck, 1967. 192 pp., ill.
—— *Moominsummer Madness.* Transl. by T. Warburton. 4th ed. London, Ernest Benn; New York, Henry Z. Walck, 1969. 163 pp., ill. Penguin Books, 1971. 144 pp., ill.
—— *Tales from Moominvalley.* Transl by T. Warburton. 5th impr. London, Ernest Benn; New York, Henry Z. Walck, 1970. 175 pp., ill.

JANSSON, T. *Who Will Comfort Toffle?* London, Ernest Benn. 1969. 31 pp., ill.

KIVI, A. *Seven Brothers*. A novel. Transl. by A. Matson. Ill. by A. Gallen-Kallela. New edn, Helsinki, Tammi, 1959. 348 pp., ill.

KOKKO, Y. *The Way of the Four Winds*. Transl. by N. Walford. London, Victor Gollancz and New York, Putnam, 1954. 286 pp., ill.

KONTTINEN, A. *Kirsti Comes Home*. The story of a Finnish girl. Transl. by O. Coburn and U. Lehrburger. London, Methuen and Co. and New York, Coward-McCann, 1961. 176 pp., ill.

LINNA, V. *The Unknown Soldier*. London, Collins and New York, Putnam, 1957. 384 pp.; Porvoo, WSOY, 1970. XIV, 310 pp., ill.

LINNANKOSKI, J. *The Song of the Blood-Red Flower*. London, Gyldendal. 285 pp.

MATTSON, G. *The Princess*. Transl. by J. Bulman. New York, E. P. Dutton, 1967; London, Heinemann, 1966. 152 pp.

MERI, V. *The Manila Rope*. Transl. by J. MacGahern and A. Laaksi. New York, Alfred A. Knopf, 1967. 141 pp.

OLSSON, H. *The Woodcarver and Death*. Transl. by G. C. Schoolfield. Madison, The Univ. of Wisconsin Press, 1965. XXXIX, 136 pp.

OTAVA, M. *Priska*. Transl. by E. Portch. London, Ernest Benn, 1964; New York, D. Van Nostrand, 1966; London, Heinemann, 1970. 176 pp.

PEKKANEN, T. *My Childhood*. Transl. by A. Blair. With an introduction by T. Warburton. Madison, The Univ. of Wisconsin Press, 1966. XVIII, 250 pp.

RINTALA, P. *The Long Distance Patrol*. Transl. by M. Michael. London, George Allen and Unwin, 1967. 184 pp.

ROSSI, M. *The Trees of Vietnam*. Transl. by A. Hollo. Mexico 1966. 21 pp., ill. El corno emplumado. Colección La llave, 1.

RUNEBERG, J. L. *The Tales of Ensign Stål*. Ill. by A. Edelfelt. With an introduction by Y. Hirn. Helsingfors, Söderström and Co., 1952. XXVI, 244 pp., ill.

SAARIKOSKI, P. *Helsinki. Selected Poems*. Transl. by A. Hollo. London, Rapp & Carroll, 1967. 48 pp.

SALMINEN, S. *The Prince From the Sea*. A novel. Transl. by E. Ramsden. London, Heinemann, 1954. 360 pp.

SARIOLA, M. *The Helsinki Affair*. Transl. by A. Blair. London, Cassell, 1970. 170 pp.

SILLANPÄÄ, F. E. *Fallen Asleep while Young. The History of the Last Offshoot of an Old Family Tree.* Transl. by A. Matson. London, Putnam, 1933. 314 pp.
—— *Meek Heritage.* Transl. by A. Matson. New York, Alfred A. Knopf, 1938. 202 pp; Helsinki, Otava, 1971. 221 pp.
—— *People in the Summer Night.* Transl. by A. Blair, with an introduction by T. Warburton. Madison, The Univ. of Wisconsin Press, 1966. XVIII, 158 pp.
STENIUS, G. *The Bells of Rome.* Transl. by I. and F. McHugh. London, Eyre and Spottiswoode and New York, P. J. Kenedy, 1961. 358 pp.
TALVI, J. *Friends and Enemies.* Transl. by A. Blair. London, Angus and Robertson, 1958. 318 pp.
TOPELIUS, Z. *Canute Whistlewinks and other Stories.* Transl. by C. W. Foss. London, Longmans, Green and Co. and New York, David McKay, 1959. 272 pp., ill.
—— *The Tomten i Åbo Castle.* Transl. by F. R. Southerington. Åbo, Åbo tidnings och tryckeri aktiebolag, 1967. 60 pp.
WALLENIUS, K. M. *The Men's Sea.* Transl. by A. Blair. London, Staples Press and New York, Oxford Univ. Press, 1955. 268 pp.
WALTARI, M. *The Adventurer.* Transl. by N. Walford. New York, G. P. Putnam, 1950. 377 pp.
—— *The dark Angel.* Transl. by N. Walford. New York, Putnam, 1952; London, Putnam, 1953. 320 pp.
—— *The Egyptian.* Transl. by N. Walford. London 1956. 504 pp. Panther Books, 567 pp.; New York, Berkley, 1970. 576 pp.
—— *The Etruscan.* Transl. by E. Ramsden. London, Putnam, 1957; New York, Pocket Books, 1958. 480 pp. Transl. by L. Leino. New York, Berkley, 1971. 512 pp.
—— *Michael the Finn.* Transl. by N. Walford. London, Putnam, 1950. 440 pp.
—— *Moonscape and other Stories.* Transl. by N. Walford. London, Putnam, 1956. 297 pp.
—— *A Nail Merchant at Nightfall. A novel.* Transl. by A. Beesley. London, Putnam, 1954. 176 pp., ill.
—— *The Roman.* Transl. by J. Tate. London, Hodder and Stoughton, 1966. 638 pp. 2nd edn, New York, Berkley, 1970. 428 pp.
—— *The Secret of the Kingdom.* Transl. by N. Walford. London and New York, Putnam, 1961. 412 pp.

FINLAND: AN INTRODUCTION

WALTARI, M. *Sinuhe, the Egyptian.* Transl. by N. Walford. London and New York, Putnam, 1953. 503 pp.
—— *A Stranger Came to the Farm.* Transl. by N. Walford. London, Putnam, 1952. 254 pp.
—— *The Sultan's Renegade.* Transl. by N. Walford. London, Putnam, 1951. 471 pp.
—— *The Tongue of the Fire.* Transl. by A. Blair. London, Putnam, 1959. 190 pp.
—— *The Tree of Dreams and other Stories.* Transl. by L. Leino, A. Beesley, P. Sjöblom. London, Hodder and Stoughton and New York, Putnam, 1969. 256 pp.
Voices from Finland. An Anthology of Finland's Verse and Prose in English, Finnish and Swedish. Ed. by E. Tompuri. Helsinki, Sanoma Oy, 1947. 296 pp., ill.

Theatre

Suomen kansallisteatteri—The Finnish Theatre. Ed. by R. Heikkilä. Porvoo, WSOY, 1962. 164 pp., ill.
Theatres in the Five Scandinavian Countries. Ed. by I. Luterkort and C. Stephenson. Stockholm, 1971. 59 pp., ill.

Music

ARNOLD, E. *Finlandia. The Story of Sibelius.* New York, Henry Holt, 1950. 247 pp., ill.
BLUM, F. *Jean Sibelius. An International Bibliography on the Occasion of the Centennial Celebrations, 1965.* Detroit, Information Service, Inc., 1965. XXI, 114 pp. Detroit Studies in Music Bibliography, 8.
Catalogue of Finnish Orchestral Works, Vocal Works with Orchestra and Opera and Ballet Works. Teosto Composers' Copyright Bureau. Helsinki, 1972.
HELASVUO, V. *Sibelius and the Music of Finland.* 3rd edn, Helsinki, Otava, 1961. 101 pp., ill.
JOHNSON, H. E. *Jean Sibelius.* London, Faber & Faber, 1959. 225 pp., ill.
KARILA, T. *Composers of Finland.* New ed. Helsinki, Suomen säveltäjät, 1965. 108 pp., ill.

SELECTED BOOKS

LAYTON, R. *Sibelius*. London, J. M. Dent and Sons, 1965. XII, 210 pp., ill.
MÄKINEN, T. and NUMMI, S. *Musica Fennica*. Helsinki, Otava, 1965. 139 pp., ill.
PARMET, S. *The Symphonies of Sibelius. A Study in Musical Appreciation*. London, Cassell, 1959. XVIII, 169 pp., ill.
RICHARDS, D. *The Music of Finland*. London, Hugh Evelyn, 1968. 120 pp., ill.
RINGBOM, N-E. *Jean Sibelius. A Master and His Work*. Transl. by G. I. C. de Courcy. Norman, Oklahoma, Univ. of Oklahoma Press, 1954. 196 pp., ill.
SIMPSON, R. *Sibelius and Nielsen. A Centenary Essay*. London, British Broadcasting Corporation, 1965. 40 pp.
TAWASTSTJERNA, E. *The Pianoforte Compositions of Sibelius*. Helsinki, Otava, 1957. 104 pp., ill.

Architecture, painting
AHMAVAARA, A.-L. *Living Close to Nature*. 2nd edn, Helsinki, Otava, 1967. 114 pp., ill.
ÅLANDER, K. *Viljo Revell. Works and Projects*. 2nd edn, Helsinki, Otava, 1967. 119 pp., ill.
Arquitectura Finlandesa en Otaniemi. Alvar Aalto, Heikki Siren, Reima Pietilä. Text in English. Barcelona, Ediciones Poligrafa S.A., 1967. 172 pp., ill.
BECKER, H.-J. and SCHLOTE, W. *New Housing in Finland*. 2nd edn, London, Alec Tiranti, 1964. 184 pp., ill.
BOULTON SMITH, J. *Modern Finnish Painting*. London, Weidenfeld and Nicolson, 1970. 48, 62 pp., ill.
CHRIST-JANER, A. *Eliel Saarinen*. With a foreword by Alvar Aalto. Chicago, Univ. of Chicago Press, 1948. 153 pp.
GUTHEIM, F. *Alvar Aalto*. London, Mayflower and New York, Braziller, 1960. 128 pp., ill.
Helsinki-Helsingfors. Architectural Guide. 3rd edn, Helsinki, Otava, 1970. 136 pp., ill.
HERTZEN, H. v. and SPREIREGEN, P. D. *Building a New Town. Finland's New Garden City. Tapiola*. Cambridge, Mass. and London, The MIT Press, 1971. 234 pp., ill.

JANSSON, T. *Sculptor's Daughter.* Transl. by K. Hart. London, Ernest Benn, 1969. 176 pp.

Finland's most Beautiful Churches. Finnish Church Architecture from the Middle Ages up to the Present Day. 4th edn, Jyväskylä, Gummerus, 1970. 184 pp., ill.

Kalela. Wilderness studio and home. Ed. by K. Niilonen. Helsinki, Otava, 1966. 95 pp., ill.

PUOKKA, J. *Hattulan kirkko. The Medieval Church of Hattula.* Helsinki, Otava, 1956. 99 pp., ill.

RÁCZ, I. *Art Treasures of Medieval Finland.* Introduction and notes on the pictures by R. Pylkkänen. Helsinki, Otava, 1960; New York, Frederick A. Praeger, 1967. 260 pp., ill.

—— *Early Finnish Art.* Helsinki, Otava, 1967. 176 pp., ill.

—— Treasures of Finnish Folk Art. Helsinki, Otava, 1969. 230 pp., ill.

—— Treasures of Finnish Renaissance and Baroque Art. Helsinki, Otava, 1969. 230 pp., ill.

RICHARDS, J. M. *A Guide to Finnish Architecture.* London, Hugh Evelyn and New York, Frederick A. Praeger, 1967. 112 pp., ill.

RIHLAMA, S. *Architecture in Tampere.* Porvoo, WSOY, 1968. 250 pp., ill.

SAARIKIVI, S., NIILONEN, K. and EKELUND, H. *Art in Finland.* 6th edn, Helsinki, Otava, 1967. 157 pp., ill.

SAARINEN, A. B. *Eero Saarinen on His Work.* 1968. 117 pp., ill.

SAARINEN, E. *The City, its Growth, its Decay, its Future.* 2nd paperback pr. Cambridge, Mass, Massachusetts Institute of Technology, 1966. XVI, 386 pp., ill. The MIT Paperback Series, 31.

SALOKORPI, A. *Modern Architecture in Finland.* London, Weidenfeld and Nicolson, 1970. 56, 64 pp., ill.

SCHILDT, G. *Modern Finnish Sculpture.* London, Weidenfeld and Nicolson, 1970. 55, 64 pp., ill.

—— *The Sculptures of Alvar Aalto.* Helsinki, Otava, 1967. 46 pp., ill.

SCHILDT, G., MOSSO, L. and OKSALA, T. *Alvar Aalto.* Jyväskylä, Gummerus, 1964. 54 pp., ill.

SUHONEN, P. *New Architecture in Finland.* Helsinki, Tammi, 1967.

Suomen piirustustaide Lauréuksesta Ekelundiin. Finnish Drawings from Lauréus to Ekelund. Introduction: J. Puokka. Porvoo, WSOY, 1966. XXXIII pp., 207 pl.

Suomen piirustustaide Schaumanista Rantaseen. Finnish Drawings from

SELECTED BOOKS

Schauman to Rantanen. Introduction: J. Puokka. Porvoo, WSOY, 1967. 226 pp., ill.
TEMPEL, E. *New Finnish Architecture Today*. London, The Architectural Press and Helsinki, Otava, 1968. 192 pp., ill.
TOIKKA-KARVONEN, A. (ed.) Homes in Tapiola. Porvoo, WSOY, 1963. 92 pp., ill.
WICKBERG, N. E. *Finnish Architecture*. Helsinki, Otava, 1965. 242 pp., ill.

Applied art
ARO, P. *Arabia Design*. Helsinki, Otava, 1958. 56 pp., ill.
Designed in Finland 1970. Helsinki, The Finnish Foreign Trade Association, 1970. 56 pp., ill.
Finnish Graphic Design. Transl. by D. Barrett. Porvoo, WSOY, 1963. 111 pp., ill.
HAYCRAFT, J. *Finnish Jewellery and Silverware*. Helsinki, Otava, 1962. 64 pp., ill.
HÅRD AF SEGERSTAD, U. *Modern Finnish Design*. London, Weidenfeld and Nicolson, 1969. 46, 62 pp., ill.
LEPPO, M. *Finnish Pauper-Sculptures*. Porvoo, WSOY, 1967. 148 pp., ill.
NIILONEN, K. *Finnish Glass*. Helsinki, Tammi, 1967. 112 pp , ill.
Old Finnish Furniture. Helsinki, SKK, 1969. 129 pp., ill.
The Ornamo Book of Finnish Design. Helsinki, Ornamo, 1962. 135 pp., ill.
SAARTO, M. *Finnish Textiles*. Leigh-on-Sea, 1954. Folio Survey of World Textiles, 6.
Scandinavian domestic Design. Ed by E. Zahle. London, Methuen, 1963. 300 pp., ill.
SIRELIUS, V. T. *The Ryijy-Rugs of Finland*. Helsinki, Otava, 1924. 263 pp., ill.
TROUPP, L. *Modern Finnish Textiles*. Helsinki, Otava, 1962. 63 pp., ill.
ZILLIACUS, B. *Finnish Designers*. Helsinki, Suomen taideteollisuus-yhdistys, 1954. 54 pp., ill.

Finnish food
BENTON, P. *Finnish Food for your Table*. Oxford, Bruno Cassirer, 1960. 116 pp., ill.

BROWN, D. *The Cooking of Scandinavia*. Publ. by Time-Life International, Foods of the World Series, 1969.
OJAKANGAS, B. A. *The Finnish Cookbook*. New York, Crown publishers, 1964. 250 pp.
SOIRO, J. *Finnish Cookery*. Helsinki, Hotel Torni, 1963. 102 pp., ill. Tornin kirjat, 5.
TOLVANEN, K. *Finnish Food. A selection of Finnish recipes*. 5th edn, Helsinki, Otava, 1965. 104 pp., ill.

Health

EISALO, A. *Effects of the Finnish Sauna on Circulation*. Helsinki, 1956. 96 pp.
Let's have a Sauna. Finnish Sauna Society. Helsinki, 1966. 22 pp.
OLIN, S. C. *Sauna — The Way to Health*. New York Mills, Minnesota, Northwestern Publ. Co., 1963. 235 pp., ill.
PESONEN, N. *Hospitals of Finland*. Porvoo, WSOY, 1964. 87 pp., ill.
Physical Education and Sport in Finland. Porvoo, WSOY, 1969. 109 pp., ill. Finnish Society for Research in Sports and Physical Education, 14.
VIHERJUURI, H. J. *Sauna, the Finnish Bath*. 9th edn, Helsinki, Otava, 1967. 126 pp., ill.

Periodicals

Bank of Finland. Monthly Bulletin.
Bank of Finland. Year Book.
Books from Finland. Quarterly Review of the Finnish Publishers and Booksellers.
Economic Review. Publ. by Kansallis-osake-pankki, Helsinki.
Finland Sells. Publ. by The Finnish Foreign Trade Association, Helsinki.
Finnish Trade Review. Publ. by The Finnish Foreign Trade Association, Helsinki.
Look at Finland. A Bi-Monthly Review. Publ. by Finnish Tourist Board and the Ministry for Foreign Affairs, Press Bureau.
Statistical Yearbook of Finland. Publ. by the Central Statistical Office of Finland.
Unitas. Economic Review. Publ. by Pohjoismaiden yhdyspankki: Nordiska föreningsbanken, Helsinki.

STATISTICS ABOUT FINLAND

OLLI SAARIAHO

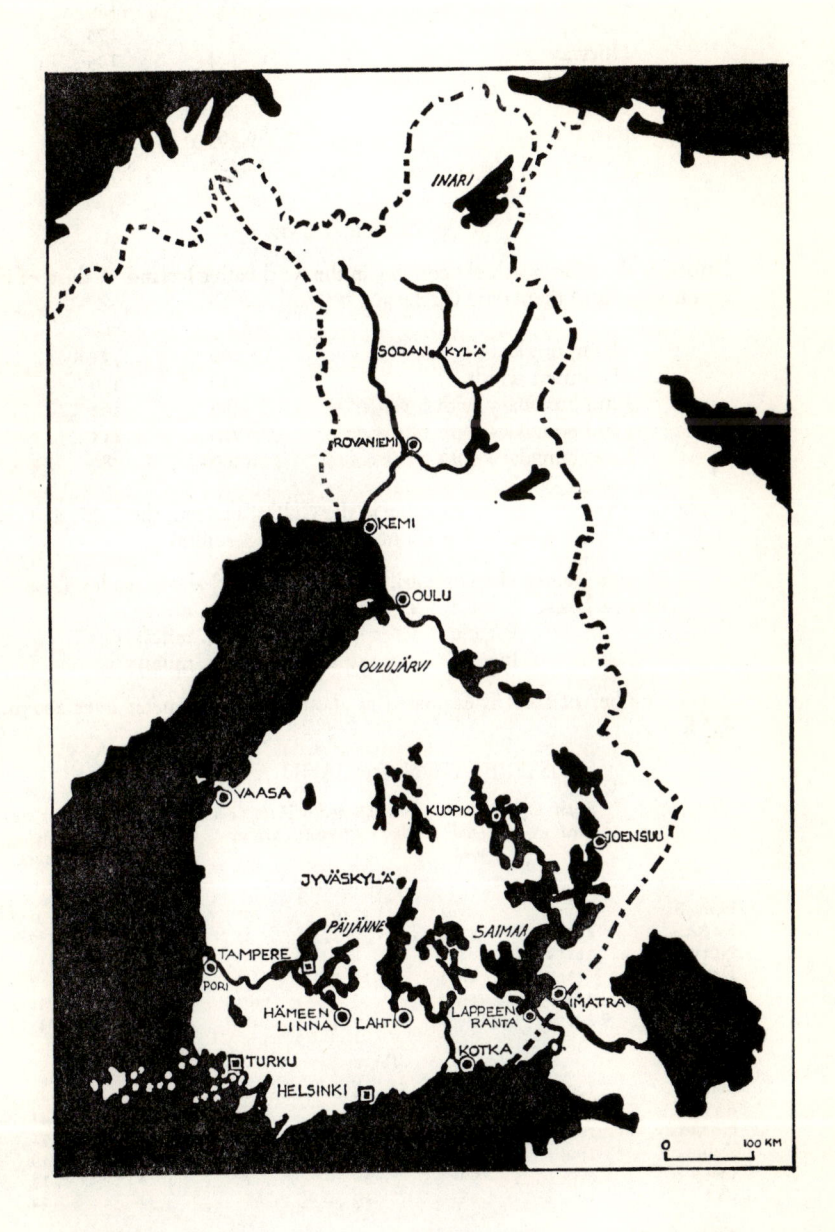

AREA AND NATURE
AREA

	1,000 sq. km.	1,000 sq. miles
Finland	337	130
Sweden	450	174
Norway	324	125
Denmark	43	17
UK	244	94
USA	9,363	3,615
USSR	22,402	8,649

GEOGRAPHICAL DATA

Finland is the most northerly country in the world after Iceland. A third of its area lies north of the Arctic Circle.

	km.	miles
Maximum length	1,160	721
Maximum width	540	336
Land boundary with Sweden	586	364
Land boundary with Norway	716	445
Land boundary with USSR	1,269	789

The length of the Finnish coastline in the Gulf of Finland, the Baltic and the Gulf of Bothnia is estimated at about 1,100 km. (684 miles).

Highest point: Haltiatunturi, 1,328 m. (4,354 ft) above sea level.
Largest lakes: Saimaa 4,400 sq. km. (1,700 sq. miles)
Päijänne 1,100 sq. km. (425 sq. miles)
Inari 1,000 sq. km. (385 sq. miles)

The number of lakes is estimated at about 55,000 (diameter over 200 m., 656 ft).

DISTRIBUTION OF LAND AREA 1968

	Total area	Total land area	Arable and other cultivated land	Permanent pasture	Forests	Other areas including lakes
	(in 1,000 sq. km.)					
Finland	337·0	305·4	27·6	0·7	217·6	91·1
Sweden	449·8	411·4	30·3	4·5	227·9	187·1
Norway	324·2	308·4	8·4	1·5	83·3	231·0
Denmark	43·1	42·4	27·1	3·1	4·7	8·2
UK	244·0	240·9	73·8	120·3	18·6	31·3
USA	9,363·4	9,191·4	1,764·4	2,591·7	2,961·4	2,045·9
	(Per cent)					
Finland	100	91	8	0	65	27
Sweden	100	91	7	1	51	41
Norway	100	95	3	0	26	71
Denmark	100	98	63	7	11	19
UK	100	99	30	49	8	13
USA	100	98	19	28	31	22

MEAN DAILY AIR TEMPERATURE 1931–60 (*in degrees centigrade*)

	Jan.	Feb.	Mar.	Apr.	May	June	July	Aug.	Sept.	Oct.	Nov.	Dec.	Annual mean
Helsinki	−5·4	−6·0	−3·1	2·9	9·3	14·5	17·8	16·5	11·7	6·1	1·8	−1·9	5·4
Kuopio	−9·8	−10·0	−6·1	1·1	7·9	14·0	17·1	15·3	9·7	3·6	−1·4	−6·1	2·9
Central Lapland	−13·5	−13·0	−8·9	−2·2	4·8	11·3	14·7	12·0	6·2	−0·5	−5·8	−9·8	−0·4
England and Wales	4·3	4·5	6·4	8·8	11·7	14·8	16·4	16·4	14·3	10·8	7·5	5·6	10·2

RAINFALL AVERAGES 1931–60[1] (*in millimetres*)

	Jan.	Feb.	Mar.	Apr.	May	June	July	Aug.	Sept.	Oct.	Nov.	Dec.	Annual total	Average per month
Helsinki	55	42	36	42	37	47	62	66	66	68	64	62	647	53·9
Kuopio	32	23	22	26	38	59	68	60	59	54	37	32	510	42·5
Central Lapland	27	26	20	32	31	56	74	71	57	43	39	31	507	42·2
England and Wales	92	66	57	60	63	55	79	81	76	92	95	88	904	75·3

[1] England and Wales 1916–50.

POPULATION
POPULATION AND DENSITY OF POPULATION 1970

	Population in thousands	Population per sq. km.	Population per sq. mile
Finland	4,695	14	36
Sweden	8,046	18	46
Norway	3,879	12	31
Denmark	4,921	114	289
UK	55,711	228	593
USA	205,395	22	57
USSR	242,768	11	28

URBANIZATION OF THE POPULATION

	Year	Per cent[1] urban	Per cent[1] rural
Finland	1950	32·3	67·7
	1960	38·4	61·6
	1969	50·2	49·8
Sweden	1965	77·4	22·6
Norway	1960	57·2	42·8
Denmark	1965	77·2	22·8
UK	1966	77·5	22·5
USA	1960	69·9	30·1

[1] N.B. The definition urban and rural varies from country to country.

POPULATION IN THE LARGEST URBAN COMMUNES 1969 (in thousands)

Helsinki	533	Vaasa	49
Tampere	155	Hämeenlinna	38
Turku	155	Joensuu	36
Espoo	93	Imatra	35
Lahti	89	Kotka	34
Oulu	87	Hyvinkää	34
Pori	73	Kemi	30
Kuopio	65	Rovaniemi	29
Jyväskylä	58	Kouvola	26
Lappeenranta	51	Rauma	26

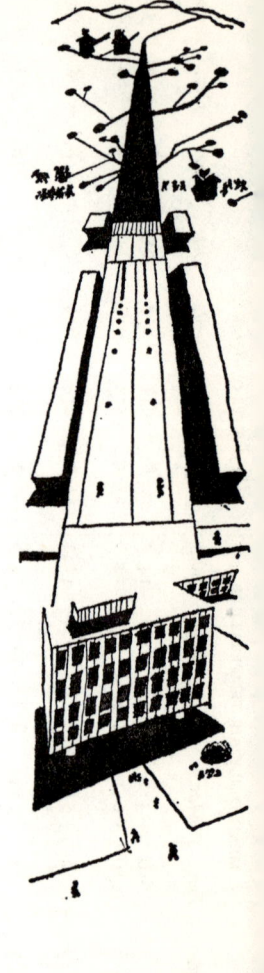

TOWNS IN UNITED KINGDOM AND USA COMPARABLE IN SIZE TO THE LARGEST FINNISH TOWNS

United Kingdom:	Year	Thousands
Manchester	1969	594
Sheffield	1969	529
Brighton	1969	164
Luton	1969	157
USA:		
Memphis	1967	537
Denver	1968	493

POPULATION BY LANGUAGE GROUPS, 1960

	Per cent
Finnish	92·40
Swedish	7·43
Russian	0·06
Lapp	0·03
Other	0·08
	100·00

POPULATION BY RELIGIOUS COMMUNITIES 1968

	Per cent
Evangelical Lutheran Church	92·7
Orthodox Church	1·3
Roman Catholic Church	0·1
Other religions	0·5
Civil register or unknown	5·4
	100·0

POPULATION BY AGE GROUPS (*per cent*)

	Ages	0–14	15–64	65–
Finland	1950	30	63	7
	1960	30	62	8
	1968–9	25	66	9
Sweden	1969–70	21	66	13
Norway	1969–70	24	63	13
Denmark	1968–9	24	64	12
UK	1969	24	63	13
USA	1968–9	29	61	10

BIRTHS, DEATHS AND POPULATION GROWTH

Per 1,000 inhabitants		Live births	Deaths	Increase of population
Finland	1948	27·6	11·2	13·4
	1958	18·6	8·9	7·6
	1968	15·7	9·6	4·2
Sweden	1968	14·3	10·4	6·2
Norway	1968	17·6	9·9	8·7
Denmark	1968	15·3	9·7	4·9
UK	1968	17·1	11·9	5·0
USA	1968	17·5	9·7	10·2

POPULATION GROWTH

1800	832,700
1900	2,655,900
1950	4,029,800
1960	4,448,600
1970	4,695,000

LIFE EXPECTANCY FOR CHILDREN BORN 1960-5

	Men	Women
Finland	65	73
Sweden	72	76
Norway	71	76
Denmark	70	75
England and Wales	69	75
USA	67	74

INFANT MORTALITY 1969

Per 1,000 live born

Finland	13·9
Sweden	13·0
Norway	13·8
Denmark	14·8
England and Wales	18·0
USA	20·7

STATE

POLITICAL PARTIES

NC National Coalition Party—founded in 1918; conservative.
PPM Patriotic People's Movement—founded in 1932; ceased to exist in 1944; extreme right.
SPF Swedish People's Party in Finland—founded in 1906.
LP Liberal Party—founded in 1918; named National Progressive Party; from 1951 called Finnish People's Party; from 1965 called Liberal Party.
CP Centre Party—founded in 1906 as Agrarian Party; from 1966 called Centre Party.
CLF Christian League of Finland—founded in 1958.
FRP Finnish Rural Party—founded in 1959 as Small Holders' Party of Finland; from 1966 called Finnish Rural Party.
SD Social-Democratic Party—founded in 1903.
SDU Social-Democratic Union of Workers and Small Farmers—founded in 1958 as an offshoot from the Social-Democratic Party; other names: Workers' and Smallholders' Social Democratic League, and Social Democratic League.
FPDU Finnish People's Democratic Union including the Communists. (The Communist Party of Finland was founded in 1918, abolished in 1930 and set up again in 1944 under the cover organization FPDU.)

PRESIDENTS OF FINLAND

		Party when first elected
1919–25	K. J. Ståhlberg	Progressive Party (LP)
1925–31	L. Kr. Relander	Agrarian Party (CP)
1931–7	P. E. Svinhufvud	National Coalition Party
1937–40	K. Kallio	Agrarian Party (CP)
1940–3	R. Ryti	Progressive Party (LP)
1943–4	R. Ryti	
1944–6	C. G. E. Mannerheim	Non-party[1]
1946–50	J. K. Paasikivi	Close to NC
1950–6	J. K. Paasikivi	
1956–62	U. K. Kekkonen	Agrarian Party (CP)
1962–8	U. K. Kekkonen	
1968–	U. K. Kekkonen	

[1] Commander-in-chief of Finnish armed forces 1939–40 and 1941–4.

DISTRIBUTION OF SEATS IN PARLIAMENT 1939–72

	1939	1945	1948	1951	1954	1958	1962	1966	1970	1972
PPM	8	—	—	—	—	—	—	—	—	—
NC	25	28	33	28	24	29	32	26	37	34
LP	6	9	5	10	13	8	13	9	8	7
CP	56	49	56	51	53	48	53	49	36	35
CLF	—	—	—	—	—	—	—	1	1	4
FRP	—	—	—	—	—	—	1	18	18
SPF	18	15	14	15	13	14	14	12	12	10
SD	85	50	54	53	54	48	38	55	52	55
SDU	—	—	—	—	—	3	2	7	—	—
DL	—	49	38	43	43	50	47	41	36	37
Other	2	—	—	—	—	—	1	—	—	—
Right	115	101	108	104	103	99	113	97	112	108
Left	85	99	92	96	97	101	87	103	88	92

GOVERNMENTS AND THEIR POLITICAL MAKE-UP 1937-72

Prime minister's party: the number is in bold.
CM = Caretaker ministers or government.

		CM	PPM	NC	LP	SPF	CP	SD	SDU	DL
12. 3.37	Cajander III	1			**2**		5	5		
1.12.39	Ryti I	1		2	**1**	2	4	4		
27. 3.40	Ryti II	4		1	**1**	1	3	4		
3. 1.41	Rangell	2	1	1	**1**	1	4	4		
5. 3.43	Linkomies	2		**2**	1	2	4	5		
8. 8.44	Hackzell	3		**1**	1	1	4	5		
21. 9.44	U. Castren	**4**			1	1	4	6		
17.11.44	Paasikivi II	3			1	2	4	4		**4**
17. 4.45	Paasikivi III	2			1	1	4	4		**5**
26. 3.46	Pekkala	1				1	5	5		**6**
29. 7.48	Fagerholm I	1						**15**		
17. 3.50	Kekkonen I				2	3	**10**			
17. 1.51	Kekkonen II				1	2	**7**	7		
20. 9.51	Kekkonen III	1				2	**7**	7		
9. 7.53	Kekkonen IV	3				3	**8**			
17.11.53	Tuomioja	**6**			3	2	4			
5. 5.54	Törngren	1				**1**	6	6		
20.10.54	Kekkonen V	1					**6**	7		
3. 3.56	Fagerholm II	1				1	6	**6**		
27. 5.57	Sukselainen I	1				3	3	**7**		
29.11.57	Von Fieandt	**13**								
26. 4.58	Kuuskoski	**14**								
29. 8.58	Fagerholm III			3	1	1	5	**5**		
13. 1.59	Sukselainen II	1					**14**			
14. 7.61	Miettunen	1					**14**			
13. 4.62	Karjalainen I	3		3	2	2	**5**			
18.12.63	Lehto	**15**								
12. 9.64	Virolainen	1		3	2	2	**7**			
24. 5.66	Paasio I						5	**6**	1	3
23. 3.68	Koivisto				1		5	**6**	1	3
14. 5.70	Aura I	**13**								
14. 7.70	Karjalainen IIa	1			2	2	**4**	5		3
26. 3.71	Karjalainen IIb	1			2	2	**4**	8		
29.10.71	Aura II	**15**								
23. 2.72	Paasio II							**17**		
4. 9.72	Sorsa*				1	2	5	**7**		

* plus one non-committed member

STANDARD OF LIVING

GROSS NATIONAL PRODUCT PER HEAD 1969

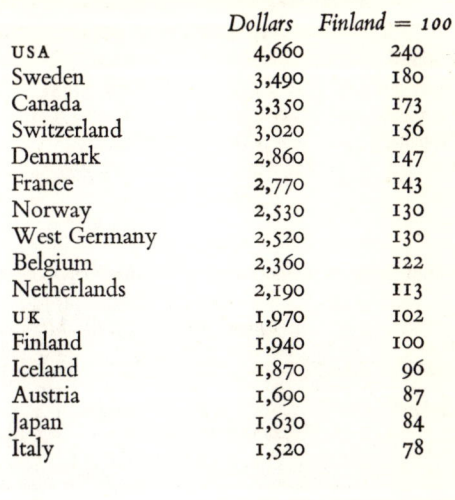

	Dollars	Finland = 100
USA	4,660	240
Sweden	3,490	180
Canada	3,350	173
Switzerland	3,020	156
Denmark	2,860	147
France	2,770	143
Norway	2,530	130
West Germany	2,520	130
Belgium	2,360	122
Netherlands	2,190	113
UK	1,970	102
Finland	1,940	100
Iceland	1,870	96
Austria	1,690	87
Japan	1,630	84
Italy	1,520	78

PRIVATE EXPENDITURE 1968 (per cent)

	Finland	Sweden	Norway	Denmark	UK	USA
Food	29	26	28	23	24	18
Beverages and tobacco	9	10	8	11	12	5
Clothing and other personal effects	8	10	13	8	10	9
Rent, water charges, fuel and light	15	14	12	12	17	18
Transport and communication	13	16	12	13	13	15
Other goods and services	26	24	27	33	24	35
	100	100	100	100	100	100

PRIVATE EXPENDITURE 1968 PER HEAD

	Dollars
Finland	1,040
Sweden	1,780
Norway	1,270
Denmark	1,600
UK	1,170
USA	2,680

TELEPHONES, TELEVISIONS AND PRIVATE CARS PER 1,000 INHABITANTS

	Telephones	Television licences	Private cars
	1968	1968	1969
Finland	215	204	137
Sweden	497	296	253
Norway	271	194	166
Denmark	311	244	209
UK	232	279	186
USA	543	409	410

CONSUMPTION OF BEVERAGES AND TOBACCO, AVERAGE PER HEAD 1964-8

	Coffee kg.	Tea kg.	Cocoa kg.	Tobacco kg.	Wine litre	Beer litre	Spirits litre
Finland	10·0	0·1	0·8	1·4	2·5	13·8	2·8
Sweden	12·2	0·2	1·1	1·6	4·6	38·1	5·2
Norway	8·8	0·1	1·3	1·5	1·7	29·0	2·7
Denmark	10·7	0·3	0·9	3·3	4·2	77·2	1·8
UK	1·4	4·2	1·5	2·4	2·5	92·2	1·7
USA	67·4	0·3	1·5	3·7	3·8	62·2	5·1

CONSUMPTION OF COAL PER HEAD 1968

	kg.
Finland	3,339
Sweden	5,360
Norway	4,259
Denmark	4,690
UK	5,004
USA	10,331

CONSUMPTION OF PRINTING PAPER PER HEAD 1968

	Newsprint kg.	Other printing and writing paper kg.
Finland	18·1	28·3
Sweden	36·4	31·7
Norway	12·9	25·6
Denmark	24·1	25·4
UK	25·7	23·1
USA	41·1	45·8

PERSONS PER ROOM AND HOUSEHOLD

	Year	Persons per: room	Persons per: household
Finland	1960	1·3	3·3
Sweden	1965	0·8	2·7
Norway	1960	0·8	3·1
Denmark	1965	0·8	2·8
England and Wales	1961	0·7	3·0
USA	1960	0·7	3·3

ECONOMIC LIFE

ORIGIN OF PRODUCTION 1968 (*per cent*)

	Finland	Sweden	Norway	Denmark	UK	USA
Agriculture, forestry and fishing	15	5	7	9	3	3
Mining, manufacturing and electricity	30	34	29	30	39	32
Construction	9	10	8	9	7	5
Transport, storage and communication	8	8	19	10	8	6
Wholesale and retail trade	10	12	12	14	11	16
Other services	28	31	25	28	32	38
	100	100	100	100	100	100

ANNUAL GROWTH RATE OF PRODUCTION 1960–8[1] (*per cent*)

	Finland	Sweden	Norway	Denmark	UK	USA
Agriculture, forestry and fishing	0·1	0·2	0·4	1·3	2·6	1·0
Mining, manufacturing and electricity	5·7	7·0	5·6	5·6	2·5	6·1
Construction	3·1	6·0	4·0	6·2	3·6	1·6
Transport, storage and communication	4·0	3·4	7·7	4·8	2·7	6·4
Wholesale and retail trade	4·6	5·2	4·4	4·5	2·2	5·2
Other services	4·9	4·7	4·6	4·5	2·8	4·8
Total production	4·0	4·9	5·0	4·5	3·0	5·1
Total production per head	3·3	4·1	4·2	3·7	2·3	3·7

[1] Sweden 1960–7.

DIVISION OF LABOUR FORCE BY INDUSTRIES (*per cent*)

	Finland 1968	Sweden 1968	Norway 1968	Denmark 1965	UK 1968	USA 1969
Agriculture, forestry and fishing	26	9	15	15	2	5
Mining, manufacturing and electricity	25	32	28	30	42	28
Construction	9	9	9	9	7	6
Transport and communication	7	8	11	7	7	5
Other services	33	42	37	39	42	56
	100	100	100	100	100	100

SAVING 1968

	Finland	Sweden	Norway	Denmark	UK	USA
Total saving as per cent of national income	23	26	20	14	13	10
Percentage distribution:						
General government	46	48	42	52	39	15
Corporations	10	26	58}	48}	29	32
Households	44	27			33	53

INCREASE IN THE COST OF LIVING 1961–70

	Per cent
Finland	59·5
Sweden	45·5
Norway	51·4
Denmark	70·4
UK	43·8
USA	29·8

DISTRIBUTION OF THE NATIONAL INCOME 1968 (*per cent*)

	Finland	Sweden	Norway	Denmark	UK	USA
Compensation of employees	65	80	67	68	76	72
Operating surplus	35	20	33	32	24	28
National income	100	100	100	100	100	100
National income 1,000 million dollars	6·3	20·4	7·0	9·3	79·8	719·8

CERTAIN PRODUCTS AS A PERCENTAGE OF WORLD PRODUCTION 1968

	Finland	Sweden	Norway	Denmark	UK	USA
Meat	0·2	0·5	0·2	1·3	2·6	20·6
Milk	0·9	0·8	0·5	1·3	3·2	13·5
Cigarettes	0·3	0·3	0·0	0·3	4·6	22·8
Sawnwood	1·5	3·0	0·4	0·2	n.a.	22·5
Wood pulp, mechanical and chemical	6·6	7·8	2·2	n.a.	n.a.	38·0
Iron ore	0·1	5·5	0·7	n.a.	1·1	13·6
Copper ore	0·6	0·3	0·3	n.a.	n.a.	20·3
Newsprint	6·6	4·3	2·5	n.a.	3·9	13·3
Other paper and board	2·6	3·0	0·8	n.a.	4·2	42·7
Cement	0·3	0·8	0·4	0·4	3·5	13·4
Steel	0·1	1·0	0·2	0·1	5·0	22·6
Copper	0·5	0·7	0·3	n.a.	3·0	25·7
Ships	1·0	6·6	2·9	2·9	5·3	2·6
Electricity	0·4	1·3	1·4	0·3	5·3	34·2
Percentage of world population	0·1	0·2	0·1	0·1	1·5	5·8

INDUSTRY

NUMBER OF EMPLOYEES AND VALUE ADDED BY BRANCHES OF INDUSTRY 1970

	Employees in thousands	per cent	Value added Mill. Fmks	per cent	Change of volume 1961-70 per cent
Mining and quarrying	6	1	360	3	53
Food	51	10	1,490	11	62
Beverages and tobacco	8	2	270	2	122
Textiles	67	13	1,000	8	48
Wood and paper	85	17	2,680	20	60
Chemicals	20	4	960	7	216
Metal products	163	32	3,570	27	73
Miscellaneous	86	17	1,800	14	103
Electricity, gas and steam	19	4	1,030	8	92
Total	505	100	13,160	100	82
Total million dollars			3,130		

DIVISION OF EMPLOYEES AND VALUE ADDED BY FORMS OF ENTERPRISE 1970
(*per cent*)

	Employees	Value added
Private companies	70	66
Co-operatives	6	5
Other private enterprises	10	7
State companies	10	18
Other public enterprises	4	4
	100	100

LARGEST INDUSTRIAL ENTERPRISES 1970

		Main products	Sales, million: Fmks	Dollars
1.	Enso-Gutzeit Oy	Wood and wood products, paper and paper products	981	235
2.	Neste Oy	Products of petroleum	907	218
3.	Rauma-Repola Oy	Metal products, machinery, ships, wood, paper and paper products	742	178
4.	Nokia Oy	Paper products, metal products, machinery, rubber products, electronics	703	169
5.	Oy Wärtsilä Ab	Metal products, machinery, ships, glass products	664	159
6.	A. Ahlström Oy	Paper and paper products, metal products, machinery, fibre boards, glass products	562	135
7.	Kymin Osakeyhtiö	Wood and wood products, paper and paper products, metal products, machinery	503	121
8.	Outokumpu Oy	Mining and quarrying, basic metals, chemicals, apparatus	502	120
9.	Rikkihappo Oy	Chemicals, fertilizers	467	112
10.	Oy Tampella Ab	Wood and wood products, paper and paper products, metal products, machinery	462	111

1, 2, 8 and 9 are state companies.

AGRICULTURE

DIVISION OF FARMS BY SIZE OF ARABLE LAND 1969
(*per cent*)

	Hectares[1]			Total area of arable land
	2–10	10–20	20–	1,000 hectares
Finland	66	26	8	2,669
Sweden	49	25	26	3,035
Norway	80	15	5	829
Denmark	31	32	37	2,694
UK[2]				7,382
USA[2]				176,440

[1] 1 hectare = 2·471 acres.
[2] Comparable data is not available.

CROPS IN 1969 (*1,000 tons*)

	Wheat	Rye	Barley	Oats	Maize	Potato
Finland	520	141	855	1,146	—	1,029
Sweden	917	178	1,523	1,133	—	873
Norway	3	5	506	130	—	765
Denmark	428	126	5,255	755	—	663
UK	3,373	11	8,698	1,334	—	6,215
USA	39,704	798	9,084	13,789	116,282	13,941

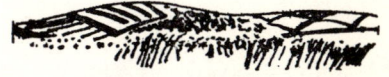

LIVESTOCK IN THOUSANDS 1968–9

	Horses	Cattle	Sheep	Pigs
Finland	111	2,153	168	792
Sweden	67	2,005	332	2,030
Norway	46	1,050	1,920	630
Denmark	40	3,002	90	8,023
UK	138	12,373	26,604	7,804
USA	7,300	109,661	21,238	57,205

PRODUCTION OF MEAT AND MILK 1968 (*1,000 tons*)

	Finland	Sweden	Norway	Denmark	UK	USA
Meat	175	397	132	925	2,023	15,982
Milk	3,591	3,308	1,805	5,122	12,478	53,197

FORESTRY

PRODUCTIVE FOREST AREA BY OWNER GROUPS (*per cent*)

	Finland 1965	Sweden 1968	Norway 1967
State forests	24·7	17·3	10·8
Other public forests	2·1	6·6	6·6
Company-owned forests	6·3	25·0	4·9
Other privately owned forests	66·9	51·1	77·7
	100	100	100
Total area 1,000 hectares	22,089	23,314	6,482

GROWING STOCK AND ROUNDWOOD REMOVALS

	Growing stock 1963 Mill. cu.m. Coniferous	Total	Roundwood removals 1968 mill. cu.m.
Finland	1,136	1,410	40·9
Sweden	1,777	2,089	50·1
Norway	357	433	6·7
Denmark	21	44	2·5
UK	51	105	3·2
USA	13,891	20,312	331·1

357

CONSUMPTION OF DOMESTIC ROUNDWOOD 1969

Mill. cu.m. excl. bark	Finland	Sweden	Norway
Sawlogs	14·2	21·4	3·5
Pulpwood	19·3	28·7	3·5
Fuel wood	8·5	3·5	0·8
Other wood	1·1	0·9	0·3
Total	43·1	54·5	8·1

Consumption in Finland by tree species

	Mill. cu.m.	Per cent
Pine	15·5	36
Spruce	14·0	33
Birch	11·7	27
Others	1·9	4
Total	43·1	100

Consumption in Finland by categories of consumption

	Mill. cu.m.	Per cent
Industries	33·2	77
Export	0·8	2
Real estate and other	9·1	21
	43·1	100

FOREIGN TRADE

IMPORTS PLUS EXPORTS PER HEAD 1969

	Dollars
Finland	853
Sweden	1,454
Norway	1,335
Denmark	1,390
UK	654
USA	361
EFTA	809
EEC	815

IMPORTS AND EXPORTS BY AREAS 1970

	Imports		Exports	
	Mill. Fmks	Per cent	Mill. Fmks	Per cent
Total		11,077	100·0	9,687	100·0
EFTA		4,332	39·1	4,198	43·4
of which					
Sweden	1,781	16·1	1,464	15·1
Norway	263	2·4	358	3·7
Denmark	327	3·0	396	4·1
Great Britain	1,455	13·1	1,690	17·4
EEC		2,977	26·9	2,252	23·2
of which					
West Germany	1,826	16·5	1,019	10·5
France	377	3·4	363	3·7
Netherlands	327	3·0	446	4·6
Italy	236	2·1	240	2·5
USA		575	5·2	454	4·7
Eastern bloc		1,811	16·3	1,572	16·2
of which					
USSR	1,391	12·6	1,187	12·3
Other countries		1,382	12·5	1,211	12·5
of which					
Japan	261	2·4	27	0·3
Total million dollars		2,637		2,306	

IMPORTS AND EXPORTS BY COMMODITY GROUPS 1970

	Imports Mill. Fmks	Per cent	Exports Mill. Fmks	Per cent
Food products	918	8·3	370	3·8
Dairy products and eggs	1	0·0	189	2·0
Fruit and vegetables	206	1·9	23	0·2
Coffee	404	3·6	1	0·0
Beverages and tobacco	82	0·7	18	0·2
Crude materials, inedible	722	6·5	2,449	25·3
Hides, skins, undressed	37	0·3	114	1·2
Round timber	110	1·0	83	0·9
Wood, shaped or simply worked	14	0·1	924	9·5
Pulp and waste paper	10	0·1	1,218	12·6
Animal and vegetable oils and fats	17	0·2	23	0·2
Mineral fuels, lubricants, etc.	1,270	11·5	80	0·8
Coal, coke, peat, etc.	256	2·3	2	0·0
Crude and refined petroleum	639	5·8	0	0·0
Petroleum extracts	346	3·1	34	0·4
Chemicals	1,080	9·7	258	2·7
Raw chemicals	278	2·5	73	0·8
Medicinal products	144	1·3	10	0·1
Plastic materials, etc.	333	3·0	44	0·5
Manufactured products	2,585	23·3	4,175	43·1
Wood manufacture, excluding furniture	37	0·3	519	5·4
Newsprint	1	0·0	631	6·5
Printing and writing paper	3	0·0	539	5·6
Kraftpaper and board	1	0·0	445	4·6
Other paper and board	6	0·1	482	5·0
Textile yarn and fabrics	638	5·8	170	1·8
Iron and steel	926	8·4	315	3·3
Non-ferrous metals	311	2·8	288	3·0
Manufactures of metal	297	2·7	159	1·6
Machinery, apparatus and transport equipment	3,607	32·6	1,598	16·5
Machinery, not electric	1,633	14·7	611	6·3
Electric machinery and apparatus	730	6·6	279	2·9
Private cars	379	3·4	29	0·3
Lorries and vans	287	2·6	9	0·1
Ships and boats	216	1·9	620	6·4
Miscellaneous manufactured products	738	6·7	713	7·4
Furniture	31	0·3	77	0·8
Clothing	155	1·4	390	4·3
Footwear	40	0·4	63	0·7
Optical and photographic instruments, watches, etc.	201	1·8	16	0·2
Other commodities	58	0·6	3	0·0
Total	11,077	100·0	9,687	100·0

TRANSPORT AND COMMUNICATIONS

DOMESTIC PASSENGER TRAFFIC 1969

	Per cent
By car and taxi	68
By bus	20
By rail	8
By lake	0
By air	1
By motorcycle, etc.	3
	100

Estimated total 30,400 million passenger km.

DOMESTIC GOODS TRAFFIC 1969

	Per cent
By road	58
By rail	28
By lake	14
	100

Estimated total 21,700 million ton km.

TELEGRAMS PER 1,000 INHABITANTS 1968

Finland	230
Sweden	500
Norway	780
Denmark	440
UK	300
USA	420

MOTOR VEHICLES IN USE 1968 (*in thousands*)

	Passenger cars	Buses	Other commercial vehicles	Total
Finland	580·7	7·6	92·7	681·0
Sweden	2,072·2	11·7	138·7	2,222·6
Norway	619·0	7·1	132·1	758·2
Denmark	954·7	4·5	254·2	1,213·4
UK	10,880·2	81·1	1,633·8	12,595·1
USA	83,281·3		16,282·1	99,563·4

GENERAL GOVERNMENT

GENERAL GOVERNMENT REVENUE AND EXPENDITURE 1968

	Per cent	Mill. Fmks	Million dollars
Current revenue	100	12,052·5	2,869·6
Current expenditure	78	9,402·8	2,238·8
Saving	22	2,649·7	630·8

Current revenue: — Per cent

Income from property and enterprises	9
Less interest on the public debt	−3
Indirect taxes	42
Direct taxes on corporations	7
Direct taxes on households and private non-profit institutions	(100) 43
of which: Contributions to social security	(28) 12
Other direct taxes	(72) 31
Other current transfers from households and private non-profit institutions	2
Current transfers from the rest of the world	0
	100

Current expenditure: — Per cent

Consumption expenditure	(100) 61
of which: Public administration	(24) 15
Defence	(10) 6
Education	(31) 19
Health services	(21) 13
Other social services	(8) 5
Transport and communication	(6) 3
Subsidies	10
Current transfers to households and private non-profit institutions	(100) 29
of which: Education	(14) 4
Health	(13) 4
Other social transfers	(72) 21
Other transfers	(1) 0
Current transfers to the rest of the world	0
	100

SOCIAL WELFARE

POPULATION PER DOCTOR

Finland	1968	1,120
Sweden	1968	800
Norway	1968	740
Denmark	1967	710
UK	1967	860
USA	1967	650

POPULATION PER HOSPITAL BED 1968

Finland	70
Sweden	70
Norway	110
Denmark	110
UK[1]	100
USA	120

[1] Non-private only.

SOCIAL EXPENDITURE 1968

In 1968 social expenditure was about 17 per cent of the national income; 4,717 million Fmks (1,123 million dollars).

Net expenditure for social services:

	Per cent
Health	28
Industrial accidents	3
Unemployment	10
Old-age, disability, etc.	34
Family welfare	13
Public and unspecified assistance	3
Relief to military or war casualties	4
Estimated tax rebates for children	3
Interest subsidies for housing loans	2
	100

Financing of expenditure for social services:

	Per cent
State	37
Communes	23
Employers	31
Registered	9
	100

TAXES AND CONTRIBUTIONS PER INHABITANT

		Dollars
Finland	1968	565
Sweden	1968	1,342
Norway	1968	892
Denmark	1967	765
UK	1968	636
USA[1]	1968	1,313

[1] Without direct taxes on public corporations.

EDUCATION

EDUCATION IN FINLAND 1969

Children of compulsory school age 729,000 of which 39,400 were school-leavers.

	Age	School years	Number
Education received in:			
Regular primary schools	7–10	1–4	313,500
	11–12	5–6	78,700
Primary continuation schools	13–	7–9	82,100
Middle schools	11–	5–9	245,200
Grammar schools	16–	10–12	70,500
Upper secondary vocational schools		9–13	102,000
Vocational schools			43,400
People's high schools			8,100
Commercial schools and institutes			18,900
Technical schools and institutes			15,000
Agricultural and forestry schools and institutes			4,900
Schools and institutes for training health personnel			7,400
Schools for domestic arts and crafts			2,900
Schools of domestic economy			5,300
Other schools and institutes			5,700
Universities and other institutions of higher education		13–	57,300
Workers' evening schools			217,200

UNIVERSITIES AND OTHER INSTITUTIONS OF HIGHER EDUCATION 1969

	Number	Teachers	Students
Universities	8	3,979	45,400
Schools of economics	5	345	5,650
Institute of technology	1	825	5,400
Veterinary college	1	46	150
Teachers' training institutes	2	123	400
Teachers' colleges	2	47	300
Total	19	5,365	57,300

STUDENTS BY FACULTY 1968–9

	Students	Per cent
Theology	1,300	2
Law	2,700	5
Social sciences	7,600	14
Arts	15,150	29
Mathematics and natural sciences	8,750	17
Education	1,150	2
Medicine and dentistry	2,850	5
Pharmacy	650	1
Agriculture and forestry	1,400	3
Technology	5,900	11
Commerce	5,000	10
Physical education	500	1
Total	52,950	100

PUBLIC EXPENDITURE ON EDUCATION 1967

	Total expenditure: million dollars	per head dollars	Capital expenditure per cent of total expenditure	Total expenditure per cent of Gross National Product
Finland	623	134	17	6·7
Sweden	1,727	220	22	8·1[1]
Norway	498	132	25	5·9
Denmark	745	154	21	6·1
UK	6,247	113	23	5·6
USA	45,300	228	17	5·6

[1] Per cent of gross domestic product.

CULTURE AND RECREATION

DRAMATIC ART

Theatres receiving State grant 1969–70
Number of: theatres 34
actors 820
performances 7,900
attendances 1,950,000

Besides the regular theatres there are amateur groups in practically every town and village. The number of amateur groups is estimated to be about 6,000.

CINEMAS

Cinemas in Finland 1969:
Number of: cinemas 341
seats 104,584
films shown 235
attendances 10,450,000

Country producing films shown in Finland:

Finland	9
England	37
Italy	26
France	30
USSR	10
Scandinavian	12
USA	86
West Germany	10
Others	15
Total	235

Cinemas and attendances:

	Year	Cinemas	Attendances per inhabitant
Finland	1968	349	2·4
Sweden	1968	449[1]	4·2
Norway	1968	207	4·0
Denmark	1968	395	5·5
UK	1968	1,631	4·0
USA	1967	13,400[2]	7·0

[1] In additon 1,064 summer theatres.   [2] Including drive-in theatres.

LIBRARIES

Municipal libraries in 1969:

	Number
Libraries	3,015
Volumes	11,282,000
Home lendings	29,513,000
Borrowers	1,167,000
Home lending per inhabitant	6·3

Larger scientific libraries in 1969:

	Number
Libraries	33
Volumes	6,141,000
Lending	1,092,500

In addition, at least 300 smaller special libraries.

BOOKS PUBLISHED IN FINLAND 1969

Works written by Finnish authors		2,583
Fiction	282	
Non-fiction	2,301	
Translated works[1]		882
Fiction	605	
Non-fiction	277	
Total		3,465

[1] About 500 were translated from English. In addition, 2,230 pamphlets were published in 1969.

DAILY NEWSPAPERS

	Year	Number	Average weekday net circulation	Copies per 1,000 inhabitants
Finland	1969	68	1,863,000	396
Sweden	1968	112	4,098,000	518
Norway	1969	82	1,493,000	388
Denmark	1968	62	1,728,000	356
UK	1966	106	26,700,000	488
USA	1969	1,758	62,060,000	305

NET CIRCULATION OF THE MOST IMPORTANT NEWSPAPERS 1970

Newspaper and Place of publication	Times published per week	Political party	Net circulation in thousands
1. Helsingin Sanomat, Helsinki	7	—	272
2. Maaseudun Tulevaisuus, Helsinki	3	[1]	150
3. Aamulehti, Tampere	7	NC	110
4. Turun Sanomat, Turku	7	—	107
5. Uusi Suomi, Helsinki	7	NC	84
6. Hufvudstadsbladet, Helsinki[2]	7	—	66
7. Ilta-Sanomat, Helsinki	7	—	64
8. Kaleva, Oulu	7	—	62
9. Savon Sanomat, Kuopio	7	CP	62
10. Vaasa, Vaasa	7	NC	57

[1] Agricultural professional paper. [2] Swedish.

MAIN SOURCES FOR STATISTICS

INTERNATIONAL:

United Nations: *Statistical Yearbook*
United Nations: *Demographic Yearbook*
United Nations: *Yearbook of National Accounts Statistics*
UNESCO: *Statistical Yearbook*

SCANDINAVIAN:

Yearbook of Nordic Statistics, Stockholm, published by the Nordic Council in English and Swedish.

FINNISH:

Statistical Yearbook of Finland, Helsinki. Published by the Central Statistical Office in Finnish, Swedish and in part in English.
Bulletin of Statistics, Helsinki, published by the Central Statistical Office in Finnish, Swedish and in part in English.
Official Statistics of Finland, Helsinki, containing extensive data from about 35 different fields, such as foreign trade, industry, population, etc. Published in Finnish and Swedish, and partly in English.

INDEX

Page numbers in bold type indicate main references; page numbers in italics refer to the section on Statistics; Pl. refers to black and white plate numbers. For colour plates see p. 15. 'Oy' (Osakeyhtiö) means limited company.

Aalto, Alvar 110, 126, 129, **191-6**, 199, 203, 204, 205, 285, 305, Pl. 28, 30, 36, 40, 42.
Aaltonen, Rauno 148
Aaltonen, Wäinö 201, 255, Pl. 16, 60
Aarikka 209
Aarnio, Eero 205, 211
Åbo, see Turku
Åboland, see Turunmaa
Academic Socialist Society 66
Äetsä 208
Agrarian Party, see Centre Party
Agricola, Mikael 179, 219
Agriculture, see also Forest Farming **70-5**, 84, 103, 131, *344, 353-7*
Ahlström, A, Oy *356*
Aho, Juhani 2, 27
Ahvenanmaa, see Åland
Air travel, see Transport
Aladin, Tamara Pl. 62
Åland (Ahvenanmaa) 47, 48, 52, **97-101**, 127, 217, 266, 267, 285, Pl. 10
Alexander I, Tsar 26, 27, 35, 301
Alexander II, Tsar 32, 90, 301
Allardt, Erik 67
American Debt, Repayment of 51
Amerplast 209
Ammus-Sytytin Oy 206
Anglo-Finnish Society 303
Anhava, Tuomas 234
Animals, see also Reindeer 96, 98, 105, 120, 129, 133-134, **138-40**, 145, 215, *263, 264*
Arabia 204, 205, 207, 209, 211, 213, 302, Pl. 63
Architecture, see also Church Architecture 182, **191-201**, Pl. 20-42
Arctic Circle 116, 129, 138, 199, 286, 287, *344*
Arctic Coast, Ocean 23, 24, 58, 116, 117, 286
Area *344*

Armed Forces **150-5**, 231, 232, *362*
Armfelt, Gustaf Mauritz 30
Army training **150-5**
Art, see Architecture, Design, Painting and Sculpture
Artek Oy 204, 211
Arwidsson, Arvid Ivar 31
Asko Oy 211
Atlas Maritimus et Commercialis 88
Atlas, Moses Pitt's 302
Atomic Power 61, 80, 81
Aulanko 285
Aurajoki, river 102, 103
Aurora Borealis 117, 286
Autere, Hannes 255, Pl. 55
Avellan, Admiral 295

Bäckström, Olaf 209
Baeckman 200
Ballet, see also Theatre 286
Baltic 18, 19, 95, 98, 102, 155, 199
Barcelona Exhibition (1929) 203
Batyushkov, Konstantin 216
Berglund, Paavo 248, 304
Bergman, Erik 248
Billnäs 104
Births *347*
Björneborg, see Pori
Bladh, Pehr 107
Blomstedt, Aulis 194
Blumenbach, J. F. 19
Bobrikov, Governor General 34
Bomarsund 101, 301
Borg, Kim 248, 304
Borgå, see Porvoo
Bothnia, Gulf of 21, 23, 117, 147, *344*
Brahe, Per Pl. 15
Brahestad, see Raahe
Breakspeare, Nicholas 178
Britain 24, 48, 49, 54, 57, 60, 61, 77, 85, 157, 166, 186, 297, 298, **299-305**
For comparative statistics, see pp. 344-367

368

INDEX

British Council   303
Brummer, Arttu   202
Brummer, Eeva   206, 208
Bryggman, Erik   196, Pl. 29
Bryk, Petri   83
Bryk, Rut   206
Bunbury, Selina   92
Byzantium   18, 20

Canada   77, 79, 295, 296
Canals, *see* Waterways
Canth, Minna   228, 260
Carpet washing   Pl. 49
Castrén, Heikki   195, 198
Castrén, Matias Alexander   31, 114
Centre Party (formerly Agrarian)   50, 63, 67, 68, *348–50*
Ceramics, *see also* Design and Individual Companies   203, 212, Pl. 63, 64
Chemical Industry   82, 84, 86, *355–6*, *360*
Chorell, Walentin   158, 230
Christianity, *see* Religion
Christian League of Finland   *348–50*
Church Architecture   188–90, 250
Church Research Institute   186
Churchill, Winston   40, 57, 218
Cinema   *365–6*
Civil War, *see* Wars
Clarke, Edward   88, 216, 217, 302
Climate   18, **95–6**, 142–9, 286, *345*
Clive-Bayley, A. M. C.   216, 308
Collinder, Björn   172
COMECON (Council for Mutual Economic Assistance)   61
Common Market, *see* EEC
Communist Party, *see* Finnish Communist Party and People's Democratic Union
Conservation Year, International   140, 141
Continuation War, *see* Wars
Cost of Living   354
Crayfish Season   268
Crimean War, *see* Wars

Dalsbruk (Taalintehdas)   104
Deaths   347
Defence, *see* Armed Forces
Denmark   20, 260
  For comparative statistics see pp. 344–367

Design   76, 82, 83, 195, **202–13**, 305, Pl. 62–67
Diktonius, Elmer   230
Dissenters' Law, *see* Religion
Dmitri, False   24
Domestic Appliances   81, 209
Duhamel, Georges   218

Edelfelt, Albert   109, 252
Education   **156–67**, 179, 220, *362*, *364–5*, Pl. 46
EEC (European Economic Community)   61, 77, 84, 85, 213, *358*, *359*
EFTA (European Free Trade Association)   61, 84, 85, 213, *358*, *359*
Ehrenström, J. A.   126
Ehrensvärd, Augustin   101
Ehrnrooth, Casimir   295
Ekenäs, *see* Tammisaari
Electric Power   81, 119, 121, *353–5*, Pl. 5
Emigration, of Finns   108, **294–7**
Enckell, Rabbe   230
Enckell, Magnus   253
Engel, Carl Ludwig   126, 200
Engels, Friedrich   64
Enqvist, Vice-Admiral   295
Enso-Gutzeit Oy   77, *356*
Ericsson, Henry   203, 208
Ericsson, Pamela   100
Erik IX, King of Sweden   178
Ervi, Aarne   195, 198, 200, Pl. 5, 32
Espoo   *346*, Pl. 34
Estonia   18, 19, 46, 49, 52, 287
Etholen, Vice-Admiral   295
Eurocan Pulp and Paper Ltd   77
Europaeus   114
Events, Calendar of   **263–70**, 286–7
Exports, 84–6, *358–60*

Fashion   76, 205, 209–10, *360*
Fauna, *see* Animals
February Manifesto, 1899,   33, 34, 301
Festivals, *see* Events, Calendar of
Finch, A. W.   204, 205, 253
Find the Finns Scheme   285
Finland, Gulf of   18, 20, 21, 24, 27, 52, 61, 104, 139, 287, 292, *344*
Finlayson-Forssa Oy   208, 302
Finlayson, James   302
Finnish-American Societies   296

FINLAND: AN INTRODUCTION

Finnish Arts Association 252
Finnish Bible Society 186
Finnish-British Societies 164, 303
Finnish Clothing Industries, Central Federation of 210
Finnish Communist Party 38, 47, 49, 50, 53, 59, **64-9**, *348-50*
Finnish Economic Society 103
Finnish Foreign Trade Association 210
Finnish Graphic Artists, Society of 254
Finnish Industries, Federation of 86
Finnish Institute of Food, Chemistry and Technology 281
Finnish Institute of Meat Technology 281
Finnish Institute of Technology 161, 190, 195
Finnish Literature Society 224, 225
Finnish Packaging Association 209
Finnish People's Democratic Union, *see also* Finnish Communist Party 38, 66, 67, *348-50*
Finnish People's Party *348*
Finnish Pulp & Paper Research Institute 79
Finnish Research Institute of Engineering in Agriculture and Forestry 212
Finnish Rural Party 63, 68, *348-50*
Finnish Social-democratic Party, *see* Social-democratic Party
Finnish Society of Crafts and Design 202, 208
Finnish Textile Industries, Association of 210
Finnish Tourist Board 288, 305
Finnish Travel Association 287, 305
Finnish Women's Democratic League 66
Finno-Ugric, language group, *see* Language
Fishing in winter 146, Pl. 14
Fiskars Oy 104, 209
Food 110, 204, **278-83**
Foreign Trade, *see* Exports and Imports
Förenade Plastfabriker 208
Forest Farming 71, 74
Forest Industries **77-9**, 82, 83, 84, 131, *353-8*, Pl. 3
Forestry Commission 141
Forssa 208
Franck, Kaj 205, 206, 207
Fredrikshamn, *see* Hamina

Friendship, Co-operation and Mutual Assistance, Finnish-Soviet Treaty of 60
Friman Oy 208
Fur Farming 105, 108, 133
Furniture, *see also* Domestic Appliances 76, 195, 203, 204, 209, 211, 212, *360*
Furujhelm, Admiral 295

Gallen-Kallela, Akseli 114, 121, 208, 252, 254, Pl. 57
Gamlakarleby, *see* Kokkola
Ganivet, Angel 163, 215
Gardberg, Bertel 205, 206, 210, Pl. 66
Gardie, Jacob de la 24
Gardie, Pontus de la 90, 115
Gas, natural 61, 80
Gebhardt, Hannes 71
Geological Research Institute 132
Germany **45-7, 54-8,** 61, 80, 85, 166, 186, 260, 297, 298
Gesellius, Herman Pl. 25
Glass, *see also* Design and individual companies 76, 202, 203, 207, 211, 212, Pl. 62
Good, John 301
Grand Duchy 26, 27, 32, 64, 105, 113, 271, 294
Granö, J. G. 96
Graves, decoration of 185, 270, Pl. 50
Great Northern War, *see* Wars
Great Wrath 25
Gummerus, Olaf 208
Gustavus II Adolphus, King of Sweden 22, 25, 179, 300
Gustavus III, King of Sweden 101
Gustavus Vasa, King of Sweden 116

Haavikko, Paavo 233, 234, 260
Hackman Oy Pl. 66
Haikko 285
Hailuoto 98
Haimi 211
Häiväoja, Paula 210
Halonen, Pekka 253
Haltiatunturi, fell *344*
Häme 20, 21, 104, 109, 110, 280
Hämeenlinna (Tavastehus) 110, 125, 189, 256, 265, 285, *346*
Hamina (Fredrikshamn) 26, 89, 105, 125

370

INDEX

Hamina, Treaty of, 1809 26
Hanko (Hangö) 54, 55, 57, 58, 105, 268
Haparanda 134
Hardy, Thomas 301
Hattula 182, 189
Hattuvaara 267
Health Services *362–3*
Heinävesi 113, 185
Heinola 267
Hellemaa, Kaarina 210
Helsinki (Helsingfors) 44, 46, 47, 49, 51, 58, 79, **101**, 105, **126**, 128, 133, 139, 140, 144, 148, 161, 165, 180, 189, 190, 191, **194–200**, 202, 204, 205, 206, 211, 216, 242, 246, 247, 250, 254, 256, 257, 258, 259, 264, 265, 266, 267, 268, 269, 270, 272, 273, 281, 282, 285, 286, 288, 299, 304, 305, *345*, *346*, Pl. 12, 13, 18, 21, 24–7, 31–3, 35, 39, 40
Hemming Oy 208
Henry, Bishop of Uppsala 20, 178
Hiltunen, Eila 304, Pl. 18
Hitler, Adolf 52, 55, 57
Holidays, *see* Events and Tourism
Hollola 251, Pl. 51
Huttunen, Erkki 196
Huutoniemi 200
Hydro-electricity, *see* Electric Power
Hyry, Antti 234
Hyvinkää 200, *346*, Pl. 37

Iijoki, river 106, 107
Iittala 203, 205, 207
Illola 285
Ilomantsi 113, 267
Imatra *346*, Pl. 36
Imatrankoski 115
Imports 84–86, *358–60*
Inari 135, 183
Inari, lake *344*
Independence Day 270, 303
Independence, Declaration of 45
Industries, *see also* individual industries 76–86, *353–6*, *360*, Pl. 5, 16
Informative Labelling Association 212
Isokyrö 106
Ivalo 138, 287

Jäger Battalion 42, 45, 46

Jakobson, Max 61
Jakobstad, *see* Pietarsaari
Jalas, Jussi 304
Jämsänkoski 110
Jäntti, Toivo 196
Järnefelt, Armas 114
Järvi, Jorma Pl. 31
Jewellery 76, 210, Pl. 65
Jews 57
Joenpelto, Eeva 234
Joensuu 161, 267, 269, *346*
John III, King of Sweden 24, 35
Jortikka, Ilkka 209
Jotuni, Maria 228
Joulumaa Oy 133
Juho Jussila Oy 209
Julin, von, family 104, 302
Jung, Dora 206
Juslenius, Daniel 220
Juva, Mikko 186
Jyväskylä 110, 127, 157, 194, 200, 212, 247, 267, 269, 272, 283, 286, *346*, Pl. 10

Kaamanen 135
Kainuu 110
Kaipiainen, Birger 205, Pl. 63
Kajaani 114, 125
Kajanus, Robert 243
Kalajoki 106
Kalevala 31, 114, **224–5**, 230, 243, 251, 252, 264, 265, 266
Kalkkinen Canal 89
Kallas, Aino 228
Kallio, Kyösti *349*
Kalm, Pehr 103
Kalvopakkaus Oy 209
Kamu, Okko 247, 304
Karelia, Karelians, 20, 21, 23, 24, 25, 31, 48, 49, 52, 53, 58, 99, 109, 110, **112–16**, 150, 186, 224, 232, 280, 285, 295
Karelia, East 48, 49, 57, 58, 185, 224
Karelians, resettlement of 72, 113, 114, 115
Karl XI, King of Sweden 29
Karl XII, King of Sweden 25, 29
Karlsson, Elis 100
Kaskinen (Kaskö) 107
Kastelholm 101
Kauhava 106
Kaustinen 247, 268, 287

Kekkonen, Urho, President 38, 39, 60, 143, 144, 165, 296, *349, 350*
Kemi 88, 108, 116, 118, *346*
Kemijoki, river 106, 107, 119, 120
Kemi Oy 132
Kemijärvi 126, 132
Keuruu 189, Pl. 23
Kevojoki, river 122
Kianto, Ilmari 228
Kihlman, Christer 234
Kilpi, Volter 228
Kilpinen, Inkeri 260
Kilpinen, Yrjö 244
Kilpisjärvi 286
Kinnunen, Leo 148
Kitkajoki, river 117
Kivi, Aleksis 156, 225, 232, 260, 268, 269
Kivimaa, Arvi 261
Kjellberg, Friedl 205
Klami, Uuno 244
Kökar 99
Kokemäenjoki (Kumo), river 104
Kokko, Yrjö 121
Kokkola (Gamlakarleby) 301
Kokkonen, Joonas 248
Kolari 132
Koli, Paavo 160
Kone Oy 81
Konevitsa, monastery 113, 185
Könkämäjoki, river 117
Konnus Canal 89
Korhonen, Toivo 201, Pl. 34
Korhonen Oy 209, 211
Korpijaakko, Pekka 209
Korsholma (Korsholm) 107
Kotka 90, 104, 107, 127, *346*
Kouvola 200, *346*
Köyliö, lake 178
Kramer, Admiral von 295
Krause, Tom 248, 305
Kristiinankaupunki (Kristinestad) 125
Kuhlefelt, Maj 205
Kullervo 228
Kultaranta 106
Kumo river, *see* Kokemäenjoki, river
Kuopio 110, 113, 125, 161, 185, 201, 208, 259, 264, 266, 286, *345, 346*
Kuusamo 116, 117, 118, 122, 264
Kuusankoski 78
Kuusinen, Otto Ville 53, 60, 65, 295

Kymijoki (Kymmene), river 104
Kymi Oy 77, 78, 104, *356*

Laakso, Totti 212
Laapotti, Jaakko Pl. 34
Laestadians, *see* Religion
Lahti 40, 110, 127, 200, 211, 264, 285, *346*
Lakes, *see also* Saimaa 18, 24, 25, 53, 58, 89, 104, 109, 110, 138, 284, 285, *344*, Pl. 1
Lake Travel, *see* Transport
Lampinen, Simo 148
Language
  Finnish 19, 21, 22, 31, 32, 35, 99, 108, **168-76**, 220, 221, 233, 292, *347*
  Finnish Language Courses 173-6
  Swedish 21, 22, 32, 35, 48, 99, 108, 220, 221, 233, *347*
  Lappish 169, *347*
  Latin 22
Lapland 17, 27, 56, 57, 58, 119, 121, **128-36**, 138, 142, 143, 145, 150, 183, 215, 263, 264, 266, 280, 284, 286, Pl. 19, 43
Lappeenranta 161, 287, *346*
Lapps 18, 116, 120, **128-35**, *347*
Lapua 50, 106
Lauritsala 90
League of Nations 48, 49, 51, 53
Lehtinen, Kauko 255, Pl. 59
Lehtonen, Joel 228, 232
Leino, Eino 114, 121, 228
Leino, Yrjö 66
Leiviskä, Juha 200
Lemmenjoki, river 122, 135
Lenin, Vladimir 44, 45, 46, 64, 65
Leningrad 23, 56, 59, 287, 294
Lepokalusto Oy 211
Lewes Jail, Sussex 301
Liberal People's Party 50, 56, *348-50*
Libraries *366*
Life Expectancy *348*
Liminka 106
Lindgren, Armas Pl. 25
Linna, Väinö 231, 232, 233, 234, 260
Linnankoski, Johannes 227
Lintula, convent 185
Lister, Lord 301
Literature **219-34**, *366*

INDEX

Living Standards 351-3
Lohja 182
Lönnrot, Elias 31, 114, 224, 225, 251
Loviisa (Lovisa) 104
Lundgren, Tyra 205
Luther, Martin 177, 179, 219
Lutheran Church, *see* Religion
Luukkonen, Risto-Veikko 201, Pl. 38

Maarianhamina, *see* Mariehamn
Madetoja, Leevi 244
Magnus, Olaus 216
Mäkinen, Timo 148, 200
Malm, Otto 301
Malm, Pehr 301
Manner, Eeva-Liisa 234, 260
Mannerheim, Carl Gustaf 41, 46, 47, 48, 53, 57, 58, 109, 256, 265, 295, 349
Mäntsälä 50
Mardall, Cyril 303
Mariehamn (Maarianhamina) 100, Pl. 10
Marimekko Oy 210
Marmier, Xavier 126
Marshall Aid 60
Martin, Elias 101
Marttini family 132
Martola, General A. E. 61, 297
Marx, Karl 64
May Day 265
Meredith, George 301
Mera programme 78
Meri, Veijo 232, 233, 260
Merick, John 24
Merikanto, Aarre 243, 244, 247
Merikanto, Oskar 243
Metals **79-80,** 121, 132, 204, 212, 353-6, 360
Metalworking Industries **80-1,** 84, 104, 132, 355-6, 360
Metsovaara-Van Havere, Marjatta 205, 212, Pl. 67
Midnight Sun 117, 266
Midsummer Day 266
Mikkeli 87, 109, 111, 126, 269
Mikkola, Kirmo 148
Milan Triennales 203, 206, 211
Military Service, *see* Armed Forces and Army Training
Millar, G. H. 97, 98
Mining, *see* Metals

Monarchy, Finnish proposal for 47
Moscow, Peace of, 1940 54, 58, 59
Moscow, Armistice of, 1944 58, 90, 113
Motor Sports 147, 148, 269
Motor Vehicles 81, 352, 360, 361
Muona, Toini 205
Murmansk 48, 57, 135
Murray, John 89, 302
Music **235-49,** 304
Muurame 212
Myllykosken Paperitehdas Oy 77, 78

Naantali (Nådendal) 105, 268
Napoleon 24
Napoleonic Wars, *see* Wars
Näsijärvi, lake 108
National Coalition Party 348-50
National Front Government 67
National Progressive Party 348
Nautor 83
Neovius Oy 206
Neste Oy 82, 356
Neutrality 37-9, 59-62
Nevsky, Alexander 179
Newspapers, *see* Press
Nicholas II, Tsar 33
Nightingale, Florence 301
Niilonen, Kerttu 211
Nokia Oy 356
Non-aggression Pact, 1932 51, 53
Noras, Arto 248
Nordgren, Pehr Henrik 249
Nordic Council 61
Nordic Economic Union 85
Norris, Sir John 300
North, George 214, 215
Northern Lights, *see* Aurora Borealis
Norway 20, 56, 178, 260
  For comparative statistics, see pp. 344-67
Nousiainen Pl. 22
November group 254
Novgorod 20, 21, 23
Nummi, Yki 209
Nurmesniemi, Antti 211
Nurmesniemi Studio 211
Nurmi, Paavo 255, Pl. 60
Nurmijärvi 268
Nuutajärvi 207
Nykarleby, *see* Uusikaarlepyy
Nyman, Gunnel 202, 208, 211

373

FINLAND: AN INTRODUCTION

Nyslott, see Savonlinna
Nystad, see Uusikaupunki

Öberg, Thure 204, 205
OECD (Organisation for Economic Co-operation and Development) 61
Oikarainen, Kalevi 144
Ojakangas, Beatrice 279
Olavinlinna Castle (Olofsborg) 112, 267, 286
Opera 244, 246, 249
Ornamo 202, 204, 207
Orthodox Church, see Religion
Ostrobothnia 50, 95, 106–8, 110, 280, 287, 300
Otaniemi 190, 194, 196, Pl. 21, 39
Oulankajoki, river 117
Oulu (Uleåborg) 106, 107, 108, 119, 125, 126, 161, 197, 300, 301, *346*
Oulujoki, river 88, 107, 118, 119, Pl. 5
Ounasjoki, river 117
Outakka 121
Outokumpu Oy 80, 110, 132, *356*
Övertorneå 134

Paasikivi, J. K. 17, 37, 55, 59, 60, *349*, *350*
Paatelainen, Raili Pl. 39
Paatsjoki, river 117, 119
Pacius, Fredrik 243
Pähkinäsaari, Treaty of, 1323 23
Päijänne, lake 89, 104, 109, *344*
Paimio 194, 195, 196, Pl. 28
Painting 250–6, Pl. 52–59
Pallastunturi, fell 286
Panula, Jorma 248
Paper Industry 77, 82, *355–6*, *360*
Paris Exhibition (1900) 253; (1925) 203; (1937) 199
Paris, Treaty of, 1947, 58, 153
Parks, National 141
Parliament, Composition of *348–50*
Paterson, John 186
Patriotic People's Movement 51, *348–50*
Peace Settlement, 1944 90, 113
Pekema Oy 82
Pekkala, Mauno 67
Pekkanen, Toivo 229
Pennanen, Eila 234
Penttilä, Timo 200

Petäjävesi 189
Peter the Great, Tsar 54
Petsamo 54, 55, 57, 58, 116
Pielisjärvi, lake 90
Pielisjoki, river 90
Pietarsaari (Jakobstad) 107
Pietilä, Reima 194, 201, Pl. 39
Pihtsosköngäs 122
Piikkiö (Pikis) 103
Plastics see also Design and individual companies 208–209, 211, 212
Pohjoiskalotti (Nordkalotten) 134
Pohtimolampi 137
Poland 49
Politics, see also Wars and individual political parties 20, 21–2, 26, 28–30, 34, 43–8, 51–2, 59, 60–2, 63–9, 165, 272–273, *348–50*
Poltava 25
Population *346, 347, 348*
Pori (Björneborg) 104, 125, 247, 267, 287, *346*
Porkkala 58, 60, 127, 152
Porthan, Henrik Gabriel 114, 120, 221, 224
Porvoo (Borgå) 26, 104, 125, 204, 285
Posio 132
Pöyry, Jaakko 83
Prästö 101
Presidents *349*
Press Club, National 38
Press, **271–7**, *367*
Prime Ministers *350*
'Pro Finlandia' Petition 34
Puijo, hill 110
Pulkkila, ridge 109
Punkaharju, ridge 109
Purnu 266
Pushkin, A. S. 217
Puukkotehdas, Oy 132
Pyhäkoski Pl. 5
Pyhä fell 286
Pyynikki, ridge 109

Quarken (Merenkurkku) 106

Raahe (Brahestad) 107
Rail Travel, see Transport
Raisio (Reso) 103
Rajajoki, river 23

INDEX

Ramsay, Henrik 300
Rapala, Lauri 83
Rauma (Raumo) 104, 125, 206, *346*
Rauma-Repola 81, *356*
Rautaruukki 80, 108, 132
Rautavaara, Einojuhani 248
Reindeer 96, 120, 129, **133-4**, 138, 139, 145, 215, 263, 264, Pl. 43
Reindeer Owners' Association (Paliskunta) 133
Relander, Lauri Kr. *349*
Religion
   Anglican 180
   Dissenters' Law 184
   Evangelicals 184
   Laestadians 184
   Lutheran 24, 25, 35, 110, 113, 116, **177-87**, 227, *347*
   Orthodox 24, 25, 116, 179, 185, 186, *347*
   Pietists 184
   Roman Catholic 180, *347*
Reserves, National 141
Revell, Viljo 194, 195, 198, Pl. 33, 41
Rew, Prescott & Co. 107
Riihimäen Lasi Oy 202, 203, Pl. 62
Rikkihappo Oy 82, *356*
Rislakki, Eero 206
Rissanen, Juho 253
Ritvala, folklore festival 265
Roman Catholic Church, *see* Religion
Rome 18, 20, 21
Roosevelt, Franklin Delano 40
Rosenlew Oy 81, 209
Rotherhithe, Finnish Church in 303
Rovaniemi 120, **127-33**, 136, 197, 264, 286, *346*
Rukatunturi, fell 264, 286
Runeberg, Johan Ludvig 31, 111, 222, 223, 264
Ruotsinsalmi (Svensksund) 104
Russia, *see also* Novgorod and Soviet Union 23, 33, 34, 37, 64, 294, 295
Ruuponsaari Holiday Village 212
Ruusuvuori, Aarno 200, Pl. 37
Ryijy, rugs 110, 206
Rymättylä 251, Pl. 52
Ryti, Risto, President 58, *349*, *350*

Sääksmäki 265

Saame, *see* Lapps
Saana, fell 286
Saarijärvi 222
Saarikoski, Pentti 234
Saarinen, Eliel 191, Pl. 25, 26
Saarnio, Bertel 200
Saimaa Canal 61, 90, 91, 115
Saimaa, lake 87, 89, 90, 108, 110, 115, 140, *344*
St Erik, King of Sweden 20
St Henry, *see* Henry, Bishop of Uppsala
Salama, Hannu 234
Salla 116, 117
Sallinen, Aulis 248, 249
Sallinen, Tyko 254, 255, Pl. 53
Salmenhaara, Erkki 249
Salminen, Sally 230
Salo, Rita 210
Salora Oy 81
Salpausselkä, ridge 264
SALT (Strategic Arms Limitation Talks) 40
Saltvik 99
Sammatti 266
Sanka Oy 209
Sansom, William 217
Sarpaneva, Timo 205, 207, 208, 209, 305
Sauna 17, 76, 83, 111, **289-93**, 305, Pl. 7, 9
Savo 110, 112, 280
Savonlinna (Nyslott) 112, 125, 247, 267, 286
Säynätsalo 149, 197, Pl. 30
Schauman, Eugen 34
Schilkin Michael 205
Schjerfbeck, Helene 253, 254, Pl. 54
Schultén, N. G. af 88
Sculpture **250-6**, Pl. 16, 51, 60, 61
Sea Travel, *see* Transport
Segerstam, Leif 248
Seinäjoki 195
Septem Group 253, 254
Sevettijärvi 135
Shipbuilding 81, 86, 102, *355*, *356*, *360*
Shuisky, Count 24
Sibelius, Jean 110, 114, **235-41**, 244, 245, 248, 252, 256, 285, 304, Pl. 18
Sibelius Academy 245
Sigismund, King 24
Siilasvuo, General 297
Siimes, Anne 205
Sillanpää, **Frans** Eemil 229

375

FINLAND: AN INTRODUCTION

Silver Line 287
Simberg, Hugo 253, Pl. 58
Sipoo (Sibbo) 189, Pl. 20
Sirén, J. S. Pl. 27
Siren, Heikki and Kaija 190, 196, 199, Pl. 21, 35
SITRA (Finnish National Fund for Research and Development) 86
Sjögren, Anders Johan 114
Skanno Oy 211, 212
Ski-ing 142-5, 286, Pl. 44, 47
Smallholders' Party, *see* Finnish Rural Party
Snellman, Johan Vilhelm 31, 226
Social-democratic League 63, *348-50*
Social-democratic Party 34, 43, 44, 45, 46, 47, 50, 52, 53, 56, 63, 64, 65, 67, *348-50*
Social Democratic Union of Workers & Small Farmers *348-350*
Socialist Working People's Party 65
Södergran, Edith 230
Soiro, Jorma 279
Soviet Union, *see also* Russia 37, **40-62**, 78, 80, 85, 90, 91, 115, 119, 160, 260, 295, *344*
Sparre, Louis 204
Sports **142-8**, 285, Pl. 44, 45, 47
Staël, Madame de 215
Ståhlberg, K. J. 47, 50, *349*
Stalin, Joseph 40, 45, 52
Stenius, Jacob 88
Stenros, Helmer 201, Pl. 38
Stenros, Pirkko 212
Stolbova, Treaty of, 1617 24
Story, John 215
Strömberg Oy 81
Student Health Service Foundation 163
Summer Theatres, *see* Theatre
Sunila 127
Suomalainen, Timo and Tuomo 194
Suomenlinna (Sveaborg) 101, 267
Suomenselkä 95
Suomen Trikoo 109
Suomen Näyttelijäliitto 260
Suomutunturi, fell 286
Suonenjoki 266
Sveaborg, *see* Suomenlinna
Svensksund, *see* Ruotsinsalmi
Svinhufvud, Pehr Edwin 45, 46, *349*

Sweden, **20-23, 35-7,** 54, 58, 60, 73, 74, 78, 81, 85, 95, 99, 158, 159, 161, 178, 179, 213, 220, 258, 260, 271, 274, **296-8**
For comparative statistics, see pp. *344-67*
Swedish People's Party 50, *348-350*

Taipale Canal 89
Talja 147
Talvela, Martti 248
Tammerfors, *see* Tampere
Tamminen, Seppo 210
Tammisaari (Ekenäs) 104, 125, 267, Pl. 17
Tampella Oy 77, *356*, Pl. 67
Tampere (Tammerfors) 47, 109, 126, 127, 161, 200, 201, 209, 231, 258, 259, 266, 268, 285, 287, 302, *346*, Pl. 16
Tapiola 126, 195, 198, Pl. 2, 32, 33
Tapper, Kain 256, Pl. 61
Tartu, Treaty of, 1920, 49
Tauriala, Anna 209
Tavastehus, *see* Hämeenlinna
Tavaststjerna, K. A. 101, 118
Taxes *362, 364*
Täyssinä, Treaty of, 1595, 24
Telephones *352*
Television *352*
Tenojoki, river 117
Terijoki 53, 65
Tervakoski Oy 78
Textiles, *see also* Design and individual companies 76, 132, 204, 205, 208, 210, 212, *355*, Pl. 67
Theatre, *see also* Ballet and Music 233, **257-62**, *365*
Thirty Years War, *see* Wars
Thomas, Bishop 21, 178
Thomson, James 215
Toikka, Oiva 207, Pl. 64
Topelius, Zachris 115, 116, 122, 222, 223, 303
Tornio 89, 118, 122, 132
Tornionjoki, river 106, 117
Tourism **284-8**, 300
Transport *361-2*
air 286, 287, 288, 300, *360*
lake 89, 90, 285, 287, *360*, Pl. 10
rail 287, *360*
river 88, 89
road 119, 135, 146-7, 286, 287, *360*

376

INDEX

Transport—*contd.*
  sea 88, 101, 102, 105, 107, 287, 300
Travers, Rosalind 305
Treaties, *see* individual treaties
Tsars, *see* individual tsars
Tuomioja, Sakari 61
Tukiainen, Aimo 256
Tulomajoki, river 119
Turku (Åbo) 21, 22, 98, 100, **102–4**, 109, 114, 125, 126, 127, 152, 161, 165, 182, 194, 195, 197, 200, 201, 243, 247, 251, 259, 269, 285, 287, 302, *346*, Pl. 15, 29, 38
Turku, Treaty of, 1743, 26
Turunmaa (Åboland) 97
Tweedie, Mrs Alec 94, 215, 305

UK *see* Britain
Uleåborg, see Oulu
United Nations 38, 61, 297
Universities, *see also* Education, *364–5*
Upo Oy 81
USA 40, 42, 60, 77, 83, 162, 186, **295–7**
  For *comparative statistics, see pp. 344–367*
USSR *see* Russia, Soviet Union
Uusikaarlepyy (Nykarleby) 125
Uusikaupunki (Nystad) 25, 81, 104
Uusikaupunki, Treaty of, 1721 25
Uusi Valamo 185

Vaasa (Vasa) 46, 97, 100, 107, 125, 195, 200, 208, 259, 266, 286, *346*
Vaisala Oy 83
Väisälä, Vilho 83
Valamo 113, 185
Valio Oy 200, 282
Valkeakoski 78, 110
Välkki, Anita 304
Vallgren, Ville 252
Valmet Oy 80, 81
Vanhalinna 102
Vanni, Sam 255, Pl. 56
Vantaa (Wanda) river 101
Vappu 265, Pl. 48
Varkaus Pl. 3
Vasa, *see* Vaasa
Vasa, Gustavus 116
Veitsiluoto Oy 132
Velkua 183
Vennola, Jorma 209
Vesijärvi, lake 89

Viikki 282
Viipuri (Vyborg) 23, 25, 54, 58, 90, 112, 113, 196
Viipuri Bay 90, 115
Vilka Oy 211, 212
Villnäs, *see* Louhisaari
Voltaire, J. F. 216
Vuokko 210
Vuoksenniska 195, Pl. 36
Vuoksi, river 55, 88, 115
Vuotso 132, 136
Vyborg, *see* Viipuri

Wainio, P. J. 212
Waltari, Mika 229
Wanda river, *see* Vantaa
War Casualties 59
War Reparations 219
Wars
  Civil War 38, 46, 47, 64, 67
  Crimean 27, 301
  Continuation War, *see* Second Finnish War
  Great Northern War 22
  Japanese 34, 295
  Napoleonic 26
  Second Finnish War 57–9, 120, 130
  Thirty Years War 300
  Winter War 53, 54, 65, 219, 230, 232
  World War I 42, 196, 203, 303
  World War II 42, 56, 65, 74, 196, 270, 303
Wärtsilä Oy 81, 302, *356*, Pl. 63
Waterways **87–91**
Weckström, Björn 210, Pl. 65
Wegelius, Martin 243
West, Werner 211
Winter Sports, *see* Ski-ing, Motor Sports
Winter War, *see* Wars
Wirkkala, Tapio **205–7**, 282, 305
Women's Vote 34
Woodworking Industries 77, 79, 84, 104, 121, 196, 203, 211, 212, *355–6, 360*
Workers' and Smallholders' Social-democratic League *348–50*
World Fair, New York 199
World War I, *see* Wars
World War II, *see* Wars
Wright, George von 300

Zilliacus, Benedict 213

377